WORDS AND MUSIC

A History of Pop in the Shape of a City

PAUL MORLEY

"This book is brilliant."

BLOOMSBURY

BY THE SAME AUTHOR

Ask: The Chatter of Pop
Nothing

'We are the music-makers and we are the dreamers of dreams'
Willy Wonka, after Arthur O'Shaughnessy

'You better lose yourself in the music, the moment you own it, you better never let it go'

Eminem

'You are the music while it lasts'
T. S. Eliot

Dedication
e.s.p.t.w.o

First published in Great Britain in 2003
This paperback edition published in 2004

Copyright © 2003 by Paul Morley

The moral right of the author has been asserted

Bloomsbury Publishing Plc, 38 Soho Square, London W1D 3HB

A CIP catalogue record for this book is available from the British Library

ISBN 0 7475 6864 2

10 9 8 7 6 5 4 3 2 1

Typeset by Palimpsest Book Production Ltd,
Polmont, Stirlingshire
Printed in Great Britain by Clays Ltd, St Ives plc

www.bloomsbury.com

CONTENTS

Part One: The journey begins

1
I am sitting in a room.

2
I can't get you out of my head.

3
At the moment I think my two favourite pieces of music are *I am sitting in a room* by Alvin Lucier and 'Can't Get You Out of My Head' by Kylie Minogue.

4
The first piece was written and performed in 1969 by Alvin Lucier, and it is an experimental piece that uses the human voice and certain simple electronic manipulation, plus the acoustic influence of the room in which the work is recorded, to create a long, formless and yet intensely controlled piece of music. Even though it is performed using purely the sound of the human voice, what happens during the recording and manipulation of the words turns the sound of the voice into a multilayered musical adventure involving a subtle mixture of tones, melodies, harmonies and rhythms.

It is music – you wouldn't think of calling it anything other than music – but it is not music in the way we usually understand the word. That is, it is musical, it resembles what we recognise as music, it is an abstract series of sound shapes and noise forms that can communicate something specific to us even without the use of words – although the essential paradox of this piece is that is starts out using words, basic, quite boring descriptive words, and then these words disappear into themselves, as if boiled down, as if they are changing from solid to liquid, forming a sensuous, absorbing musical form that implies how all music began with the sound of the human voice. The sound of the human voice imitating sounds around us; the sounds of nature, animals, even the sound of silence. The sound of the human voice copying the voice of God.

But it is not made using instruments, there are no notes, you could not find sheet music for this piece. You would find a list of instructions for how to create the sounds, but you wouldn't be able to sit down at a piano and follow those instructions in the way you would read a sheet of music. It is an example of an art of music-making, a theoretical interest in sound for sound's sake, in the music that resides inside sound, and inside silence, ready to be liberated, that has created some of the most important and influential music of the past 100 years – an abstract music that blurs the lines between art, music, talking and performance.

It represents the side of me that loves music for the way it constantly surprises, changes what it is, moves with the times, moves through time, creates space within itself, reacts against the past and finds new ways of saying perhaps the same thing. What this 'same thing' actually is, and why the variety of this 'same thing' is constantly stimulating, makes listening to music just as challenging an idea as the making of it – and can make listening a musical act, so that the listener can, in ways, be described as a musician, participating in the making of the music.

Without the listener, there is no music. The listener completes the musical circuit, and, even though I am not a musician, I feel as if I am a form of musician when I listen to something like *I am sitting in a room* and believe that, by hearing the piece, by responding to it with my thoughts of what it is and what it is doing – what it means – I am actually helping to finish it off. As the listener I am the final element in the making of the music. I have made the music useful. I have put it into a context: the context of my own life, and my own perception of what music is, and why it exists.

'Can't Get You Out of My Head' is something else altogether, and yet is not that different. Like *I am sitting in a room*, 'Can't Get You Out of My Head' has a title that instantly describes what is going on. And what is going on is exactly what is going on. In a way, it is as far removed from an ancient idea of music as composition, as arrangement of emotion through the following of certain rules and regulations, as *I am sitting in a room*. It is, for all its need to comfort and charm, as abstract as *I am sitting in a room*, as conceptual. We are led to believe, by the commercial paraphernalia and the hard gloss of soft persuasion surrounding 'Can't Get You Out of My Head', that it is a pop song with limited life, no better, no worse than thousands of other equally slick, shiny constructs.

But something happened during the production of the song, during the processes that built the song up from an idea into a thing, that made it something more, a piece of music that is much more than the sum of its parts – in fact, its clear abstract likeability outstripped the momentary hopes for its commercial likeability because somehow it became not a calculated representation of a great pop song but actually a great pop song full stop.

How this happened is, essentially, impossible to detail or summarise, except perhaps by placing it inside the context of a whole history of music and art and entertainment that helps us to work out what might be its true value, its true life expectancy. Why is it better than other pop songs that appear to be of similar weight and density? Why does it work in the way that it works as whatever it is working at? And, while we're at it, why does *I am sitting in a room* work as a piece of music when it is, really, merely a theory about sound that could easily end up sounding like someone talking to himself for a bit until the sound gets horribly muffled? Is it possible to write about the reasons? Or do these things just happen in their own way, in their own spaces, leaving other people, non-musicians, non-artists, simple writers, puzzled to bits by the way these things happen, to try to explain the magic in a way that reveals the trick or even explains the real magic behind the apparent magic?

They're both sounds that seem to emerge out of dreams – the Lucier piece a dream about speaking, the Minogue piece a dream about singing. They're both operating inside spaces – a room, a head – that offer more freedom and more possibility for adventure than seems immediately apparent. Lucier is all talk, leading to mutant melodic surprises. Minogue is all flirt, leading to rhythmic flight. *I am sitting in a room* is a natural sonic sculpture. 'Can't Get You Out of My Head' is synthetically tuned pop art.

3

Kylie's song, a lovely little drama about love and loss, a mesmerising observation of obsession, is certainly a pop piece, but there is art to it as well. It can be as satisfying mentally as the Lucier piece, as tantalising and as mysterious for all its aggressive, even cynical, commercial glitter. Lucier's piece, not a song, aches with artistic intent, but it is also, in its way, about love, loss, obsession, and is as satisfying physically as Kylie's song. It is as sexy, maybe in the way it combines tension with relief, repetition with surprise, lubricating the imagination with gentle twists and turns, opening up emotional possibilities with little drops in temperatures and subtle increases in pressure. Within the space of their space, both create a sense of space that seems to reflect the vastness of space and yet protect you from that vastness by using sound to make you feel connected to other people, to remind you that you can be lonely but that you are not alone. Both pieces were made using microphones, and you will use headphones or speakers to listen to them. They are the same thing and they are very different things.

Perhaps what connects the two pieces of music is a tunnel, a hole in the ground, which you fall down and into and down, changing dimension, direction and context as you tumble. Or maybe whatever connects the two pieces is a road, a highway, an *autobahn*. A straight line between one way of making music and quite curiously another. Of course, no line is really straight. All straight lines actually contain kinks. Everything is curved.

In the end, for our immediate purposes, to get from here to where we're going, what connects the two pieces is a page in a book. The road travels across the page. The road takes us from page to page. The tunnel also takes us from one page to another. The tunnel connects sound. Sound runs, melts, drops down the tunnel into our ear. The tunnel connects our ear to our brain. In our brain, where we are large and small, weak and strong, sure and unsure, loud and quiet, the story I am about to tell really begins.

5

The road and the tunnel or both take us between my two favourite pieces of music. Inevitably, because life can be like that, and journeys often don't end up as you planned them, this could very easily change. In another book written in another universe where other moments are occurring by the infinite bucketload, and where another tunnel is materialising, then

4

there will be a different beginning to this book. For instance, in another moment, in another universe, along another motorway, then it could be a case of . . .

1

I feel love.

2

I feel like I'm fixin' to die.

The beginning of that book would be dealing with Donna Summer and Country Joe & the Fish. That's a weird universe to be in, but then aren't they all? At a guess, that book would be about love and death. Other books might open with Olivier Messiaen and Digable Planets – a book about mess and moisture – or George Crumb and the Kinks – waste and wit – or Herbaliser and the Dave Clark Five – a pop-up beat annual – or Björk and Harry Partch – the inhuman body – or Matching Mole and Madonna – a novel about mathematics and rhythm – or Arvo Pärt and Spike Jones and his City Slickers – prayer versus the pratfall.

In fact, we could begin as we possibly mean to go on, with a list loaded with suggestion. A list loaded with pure, simple list. A list that is what it lists. A list of, say, forty musical pairings that would fill forty books that exist in forty parallel universes. You can use this list simply as an entertainment in itself, or to get your bearings regarding the kind of music that will be mentioned in this book, or to imagine the kind of books that could be written if they began with the following pairings (perhaps the books would all be identical to this one, as long as they were written by alternative *me*s), and also to work out if you're in the right book. After all, for all I know, there might be a photograph of Kylie Minogue on the cover of this particular book. You might be reading this book as a fan of Kylie, thinking you will be finding out about her favourite moisturiser and perfume, and so I think it only fair this early on to say that, while Kylie will play a large part in this story – not really as the love interest, nor will she be written about as a moll, as such, and she isn't the villainess – it is not a book about her. I suppose in the following story she's somewhere mechanical and human between entertainer and dream, if that's not giving too much away. She might be simply playing a driver. (For those of you who suddenly perked up, expecting some steamy, even bloody auto erotica, there will be no car crash. Kylie is a very safe driver. And, alas, in this book at least, she never gets to meet J. G. Ballard. Then again, we are only at the very beginning of the book, and anything can happen; minds can change, including mine, and Kylie's, and Ballard's. Kylie in a car crash might be a very commercial event, and in a book that is going to spend some time discussing the history of abstract music that began in the distant beginning and ended up in obscure twentieth-century distortion, then a mystery involving Kylie might be, in various ways, quite useful.) Whoever, whatever, Kylie is in this book, a key thing to remember might be that Kylie never really speaks her own lines. Alvin Lucier always speaks his own lines. Then again, again, this thought might be no help at all, and might not actually be that true.

If she is on the cover, well, I don't suppose I really have to explain why she would be on the cover and Alvin Lucier would not be. Even if Lucier was not a middle-aged man when he produced *I am sitting in a room*, with all the visible and quite moustached and behatted signs of being a middle-aged man a little on the eccentric side, you would still expect Kylie to be on the cover of this book. As soon as it was noticed that there was mention of Kylie, the cover of this book was planned, by those forces beyond the current sight of myself, who is merely the author simply struck by an occasional shiver of inspiration.

I'm sure in the universe where this book begins with Donna Summer and Country Joe & the Fish, Donna is on the cover and not Joe. Although the writer – hello, is it me you're looking for? – doesn't know for sure. He knows nothing for sure, except what's coming next, and even that is, ultimately, in the lap of the gods who dictate the shape and length of the tunnel he is plunging down.

In the following list, part of the fun will be working out who, of the pairings, would be on the cover of the book they appear at the beginning of, whatever story they find themselves at the beginning of. Also, if you're aware of at least twenty per cent of the following, then you are reading the right book. If you are aware of less than twenty per cent, then I would still recommend that you keep reading – because by the end of the book you will be aware of well over twenty per cent of the following list, and you can start the book again, with a better sense of the scale of everything. If you're here merely for Kylie, well, stick around if you're interested in the content of Kylie as well as the form. If you just fancy Kylie, are just lusting for a quick throbbing fix of images and curves, and have no real interest in music, or even her music, then, yes, you are in the wrong book, and I'm afraid we must now part. The soundtrack for this parting could well be supplied by the first piece of music from the following list.

6

'Hallo Gallo' by Neu! and 'Goodbye to Love' by the Carpenters

'Golden Age' by the Legendary Pink Dots and 'Route 66' by Nelson Riddle

70 Minutes of Madness by Coldcut and 'It's Too Late' by Carole King

'Friendly as a Hand Grenade' by Tackhead and 'I Honestly Love You' by Olivia Newton John

'By the Time I Get to Arizona' by Public Enemy and 'Midnight Train to Georgia' by Gladys Knight & the Pips

Feed Me Weird Things by Squarepusher and 'Downtown' by Petula Clark

'A Man Under the Influence' by Alejandro Escovedo and 'Funky Town' by Lipps Inc.

''Out-bloody-rageous' by Soft Machine and 'Happy Together' by the Turtles

'Repeat' by This Heat and 'Oops Oh My' by Tweet

Free Jazz by Ornette Coleman and 'Fucking the Pain Away' by Peaches

'Gravity' by Fred Frith and 'Ain't No Mountain High Enough' by Diana Ross

They Wash Their Ambassadors in Citrus and Fennel by Jon Christopher Nelson and 'Crazy' by Patsy Cline

Stormcock by Roy Harper and *Janet* by Janet Jackson

Zaireeka by The Flaming Lips and 'All Through the Night' by Cyndi Lauper

The Tony Bennett Bill Evans Album and *Naked City Live at the Knitting Factory, 1989*

Charlie Parker with Strings: The Master Takes and 'Love Grows where My Rosemary Goes' by Edison Lighthouse

Y by the Pop Group and 'Love and Affection' by Joan Armatrading

Filtered Through Friends by Spunk and 'Be My Baby' by The Ronnettes

Phallus Dei by Amon Düül II and 'Have You Ever Seen the Rain' by Creedence Clearwater Revival

Chiastic Slide by Autechre and '9 to 5' by Dolly Parton

cLOUDEAD by cLOUDEAD and 'Help Me Make It Through the

Night' by Kris Kristofferson

Alfred Schnittke Complete String Quartets by Kronos and 'Heart of Gold' by Neil Young

The Pavilion of Dreams by Harold Budd and 'Proud Mary' by Ike & Tina Turner

Emperor Tomato Ketchup by Stereolab and 'Stoned Out of My Mind' by The Chi-Lites

The Hangman's Beautiful Daughter by the Incredible String Band and 'A Foggy Day in London Town' by Ella Fitzgerald

The Raincoats by The Raincoats and *Spice* by the Spice Girls

On Land by Brian Eno and 'Crazy Horses' by the Osmonds

'Alles ist Gut' by DAF and 'If I Had Possession Over Judgement Day' by Robert Johnson

Dread in a Babylon by U Roy and 'Sugar Sugar' by the Archies

Forbidden Planet soundtrack by Louis and Bebe Barron and 'A Song from Under the Floorboards' by Magazine

The Gilded Palace of Sin by The Flying Burrito Brothers and *Music in a Doll's House* by Family

Fitzcarraldo soundtrack and 'The First Time Ever I Saw Your Face' by Roberta Flack

Playing with a Different Sex by Au Pairs and 'Feeling Good' by Nina Simone

Fly by Yoko Ono and 'Do You Remember Rock'n'Roll Radio?' by The Ramones

Oui by Sea and Cake and 'How High the Moon' by Billie Holiday

'Right Now' by Pussy Galore and 'Love in an Elevator' by Aerosmith

I Am The True Vine by Arvo Pärt and Get Ur Freak On by Missy Elliott

Oh Yeah by Charles Mingus and 'I Wanna Be Adored' by The Stone Roses

Paris 1919 by John Cale and 'Tainted Love' by Gloria Jones

Intellectuals are the Shoeshine Boys of the Ruling Elite by Killdozer and 'Wordy Rappinghood' by Tom Tom Club

7

But, listen, in this book, in this world, at this moment, a moment we must stick with so that we may progress into a story, my two favourite pieces of music are by Alvin Lucier and Kylie Minogue. And this is, to a degree, a book about music, as if it all can be tidily explained – from the third century BC to 2003, from before then to after now, from the Italian futurists to 'File under Futurism', from human voice to processed vocoder, from 78 rpm to MP3, from jukebox to iPod, from the heat of early-twentieth-century modernism to the chillout of early-twenty-first-century lifestyling, from the one second of the Descendents' 'All' to the twenty-nine minutes of Iron Butterfly's 'In-A-Gadda-Da-Vida', from The Moody Blues recording a full orchestra on to a four-track tape machine in 1967 to Nine Inch Nails mixing their album on a laptop in a hotel room in 1990, from before pop was compiled on album collections broken up into a hundred genres, to when it became nothing but compilation. From the hip of Elvis Presley to the lip of Eminem.

Kylie and Alvin's two pieces are, conventionally speaking, as far away from each other as you could imagine in a universe we try hard to make as familiar as possible in order not to panic ourselves to death. Yet they are a lot closer than you can imagine, in the fact that they both emerged out of the minds, hands, fingers, dreams, machines, emotions and instincts of human beings not too far apart from each other inside the space and time of this planet, whatever you choose to call it. Because I have a plan, and a vague sense of where this story is heading, it is a lucky coincidence that my current favourite pieces of music are by Minogue and Lucier, because it enables me to tell that story:

Without making too much up

By sticking to most of the salient facts and yet noticing surprising and satisfying connections

By keeping within enough of the established histories of music to avoid seeming like I don't really know what I'm talking about

By sticking loosely but gamely to a structure that is almost musical in the way that it has a beginning, a middle and an end

By revealing things that you might not know and that are both real and imagined

By introducing very early on two characters whom you will get to know, and possibly even love, or at least admire, although not so much that you are totally devastated when they disappear from the story. Not that I'm giving anything away about the story by saying that there will come a time in this book when both Alvin and Kylie fade away. Indeed, one of them might be killed off – and the list of suspects will include Madonna, Harry

9

Partch, Kid 606, Audioslave and, a real dark horse, Robert Fripp.
The Beastie Boys will need a better alibi as well.

8

Before she sets off on what will become her journey, Kylie Minogue
sits with her younger sister in a bright-yellow field. It's a lovely hot day,
but they are a little bit bored, a little sleepy, and Kylie in particular would
fancy an adventure. Little does she know what is in store for her.

A beautiful sports car designed by devilish angels appears out of
nowhere. Kylie being Kylie – or, as the case may be, not being quite
herself – climbs into the car and, seeing a key in the ignition with 'TURN
THIS' written on the key-ring, starts up the engine. The fresh clean noise
of the engine sounds like music to her ears. She finds herself driving
the car down an empty motorway carved proud with exciting curves
that seem to emerge out of her own body and take off into the future.
It's as if she has imagined the road that she is now driving down and it
has come true. She fits tightly into the car, which fits tightly on to the
road, as if they have been built to belong to each other: girl, car, road.
A landscape of shapes and shadows appears all around her as suddenly
as the car appeared. The sky looks so real it can't be real. The sun is
shining in a glittering stream.

Before she can really think about what's happening, her journey has
begun, in much the same way that a story begins, that a rhythm begins.
She has a strange feeling that things will happen to her on this journey,
and she feels so happy about this that she starts to sing. Her journey is
a song, a series of songs, perhaps all the songs in the universe. She's on
her own, but she senses that this won't be the case for long.

The actress playing Kylie Minogue, who just happens to be called
Kylie Minogue, is driving through an industrial landscape towards a city.
She has to be driving, not walking, because her journey, a journey that
is at the heart of this story, is all about her interaction with machines.
She is driving at night or day along a highway through miles and miles
of factories. She is driving towards a city full of anonymous, mysterious
lit-up buildings. The city is perhaps the capital city of Pleasure. Or it is
a city with no name that resembles, in your computer dreams, Toronto
or New York or Düsseldorf or Sydney or Tokyo. She's in a fast car driving
towards the city where everything important in modern life is happening.
There is no great detail in this film of her drive into the city. On the

other hand there is a lot of quite intense detail. So much detail it creates a kind of enigma; so little detail as to add to the enigma. She drives through a digital world that reveals itself as she drives through it and then disappears as she passes by. The world is as real as a cartoon, and is there anything as real in this universe as a cartoon? Look around – this universe may well be a cartoon, or at least is packed into a shoebox that is part of a cartoon, a shoebox that is in the glove compartment of the car that Kylie is driving.

The highway is smooth and empty. The road is a grey ribbon. White stripes, green edges. Her car is sleek and sensual. She fingers parts of it as if she is fingering a lover or flicking the switch on her favourite machine. It responds to her wishes before she has even thought of them.

She looks pleased with herself. Liberated from the everyday. Her eyes reflect the fate-grey and shimmering colour around her, so that her eyes seem the colour of her journey, the colour of a song, lit up by motion, the iris a sea-blue melody hinting at secrets and sensation, the pupils a simple but mysterious rhythm in the regular shape of forever. She looks as if she is hearing sounds that are the soundtrack to her journey. Soon she will be with some friends who appear lost in her new world. They will all dance together in an attempt to locate just where they are, finding great security in the way their bodies fit together. She will meet strangers with interesting stories to tell. These friends and strangers will look like they might be robots. Kylie herself could be said to look like a robot. A robot version of herself in human form, a version of herself manu-factured in the minds of robots. The buildings around her might exist only in the imagination of the robots. The sound we hear, the sound-track to her journey, might exist only inside the imagination of the robots. A car overtakes her, surely as fast as sound, and the driver of the car is a white robot, as white as nothing, whiter than white, as clean as a whistle, who is obviously late for something. The white robot in his car races off, chased by the beat of time, and Kylie wonders whether she will ever see him again.

A grid of light and dark, buildings and shadows, city and ghost city, stretches to the horizon in every direction. Everything is connected to and from the highway like a vast circuit-board. The creature designed to be Kylie exists in her car riding and sliding straight down the highway like a spark down a wire. The tyres of her car speed to a rhythm. But she can't hear the noise they make, because her car stereo's on, a big booming stereo filling her own private space inside this machine, providing a soundtrack to her own private movie, the movie of her song, the song she's here to sing, the movie that passes across the windscreen of her high-speed sports car, the movie of her life, a life as singer, her life as a singer speeding into the city to dance to the rhythms of her own song, the song of her life, the song of the city. This is a modern landscape and this is a modern drama designed for sophisticated consumption and on she drives straight on and towards the city where nothing exists without electricity and machinery and the human need for distraction and excitement.

Her adventure has begun. An adventure in sound, in history, in love, in legend. She feels so alive that she forgets the world she has left behind. She forgets her sister. She forgets that she was bored. She forgets what day of the week it is, or even if she ever knew what day it was. Sat in this car, which is the shape of a fantasy, she knows only that this is a new day which won't be the same as the day before or the day after. She drives out of her past into a future that will shape her memory into a new form.

It is just her, the car, the open road, the city in the distance, her dreams that fill the city. She feels so alive that she can't believe that she will ever die. She increases her speed, she increases the volume of the music, and the rhythm all around and inside her pushes her towards the city, a city full of wonder. The city waits for Kylie. Kylie's coming. She doesn't know it yet, but her drive will reveal to her the secret of her own existence, the magic of her relationship to a whole history of music, and it will end, somewhere in the city, so inside the city there seems no way out, as mysteriously and as abruptly as it began.

She may feel immortal as she speeds towards her destiny, but ahead of her lies something quite close to her end; because all stories and all songs and all lives must end. If they had a beginning they must have an end. The end is what tells us how vivid what comes before really is. And was. And will be.

For now, let's look at Kylie in the car, her pink mouth and her white skin, her riveting absent-minded smile; look at Kylie as she goes faster and faster, faster through the tender landscape that dissolves into itself, faster as she chases the white robot, who's white like light, the light that illuminates the dark, the robot, shining bright, who's late, who's rhyming with the last thing he thought, faster, as the car is fuelled by the energy of her fame and the electricity of her femininity. She's intimately part of the car, coupled with its parts, penetrated by its purpose; linked to the machinery of the car, eyes full of anticipation, body relaxed for action, singing to herself, to an imaginary audience, as alive as she will ever be, smiling through history, flirting with fame, on top of the world, skimming its surface, not thinking for a moment how the car and the city and the road that takes her from one to the other will conspire in her brutal, untimely, yet somehow beautiful death.

9

I like *I am sitting in a room* not just because it's one of the very few albums you will find with a title that begins with 'I', and, for reasons that will become apparent as one of the main characters in this story – me, I'm afraid, but I have a great alibi – is introduced more and more, it is important that the first word in this book is 'I'. I also like the piece because I'm not actually sure it exists.

Certainly, I don't own a copy of it, and I can't exactly remember a time when I actually did. I don't wish to annoy you, not yet anyway; I'm not toying with you. It's possibly quite a serious point – the piece is so obscure, so remote from the mainstream world of music, that it becomes a little like a memory you're not sure is real, or that is based on a dream, or based on false recollection. *I am sitting in a room* is like that for me – I think I remember hearing it, and enjoying it, and all my feelings about it are based on the possibility that I heard it and made up a series of assumptions about what it is and where it belongs and what I got from it as a communication, a work of art, an entertainment. I have a memory about the music, and all the following reports about the music are based on that memory. I'm not actually playing the music as I write this story. Well, I am playing it in the sense that I'm playing it in my mind, I'm reconstituting the sense of the sound as I recall hearing it, and calling up the emotions I seemed to be having as I heard it, but it's not actually physically available for me to play. In case you are wondering why I don't do a bit of research work and go out and buy it, let me just point out that it's not exactly available in any old local HMV, and even amazon.com seem to be able to supply me with a copy only by waiting for someone to sell one and then making it available to me. I imagine I am the only person on the waiting list for this disc. I also imagine that there are not many people considering selling this disc. It's not something I believe you might think of a morning – 'Today is the day that I must sell my copy of Alvin Lucier's *I am sitting in a room* in the hope that amazon.com can find a buyer.'

So, I am relying on my memory of the music. This is fine. The fact that the music has stayed in my mind, where there is so much coming in that a fair amount has to leave in order to let the new stuff enter, means that it has a strength and a presence that proves it is a great piece, and I also know enough about it as a piece to know it belongs exactly where it is going to be put in this story of music. It is also somehow appropriate that such a shadowy piece – and, believe me, it is a series of musical shadows that throw shadows until the shadows come home – features in this story as a kind of shadow. (Shadow is such a great word, and I know you won't mind the tiny detour to point out that a group called The Shadows should have been better and stranger than the group called The Shadows actually were. You would want them to be making albums with titles like *White Light from the Mouth of Infinity* or *Venus Lexure No. 1 Baby* or *Mekanik Destruktiw Kommandah* or *For How Much Longer Do We Tolerate Mass Murder?* or *Songs of a Dead Dreamer* rather than *The Best of the Shadows*. You would have wanted their greatest hit to have been called 'My Guitar Wants to Kill Your Mama'; those of you who know that that was actually a Frank Zappa song, and are therefore trying to look ahead and are considering that Zappa might be responsible for whatever murder may or may not take place later in the book, well, you're wrong, although he is something of a character in the story, if only to the extent that many of his records will be mentioned. At the moment, this is as far as I've got with the planning: Frank Zappa kills no one; and a lot of his records are mentioned, as they should be if you are intending to tell a story of musical development from, say, Louis Armstrong to, say, John Zorn, or, for the sake of argument, Robert Johnson to Tortoise and Bach again. I've just spotted in my notes concerning the planning of this book that Zappa does have a bit of a run-in with Lee Scratch Perry, and forms a small army with Durutti Column, Judee Sill, Bark Psychosis and Jacques Brel, but God knows how I'll work that in. I would also like to feel, when I finish falling down this particular tunnel, stretching between these particular brackets, that I might be able to take a pill that will create a world in which DJ Shadow actually had hit records with The Shadows and not with Cliff Richard. This will also be a world where I don't actually have to answer the question, in immediate regard to the idea of DJ Shadow and the Shadows, of 'Why?' Unless, of course, I can simply reply . . . 'Because. Just because.'

This, in the shadowy world I makebelieve I find myself, would be the title of the latest DJ Shadow and the Shadows hit. 'Just Because' – taking a break from the ordinary, beating sensation by a light-year, twisting like thought, cutting up itself, slicing through its insides, just because it does. It's a great world, a great track – who says there are no instrumental hits? – and I feel a little sorry that I am just about to hit the closing bracket, a bracket which must be the pill that puts everything back where it once was, or where it continues to go.)

This side of the brackets, though, I like *I am sitting in a room* because it also encompasses many of my favourite musical things. There's a flat, filled droniness to it that I've found personally thrilling since I first heard Tangerine Dream as a fourteen-year-old – I think hearing Tangerine Dream meant I didn't lose my virginity for many, many years, because their music, and the music it led me to listen to, seemed like the most sexual experience you could expect from life. The music of Tangerine Dream, which tripped inside and outside itself, somewhere spacious between inner space and outer space, also gave you a convincing sense that you were stoned; it altered reality and deranged the senses. So while my parents – faced with my antisocial behaviour and the way I seemed to be slipping off the planet's surface – might have been worried that I was on drugs, or was a secret cider-drinker, the truth was in fact more complicated. I was addicted to Tangerine Dream. The after-effects of this addiction may have lasted longer than those I might have experienced had I been into drugs or drink: I am still using music to push reality into different shapes.

As a fourteen-year-old, I perhaps used my addiction to Tangerine Dream as an excuse not to experiment with drugs or even drink. This might have been because then and all through my teens I was scared of losing control, and the way that Tangerine Dream abducted me, lifted me out of reality and did things to my mind and body, seemed like a better means of escape than drugs and drink. It seemed the best way imaginable to lose control. To lose control and find yourself inside the vastness of the mind, where suddenly unresolved emotions and strange images seemed to make sense, once they were filtered through the drone drowsiness of this space-stretching time-twisting sound.

Of course, alas, I've since realised that, when it comes to drones, Tangerine Dream are quite middle-of-the-road, not really drony at all, in fact quite melodic and rich. Positively sumptuous, when what you really want from a drone is a sense of starkness that when you are in the midst of listening to it feels like it can go on forever. Therefore, you will live forever, inside the drone, the drone of existence. Tangerine Dream droned, but they're really, when all is said and done and listened to forever, the Barry Manilow of the drone universe. And yet, they were my first. If I try to source back to my original interest in abstract avant-garde music, try to remember where it all began, I get to Tangerine Dream and an album I bought in Virgin Records, Manchester, for £2.15 – full price. The cover looked like a piece of blue-green soft metal – and it looked to be in motion. It turned out that it looked how the group sounded: molten, swirling, changeless, changing, weird, a long way from home, a long way from where I found myself stuck inside a small room in a small house in the backstreets of a small town. This kind of music could lift you outside yourself and your environment, and take you on a journey, a journey into a spaced-out city set on a strange planet light-years away, where emotion was a rhythm and you weren't alone. You were with this sound, which seemed to be the sound of love, of sex, of intoxication, of the future. It was in your mind and you were in its mind. It all seemed to be impossibly intimate, and the intimacy could be greatly increased if you played the record in the dark. If you also played the record at 16 rpm – half the speed at which it should be played – you felt that you were holding hands with a close acquaintance of someone who was right to claim he was God. If as a teenager you feel music this powerfully, it is very difficult to grow up and grow out of it. You are in fact likely to spend the rest of your life searching for similar experiences, even at ages when other life experiences should have suggested that there is a kind of immaturity in feeling so strongly about what is, after all, merely music, which is merely a form of guesswork about consciousness.

At the time, in the early seventies, *Phaedra* was relatively revolutionary. It soon got overtaken, sonically, experimentally, technologically. I can't remember when I last played this music, but it was somewhere between the time I first heard it and now. What I remember of it may well be not much to do with what it is, which is sometimes why you don't really want to really hear things in the present. You want to retain the memory of the experience, rather than listen through the ears of what you have heard since, of what has developed and expanded those ideas, making them now seem more traditional than radical. I always want to think of *Phaedra* as a radical, groundbreaking work that doesn't remind me of music that has happened since. I want the music that has happened since to remind me of *Phaedra* – even though that music might be spacier, better-sounding, more advanced. I want to remember that it couldn't have happened without Tangerine Dream. I want *Phaedra* to always sound as if it is the most forward-looking, mentally exhilarating, physically liberating musical work of all time, the way it sounded to me the first time I ever heard it. If I played it now it might not actually sound like the music I have in my head, the music I felt was the sound of the future, of everything, music that could never be out-imagined. I never thought anything could stretch beyond the sound of Tangerine Dream; and, although I know in my mind that even twenty-first-century MOR pop records machine-tooled in the name of Atomic Kitten or Liberty X can sound as spaced-out as Tangerine Dream did, in my heart I want Tangerine Dream to be untouchable, outside the wounding, diminishing effects of time and fashion, immune to the vast leaps across logic that computers have made in the past thirty years. Tangerine Dream were my first sound, the sound to which I lost my existential virginity. I want to remember them as perfectly eternal. I have created an image of what the four pieces on *Phaedra* are like; I have created a series of interpretations that connect with my memories of the experience I had listening to the album. And I am reluctant to challenge these things.

Sometimes, you want to play great music again and again. Some music can take being replayed. Other music is best suited to sitting in a special place in your mind, a kind of museum where you can visit the memory of the sound rather than the sound itself. I may be wrong, but I think *Phaedra*, because it is an electronic album of minimalist rockless rock music, made before the massive advances in electronics in the eighties and nineties, before the vast leaps in post-rock techniques, will now sound disappointing. Or, at least, it will disappoint the high hopes I have that it is as perfect, as beautiful, as I imagine it is.

Perhaps it is the same with *I am sitting in a room*: I do not want to hear it now because I have made my mind up what it is, and what it represents, and I am worried that it will become a different piece of music, a lesser piece, a plainer piece, if I hear it again. Other things I have heard since might reduce it in my mind, and not in ways I want it to be reduced; for me, it is a remarkable reductionist reaction against overcomplicated, needlessly dense music, something that ultimately communicates more than the complicated music does. Advances in technology and style don't particularly threaten the music of Miles Davis or Faust – the energy and audacity of such sounds can resist change – but the music of Alvin Lucier and Tangerine Dream seems less secure, perhaps because of the way it entered my imagination in the first place, and the way I generated a response. Then again, I might play *Phaedra* now and feel that it is exactly as transcendentally atmospheric and emotionally stimulating as I have always thought it is. I just don't want to take the risk. I like what I think it is in the way I like a painting by Picasso or an object by Duchamp that I have only ever seen once for real. (As I write these words, I have the album in front of me. If it was on vinyl, as it was when I used to play it, with its deluxe gatefold sleeve opening up to suggest the tenseless glories of its rolling-drone drama, then I might be tempted to play it. The flimsy floppy CD version seems far less ravishing than the old LP. Then again, the title of the second track alone, 'Mysterious Semblance at the Strand of Nightmares', is tremendously tempting. The cryptic allure of those words and the promise that I will be led by the sound of the piece back, or forward, into a braced state of mind where life seems so purely terrifying and tantalising is extremely strong. Strong enough, ultimately, to allow me to resist the pull and rely on the memory alone to get in touch with the feeling that I could reach out and touch the stars and be the stars. Just to be safe, though, I will put the CD, this repackage of uncompromised recollection, away. I will save returning to the music until later – much later – in my life. Perhaps it is the music I should be playing at the exact moment I die. I slip and slide across the moving surface of its momentous drift out into the tunnel of death, and the music carries me into eternity, where it will accompany me forever through the galaxies to the edge of heaven. Or, just in case it will be a disappointment to hear it, and not the kind of regret you really want as you die, perhaps it is something that can be played at my funeral – a reminder of when life was just beginning, and when the sound of sound, just sheer sound surrounding itself with more sound, seemed to make the world such an extraordinary place to be. The congregation might be puzzled as to why I placed so much importance on the sub-grandiose sound of a few low-fi electronic instruments squiggling about as if the group were attempting to play Holst's *The Planets* with their eyes and ears shut, but they will have to respect my wishes, and ignore my aged youthful zeal. Besides, after that they can sing along with Judy Garland's 'The Man That Got Away'.)

The Tangerine Dream name alone is relatively extraordinary. You couldn't make it up to describe a group who made electronic music that seemed to keep the planet revolving with its ebb and pulse; it would seem too obvious. Except they did. It is one of the wonders of modern music that there is a group called Tangerine Dream whose first album was called *Electronic Meditation*. It's so perfect, and they are exactly the group you would hope to have thought of a name like that, and who are actually called that, and who make music that sounds just like the music of a group called that who make albums called *Electronic Meditation* would sound. Eventually they wrote soundtracks for second-rate Hollywood movies. That was not so perfect, and yet was somehow quite inevitable. They started out the day after tomorrow on another planet and ended up in the next door to the everyday.

The first musician I ever interviewed as a music journalist was Edgar Froese of Tangerine Dream. I interviewed him in a hotel lounge in Madrid. It was the first time I had ever been abroad, and the second time I had ever stayed in a hotel. I had loved the music of Tangerine Dream so much, but at that point, because it was 1977 and punk was raging across the pages of history, it wasn't too cool to admit to a liking for these hippy dreamers whose music seemed to hint even embrace the type of pomp and self-centred introversion that punk was erasing. I secretly thought that Tangerine Dream were truly amazing – this was something you could admit again by the nineties, and, as we speak now, in the twenty-first century, it's becoming more and more acceptable to count the group as a major part of your musical upbringing. But I had a twenty-year-old rock-fan baby-music-journalist snob confusion as to how much I could reveal about what I felt about the group, to Froese in particular and the outside world in general. Also, I was very nervous about meeting him. After all, his music had seemed to melt into my ears from outer space, and it poured through my pleasure centres, and he was surely even more alien than just being a German who couldn't actually speak English. I was a little embarrassed to look him in the eye.

At least, my memory of the occasion is that he couldn't speak English.

I shared the interview with a *Sounds* journalist, and he promised me that he would send me a tape of the interview after he had done with it. I was stupid enough and naïve enough to believe that this was an everyday sort of arrangement, and waited many weeks for a tape to arrive before I realised that the *Sounds* journalist wasn't going to send it. By then, the paper I wrote for, *New Musical Express*, was demanding the piece, and so I wrote something with some quotes that seemed vaguely appropriate to how I imagined Edgar Froese had talked during the interview. There was also the Virgin Records press officer with us during the interview, and I think he translated what Edgar was saying. I don't really know. I was so nervous, and so crushed by Froese, and so puzzled as to why he looked like a frazzled Santa Claus who may or may not have been psychotic, psychedelic and slightly deaf, that I didn't really pay any attention to what he was saying, or, rather, to to the translation of what he was saying. In a way, being big, bearded, wearing white, very calm, slightly aloof, he could be seen as a child's vision of God.

Actually, he might well have been speaking quite good English, but I was so nervous it just sounded like what he was saying needed translation. I would like to think I asked intelligent, probing questions about the nature of his music, his relationship to it, how it developed. I've got a feeling I didn't, in the end, ask anything at all. And so in some respect I came away from meeting a member of this strange, other-worldly group with an even greater sense of there being nothing ordinary about them. The exquisite sense of exotica I felt about the group, and the quiet awe I felt about their ability to produce such naturally soulful sounds using their mysterious metal and wire machines, was considerably enhanced.

I have lost the original piece, but I found a part of it on the Net, in Japanese, and what follows is how it was translated back into English. The translation was made by a machine, which seems entirely appropriate, and I think the piece has found something in the process:

In the beginning knew to begin no so quiet somewhat thereby: synthesiser, sequencer, keyboards, random number generators and oscillators. Does not prevail also today and yet everywhere and with each clarity over it, but music electronics became nevertheless more understandable. While stick living klangbilder were searched still for geometrical and mathematical structures, in order then, with samples it provides, the understanding association and the way to offer, it succeeded to other German musicians to darzubieten the electronically produced music in such a way the listener that they – despite atonalism and saw tooth structure – could find a direct emotional purchase.

Perhaps the music of the future becomes from this electronic sound – and clay/tone university verses come – who knows. Safe is only: the ranges, which cannot do today to no more without quality and statement loss without electronics, are not understanding nearly any longer. The evaluation of this music becomes simultaneous ever more with difficulty. According to which criteria one is to proceed, with which means one is to try to seize this music verbal it in purchase to humans to set, if their do not even know to control Beherr the possibilities of this dargebotenen inexhaustibly completely. Or shouldn't one perhaps at all ask?

No, with security no. The acoustic experience of spontaneous hearing one can penetrate let, one can to be floated be able, one can emotional to be motivated to be able. And because like that is, therefore also this music must be asked.

But the spirit separates here. Here the problem begins. As one asks music, which comes from synthesisers, if one has the same purchase to the synthi as to the vacuum cleaner. How does one ask music which comes from synthesizern if one loves it only because of their clear pures tones? How does one ask music which comes from synthesizern if random generaters and oscillators producer inadvertently sounds, which play the musician? How does one ask this unit from humans and technology, in whom once machine, and another time become humans the subject?

Relatively simple succeeds still, if one can put on assistance. If one can observe the synthi musician in interaction with conventional instrument valleyists or with singers. Also one can understand and understand an individual synthimuziker still relatively clearly and clearly, and experienced ears succeed in ever more frequently understanding this Zweisprache, which is actually a self-discussion between humans and machine. Obscurely however this music, if it, as with Tangerine Dream, comes from three individual personalities, becomes particularly if still everyone of these personalities with itself, with which and with the synthi in the conversation stands for others. Then everything becomes the complex and multilayered unit. From the P.A. towers then stereophon the comprehensibe statement of three brains, three bodies sounds – with only one tongue. In all its warmth, in their perfect rhythmik, in their floating, swelling and then again emotional clay/tone pictures sinking in the endless this music is neverthless compromiseless. It is perhaps still more uncompromiseless than the hardest skirt. On another level, but the Kompromisslosigkeit is boundless. No music demands as the total openness of the listener as this music.

Safe is only indeed. I think the excerpt just about sums the group up – and some of the ideas can be transferred to Lucier, whose music also flirts with 'sinking in the endless'. This just goes to show that writing about music can occasionally, even if in an unexpected way, get to the heart of just what it is that music is, or resembles.

Tangerine Dream, with songless timeless limitless non-urgency, foaming up out of the freaky end of Pink Floyd and the softer centre of Stockhausen, the comprehensible statement of three-brains, three-bodies sounds, with only one tongue, set me off on the drone road; and, within the room of Lucier, I can hear drone. Drone that is both musical and anti-musical, where nothing really happens, no voice, no melody, no rhythm, nothing except, ultimately, nothing. But a nothing that is rich with something. Something that is completely musical. Something that explains something about the world and where you are in connection to it that words cannot.

I hear drone. The drone of existence. The drone of meaning, and of no meaning. Drone as repetition and monotony and a reminder of something that is either the sound inside the womb, the sound of your thoughts before words become your thoughts, the sound you expect after death, or all of that plus sounds that seem to confirm not only that there is life on Mars, but that there is life on earth too. Within the drone, you can hear noises that, quite simply, seem to be coming from the darkness, strange whispers that you are quite possibly imagining, and an echo of the sound of highly evolved insects reading aloud from a script by Samuel Beckett. This, despite evidence to the contrary, can actually be quite comforting.

There is also, within *I am sitting in a room*, a honeyed agitation of variety that is actually extremely non-drony. I can hear the kind of beat and anti-beat – one beat per year, a thousand beats per second, which can, oddly, end up sounding the same – that would surface throughout some of my other favourite music, music that would have labels such as post-rock, hyperdub, click hop, flip hop, click house, heroin house, click clock, click clack, laptoploop, think float, japanoise, technotonic, mixtweak, deep charge, math rock, dronehypenate, drip hop, dropdown, three beat, four top, five alive, six back, seven89, tensionease, chilled beat, grilled beat, thrilled beat, stilled beat, filled beat, platypus duck-billed beat, trilled beat, killed beat, ambient, illbient, finebient, straightbient, bentbient, wentbient, washbient, bientbient, mercedesbient. I like *I am sitting in a room* – it's sort of think float meets tensionease with a drip hop of ambient, a slowmo dose of heroin house and a hint, click, of hyperdub – because it is very beautiful, very peculiar, and completely natural, and because it makes me fancy myself for liking it, because it seems so unusual and intellectual. Above and beyond anything else, it simply is. Music reduced to such psychic simplicity that it cannot really even be labelled as music, let alone as anything else.

10

I like 'Can't Get You Out of My Head' because it has such great shape and it moves with such great confidence. It is built in the image of Kylie's eyebrows, those plucked minimal curves of severe simplicity that transform Kylie's face. It bounces off the discreetly sensual and deeply fictional plumpness of her lips. It reflects the artificially realised but naturally enticing line and shade of her body. It shines like her hair. It swirls like her eyes. It travels in a straight line from A to B but as it travels on this straight line it zigzags and curls up and stretches and shudders. It plays to her vocal strengths, the ease with which her thin, sweet voice can be processed without damaging its essential tough-naïve qualities. The singing of this song requires the kind of understatement Kylie can pull off in her sleep; she is talking her way through the song, allowing a machine to inject the traces of melodic action that slide emphatically and appropriately, but with no immediate sense of fuss, into your head. The song is a pulsating dotted line that connects Kylie's mysteriously submerged soul with the radiant action of the outside world.

It's as if the composers of the song were writing the song in an attempt to compress into song form just what it is about Kylie Minogue that makes her such a great image of an entertainer – her physical representation of the pleasures of pop that mysteriously shimmer in the spaces between innocence and sensuality, between the natural and the artificial. It articulates the sheer professionalism of her presence, a professionalism that can verge on coldness, remoteness, but it captures the ultimate warmth of her absolute need to please her audience, the need of the actress dedicated to success. It's built with ruthless precision so that everything happens just as it should, when it should; it's extremely punctual, understanding exactly a schedule of pleasure that knows the rhythm must happen in a certain way at a certain time – it's obvious but done right this can be sublime – and the hook arrives dead on time, the hook built in the image of Kylie's look, the way she looks, how she looks, where she's looking, right at the camera, into the camera, out into the world, into your world, a world she maintains is just between you and her. The song outlines the distance there is between the girl pop singer looking into the camera and the audience, the voyeur, the invisible mass on the other side of the camera. The song is a diagram of the journey her look, the combination of her looks, takes as it travels from inside her mind via inside the camera to inside our mind.

The impression we might get is that Kylie does nothing but look into a camera, because pretty much the only time we ever see Kylie it will be because she looked into a camera, and that sense of super-real photographic closeness is beautifully captured in the song. The song wasn't particularly written for Kylie Minogue. It could have ended up in the repertoire of Hear'Say, or Cher, or The Sugababes. But it only really makes sense as a Kylie song, as the soundtrack to her life of fame, the soundtrack to her life that is all about fame, the soundtrack that abstractly refers to the life of a singer. The song gives nothing away about the everyday life of Kylie, but gives everything away about the fantasy of Kylie – which is the most important part of Kylie, the only part that need concern us.

It has been cleverly designed by experienced songwriters aware of a history of pop music stretching from the cosmetic repetition of glam to the spatial repetition of house, from the satin repetition of disco to the optimistic repetition of pop, to incorporate all the important elements of a great pop song. It's a paraphrase of the snap and motion, the slink and shine of great dance pop, the pop that moves you to move if only inside your own mind, where all the greatest movement actually takes place.

To make something so simple seem so detailed and seductive is not at all easy. A little less detail and there might be nothing there. A little more detail and it would seem overwrought, unbalanced. Nothing in the previous history of the songwriters – Rob Davis, formerly in the seventies hack-glam band Mud, and Cathy Dennis, a rough, much less fascinating version of the Kylie girl-singer model – would suggest that they were familiar with techniques of Steve Reich and Philip Glass, but their control over the sparse, minimal elements of the song, and their smart development of the monotony, suggest that they were as aware of this area of music as much as they were aware of Kraftwerk, Giorgio Moroder, Abba, New Order, Frankie Knuckles, Madonna and Daft Punk. Their knowledge of the beats, textures and wiring of dance music is attached to an experienced sensitivity towards song arrangement and structure, and spiked with this mysterious respect for the nature, and deceptiveness, of sheer nerveless repetition.

Their accidental or intentional mix of these hedonistic electro elements and the cool dramatic presence of a more academic minimalism left an impression that they were creating a ghostly history of dance music in the grooves of the song. This sense of history then passed over to Kylie, as if it was Kylie herself who was taking us on this journey through dance music, through rhythm, through pop entertainment, as if she was in control of this whole world of dance, of pop, and this whole world had existed just so that it could lead to this song. So, it is Kylie's song, part of a modern pop world at the beginning of the twenty-first century, that is a programmed, processed compression of rhythm, image, myth, tease, money, sound and some kind of promise; and it is a great part, some kind of classic. It is possibly my job, in this story, on this journey, to explain what is actually meant calling it a 'classic', and I shall do my best, by asking you to look at the view all around you, as Kylie drives along, singing the song, dancing to it, meeting people, making friends, sexually supposing and just generally posing, and using the fantasy of her own character to convince a watching, listening world that she is special.

'Can't Get You Out of My Head' has instant appeal, and is so well pieced together, and prepared, following the rules of a pop song in the relationship there is between the rhythm, the words, the melody and the flow, that it is a song you are always pleased to hear. The way that the beat, the lyrics, the harmony and the movement of the track fit together add to so much more than the sum of the parts. There is something abstract and mathematical going on, in the way that the appeal of the song multiplies because of the way that everything connects, and that each part helps another part be a better thing because of the way it has all been joined together. The melody is made better because the rhythm just seems so right. The rhythm is better because of the way that sounds are subliminally laced around it to create a pattern of propulsion that seems so natural and pure. The voice is angled and synthesised to exist perfectly in sight of the pulse, and this helps the rhythm enhance the melody even more, so that the whole thing is a circuit of sound and sensation that appears to emerge out of the air. It sometimes seems as if it is built out of some kind of static dust that exists on the surface of silence. It's a beautifully groomed pattern of noise, a smartly coordinated arrangement of shapes and surfaces. Some of these surfaces are matt, a few are shiny. The shapes are all very regular, but when they combine it is not boring; in fact it is very attractive, even addictive. It is all very tidy, but somehow still very exciting. You get the feeling that even those bits of the song that you can't really see or hear, the parts hidden deep in the mechanism, are polished to within an inch of their artificial life.

The surprises in the song are subdued, but seem more exciting because they are so underplayed. Small shifts in the sound are deeply satisfying, coming as they do out of a deadpan sense of motion that is possibly about the absence of pleasure as much as it is a celebration of it. The little details of gentle thrust and delicate throb are ultimately more interesting because they tease and tempt rather than scream and thrash. There appears to be a lot of space in the song – you can sense huge pools of silence around which the music trips, dives and cavorts, silence that forces the music to change shape, to change direction, to think for itself – and it's the space in the song, the space filled with spaces, that makes the whole thing more stimulating than it would be were it crammed with obvious hooks and routine pop action. It never sounds needy; it never sounds unbalanced by any anxiety about not doing enough. It is an elegant demonstration of the way that all great music is about a relationship between sound and silence, between holding and letting go, between motion and pause.

The song is a fluid thing of deep, deepening mystery, perhaps because what could be so corny, a pop song about love and desire, which doesn't mean anything beyond its own limited world, has become something so profound. A pop song about love and desire that succeeds in communicating millions of unique things about the unlimited worlds of love and lust. The song is about secrets, the unknown, the obvious and the everyday. It's about how everyday life and love are a shifting set of compromises between the ordinary and the extraordinary. It's about how pop music at its best is a simple, irresistible reflection of those compromises. It's about how pop music brings together the mundane and the transcendent – the familiar gets ravished by the unfamiliar and Kylie and her people, for the moments in which this song is of the moment, capture this ravishing state with definitive poise.

It's a wonderful trick, the way that the song is a collection of clichés, nothing you've never heard before, and yet seems brand-new. It's full of shapes and rhythms that have been around for decades; it's a collection of repetitions that could collapse into tedium – Kylie sings from the heart of an off-the-shelf machine – but somehow it ends up being as distinctive as anything that has come before. Maybe what helps the song to transcend the clichés, the formula, has something to do with its title, which comes straight out of a chorus that compresses right into the very centre of a pop song the whole idea of what a pop song should do. A great pop song about love should try to define what it is to feel love for someone else, and should imply how that love will one day come to an end, one way or another, so there is a kind of melancholy lacing the joy; and the song should achieve this in a way that means when you listen to it you can't get it out of your head.

You can't get 'Can't Get You Out of My Head' out of your head, and the song actually refers to this fact all the time, so the song, even as it is about a girl and a boy, or about someone who is talking and someone who is listening, or about sex, or about the movement between one state of mind and another, is about itself. The song is about itself and about the fact that it is about itself. This is not so bizarre a thought as to be frightening or confusing, but it is just ingenious enough to wrap the collection of received sounds and stolen rhythms with a seal of novelty, thus making it not a parody or a homage or a copy of other things, but something that has been made modern and knowing enough to add to the history of a certain kind of pop music. This is because it contains all the elements a great pop song needs, which can never be listed, because some of the elements are known, and can be judged, but many of them are elusive, and can't really be described. This is possibly because what makes a great pop song is not only the correct use of rhythm, form, content and glamour, but also the right atmospheric, emotional connection with performer, time, listeners, the fashion of the moment and the way the present seeps into the future. So you can say that a great pop song needs to be a certain number of things – fresh, familiar, new, traditional, catchy, banal, brilliant – and it also needs to be a number of other uncertain things that are not part of a formula but must not unbalance those elements which are part of a formula, in fact which complement, enhance and re-contextualise those elements. And, of course, the composer of the great pop song is aware of all of this and yet not aware at all. The composer is simply working hard at getting things to sound right given the period of time within which they are working, and at making sure that what the song communicates is unlike anything else before and yet totally like everything that has gone before.

The song also features a thrilling hint of fairly out-of-place droniness. You can imagine it eventually tailing off and becoming a drone that stretches all the way down the highway that Kylie is driving along, showing every sign of getting somewhere, if not nowhere. The song is a sort of mixture of a snipped-off thread of a drone and a precisely tooled pop song featuring elements of some of my other favourite musical things, things I like so much I love making up names for them: a glitter of glam glamour, a stream of new pop shine, tick tock tack beats from a disco dream, unspecified noise shimmers that seem scientifically subsonic, and swanky, caressing, pulse-sonic purpose. Plus, of course, there is, to some extent, a synthesised female voice, with all that that can imply to a listener whose first sexual experience involved a mental embrace with the random momentum music of Tangerine Dream as it dazzle-dissolved my mind on a slow-analogue route to Alpha Centauri.

Whatever world it was that Tangerine Dream travelled from on their way to the Hollywood Hills via dronetown, a metal world wired for sound and breathing, thought and pleasure, then Kylie once visited this planet under the name Barbarella. Wires were inserted into her body, circuits slotted into her mind, and years later she emerged, video-driving towards a city on the other side of the imagination, as a finished mix of dream machine and celebrity. Somewhere in some universe down some wormhole on the edge of some supernova, Tangerine Dream were a time-travelling science-fiction boy band, and Kylie, as a coltish, bare-cheeked Barbarella, guested on their biggest hit, a song that went on for centuries and whose lyrics consisted simply of the sounds 'la la la la la la la'. Here she is on another adventure – it looks to me as if she, with a song and a smile, is being magnetised on to videotape, digitised and projected electronically miles into space, angled off the face of a satellite, back down to a central relay system, amplified, synthesised, re-digitised, sent to peripheral relay posts, forked out to local signal sites, re-magnetised, and sent on her way along primitive copper wiring into homes around the world.

Her expression as she drives and sings seems to be right at the perfect drop-dead living-doll centre between biology and engineering. She is thinking, and she must be right, that she is in a pop video, and we are looking at her live her life inside a pop video, finding just the right preened and provocative ways to match the movement of her body with the movement of her music. As we watch her drive into the city, dancing inside and outside her car, which is dancing through a landscape that is itself dancing, we might be reminded of something that Igor Stravinsky once said.

'I have always resisted the idea of listening to music with eyes closed, i.e., without allowing the eye to plan an active role. If one wants to grasp music in its full scope, it is also necessary to see the sensitivity and movement of the human body by which it is produced.'

II

The likelihood is that you will have heard 'Can't Get You Out of My Head'; and, whether you like it or hate it, I don't suppose you can get it out of your head. That is a part of its great success as an entertainment that verges on a work of art. While it is moving along, the set of signals setting off in their particular way towards a satisfying end that leaves you wanting more, it is communicating its own purpose. The song itself is about itself, as well as being about desire, lust, electricity, attraction, movement, appetite, and so on. As it carries on, lazily creating its own light energy, it talks to itself about just what it is that makes it so alluring. It comments on its own appeal, an appeal that is somewhere between stimulating and comforting.

The song is a very public piece of music. It was built, designed, worked out so that it would make its presence consistently felt in the real world of commercialism. It has been designed to be wanted – this is something else the song talks about: its own need to be wanted, matching the need to be wanted that is part of our daily negotiation with existence. You might say, if you were so inclined, that there is a little sliver of postmodern finery in the area of the song, if that didn't make the song seem deeper and darker than it actually is. Then again, what makes it a postmodern masterpiece is its ability to combine slick self-awareness with a bouncing strut of innocence. The song seems sinful to those who know their sin, and virginal to those who have yet to cross their wires with the charge of sin. You see and hear in the song what you want to see and hear in the song. In the flat, barely furnished simplicity of the piece lie enough blank surfaces for you to etch on your own interpretation of what might be going on. You can see your own levels of sophistication, or unsophistication, reflected in the parts of the song that are mirror-shiny, and the parts that magically hide in the shadows taunt you with shadowy hints of things about yourself that you don't yet know, and that are yet to be revealed.

But you will know the song. The 'la la la's will be already well inside your head. I'm guessing here, but I would presume if you have found yourself reading this book you will be interested in the popular end of music, or at the very least in the electronic fringe of the popular end of music. If you are interested in buying any sort of paperback book written by someone born in the second half of the twentieth century with a cover boasting a certain kind of graphic design and a particular typographic arrangement, then it's ninety-nine per cent certain you will have heard the song. And, of course, there is every likelihood that Kylie is on the cover of this book, and you bought it because of that, and so feel as if you have known the song all of your life. Which in many ways you have, because it sounds as if it has been around forever, even as it sounds very much like a 2001 pop song. A song Kubrick could easily have had HAL sing in *2001: A Space Odyssey* as he broke down, as opposed to 'Daisy Daisy'. It's a song that might have been around in 1968 even though it could only have been made after the technological developments and movements in pop style and electronic dance music over the last thirty years. The transparency, smartness, shape and space of the song would have suited *2001* the film. The sense that it is from the past yet of the future even as it arrived squarely out of the present. A song that belongs in a fictional 2001 as well as a factual 2001.

It was again very smart of the composers, the constructers, the programmers, the architects, the makebelievers of this song that they realised that a succesful pop song in the early twenty-first century has every chance to get right inside the heads of most of the populations of most of the areas of most of the world that is wired into sound. Once the song was working commercially and getting inside people's heads like an irresistible command, the song became more and more real, more and more an accurate self-reflection of its own reflective surfaces, and grew in strength and power, becoming, if I'm not missing the point, if there is one, a pop classic.

I'm also probably right in thinking that most of you will not have heard *I am sitting in a room*. Even I, for whom it is a favourite piece of music, am not completely sure that I have actually heard it. I'm confident enough to consider that I can write about it with enough of a sense of expertise to push the story in this book along to wherever it needs to get pushed, but I remain puzzled as to the circumstances in which I originally heard it. In some ways I can remember the moment I first heard the piece; in other ways, it is an elusive thought, something I can't quite pin down. Then again, I feel the same way about the first time I heard Hendrix, or Peter Hammill, or Henry Cow, or Helmet. They all just seemed to appear in my life as something I had listened to. I might have stopped listening to them. Certainly Henry Cow and Helmet are artists I haven't listened to for a while, whereas I would say that I have listened to Hammill and Hendrix quite recently; but, now I think about it, I may not have listened to Hendrix as recently as I thought. In fact, it may have been as long a time as it has been since I listened to Helmet; it just seems more recently. I suppose the difference is that when I listen to Hendrix there will be a week of Hendrix. I will live with Hendrix in a great penthouse apartment with a view of eternity. With Helmet, it will be a hop, skip and a jump through a CD. It will be a few minutes of it. I will fumble with Helmet in a back alley. I guess, with Lucier, there was a time when I played it a lot, although I can't remember when that was. I can believe I once had the time, but I think that about a lot of the music I know and like – to have the time to play all the music I may end up mentioning in this book, this book-like history of music, I would have to live for about 343 years. But that's another story, another seven stories, and I'm not going to get there for another two or three books, when I will write the novel about my 416-year life span which I needed just to listen to every jazz album I want to listen to, let alone every pop and rock and so on CD. So I can't remember making the time to get to know Lucier's *Sitting Room*. I can't remember sitting in that time to listen to the *Sitting Room*; I just believe that there was once such a time, I found the time, I made the time, I created the time, or Lucier created the time for me, and it changed the way I feel about music, subtly and yet profoundly. I can hear the music develop in my mind as I think about it, I can feel its weight, and understand its magic. It has a magic that is to do with time, and how you find time, and how time finds you, and what happens when you meet, time and you, in the middle of nowhere, timed to meet, timed to perfection, from time to time, time stops, in the middle of music, which is all about time, and about the way that time and timing is everything, and music is time itself turned into form, time is the past and the present turned into content, form and content connect blend float across time, time for thought, time to listen, time to feel, time to end this sentence, which was written while listening to a CD by Matthew Shipp called *Pastoral Composure* which creates a pretty abstract picture of time.

I am sitting in a room is a private piece of music. It was not composed with the idea of entering a commercial zone, it was not designed with the thought of creating a soundtrack to youthful energy, and it was not created in order to make money. It was improvised as an experiment in sound to see what would happen if you followed the exact instructions involved in performing certain tasks involving sounds and the recording of them.

If 'Can't Get You Out of My Head' is a musical representation of commerce, of the buying and selling of moods, clichés, comforts and styles, is music conceived out of the conniving busy-ness of business, then *I am sitting in a room* is a musical representation of personal philosophy, a demonstration of privacy and introspection, a lonely pursuit of mysterious company, a quiet way of working out what to believe in, and why. If Kylie's song is city music, made to be played in cities all the time so that it becomes part of those cities' complicated structure, Lucier's piece is water music, vast, adrift, deep, fluid, dark and a little scary.

This doesn't explain exactly what it sounds like, and this clearly has to be the next stage of this story, the stage after the beginning that begins to move the story out into its world of adventure. It doesn't matter so much that I cannot really describe what the Kylie Minogue song sounds like, even though that's meant to be my job, because I can really take it for granted that you've heard it. Whatever I say about it confirms your own sense of what the song sounds like. Sometimes I will write something you agree with, sometimes something you don't agree with, but mostly you will think, Yes, he is talking about the song I know. I just have to go 'La la la, la la la . . .' and you will be in the song, the song will be in you.

But if this story is to develop towards the essential middle, and get a sight of the all-important end, then we need to know what happens next. And because of the way things have been set up, what happens next is a need to know exactly what *I am sitting in a room* is, and what it sounds like. How this work connects, in the way it combines space, thought and sound, to 'Can't Get You Out of My Head', and beyond that a whole world of music, from Mozart to maybe Moby, a world of music that is the main setting for this story. Actually, the world of music, according to my notes, appears to be not only the setting for this story, but a major character as well, and also the main sex/love object. It will not be murdered. It is immortal – not to make the story fantasy or science fiction or anything. It will not perform murder – it is beyond good and evil, not to lose my mind or anything.

12

Alvin Lucier's *I am sitting in a room* is an electro-acoustic classic. It is a cornerstone in the world of resonant frequencies, a fascinating exploration of acoustical phenomena. I think it is a clue to its existence that it can be described as such, and also as a looping classic, as a minimalist classic, and I have seen it in numerous lists of important, influential music. Hopefully, by mentioning electro-acoustic, resonant frequencies, minimalism and looping, you are beginning to see more of the decoration in the room that Lucier was sitting in. The decoration is particularly minimal, but not without extreme interest. You can in fact begin to make out the shape and size of the room if you listen to the music, from the way the music begins to develop in sonic reaction to its surroundings. The sound as it progresses creates a kind of aural diagram of the room: the sound becomes the room, an impression of the space the room fills. Of course, you need to hear the music to get a picture of what kind of room it was made in, so that you can look at this mental picture of the room and work out how the room would sound. So this isn't really helping us work out how the piece sounds; it just emphasises that the piece was written to be performed inside a room, which is then the amplifier, the illustrator, the container of the music. The room collaborates in the composition of the music. It supplies the dimensions and the atmosphere of the world that the music exists inside, and this world makes the rules that dictate how the music sounds.

The work, which questions the distinctions between speech and music, is conceptually rich, sonically lovely and is achieved with an extraordinary economy of means. It consists of Lucier sitting in a room with two distant microphones, two tape decks, and speakers. The recording begins with Lucier verbally describing the process of the piece, which is that he is recording his voice and, after the recording has been made, he will play it back through the speakers, and record that through microphones on to the second tape deck. This continues for about a variable amount of generations – anywhere between twenty-five and fifty. 'I am sitting in a room,' begins Lucier, 'a room that is not the same as the room you are sitting in.' The explanation of the process becomes the work itself. The work is commenting on itself, creating itself out of its own text. It exists because it says that it must exist. It comes into existence, the sound of something appearing out of the sound of nothing, the room of the universe appearing out of the nowhere of nowhere, in the way that the Bible says our universe was invented. In the beginning was the word. And God said, 'Let there be noise.' And there was noise. There was silence, then there was a word, then there was sound. And God eventually, after a bit of prevaricating, found a way for it all to be recorded. Music will be mostly recorded in a recording studio, a room, and it is in rooms that music gets made, and is played, and it is the room that Alvin Lucier is in that is set in the past but relates to the future and therefore has more than a nodding acquaintance with some kind of present, and it is this room, this room that is the environment for Lucier's text to evolve into sound, that is a metaphor for all music that exists because of a room. The room in which it was made and the room in which it is then listened to. The room which liberates and then contains the music. The music you can't get out of your room. If you travel listening to music in a car, then the car becomes the room. If you listen to music on the move with the help of headphones, then your head becomes the room. You can't get music out of your room, your head, the places that make sure we don't leak out into the universe, the spaces that hold us in place. The places and spaces that allow time to have a boundary, that allow music to maintain its shape.

Listening to *I am sitting in a room*, as I remember I once did, some-where, somehow, in some way, made me think of the very beginning of time, even the time before time, if that was time. It made me think of a place where there was no space and no place for space. It slipped me back in time to when there was no time. As the sound of the piece developed, I drifted into the musical patterns that were forming as sound collapsed and reformed, and thought of how this musical story began at the absolute beginning of everything, when there was nothing but a beginning. Along the significant lines of:

10–15 billion years ago The universe is born.

10,243 seconds later The temperature cools to 100 million trillion trillion degrees and gravity evolves.

10,234 seconds later The temperature cools to 1 billion billion billion degrees and matter emerges in the form of quarks and electrons. Antimatter also appears.

10,210 seconds later The electroweak force splits, becoming the electromagnetic and weak forces.

1,025 seconds later With the temperature at 1 trillion degrees, the quarks form protons and neutrons and the antiquarks form antiprotons. The protons and antiprotons collide, leaving mostly protons and causing the emergence of photons (light).

1 second later Electrons and electrons (positrons) collide, leaving mostly electrons.

1 minute later At a temperature of I billion degrees, neutrons and protons coalesce and form elements such as helium, lithium, and heavy forms of hydrogen.

300,000 years after the Big Bang The average temperature is now around 3,000 degrees and the first atoms form.

1 billion years after the Big Bang Galaxies form.

3 billion years after the Big Bang Matter within the galaxies forms distinct stars and solar systems.

5–10 billion years after the Big Bang, about 5 billion years ago The earth is born.

3.4 billion years ago The first biological life appears on earth – single-celled creatures.

1.7 billion years ago Simple DNA evolves.

700 million years ago Multicellular plants and animals appear.

400 million years ago Land-based plants evolve.

200 million years ago Dinosaurs and mammals begin sharing the environment.

80 million years ago Mammals develop more fully.

65 million years ago Dinosaurs become extinct, leading to the rise of mammals.

30 million years ago Advanced primates such as monkeys and apes appear.

15 million years ago The first humanoids appear.

5 million years ago Humanoid creatures are walking on two legs. *Homo habilus* is using tools, ushering in a new form of evolution: technology.

A slight flutter in the acoustic texture of *I am sitting in a room*, and I am flung into the future, I am brought back, more or less, to earth. But there is something about the way that Lucier's piece grows and slows and speeds and shrinks that makes you wonder how sound, and the way we hear it, and how it connects to us, all began.

13

Vibration and regular repeating patterns are the foundations of matter and energy. On a scale more accessible to humans, rhythmic repetition, oscillation and pulsation are dominant qualities of nature known to everyone. Waves on a shore, moon phases, day and night, the seasons. There is pulsation and rhythm in our own body. Heartbeat, breathing, the steady rhythm of walking that was imprinted in our genetic memory during our life as nomads. These basic experiences of life have long ago formed our love of rhythm. While developing a sense of rhythm, our ancestors found that it was fun to sing along with the rhythm. Our first melodies were taught to us by birds and other animals, all of whom employ repetitions in their songs.

14

At the beginning of Lucier's work, you can imagine the shock of the moment in which something first murmured a noise out of nothing, a shock we are all still trying to recover from. Lucier begins with a basic description of a setting and suggests how that setting might change through some simple commands; and then, slowly, and then faster, at its own speed, a whole new world of worlds within worlds evolves and takes shape. It is a piece of music that therefore reminds us both of the miracle of existence and the miracle of music. It makes you think that the first sign of existence was noise, that noise came first, noise before consciousness, and that our eternal unquenchable fascination with music is partly a consequence of some irreversible genetic memory we have that before us there was noise, and this noise is what all music is based on. All music echoes the very beginning of time. Some of those echoes are more profound and possibly accurate than others.

As Lucier's text is repeated over and over in the room, the acoustic properties of the room become apparent. Each room you perform the piece in will make a difference to the sound. The room acts as a filter to the sounds being produced, and each room would create a different sort of filter, meaning each performance would be different, each decomposition of the vocal instructions would alter at a different rate, with different textures emerging at different places with different sounds being eliminated at different places. The piece can never be the same twice, and Lucier, in his instructions, explicitly encourages experimentation.

> Make versions in which one recorded statement is recycled through many rooms. Make versions using one or more speakers of different languages in different rooms. Make a version where, for each generation, the microphone is moved to different parts of the room or rooms. Make versions that can be performed in real time.

Echoes begin to elongate and smear the speech, and the resonances of the room enhance some of the frequencies present, while others disappear. Gradually, the speech is shaped into a kind of music. Melodies and harmonies start to appear – accidentally, and yet with apparent purpose. The words become a complex weave of pitches based upon the intersections of the recorded voice and the resonant frequencies of the room. The words become less and less distinguishable as words – they become part of the mechanics of the noise, circuit resonance and tape dropouts, they bend and blend into abstract sounds, they reconstruct themselves as the process reverses, and the sense of the words turns into a new, more abstract kind of sense, a sense you can only imagine, or imagine you can interpret. The specific demands fixed language places on the way you respond to the work dissolves into other kinds of demands, and you are inspired to respond to a more and more nonliteral sequence of events that ask for a more complicated, less traditional response.

Hearing a plain descriptive text evolve into something so abstract and beautiful is very moving. You feel yourself sinking through language itself into thought and beyond that into the impulses and instincts that lie beyond thought, into the very depths of the soul that music represents and reflects. It's as if you are drifting back through time, to a period before language, when existence was a pure, unformed smear on the surface of an abyss. The piece becomes a provocative meditation on the relationship of man and machine, meaning and form, art and technique, past and present, present and future. It is also incredible to realise that something so sumptuous and strange was essentially created using just one voice and two tape recorders – and, of course, a room, the room being just as important as the voice and the machines. The room creates the surroundings for the piece, the sound of the piece, and both limits and unlimits the nature of the piece. It supplies the colour, the depth, the kind of echoes, the way the sound rubs and dissolves and replicates itself. You hear melodies, dynamics and rhythms that remind you of every type of music you have heard and have yet to hear. All of this sound, enough to hint at the possible size of the universe, exists because one mouth reads out simple instructions worked out by one mind, which are then roughly filtered through some primitive if ultimately magical electronics equipment. It exists because, somewhere in the universe it is estimating the size of, in the universe that is bigger than a room and smaller than a mind, there is someone thinking about its existence.

It is a piece belonging to that area of music which responds to ideas, and to what ideas are and what they can do, rather than to music as a purely musical end in itself, or to music as a way to make money, or generate fame. The idea is as important as the music. In fact, the idea *is* the music, not in a traditional compositional way, but in a way that floats far outside the conventions of music. It is not as such a musical piece, but musical things happen, in the most transcendent and uncompromising way. It is, in its way, more purely musical than a piece of music written to be played and listened to as a piece of music. It taps into the musical elements that exist in the great silent nature of existence, it captures the sound inside reality, it reaches out into the vastness of the universe and finds a way to transmit the pulse and harmony, the very matter floating throught itself, that there was before us, and that there will be after us – the music of the spheres that genius composers have struggled to contain using traditional instruments and the inherited conventions of musical structure. Lucier crosses the universe of sound using just his voice and a simple set of electronic equipment.

Tattooed at the nape of Kylie's neck, in print so small that not even her closest lover has actually read the words, are the following paragraphs, presumably there to help us with our history of music. Because Kylie is a main character, it is only right that she should be so helpful in participating in this explanation. She herself has no idea that these words are collected at the top of her spine. She has never fully appreciated how she is up to her neck in history. As far as she is concerned the mark is not even a tattoo – it is simply a birthmark that one of her lovers remarked seemed to be in the shape of a rabbit. Or a robot. Or a robot rabbit. As she drives her car into the centre of the city with no centre, feeling more and more as if her journey resembles a tumble down a tunnel, her long, light-brown hair covers up the robot-rabbit mark, the text tattoo, and it is only from our particular position of privilege, as writer and readers of this musical fantasy, that we can see the following words:

Prehistory	While the voice is the original musical instrument, tools and instruments are developed to make sounds, probably for ritual, spiritual, ceremonial and entertainment purposes.
Ancient times	Mechanical sound-making instruments are created, for which the energy source is no longer directly that of the lungs or hands – for example, bagpipes, where the energy is stored in a bag; and water organs, where flowing water pumps the air.
Fifth century BC	The monochord is developed – a one-string instrument used to explore the relationship of intervals.
	Pythagoras says: 'There is geometry in the humming of strings. There is music in the spacing of the spheres.'
Fourth century BC	Chinese musical writings emphasise the philosophical, cosmological and educational values of music.
100	Claudius Ptolemy writes *Harmonika*, a treatise on harmonics, acoustics, interval theory, tetrachords, modes, the monochord, and the relationships

between notes, parts of the body and heavenly bodies.

325 Constantine declares Christianity the official religion of the Roman Empire. The spread of Christianity in the Western world spurs the development of European music.

600 Pope Gregory the Great codifies and collects the chant, which is later used in Roman Catholic services and is named the Gregorian chant in his honour.

850 Western music begins to move from monophony to polyphony with the vocal parts in church music moving in parallel intervals.

1030 Guido of Arezzo, an Italian monk, develops a system for learning music by ear. Voice students often use this system for the naming of notes, solfeggio, to memorise their vocal exercises. In the nineteenth century, solfeggio develops into the tonic sol-fa system used today, at least by Julie Andrews.

1180 Troubadors appear in Germany and call themselves *minnesingers*, 'singers about love'.

1565 Castration emerges in Italian music as a means to imitate the sound of a woman's voice; deemed necessary because of St Paul's dictum prohibiting women from singing on stage and in churches. The practice becomes commonplace by 1574.

1588 The English Madrigal School is firmly established. The movement, led by Thomas Morley, produces some of the most delightful secular music ever heard, with the Madrigals often telling stories of love or grief.

1619 Johannes Kepler writes his *Harmony of the Worlds*, seeking celestial harmony – chaos is but unperceived order. Kepler argues that the human soul was endowed by God with the ability to intuit the harmony in the universe.

Kylie doesn't know this either, but the small birthmark on her left ankle in the shape of the number 720 is actually a tattoo of something said in first-century BC China: 'When numbers assume form, they realise themselves in musical form.'

16

In the car Kylie is driving into the centre of the city with no name, Alvin Lucier is reciting the instructions for his piece *I am sitting in a room*.

> I am sitting in a room different from the one you are in now. I am recording the sound of my speaking voice and I am going to play it back into the room again and again until the resonant frequencies of the room reinforce themselves, so that any semblance of my speech, with perhaps the exception of rhythm, is destroyed. What you will hear then are the natural resonant frequencies of the room articulated by speech. I regard this activity not so much as a demonstration of a physical fact, but more as a way to smooth out any irregularity my speech might have.

The words to *I am sitting in a room* came to me in a dream I had about words and music. Or they came to me in a dream I had about a dream Kylie was having about a city at the edge of her imagination. Or they came to me after a trip across the Internet to see what the words were. Or they came to me when, some time ago, I heard the words, and they made such an impact on me I can quote them straight off. Except when I forget them. Or, possibly, they came to me in a dream I had about a Web search where I found the words to *I am sitting in a room* and realised as soon as I saw them that I already knew them, from the time I listened to this piece of music so many times I couldn't get the words out of my head. Or perhaps the words came to me as soon as inscrutable Alvin quoted them to inquisitive Kylie in a car the shape and size of a memory that exists in a dream.

These words are, if you like, the lyrics of the piece. In this kind of process music, the instructions are everything. It is as if you say that you are going to push a swing. Then you push a swing. Then you watch the swing as it swings, as it slows down, as it comes to a halt. That is what happens here. Lucier thinks of the text. He speaks the text, he follows the instructions. Then he sees what happens. He lets things happen until the things that are happening come to a stop.

As he speaks, it becomes clear that he has a slight speech impediment, a little stutter. He makes himself more eloquent and aurally interesting by distorting his voice so that it evolves and resolves into a pure abstract sound that has no perceivable relationship to text or even the human voice. Lucier's stutter is obliterated and we are left with pure sound. A sound as modern – or as ancient – as anything. A sound that emerged out of the machinery that is the mind through the machinery of the mouth into two microphones and then down wires and along the edge of reason out into a world of perception and memory. A sound that tunnels between thought and feeling, between surface and depth, between sense and more, or less, sense.

As automatic Kylie steers the glossy car down the centre of the highway towards the abstract city of dreams, we have moved from the symbolic to the sonic and, perhaps, back again.

17

If you still cannot imagine what *I am sitting in a room* sounds like, even though you now know the lyrics, so to speak, then perhaps references to other music might help you locate it. To start with, a classic list of twenty pieces of music that helps to define the way serious music progressed – as an intellectual, emotional, sensualised adventure – during the last 100 years could be:

Claude Debussy, *Prelude to the Afternoon of a Faun*
Scott Joplin, 'Maple Leaf Rag'
Igor Stravinsky, *The Rite of Spring*
Arnold Schoenberg, *Pierrot Lunaire*
Charles Ives, *The Concord Sonata*
George Gershwin, *Rhapsody in Blue*
Maurice Ravel, *Bolero*
Olivier Messiaen, 'The Quartet for the End of Time'
Aaron Copland, 'Appalachian Spring'
John Cage, *Sonatas and Interludes*
Alan Hovhaness, 'Mysterious Mountain'
Terry Riley, 'In C'
Steve Reich, 'Drumming'
Alvin Lucier, *I am sitting in a room*
Ben Johnston, 'String Quartet No. 4'

Philip Glass, *Einstein on the Beach*
Robert Ashley, *Perfect Lives*
Laurie Anderson, 'O Superman'
Arvo Pärt, *Miserere*
Meredith Monk, 'Atlas'

Of those, direct clues to the density, delicacy, relentlessness and other-ness of *I am sitting in a room* would come from having heard the uncertain, definite sounds of records by Riley and Reich, the inscrutable, hypnotic way Ashley narrates his opera *Perfect Lives* and the way it demonstrates the musicality of the spoken word, and the sense of philosophical playfulness and seriousness in the works of John Cage and Laurie Anderson. This, anyway, will be pushing you into the right areas, and somewhere in there is the exact area, and inside that area is the actual room in which *I am sitting in a room* is sitting. Sitting as if it is hovering. Hovering as if it is meditating. Meditating as if it is dreaming. Dreaming as if it is alive.

A record I've always loved, and that is in an area possibly in the next field of imagination to *I am sitting in a room*, is *No Pussyfooting* by Robert Fripp and Brian Eno. (Eno is a major character in this book; and, although he is not the murderer in the murder that may or may not occur during the story, he certainly went to bed, or fantasised that he did, with the best friend of the person who is murdered.) *No Pussyfooting* is another stunning sonic sculpture that, when you listen to it, feels as if it has taken shape in the room with you. It seems alive. It has substance, and it moves, towards you, away from you, inside you, all over you. It's thick and oozy, and you hear it and you think, 'If the universe cut itself shaving – and it has to shave now and then (it is the universe, after all) – then it would bleed the sound of *No Pussyfooting*.'

Related to Lucier's experimentations in the way that it is one instrument, in this case guitar, treated by electronic sources to sound like something else, to sound bigger and odder and more flexible, it conjures up similar levels of abstraction that seem to get extremely close to the absolute essence of what music is, and how we experience it, and why we experience it. The music takes on the shape of our thoughts in a dream about our thoughts. What seems at first listening to contain no details, to be monotonous and austere, proves with repeated listenings to be a mass of details and variety. *No Pussyfooting* was the second stop

– to some extent I am still at the stop, stopped inside the drone as it stops time until it seems so stopped it's actually moving – on my journey into a life of drone. If Tangerine Dream was a lover, then I left that lover for *No Pussyfooting*, and it was this record that further, and more comprehensively, prepared me for serious drone travel. *No Pussyfooting* contained a series of codes that a young listener could use to crack a new musical world that was without limit – music so monotonous and minimal actually showed that music could be anything. This nothing. This everything. Since the early seventies, because of *No Pussyfooting* and the music that liking Fripp and Eno, and Eno and Roxy Music, led me to – Can, Faust, Cluster, Ornette Coleman, Terry Riley, Miles Davis, La Monte Young, Spontaneous Music Ensemble, added to an early love for Iggy and The Stooges, The Velvet Underground and King Crimson – no musical development has seemed too far out, too intimidating. Eno's exploration of the drone and the dynamic of music, their differences and their similarities, prepared me, in this story, for everything that has been and was to come. Including *I am sitting in a room*.

For the sake of this story, the musician who first wrote a piece of music for which the score comprised instructions was Erik Satie, in 1893. 'Vexations', a masterpiece of musical mischief, was a piece where the performer was asked to play two lines of chromatic, diminished triads. This would take a minute or two to play. You then repeated this. Then again. And again. And again – 840 times. Satie suggested that, before the performer played this piece 840 times, they should prepare in deep silence and serious immobility. When repeated for hours, it was said, the music developed a deep and quiet kind of beauty. With its large-scale repetitive structure, the absence of strong contrast, the intent to transform consciousness through the hypnotic intensity of the sound, it was in many ways the very beginning of looped, minimal music, and therefore the very beginning of a kind of music that stretches all the way through Riley, Lucier, Fripp and Eno, and then out through Kraftwerk, Grandmaster Flash, and further out into electronic dance music, taking off up to the far-out, fucked-up, MOR computer-programmed sci-fi R&B of Dr Dre, the Neptunes and Timbaland, and all popular music made on computers, which includes just about all popular music. It can all be traced back, honestly enough, to the early part of the twentieth century, when Erik Satie fancied fooling around with the limits of music as he saw and heard them. He started to cut up music, to move it around, to wrap it around the little finger of the future, to imagine how sound would be transformed by technology and how technology would transform the imagination.

For years 'Vexations' was thought of as a musical joke. An impossible, not to mention very boring, task. John Cage took it very seriously indeed. For him, there was something to worship in the idea; it was positively mystical – this way of reducing music to next to nothing, and then increasing it to a point where time ceases to have meaning, and is therefore a place that is reached on the edge of forever.

Cage, the master of turning ideas about sound into the sound of ideas, premièred Satie's 'Vexations' on 9 September 1963, when eleven players, including Cage, took turns to play the piece. The performance went on for almost a day – eighteen hours and forty minutes. While we contemplate Cage contemplating a piece of music that excites him so much because it is so seriously about time, humour, and mystery, for the sake of progress let's point out a quick set of links to the rest of the book as much as it relates to Brian Eno.

Eno, because he was a pop star in glam-galore Roxy Music, who orchestrated a style collision between the drones of La Monte Young, the stress of the Velvet Underground and the fire of the Who, who hooked up Coward with Kraftwerk, took the advanced theories of Erik Satie and John Cage, who had taken the advanced theories of Luigo Russulo and Marcel Duchamp, and transformed them into an intelligently neo-commercialised semi-mainstream, and changed all music because of it. There will be other references to Eno's genre-shredding, idea-embedding influence on music elsewhere in this story, but they will all be variations on this simple formula: Satie + Cage X the Velvet Underground ÷ himself = Eno.

Don't worry if this make no sense – there is no sense in worrying about such things, and the nonsense of worrying cancels out the nonsense of the formula, and somewhere in there is the absolute quandary, and delight, of writing about music, and the whole problem of trying to write about music may get so fraught as this story develops that it might end in a murder or two. Or at least a disappearance of sorts. If there is a murder in this story, then Eno is not the victim, nor is he the killer. He is, let's face it, the detective who'll reach a solution in the most ingenious manner.

He will refer to some notes by Satie to help him in his quest.

18

The following is something I wrote when Eno asked for my statement while investigating the murder that will or will not take place. I could just be describing myself here, my own taste in my own terms, but, not surprisingly, I consider the following to be how it is, not how it might be, in terms of a rough description of the advancing twists and turns rock music has made since music turned to rock.

If you were in your mid-teens in the mid-seventies and you were particularly obsessed with what is, in this story, a holy trinity of The Velvet Underground, Kraftwerk and Can, and if, at the edges of the centre of the trinity, your taste was for Beefheart and Zappa, T. Rex and Alice Cooper and David Bowie and Roxy Music, MC5 and Iggy and the Stooges, Tangerine Dream and Neu! and Faust and Cluster, then a little incidental journey can be mapped out here – one that will eventually take us back to the highway that Kylie and Alvin are speeding along as they make their way to the centre of the city, the city where all music eventually arrives. I'm not sure what happened to the Beatles, the Beach Boys and Chuck Berry, other than their perverse influence on some of the above. I can see Radiohead in the distance, but I'm not sure their car is moving as well as it might. The book you are wanting if you are more of a Beatles, Beach Boys, Berry kind of a person features George Michael and Electric Light Orchestra, and in it George Michael is taking a walk through the park in the centre of a city that is a little like the one Kylie is driving towards, but perhaps not as, shall we say, *plugged in* as Kylie's city. That book, as you can imagine, is a very different travel book to this one, but I am sure it is very readable. It just doesn't taste anything like the same as the city in this book, and my own feelings are that the city in this book has more of a future than the city in that book, or at least is better suited to the future, at least a future that seems like a future from where we are in the present.

The journey in this book means that you would, starting with the Velvet Underground and Can, moving forward in time, have found space and time for The Sex Pistols, Wire, The Fall, Buzzcocks, Cabaret Voltaire, Throbbing Gristle, Joy Division, Television, Patti Smith, Pere Ubu, the Modern Lovers, The Human League, The Smiths, Sonic Youth, The Pixies, My Bloody Valentine, Nirvana, N.W.A., Tortoise, Pavement, Underworld, Björk, Four Tet, Godspeed You! Black Emperor, Múm, Missy Elliot . . . (Somewhere in the late nineties, due to my age, or the age of rock, the amount of time there is in a day, the way that rock was eating regurgitating echoing shadowing repeating replacing reworking repackaging renaming itself, I drifted off a little, and lost interest in groups with names like Muse, Coldplay, Coral, The Music, who seemed to have all the right moves, learned like rock was a university subject, but no stunning sense of motion; nothing other than an exuberant competence, a sweetened blandness. Groups like Oasis and The Strokes seemed as exercises in recreation that made no sense if you were not of an age where you were simply passing through music, as part of your education in the ways of modern simulation, and were simply demanding to be entertained in a way that seemed appropriate to how you were meant to behave at a certain age according to the well-established laws of pop-culture rebellion, a rebellion that by the end of the nineties actually meant a commercially controlled conforming to ways of behaviour that must be maintained if the original energy of rock and roll was to be exploited in ways that sustained business and the illusion of rock excitement. As part of the new chaos of the world, music split into its own versions of reality – the reality of a music made for original reasons to do with developing and refining influences, and the reality of a music that was pretending to develop the history of rock even as it went back on itself, and went back on its word, and fixed itself to various dates in the sixties, seventies and eighties. There was music that was made with machines and sounded as if it was made with machines and was the music of the moment. And there was music made with machines that pretended to a kind of authenticity established in the sixties and seventies that was long out of date, worn out by the new world of virtual sensations. A lot of the new rock sounded to me, of a certain age, with a certain predilection for the glamorous, the exotic and the experimental, like the same old can of beans, but with a new label, a new product shape, a couple of synthetic extra ingredients. It seemed to be a revivalist kind of music, paying homage to certain periods of rock, but lacking the vital element of sonic, philosophical surprise. This perhaps suggested that somewhere along the way, maybe as early as 1969, or 1977, or as late as 1990, rock music, if you know what I mean, had reached its ultimate potential as a combination of sound, energy and meaning, and everything else was just a case of finessing, modifying, recalling. Now and then there could be a sudden shift, a fashionable shift, a hype-able shift in tension and attitude, a change of emphasis in the sound possibility, but essentially it was the same old sound, the same old idea of a sound, in a different time zone, a different context. By the beginning of the twenty-first century, this meant that there was a peculiar paradox in music where some pop records of the day were made in a more sonically original way than the rock records, so that what could be described as teenybop music, mass-marketed pop for teenagers, sounded more modern, intense and strange than the serious rock, which just sounded like rock had always sounded. Which meant that in the case of, say, The Strokes, it sounded like a group making music that would have sounded fantastic in 1977 New York, but which in the twenty-first century sounded like something old that was in fact new, like a music that had travelled through time from a time where it never was in the first place. It had a period quality, but in a modern sense. Or it had a postmodern quality, but in an ancient sense. It was on the edge of novelty, novelty with an edge of attitude, but it lacked the edge of now. The Strokes were great at re-creating moments but not as great at creating moments. They were conservative (they conserved); they weren't radicals (they didn't remake the world). Their music was a tribute to a radical spirit, while missing a radical spirit. Ultimately what was lacking was the sense of newness, the sense of coming-out-of-nowhereness, that gives essentially simple, obvious bursts of communication a power beyond the immediate. If Television had not made 'Little Johnny Jewel' in 1975, and we had first heard it in 2000, it would have still been as uncanny a piece of music (and, in a way, perhaps the Strokes have produced music as brutally dreamlike) but it would have had twenty-five years of other things that have happened to contend with – like the fact that sounds as bent, warped and nervy as it contains now streak the most everyday of pop singles. So, it would have been a near classic, but somehow it would have had a quaintness about it that would ruin the apparent power.

If 1949 Charlie Parker had in fact first popped up in 1964, well, it would have been quite arresting but, really, pretty pointless. This is the problem I began to see at my age as rock music started to photocopy itself: what was lacking for me was the suddenness that must be attached to the sound, the suddenness of its appearance and its newness. The suddenness of sound when it sounds like new sound connected to but adrift from other sounds.

It's as if a filmmaker now made a film carefully re-creating all the techniques Welles developed in *Citizen Kane*, but neglecting to incorporate everything that has happened in film since. Clever, perhaps, even fascinating, but a little dull, even a little sad. The Strokes sound like they're new in an old-fashioned way, and something that needs to be new cannot also sound old-fashioned it if wants to be anything other than just another sound in the same old kitchen. Actually, with the Strokes, it's like a comedian post-Milligan/Cook/Monty Python/Reeves and Mortimer coming along with an act exactly like Charlie Chaplin. You'd laugh if you were young enough not to remember the original, but at a certain age you would think, 'Those trousers look really stupid.' In fact, I quite like the Strokes as a comedy group, and I very much like the Strokes when their music is mixed up, in a bootleg sense, with the music of pole-dancing pop fiasco Christine Aguilera: 'A Stroke of Genius' – a blasting together of one Strokes thing, 'Hard to Explain', and one Aguelera song, 'Genie in a Bottle' – conjures up the reality-bending shock of the new that the Strokes lack. The stupid sublime stitching together of heated machined pop dripping with money and reheated NY punk scratched out of the fake history books creates a ravishing blur of signals, signatures, speeds and gaps in time that please me in the places where I like to be pleased, the places where the mind and body cannot make up their mind and body who is in charge. It's got the best beat the Strokes will ever have, because where they look back to for sound was a bit pre-beat, a bit pre-post-punk, a bit pre-computer time-shifting. 'A Stroke of Genius' sounds like new sound; and, at the end of the twentieth century, into the beginning of the twenty-first century, it was commercial pop that was sounding more exciting than commercial rock. The hybrid that made up pop, borrowing from all over a glamorous machine century of sound and image, style and sensation, had more impact than the hybrid that made up rock, which borrowed from rock, and from just within rock. Sounds stripped down in number-one songs, sounds creeping around the back of pop hits, were more experimental than rock bands lifting ballads out of a world where Elton John duetted with Radiohead. I don't know what this means, except that I found more modern delight in listening to the Sugababes than in listening to Coldplay. Coldplay seemed stuck in the middle of the road with mid-period Stealer's Wheel; the Sugababes seemed to be driving through the digital dust of a modern city with Joe Meek, Steve Reich and mad-period Can. Missy Elliot is more avant-garde than mod-period Oasis by a million micromassive granulated miles. But then, so are Mis-teeq.

Yes, by the time Oasis arrived, and then the Strokes, I was getting old, remembering too much, yearning for my own kind of youth, and my own set of circumstances, nostalgic for my own version of rebellion. I was out of touch, with the very nature of what it is to be a rock-and-roll fan, the given context of the time; and in this case that was rock recycling itself having gone, a few times, as far as it could, in terms of the guitar, the chord, the songs of lust, lewdness and loss. But, in another way, I was getting younger; I was wanting rock to be as strange as the times in the way that its history of strangeness had predicted the times of strangeness we were living in. I wanted science-fiction music, not the non-fiction of the new type of rock. I wasn't as such actually too old, or getting younger; I was becoming less real in a world that was becoming less real, and at the same time I was gaining in reality in a world that was gaining in reality, the reality of being able to live across time zones, across cities, across space. For years rock and pop thrived on a kind of energy and madness that predicted the sounds and sights of the future; and then a lot of the more popular rock, the festival rock, the melodic-guitar lovelorn rock baked in a past of Beatles and Byrds, started to look back, to predict nothing other than the past, the olden days. This all means very little other than what it means unless you believe that something can be better than something else, and that one thing can have greater value than another thing, and that it is worth us wanting things to be new, because therefore the future is different and progressive.)

Thinking about how rock once liberated me, introduced me to new ideas and new ways of thinking, because of the type of music I was listening to, because of the way it pointed out there, beyond, elsewhere, around the bend, I found a future and a present in the past containing Miles Davis, John Coltrane, Eric Dolphy, Cecil Taylor, Derek Bailey, Evan Parker, Charlie Parker, Thelonious Monk. I moved in two teenage moves of curiosity and lust from the fast tongue of Iggy Pop to the sheer gall of Charlie Mingus. There were two degrees of speeding adolescent desperation between the brains of David Bowie and John Cage.

And a playlist to accompany my statement to Eno, a playlist that sums up where I made it as a listener because I began where I begin, a playlist that offers further clues as to the elusive nature of *I am sitting in a room* and even the obvious elusiveness of 'Can't Get You Out of My Head', would consist of music by: Joe Meek, the Syncopated Elevators Legacy, Dub Sonic Roots meets Nerve Net Noise, To Rococo

Rot and I-Sound, Quantic, Oval, Tanya Tucker, Clinic, Beatnuts, Dolly Parton, Supersilent, Shuggie Otis, Blue States, I am the World Trade Center, David Sylvian, Jewel, His Name is Alive, Nils Petter Molvaer, Layo and Bushwacka, Bobby Hutcherson, Alva Noto, Spunk, Laurie Anderson, Paul Bley, Bardo Pond, Brad Mehldau, Manitoba, Human League, Stars of the Lid, Mum, Fila Brazilia, Bed, the Silver Mount Zion Memorial Orchestra and Tra-La-La Band, Baby Mammoth, Farben, Nina Simone, Plaid, John Surman, Hint . . . This is a list surrounded by other lists leading to other lists, lists that are at the centre of this book, the lists that explain everything by being gateways into worlds of sound, feeling and information, but Eno seemed worried that my statement was wandering a little from what was once the point.

I remember a lot of this music, even if I'm not totally sure I've heard all of it. It occurs to me that keeping track of all the music that there is now connecting with the past and across itself, emerging out of a public and private, commercial and artistic, wordless and wordy world, is more and more a matter of memory, and a matter of believing that you have heard it, because you know music a little or a lot like it.

The aforementioned is also the playlist of the leading radio station in the sensational city that's always in view, the city Kylie can't help but drive towards. She's famous enough to go as fast as she wants, and not even Inspector Eno is able to stop her.

Eno, meanwhile, tells me that my statement was a little longer, and more detailed, and slightly more bewildering, than he was expecting. Ah, I said, that is perhaps because I am writing about music, and perhaps music should not be written about. So why was I doing it, Eno asked suspiciously.

My reply was brilliant, and can be found in various forms at various stages of this book, this journey, this mystery. It helped that I stole the Satie notes that Eno was referring to.

19

I should point out here that if there is a positive quote from Brian Eno on the front cover of this book, possibly above the photo of Kylie Minogue that may or may not be on the front cover of this book, then Eno isn't being particularly self-aggrandising. He may be quoted as saying how much he likes this book, and thinks that it does such-and-such a thing in purveying this or that, but I can assure you that he hasn't actually read the book, and doesn't know that he is featured in what we might describe as heavy rotation. I often ask Eno if he might like to supply a marketing quote for some book that I might have written – 'By the way, buy this book' – and he often registers interest in doing such a thing, with one condition: 'I won't have to read the book, will I?' He might have kindly supplied a quote, but he will not know how flattering I have been.

It might be best, all things considered, if the cover of this book in fact featured a photograph of Brian Eno and a quote from Kylie Minogue.

If Donna Summer is featured on the cover of this book, then I imagine the quote is by Neil Tennant. If Olivia Newton John is on the cover, then the quote will be by Bryan Adams. It will not necessarily be an endorsement.

20

Eno, to edit a long story short, coined the word 'ambient' to describe a kind of intellectual easy-listening music. An easy-listening music that has certain levels of difficulty in its make-up. A background music that you could take – as a weighty, slight provocation – or leave – as a sound drifting around its own pretty pointlessness. It was the missing link between dubious muzak and artful minimalism, between the whispering of space and the whispering in space, between form and formlessness, between content and contentment.

As was often the case, Eno was not the innovator of an idea, but was its populariser – if that word is appropriate, given that the music's still fairly marginal. Eno was developing an idea that was originally considered by Satie, and that then became more and more apparent in the century of film soundtracks, where music was considered to have succeeded when, in a way, you ignored it and yet were very conscious of its effect. By the twenty-first century, all music was ambient, part of the adventure of the world as it turned into a version of itself, in the background, even when the background was the foreground.

Erik Satie, who has been patiently waiting for us, because here is a composer who undertands patience better than any other, was the first composer to write music explicitly as something that was to remain in the background, as a backdrop to other activity. In 1920 he wrote a piece for a string and wind quartet which was to be played in the intermission of a concert in a Paris art gallery. It was not necessarily meant to be listened to. It was not there to be 'memorable'. It was to simply be there in the background to general activity and chatter. The music was just a series of simple patterns repeated endlessly. Short phrases – some a mere four bars – that were to be repeated an unspecified number of times, acting as articles of sonic décor. Satie wrote several pieces in this style and gave them titles such as 'For an Assembly Hall', 'For a Lobby', 'For a Shop Window'. He was a little too early to write 'For an Airport'. And he didn't term this music 'ambient' – for Satie it was '*Musique d'ameublement*'. Furniture Music. It was a part of the process he began with 'Vexations'. 'Vexations' was the one-off art piece, Furniture Music, ideally, the mass-produced reduction of the idea into a manageable proportion. It was an attempt to break away from the traditions of the concert hall, anticipating a world yet to come when people would listen to their music in their homes, in their workplace, as they travelled.

Satie wrote a manifesto about Furniture Music: 'Furniture Music creates a vibration, it has no other goal, it fills the same role as light and heat – as comfort in every form.'

Other titles for this music suggested functional two-dimensional surfaces – 'Acoustic Floor Tiling'. 'Wrought Iron Tapestry'. In order to fulfil its function, Furniture Music was not meant to attract undue attention to itself, and was to offer no encouragement to those who might attempt to actually listen to it. The pieces were musical 'objects' to use, not works for 'interpretation'. It didn't exactly work. At the first performance as soon as the music started everybody stopped talking and returned to their seats, assuming they were supposed to pay attention. Satie was forced to implore the audience to return to what they were doing, to carry on talking.

'Don't listen!' he shouted. Eventually, the other side of the century, people would be used to not listening to music played in public places.

Satie's 'Vexations' is in an area close to Lucier's *I am sitting in a room*, although it's an area surrounded by a very high fence, and fewer people alive today have heard 'Vexations' than have heard *I am sitting in a room*. But comparing the two should give you an idea of the spirit of Lucier's piece, the way it takes nothing for granted, accepts no limitations, and wants to find ways to break outside accepted thinking in order to find new ways of doing things. Thinking about the idea of creating music by thinking about a composition, writing down those thoughts, and then acting them out in order to create sound – this will further help understand *I am sitting in a room*. Also note, in a music that is not necessarily about notes, the sense of humour shadowing, even undermining, if not overwhelming, the deep seriousness in all such ventures.

21

John Cage, who could find himself anywhere he wanted once he put his mind to it, is for the moment sat in the enchanting smart car with Kylie Minogue as she glides towards the city lit up by its own energy and expectations. He is reporting on his experience being part of the performance of 'Vexations'. (Sixty years after 'Vexations' Cage was to write a sort of first movement to it with his celebrated silent piece *4'33"* – a composed realisation of Satie's instructions for how to prepare to play the piece, the 'deepest silence' and the 'serious immobility'.)

He is explaining, as they pass building after building that looks the same and pass parts of the landscape they seem to have passed hours before, that even a work based solely on repetition changes dramatically as it unfolds, and the cumulative effect can be profound. Kylie occupies a zone somewhere between where she is and where she imagines she is, and Cage teaches her a bit of Zen. 'If something is boring for two minutes, try it for four. If it is still boring, try it for eight, sixteen, thirty-two, sixty-four, and so on. Eventually, one discovers that it is not boring at all, but very interesting.' The whine of a mosquito passes between them, and for some reason in both of them it evokes a fleeting memory of something infinitely remote, to do with late bedtimes during childhood, something sad, yet happy.

He recalls the profound experience he had being part of the performance of 'Vexations', when he and his team of ten performers worked in shifts to play all 840 repetitions without a break. 'The experience over the eighteen hours and forty minutes of those repetitions was very different from the thought of them or the realisation that they were going to happen. For them to actually happen, to actually live through it, was a different thing. What happened was that we were very tired, naturally, after that length of time, and I drove back to the country. I slept an unusually long period of time, and when I woke up I felt different than I had ever felt before. And furthermore the environment that I looked out upon looked different than I had ever felt before. In other words, I had changed, and the world had changed.'

As he talks, Kylie feels as though she is in the audience, watching the performance.

'The music first becomes so familiar that it seems extremely offensive and objectionable. But after a while the mind slowly becomes incapable of taking further offence, and a very strange euphoric acceptance and enjoyment begins to set in . . . It is only boring at first. After a while the euphoria begins to intensify.'

In a state of euphoria, John and Kylie speed past a billboard featuring a big poster that appears to be advertising some of the elements of minimalism, which is particularly handy in helping us consider the object that is *I am sitting in a room*. And, indeed, the electronic pop music developed over the past, let's say, thirty-five years that has led to the sensual, repetitive intensity of 'Can't Get You Out of My Head'. On the poster are the words:

Minimalism is typically characterised by:
1. A minimum of means. In paintings, this may be characterised by a monochromatic canvas; in music, by brief motifs with a very limited number of pitches and fixed dynamics; and in sound poetry, by a few words or limited utterances.
2. The work is static or immediate by way of extensive repetition of a single image, gesture or gestalt.
3. The avoidance of complexity. In music, the works tend to be tonal or modal rather than dissonant, rhythms and pulse are regular, even mechanical. In the visual arts, colours are pure and unmodulated, forms are symmetrical or otherwise regular.

They drive on, past buildings set against other buildings that form patterns both because of their shapes and the way that within these shapes are buildings lit up in random and sometimes regular patterns. Other billboards flash up messages about minimalism that also hint at the form and content of *I am sitting in a room*. It isn't clear whether Cage and Minogue are paying too much attention to the messages. But then, it doesn't matter particularly whether they do or don't notice the messages. They have other things on their minds. Their minds might not even be with them in the car. Even their bodies might be elsewhere.

The messages printed on billboards along the side of the highway say things such as:

Not everything about a piece of minimalist art can be anticipated ahead of its realisation. The actual work contains elements, whether manifest or implied, which cannot be conceived without its realisation.

The intellectual and aesthetic content of a stripe painting by Frank Stella is as sophisticated and elegant as that of a Bach fugue.

Minimal music is just so spacious.

The more surprising elements take place, the quicker time passes. The more repetitions there are, the slower time passes.

One moment does not lead to the next. Rather, one moment is simply followed by the next.

A great deal of the boredom associated with minimal art is in the mind of the beholder.

The virtues of a thing do not come from it, they go to it.

There is a smile on the face of John Cage that is not like the smile that is on the face of Kylie Minogue, but both smiles are in response to the view all around them, and the sound in their heads, as they carry on down the highway towards a city that is certainly getting closer. A city that you would be able to listen to. A city with pitch. With small variations in pitch. The car sweeps towards the sound of the city. John and Kylie keep smiling.

He says to her: 'You have a body like a machine.' And then he says: 'The song you are singing is a machine made up out of words, rhythm and sound.' He also says: 'The idea becomes the machine that makes the art.'

She replies: 'The whole universe is a machine.'

The music inside the car, which is a private space on the public highway, reflects this thought. It supports the idea that she is a machine inside a machine driving through a landscape of machines towards a city powered by machine on a world machine spinning around inside a galaxy you can find, if pushed, inside the ultimate machine of them all, the universe. The music repeats itself and yet changes in a way that the world around them seems to repeat itself and yet change.

A billboard flashes past advertising a thought:

The subconscious is a factory, a machine for production.

Kylie asks John if he thinks that one day we might have a computer that seems to have a mind of its own.

'Yes,' John replies. 'But I doubt that the computer will ever be taken in.'

John or Kylie, one of them, points out that 'Vexations' is never really meant to finish. The 840 repetitions are themselves but an instant in the eternal present in which the music exists, like some platonic form, obliterating memory, eluding analysis. 'The music continues. It is we who walk away,' says Kylie, or John, or both of them together, in dreamlike harmony.

A message lit up in golden neon flashes by:

Machinery is the soul of the modern world.

This is closely followed by another neon slogan:

There's a rhythm to the natural world.

The music suddenly stops, and for a while Kylie and John drive on in what seems to be silence. Silence with attitude.

22

There is someone new sitting in the car with Kylie. Who can it be this time?

'Knock knock,' he says.

'Who's there?' replies Kylie, with a girlish giggle.

'Knock knock,' he says, not a little sternly, and yet with a kind of kindness.

'Who's there?' replies Kylie, not taking her eyes off the road.

'Who's there?'

'Knock knock.'

'Who's there?'

'Knock knock.'

'Who's there?'

'Knock knock,' he says, still managing to keep his face quite straight.

'Who's there?' replies Kylie, who has in fact learned fast how to keep a straight face, although she's laughing inside.

'Knock knock.'

'Who's there?'

'Knock knock.'

'Who's there?'

'Philip Glass.'

Kylie doesn't get it. Not yet anyway.

In time, she will. In time, she might find herself in the car with Plato, who will tell her that time is that which is and never becomes.

She will share some car time with Aristotle, who will explain how time is a succession of nows. Einstein will drop in to suggest that time deals with consciousness and cannot actually be held in the memory. Freud calls in on Kylie's mobile to agree.

He, too, tells her a knock-knock joke. The punchline is, somehow, 'Music is the very thing which gives this life meaning.' She finds the time to laugh.

23

More help in locating the sitting room that was the private space of Alvin Lucier will come from moving into the area occupied by Steve Reich's 1965 'It's Gonna Rain'. Reich's greatest contribution to minimalist music was a process known as phasing. Phasing involves two or more loops of identical material being played side by side. One of the two pieces then starts to speed up slightly, or slow down slightly, or is manipulated in some other way. Reich first tried these techniques on 'It's Gonna Rain'. One Sunday afternoon, Reich, who had been experimenting extensively with tape loops since 1963, recorded Brother Walter, a black Pentecostal preacher who was speaking his thoughts on what would happen at the end of the world. Walter's voice was highly musical, and his sermon was almost chanted or sung. Reich made two loops of the same material.

By accident – because of small motor variations in the speed of the two tape recorders – Reich discovered what happens when two identical tape loops gradually fall out of synch from each other.

In the first part of 'It's Gonna Rain', he looped the two recordings of the voice together, moved them out of phase with each other, slipped them back into unison again. In the second part, he used loops of a longer length, and moved them out of phase with each other. Thus what starts out as a two-voice sound becomes four voices, with one pair out of phase with another pair. Finally it breaks into eight parts, and the effect is, as Reich described it, 'a kind of controlled chaos which may be appropriate to the subject matter – the end of the world'.

This way of creating new meanings, new sounds, unexpected rhythms, shifting polyphonic textures and secondary melodies by manipulating and treating taped voices, again points us towards the area where Lucier is sitting in a room, a room not like the one you are sitting in. Momentum is created through the way the voices react against themselves to generate rhythmic pulse that is related to no known meter or time signature. Musical effect is created through a process of thought that applies itself theoretically as opposed to using normal musical technique. A combination of text, tape, manipulation and a score that describes a process to be followed creates sounds that generate new musical possibilities. Lucier is in the tradition of musical inventor who observes that music is in essence a transformation of sound into something that is ordered, or disordered, enough to inspire a reaction, and that this can be done without musical instruments. It can be done through the use of voice, thinking – planning – and electronics. The beauty, as well as disorientation, found by Reich, Fripp and Eno and Lucier shows that, whatever music is, it is not necessarily defined by the use of traditional music instruments, nor is it reliant on ordinary musical instruments. In many ways, acoustic instruments have merely been a preparation for electronic instruments that take us both further out from nature and closer to it. It is electronic music that creates noise that can represent when and where inside the mind the universe finds ways to begin and end.

24

Kylie gradually increases the speed of the fast car, faster, faster, er, fast, er, fast. Er. She turns with a teasing look flashed through a lock of hair falling over one eye, a trick she has practised for years, to peek at her passenger, who is suddenly Steve Reich. There is a narrative reason for the abrupt coupling of Reich and Minogue. For the purpose of this part of this story, we note the edgy repetition and edgeless hypnotic quality of Reich's music. Say, the eighteen minutes of 'Eight Lines', a tactile cloning of drone and tone that goes on in much the same vein for eighteen minutes that might be timed at a few times that length, depending on your mood. It's typical of the avant-garde minimalist tradition in the way it defies traditional conventions of build-up and release, of tension and relief, of ways of getting from A to B that make accepted sense. It seems quite happy to get on people's nerves, to annoy listeners, to make them think that what they are listening to is not, as such, in any way or form, music. And yet such ideas of repetition, narrative perversion, rhythmical pressure and spatial adventure have led to great populist movement in new music. Rhythmic minimalists since Reich have turned to very accessible tunes, very conventional tunes. There's no great surprise in seeing Steve Reich and Kylie Minogue share a fast-forward car in this dream story of music that travels from the mind's ear of an avant-gardist to a nightclub in a dream city. I'm sure later in the story we'll find out just how we can move from Steve Reich to Kylie Minogue, in much the same way as we can plot a movement from Edgard Varese to Missy Elliot, from Messiaen to Radiohead, from Brahms to Tortoise, or from Duchamp to Björk. Before that, Kylie, proceeding with charming but clinical caution, must increase the speed of her car so that she can catch up with the car carrying Kraftwerk.

25

As she accelerates, she turns to her latest passenger, who is, abruptly, La Monte Young. She has reached that part of the song where she, acting out her part to the eternal limit, is singing, 'Forever and ever and ever . . .' Young is particularly taken by this, as there is some of his music, some limitless drone alone without a telephone, that began, just started of its own accord, with a little nudge from him, in 1959 and is still continuing. It will continue, if only you could hear it, forever and ever and ever (this sentence continues forever, or until something happens to it), filtering out into the white-light darkness of infinite space.

Kylie starts to say something to Young, but she is a little nervous. Even celebrities get nervous. She stutters. She tries to say his name. She says, 'La, la, la . . .'

26

The area I am looking for, the area of the sitting room, is found by imagining music that combines electronic equipment with novel theory, spatial awareness and intellectual curiosity. The sound made in these areas manages to sound fast and slow at the same time, it is simultaneously solid and hollow, big and small, light and heavy, boring and exciting, plain and mysterious, predictable and surprising, tight and sharp, loose and expansive. It would be of great help when searching for the area of the sitting room if you know the work of Terry Riley. He is, for the sake of this story, the inventor of the time-lag accumulator tape-delay system, which uses two Revox tape recorders to create loops. Although his music would have been originally filed under classical/avant-garde, he was an early example of a classical musician marketed by a record company towards a more mainstream audience – in his case, because his major works were made in the late sixties, towards a rock audience sampling avant-garde techniques through the music of the Grateful Dead, the Beatles, Pink Floyd and, sensibly, so on. Riley would feed traditional instruments such as organ and saxophone through his tape-delay system to transform the sounds and the structures they would usually make into sounds and structures that sounded like nothing else in structures that, at first thought, were without structure. His music flirts with chaos, but also makes eyes at complete control, and is quite happy to seduce whatever happens by pure chance. Riley's music, as with everything in areas close to his area, can sound as if it is happening automatically, as if the music is writing, or processing, itself; and in a way what makes it so natural, as well as supernatural, is the fact that a collaboration between human beings and electronics is being used to produce music that seems to connect with the sounds of the universe that you can imagine existing before anyone was around to hear them, or indeed re-create then. It is a good definition for great music of all kinds – that it appears to sound as though it has just happened, just is; that it is an unforced, perfectly sequenced order of the right notes and the right spaces combining in a way that reveals/responds to that part of the human experience that is, or wants to be, spiritual.

Elsewhere, to hover almost above the area of the sitting room, consider these drones meta-drones, neo-drones, sub-drones, dub-drones, post-drones, etc-drones, sad-drones, peace-drones, spin-drones, noise-drones, plus-drones, minus-drones, divided-drones, lost-drones, song-drones:

Labradford, *Prazision*
Pengo, 'Climbs the Holy Mountain'
Tony Conrad with Faust, *Outside the Dream Syndicate*

⅓ Octave Band, 'Fading Light from the Distant Suns'
Barry Adamson and Pan Sonic, *The Hymn of the Seventh Illusion*
Carrier Band, *Automatic Inscription of Speech Melody*
Earth, *Earth 2*
Alan Lamb, *Primal Image/Beauty*
Michael J. Schumaker, *Fidicin Drones*
La Monte Young and the Theatre of Eternal Music Brass Band, *The Second Dream of the High-Tension Line Stepdown Transformer from the Four Dreams of China*
Robert Rich, *Trances/Drones*
Peter Wright, *A Tiny Camp in the Wilderness*
Boris with Merzbow, *Megatone*
Thomas Campion, *Six Poems on a Fantasy*
Robert Ashley, *In Sara Mencken Christ and Beethoven There Were Men and Women*
Swswthrght, *Essence or Residue*
Keith Fullerton Whitman, *Playthroughs*

For further information regarding the area where Lucier set his room, dream yourself stupidly smart to the following deeply subdued ambient selection, where the sound that happens doesn't ever seem to be happening until the very moment that it does, just, make a sound, and merges that sound into another sound that closely resembles itself:

Brian Eno, *Discreet Music*
Information, *Biomekano*
Takehisa Kosugi, *Catch Wave*
Edgar Froese, *Epsilon in Malaysian Pale*
Klaus Schulze, *Mirage*
Paul Horn, *Inside the Taj Mahal*
Prelim, *Pulse Programming*

Get as close to the Lucier area as you possibly can without actually ending up so far away you lose sight of your ears by spending some time with the following, which can be categorised only as being 'experimental', which means they cannot be safely categorised, and never accurately, adequately explained, which means they only really point towards Lucier in that they are beyond explanation, and most other things, including time, space and interpretation, give or take the fact that they all seem to be about meaning, and the meaning of meaning, and, ultimately, the paradox of meaning in what might yet prove to be a meaningless universe:

AMM, *Tunes Without Measure or End*
Birchville Cat Motel, *We Count These Prayers*
Entire musical works of Marcel Duchamp
Philip Jeck, *VinylCoda 1–3*
Dieter Moebius, *Blotch*
Arnold Dreyblatt, *Nodal Excitation*
Merzbow, *Loop Panic Limited*
Terry Riley, *You're No Good*
Susumu Yokota, *The Boy and the Tree*
Fennesz, *+47 degrees 56'37" – 16 degrees 51'08"*
Ilitch, *10 Suicides*

Probably you will not have heard most of the above. I'm not sure I have, although I'm pretty sure I have. As the writer of a book very like this one, as an expert in music so quiet or obscure or distant it barely exists, I must surely have heard these records. I can imagine them, so I must have heard them, or at least ones I can imagine are very like them. (Some of them have only been heard by somewhere between one and 1,000 people; some of them have not even been heard by the people who made them. Nonetheless, put Eno and Duchamp together and their combined influence touches everything artistic you will see and hear today.) But, I think, for the sake of directing you towards just what *I am sitting in a room* is like, as a thing, a process, a work of art, a series of messages, then the titles alone will be a help. Except possibly *Earth 2* – although that '2' might be a help, if we think that music, and everything it attempts to represent and describe and enhance, is a case of numbers, in some order, one way or another, with a little bit of light added for the sake of, in a very real sense, reality.

The fact that in the above list there exists the entire musical works of Marcel Duchamp, and that they are exactly as you would imagine, and yet not as you would imagine, even to the extent of being inside, outside or inside-out the radar of your wildest fancy of what they might be, is evocative enough for you to have half a think about Lucier's piece.

You will, I suppose, be considering that we are in an area bordered by the cosmic and the conceptual, and you might be on the right motorway. After all, after Duchamp, all art is conceptual in nature, because art exists only conceptually. And the cosmic takes care of itself. The cosmic just happens and we go along for the ride. Then we make theories about the ride, and Kylie comments in a simulated sleepy sing-song voice that the whole thing is spinning around somewhere between curiouser and curiouser.

27

Then again, despite the titles in the above selection, despite the narrative wink towards the notion of the cosmic and the conceptual (the hallucination of sound versus an objective belief in the existence of noise, as the bishop said to the Mad Hatter), you might still be no better off imagining what *I am sitting in a room* sounds like. Even Eno's continuing investigations into repetition and the murder of variety, and the reincarnation of variety in various forms, might not help you imagine the sound of the room Alvin is, was, will be sitting in.

Even if you spend some time getting hold of the music listed above, and spend a lot more time listening to it, you will only be guessing as to the exact nature of *I am sitting in a room*. But at least you will be a lot closer than you were before you were aware of the above. Be grateful for small mercies.

To get closer and closer and closer to the area where we can sneak a peek through a window into Lucier's sitting room, we perhaps need a quick detour through some history. A history of music, and a history of the things that influenced music, that environmentally and emotionally pressed it to move on, to change and respond as the world around it changed shape and atmosphere.

And don't think Kylie has been forgotten – because, in many ways, the following detour is also relevant when considering how music reached the stage of 'Can't Get You Out of My Head'. In fact, everything written in terms of trying to locate the area of Lucier's sitting room has a relevance regarding the Kylie song. Because, without the experimentation, consideration, rebellion, meditation, invention and playfulness involved in the works of Reich, Riley, Eno and Lucier – and the others in their area before and after and during their time in that area – an electronic pop song like 'Can't Get You Out of My Head' would never have happened. The sources used by Reich and Riley and their questing cohorts in the sixties as they merged radical electronic experimentation with historical interest in music and art stretching back centuries eventually became an influence on the experimental areas of rock and pop that eventually filtered over into the mainstream through Kylie's electronic mouthpiece. Pop, the young yet old bastard, thrives on the journeys and discoveries of others to help give it so much novelty, so much energy, and its occasional odd shine of mind-changing art.

The following historical detour eventually leads us in the direction of the repetition and variety, beat and melody, pun and persuasion, rhyme and thought, emotion and electronic manipulation so winningly exploited on 'Can't Get You Out of My Head'. Treat the following as a way to find *I am sitting in a room* on the musical map that is relevant to this book, but also as a way of discovering how centuries of exploration eventually made it possible for Kylie Minogue, or an actress playing Kylie Minogue who just happened to be called Kylie Minogue, to find herself sitting in a car ready to drive into the hypersonic modern city and dance forever to a track called 'Can't Get You Out of My Head'.

In the following list, as we move through a history of musical moments, human advancement, artistic change, random generation, general events and major inventions, you can see how, once electronics were involved in the recording and storage and then the actual making of music, the sound of the music, as opposed to its compositional structure, became more and more the most important thing. This reaches its apex with an electronic pop song like 'Can't Get You Out of My Head', which has all the appearances of a song but is actually an electronic sequence of events layered and falsified into a series of shapes biased towards the appearance of a song. It's much odder than it seems, much more of an illusion, much more a series of ideas and theories about music than a straightforward song written using piano and voice. The gradual progress that has been made during the last forty years of pop change disguises its oddness. We have been slowly prepared for such a sound. What makes the song more special than it might have been is the fact that involved in its make-up are elements of experimentation and thinking that initially had nothing to do with pop music, but have been introduced so that the possibility of what a pop song can be and sound like has greatly increased.

And watch as art and entertainment move closer and closer together, pulled towards each other by the rise and rise of technology, and electronic communication, and image fixation, and the wit necessary to deal with the collapse of systems and the evolving extravagance of fragmentation.

28

At this stage of the book, the list of characters is about to be considerably expanded. Kylie, sweet, serene and innocent in her invincible car, alive with shape and excitement, drives relentlessly forward towards a whole city of meaning. One pill makes her larger. One pill makes her smaller. One artist scrambles her features. One artist saturates her with colour and turns her into the flattest of surfaces. Another reduces her to a dot. Still another artist renders her invisible. A series of machines wired together by programmers, who are, ultimately, an emotional lot, make up a soundtrack to this elusive hypercoloured scambled dot that statically rests on the near-far side of widescreen vision.

Let's say, for the sake of quite a complicated argument, that the following list of life and death, sound and silence, art and design, movement and music, thought and escapade, innovation and intuition, style and fashion, dream and reality is the landscape on the outskirts of the city she is driving towards. These processes, motions, events, actions, deeds are some of the major buildings, sculptures and natural features on the edge of the city of secrets, wires and publicity that Kylie is driving towards. They make up the false sky and the misleading horizon. The strange light and the stranger dark. The flat surfaces and the energetic curves. The sights and the scenes. This list of dates and dreams is a grand panorama stretched over the history of the universe, and Kylie is driving straight down the middle, and at the end of her journey is the city of space and closed-up space where everything is always starting, beginning, new. It is, to be specific, one version of what can be seen as we speed into the city; it is a diagram of what can be seen, a hint, a suggestion – it is the beginning of the shape of the story, a series of shapes that lead to other shapes, other stories, that accumulate to tell a kind of truth about what can be seen and heard in this universe most of us have gathered at this point to share.

Note that, as she heads towards the city, which for the sake of this story is located in 2003, the landscape just can't help but get more and more artificial, more modern as we understand the idea of the word as we live today. It becomes more a reflection of the shape of entertainment, increasingly lit by information. The landscape Kylie is driving through evolves into an entertainment-scape, and the chronologically indifferent city she moves towards is built on the principles of information, information that is more and more dedicated to pleasure and the simultaneous experiences of real and virtual experiences.

The wheels on Kylie's car go round and round as they drive on between the past and the future. Nothing changes inside Kylie's car, except the look on her face, and the way she moves her body as if in tribute to the landscape that spreads around her windscreen. Outside, everything changes, a perpetual motion of racy static pixels.

You are welcome to take photographs of the sights and tape the sound as the car skims over a makebelieve road towards a simulated city on a fake horizon. By the end of the following list, the following collection of dates and words, this dreamed-up series of landmarks, views and buildings, we will be at the edge of the city, and the brilliant lights and the sky-scraping buildings will begin to absorb Kylie. The motorway will begin to enter the city, curl and rise and fall around into the city, and become another kind of road, a network of roads, a variety of directions and destinations, entrances and exits. One road will become many. One road will become splattered throughout the city, transplanted right into the essential fibres of the city, become as integral to the functioning of the city as are the wires that supply the electricity and the dreams that supply the realism. Kylie is on the road to the city of bits, the software city without solid presence where Kylie will really begin to live and experience and learn, the city that spans all time zones where Kylie really will meet her death, the death of her image, and the image of her image. Look out of the window. The view is amazing. Kylie has never seen anything quite like it. It stretches as far as the eye can see, the ear can hear and the mind can understand.

29

1624   The English philosopher and essayist Francis Bacon writes about a scientific utopia in his *New Atlantis*. He states, 'We have sound houses, where we practise and demonstrate all sounds, and their generation. We represent and imitate all articulate sounds and letters, and the voices and notes of beasts and birds. We have also diverse, strange and artificial echoes, reflecting the voice many times, and as it were tossing it: and some that give back the voice louder, shriller, deeper. We also have means to convey sounds in trunks and pipes, in strange lines and distance.'

1637 Descartes – 'I think, therefore I am.'

1641 Blaise Pascal develops the first calculating machine.

1666 The first Stradivarius violins emerge from Antonio Stradivari's workshop in Cremona, Italy.

1685 Johann Sebastian Bach born. Later, he and George Frederic Handel are considered to have been the principal classical composers of the Baroque period.

1725 Antonio Vivaldi, *The Four Seasons*.

1738 The Industrial Revolution begins to flourish. There are attempts to harness steam power to mechanical computation machines.

1750 Bach dies.

1759 Clavecin Electrique invented by Jean-Baptiste de Laborde. Low-voltage electricity applied to a harpsichord-like keyboard rings bells so long as the key is depressed.

1761 Maelzel, inventor of the metronome and friend of Beethoven, invents the Panharmonicon, a keyboard instrument.

1770 Ludwig van Beethoven born.

1786 Wolfgang Amadeus Mozart, *The Marriage of Figaro*.

1787 Mozart composes the *Musikalisches Würfelspiel* (*Musical Dice Game*). This composition is a series of precomposed measures arranged in random eight-bar phrases to build the composition. Each throw of the dice represents an individual measure so that after eight throws the first phrase is determined.

1796 The invention of carillons: 'A sliver of steel, shaped, polished, tempered and then screwed into position so that the projections on a rotating cylinder can pluck at its free extremity.'

1800 Mozart, *Requiem*.
Beethoven, *Sonata No. 2 (Moonlight)*.

1804 First use of the term 'Art for art's sake'.

1808 Beethoven, *Symphony No. 5 in C Minor*.

1811 Jane Austen, *Sense and Sensibility*.

1813 Richard Wagner born; it does not take him long to realise he is all on his own.

1818 Thomas Bowdler's *Family Shakespeare* has rude words expurgated.

1819 Mary Shelley, *Frankenstein*.

Artur Schopenhauer, *The World as Will and Idea*.

Lord Byron, *Don Juan*.

1820   John Keats' 'Ode on a Grecian Urn' is the height of literary romanticism.

1821   Charles Baudelaire born; it does not take him long to realise that every word has its own special aroma.

Manchester Guardian begins publication.

1822   Louis Daguerre's *The Diorama* opens in Paris.

Franz Schubert's *Symphony No. 8 in B Minor (Unfinished)*.

1825   George Stephenson's 'Locomotion Number One', the first steam engine to carry freight and passengers on a regular basis, makes its first trip.

1827   Beethoven dies.

1831   Victor Hugo, *The Hunchback of Notre Dame*.

1832   Samuel Morse invents the telegraph.

Frédéric Chopin, *Mazurkas*.

Johann Goethe, *Faust*.

1833 –34   Charles Babbage builds the 'difference engine', a large mechanical computer.

1835   Robert Schumann composes the *Carnaval* pieces, twenty-one short pieces for piano. Each piece is based on a different character.

Hans Christian Andersen publishes his fairytales.

Charles Dickens becomes famous with the publication of *The Pickwick Papers*.

Louis Daguerre creates daguerrotype, begins photography craze.

1837   Dr C. G. Page of Massachusetts reports his accidental discovery of 'galvanic' music, a method of generating a ringing tone using horseshoe magnets and a spiral of copper wire.

1839   The first fuel cell is developed by William Robert Grove.

The invention of the first camera manufactured for sale: the Giroux dageurreotype.

Chopin, *24 Préludes*.

Electricity runs a printing press

1841   Edgar Allen Poe's 'The Murders in the Rue Morgue' sees the start of the modern detective story.

Ralph Waldo Emerson, *Self-Reliance*.

1842   Morse wraps a telegraph wire to carry messages through water.

1843   Poet Gérard de Nerval walks a pet lobster through the park of the Palais Royal in Paris on a pale-pink ribbon. Says he likes lobsters because they don't bark and because they 'know the secrets of the deep'.

Søren Kierkegaard; *Either-Or.* Will later become basis of existentialism.

Bryon's daughter, Ada Lovelace, explains concept of computer programming.

The *Economist* is founded.

Poe, 'The Gold Bug'.

1844   Friedrich Nietzsche born; it does not take him long to realise that the world is in bits, truth is in bits, God is in bits, his mind is in bits, language is in bits.

Paul Verlaine born.

Morse develops Morse code.

1845   Friedrich Engels, *The Condition of the Working Classes in England in 1844.*

Poe, 'The Raven'.

1846   Edward Lear, *A Book of Nonsense.*

1847   Emily Brontë, *Wuthering Heights.*

1848   Karl Marx and Engels, the *Communist Manifesto.*

1849   Armand Fizeau calculates the speed of light as 300,000 km per second.

1850   D. D. Parmelee patents the first key-driven adding machine.

Antonio de Torres Jurado fine-tunes a stringed instrument into a form that we recognise today as the modern guitar.

Ballroom dancing divided into round dancing and square dancing.

1851   Herman Melville, *Moby-Dick.*

1852   Peter Roget's *Thesaurus of English Words and Phrases* is published.

Dickens, *Bleak House.*

1853   Vincent Van Gogh born.

1854   Arthur Rimbaud born; it does not take him long to realise that he wants to be a poet, to make himself a visionary, to arrive at the unknown . . . 'through a long, a prodigious and rational disordering of all my sense'.

Paris and London are connected by telegraph.

1855   Gérard de Nerval hangs himself with what he claimed was the Queen of Sheba's garter. His pet raven is found flying around his

head crying the only words Nerval taught it: 'J'ai soif.' I'm thirsty.
Walt Whitman, *Leaves of Grass*.

David E. Hughes invents a typewriting telegraph utilising a piano-like keyboard to activate the mechanism.

1857 Baudelaire, *Les Fleurs du mal*.

1859 Charles Darwin, *On the Origin of Species*. All copies sell out in one day, but the book creates fury.

1860 The age of plastics begins – Alexander Parkes produces celluloid *c*. 1860.

The slave trade introduces West African rhythms, work songs, chants and spirituals to America, which will later strongly influence blues and jazz.

1861 Telegraph lines connect New York and San Francisco.

1862 Claude Debussy born.

1863 Hermann von Helmholtz publishes *On the Sensations of Tone as a Physiological Basis for the Theory of Music*, an important early treatise in the principles of acoustics.

Édouard Manet shocks with the nude *Déjeuner sur l'Herbe*.

1864 Jules Verne, *Journey to the Centre of the Earth*

1865 Lewis Carroll (mathematician Charles Dodgson), *Alice's Adventures in Wonderland*; it does not take Alice long to realise that she doesn't know where she is or who she is, but a number-one single would help her find out.

Richard Wagner, *Tristan und Isolde* – in the years before this opera, the tonal consistency of classical music, its attachment to a central uniform key, had begun to waver. The giants, Bach, Mozart, Beethoven and Tchaikovsky, would sometimes deviate from the original key, a c minor or a f minor, modulate through a few other keys, but they would nearly always return to where they started. As the nineteenth century developed and the Romantic era evolved into the late Romantic era, composers drifted away from the home key more and more. It became less clear which key the music was heading for next. The predictable nature of a music remaining close to its starting place was changing, the certainty of classical music was blurring at the edges – and this blurring of modulations came to a head with *Tristan und Isolde*. The opening is entirely ambiguous with regards to key. Tonality was breaking down.

1866 Erik Satie born; it does not take him long to realise that size isn't everything, which therefore means it is.

1867 Marx, *Das Kapital*.

Johann Strauss, *The Blue Danube*.

1868 Scott Joplin born.

Publication of *Enquire Within Upon Everything* – 'Whither you wish to model a flower in wax, to study the rules of etiquette, to serve relish for breakfast or supper, to plan a dinner for a large party or a small one, to cure a headache, to make a will, to get married, to bury a relative, whatever you may wish to do, make, or to enjoy, provided your desire has relation to the necessities of domestic life, I hope you will not fail to "enquire within".'

1869 Leo Tolstoy, *War and Peace*.

1870 Verne, *Twenty Thousand Leagues Under the Sea*.

'Cardiff Giant' hoax inspires comment: 'There's a sucker born every minute.'

John Hyatt's work with celluloid will lead to phonograph records and telephones.

1871 Verlaine and Rimbaud form relationship – and will be insepar-able for years.

Verne, *Around the World in Eighty Days*.

P.T. Barnum opens a circus, calls it 'The Greatest Show on Earth'.

1873 Rimbaud, *Une Saison en Enfer*.

Verlaine shoots Rimbaud in the wrist

Development of the pseudo-scientific 'QWERTY' keyboard.

1874 Arnold Schoenberg born.

Modest Mussorgsky, *Pictures from an Exhibition*.

Thomas Hardy, *Far from the Madding Crowd*.

1875 Maurice Ravel born.

Typewriter invented.

1876 Alexander Graham Bell transmits voice using electrical current. He is granted patent number 174, 465 for the telephone. 'Mr Watson, come here, I want you.'

Mark Twain types out *The Adventures of Tom Sawyer*.

Johannes Brahms, *Symphony No. 1*.

1877 Thomas Edison invents the phonograph for playing back-stored sounds. The first recording he makes is 'Mary Had a Little Lamb'.

It is not long before *Harpers Weekly* is reporting on the new phenomenon: 'If it were not that the days of belief in witchcraft are long-since past, witch-hunters such as those who figured so conspicuously in the early history of our country would now find a rich harvest of victims in the Tribune Building. Here are located the two marvels of a marvellous age. The telephone, which created such a sensation a short time ago by demonstrating the possibility of transmitting vocal sounds by telegraph, is now eclipsed by a new wonder called the phonograph. This little instrument records the utterances of the human voice, and like a faithless confidante repeats every secret confided to it whenever requested to do so. It will talk, sing, whistle, cough, sneeze, or perform any other acoustic feat. With charming impartiality it will express itself in the divine strains of a lyric goddess, or use the startling vernacular of a street Arab.'

Anna Sewell, *Black Beauty*.

1878   Gilbert and Sullivan, *HMS Pinafore*.

1879   The first incandescent light bulb that burns for a significant amount of time is invented by Edison.

Fyodor Dostoevsky, *The Brothers Karamazov*.

George Eastman builds a machine to mass-produce photographic dry plates.

1880   Bell finances his own laboratory in Washington DC. Together with Charles S. Tainter, he devises and patents several means for transmitting and recording sound.

Carlo Collodi, *Pinocchio: The Story of a Puppet*.

1881   Pablo Picasso born; it does not take him long to realise that he is Picasso.

1882   Igor Stravinsky born.

Wagner's final opera, *Parsifal*.

1883   Edgard Varese born.

Nietzsche, *Thus Spake Zarathustra*.

1884   Establishment of Greenwich Mean Time.

1885   Gilbert and Sullivan, *The Mikado*.

Richard Burton, *The Arabian Nights*.

1886   Robert Louis Stevenson, *The Strange Case of Dr Jekyll and Mr Hyde*.

1887   Marcel Duchamp born; it does not take him long to realise that art is whatever you say it is.

Arthur Conan Doyle writes his first Sherlock Holmes story.

1888   *National Geographic* is launched.

Heinrich transmits what are now known as radio waves.

Considered an office machine, the phonograph is franchised. Speech has become immortal, sound travels beyond the limitation set by time, space and death. The beginning of a process whereby a newly conceived reality is wholly subsumed within the virtual realm of technology.

The first beauty contest is held in Spa, Belgium.

1889   Satie, *Trois Gymnopedies* – three pieces of music conceived as different versions of the same composition. Thus Satie is at the very beginning of the idea of the remix. There are also early whispers of what will one day be called ambient – whispers that began way before there was a necessity to label music, to name sound, when the mystery of music had not been damaged by mass production, when the aolean harp, as mentioned in Homer's *Odyssey*, would be hung outside on a tree, and the wind rustling through it would produce sound.

1890   Van Gogh commits suicide aged thirty-seven.

Man Ray born. It does not take him long to see the light.

Oscar Wilde, *The Picture of Dorian Gray*.

1891   Rimbaud dies.

1893   Antonín Dvořák, *Symphony No. 9 (From the New World)*.

Fred Stone, 'Ma Ragtime Baby'.

Edvard Munch, *The Scream*.

Coca-Cola is registered as a trademark by a pharmacist in Atlanta.

Satie, 'Vexations'.

1894   Claude Debussy, *Prelude a l'après-midi d'un faune* – Debussy responds to the tonal adventures of Wagner and ventures further out than anyone, in directions no one had yet ventured. Essentially, this is the first piece of modern music – whilst still in sight, or sound, of tonality, he leaps away from the existing logic of musical thought by ignoring traditional rules. He achieves a kind of pan-tonality by trying such things as shifting block chords sideways, and music seems to melt into the future in ways that at the time was perceived as being 'impressionist'. It was not soft music, though, and where for Wagner the key was ambiguous, a tentative opening of the door to a future, for Debussy it was irrelevant, and the door pretty much fell of its hinges.

Edison, *Kinetoscopic Record of a Sneeze (Fred Ott's Sneeze)* – the earliest surviving copyright Edison film. A soundtrack was recorded separately.

The word 'spaceship' appears in print.

1895 Debussy, *Pelléas and Mélisande*.

H.G. Wells, *The Time Machine*.

Hardy, *Jude the Obscure*.

Luigi Russolo born.

The first jazz band, The Spasm Band, performs in New Orleans.

1896 Ragtime, a combination of West Indian rhythm and European musical form, is born.

Henri Bergson, *Matter and Memory*.

Alfred Nobel creates the Nobel Prize.

1897 Henry Cowell born.

E. S. Votey invents the pianola, an instrument that uses a pre-punched, perforated paper roll moved over a capillary bridge. The holes in the paper correspond to eighty-eight openings on the board.

1898 Valdemar Poulson patents his telegraphone, the first magnetic recording machine. The device uses a microphone, itself something dating back to Bell's earlier experiments in telephony, to drive an electromagnet which alters the magnetic pattern on a coil of steel piano wire.

Auguste Rodin, *The Kiss*.

René Magritte born; it does not take him long to realise that art evokes the mystery without which the world would not exist.

1899 Joplin, 'Maple Leaf Rag'.

Schoenberg, *Verklärte Nacht*.

Edward Elgar, *Enigma Variations*.

Duke Ellington born; it does not take him long to realise that if it sounds good, it is good.

William Duddell develops the singing arc, the first fully electronic instrument.

Sound is recorded magnetically on a wire and on a thin metal strip.

1900 Giacomo Puccini, *Tosca*.

The telegraph now connects the entire civilised world.

L. Frank Baum, *The Wizard of Oz*.

1901 Sigmund Freud, *The Interpretation of Dreams*.

Frank Lloyd Wright, *The Art and Craft of the Machine*.

Picasso begins his Blue period.

In Newfoundland, Marconi receives a radio signal, the letter S, from England.

Louis Armstrong born. His nickname will be Satchmo (he received ths nickname in the early 1930s when the British heard his original nickname, Satchelmouth, incorrectly). Armstrong is recognised as jazz genius number one because the entire concept of swinging (playing off the beat) is attributed to him.

Blues becomes a standard feature of honky tonks and dancehalls. Horn players imitate the human voice with mutes and growls.

1902 Joplin, 'The Entertainer'.

Jelly Roll Morton claims to invent jazz as a combination of blues and quadrilles.

Ten-inch Red Seal records feature tenor Enrico Caruso.

Melies's *Voyage to the Moon* film pioneering special effects and 'trickery'.

In Los Angeles, a theatre succeeds by showing movies only, no vaudeville.

People begin to buy phonographs and cylinders for home use. This enables the rapid spread of popular music.

1903 *The Great Train Robbery* introduces editing into movies and creates demand for fiction movies.

1904 Richard Strauss, *Salomé*.

Salvador Dali born. It does not take him long to get laid by fantasy and money and the fantasy of money.

1905 Albert Einstein formulates Special Theory of Relativity.

1906 Thaddeus Cahill invents the dynamaphone, an instrument weighing more than 200 tons and which generates sounds electronically, resulting in the first commercial effort to distribute music over the telephone. Later, Cahill is therefore considered 'the father of muzak'.

Victor Herbert, *Love is Like a Cigarette*.

Records may be 6⅔ inches, 7 inches, 8 inches, 10 inches, 11 inches, 12 inches, 13¾ inches, or 14 inches wide.

1907 Elgar, *Pomp and Circumstance*.

Schoenberg, *String Quartet No.2*. Judging that tonality had nowhere else to go, Schoenberg completely abandoned it in the final movement. As if he was symbolising this dramatic moment, the voice he has radically introduced in the previous movement of what is after all a generally voiceless string quartet sings: 'I breathe the air of other planets.'

Dr Lee De Forest patents the audion tube, which allows a small signal to be amplified and played over loudspeakers.

Picasso and Georges Braque invent an art that will be called cubism. *Les Demoiselles d'Avignon* by Picasso is the beginning of cubism without really being all that cubist. Picasso paints not what you see but what you know is there. Drawing inspiration from the simple geometry of African sculptures, the cubists dematerialise objects, breaking them down into their basic geometric forms.

1908   Joe Howard, 'I Wonder Who's Kissing Her Now'.

Ravel, *Bolero*.

Anton von Webern, *Five Movements for String Quartet*.

Olivier Messiaen born.

Elliott Carter born.

Orville Wright's first hour-long aeroplane flight takes place.

Columbia produce the first two-sided disc.

1909   Declaration of the futurist manifesto, *The Art of Noises*, in *Le Figaro* by Filippo Marinetti: 'We declare that the splendour of the world has been enriched with a new form of beauty. The beauty of speed.'

Schoenberg, *Three Piano Pieces*. They are not written in any musical key or tonality. They're made from a series of notes, musically unrelated. The series has little of what is usually called a melody. Because there is no tonality, this music was called atonal, which to most people means tuneless. By abandoning the previous system of ordering sound into harmonious tunes, Schoenberg is beginning the century's musical experimentation with less harmonious sounds. Disordered sound. Noise. At the beginning of the century, noise is everywhere. The melodies of Edison's phonograph, the roar of the automobile, the wireless wonder of Marconi, and Einstein's Theory of Relativity have ushered in a new age.

Irving Berlin, 'Alexander's Ragtime Band'.

The term 'jazz' is used for the first time in the song 'Uncle Josh in Society'.

Magazine publisher Condé Naste acquires *Vogue*.

The New York Times publishes the first movie review.

Winsor McCay produces first animated cartoon, *Gertie the Dinosaur*.

1910 The first radio broadcast in New York City.

The first commercial neon sign in Paris.

Stravinsky, *The Firebird*.

1911 J. M. Barrie, *Peter Pan*.

1912 Russolo publishes the futurist manifesto, which proposes the composition of music based entirely on the use of sound sources from the environment. Russolo and the Italian futurists investigate, classify and produce new noise instruments – 'Our ears . . . keep asking for bigger acoustic sensations.'

Duchamp, *Nude Descending a Staircase*. A human body is represented as geometric, shifting planes, a compilation of angles and etched curves. He has produced a body that is like a machine.

Henry Cowell introduces tone clusters in piano music.

Picasso, first collage.

Queen Elizabeth starring Sarah Bernhardt is first feature-length movie.

Stravinsky, *The Rite of Spring*. While Schoenberg experimented with atonality, Stravinsky tried using more than one key simultaneously. He used familiar melodies and traditional techniques in often dissonant contexts.

Debussy, *Jeux*. Debussy begins to use cinema-like jump cuts in the music, deciding there is no need to always maintain smooth transitions from one section of a composition to another. Stravinsky, meanwhile, even more extremely than Debussy, seems to anticipate in the way his music jumps and moves from one style and rhythm to another, the late twentieth-century techniques of tape and digital editing – he would write music of individual character and then intercut the pieces, previewing how music would fragment as the twentieth century itself fragmented.

Schoenberg, *Pierrot Lunaire*.

John Cage born; it does not take him long to realise that the fundamental aspect of music is duration.

Jackson Pollock born; it does not take him long to realise that every good painter paints what he is.

Gil Evans born.

1913 Webern, *Five Pieces for Orchestra*.

Benjamin Britten born.

Braque, *Musical Forms*.

Duchamp, *Bicycle Wheel*. He renounces painting for the ready-made. He also composes *Erratum Musical*, where he draws musical notes out of a hat.

Gabrielle 'Coco' Chanel opens boutique in Deauville, France.

Billboard magazine publishes a list of the most popular vaudeville songs. It is the predecessor to their trademark charts.

Kasimir Malevich, *The Void* – a single black square on a white canvas. A defining minimal moment; much complexity will follow before Malevich's formal reduction, achieving mystical 'Artistic Truth' through supreme discipline, is echoed half a century later by Reich, Riley, Young, and the dance music that repeat echoed them, through rhythm, repetition, release, process, progress, technology, and back again, in moments of artistic breakthrough, to truth. Malevich called his new geometric visual language Suprematism. He wrote of visualising a 'state of feeling', of creating through abstract painting a sense of bliss and wonder. The square equals feeling, the white field, the void beyond feeling. The square equals rhythm, the white canvas the space around the rhythm. A single black square on a white canvas is at the very beginning of modern electronic dance music. And whether the black square is the cradle of twentieth-century art, a two-dimensional swindle, a representation of nothing, a black void, it also predicts the minimal appearance of the universal product code, the barcode, featured on every single piece of modern consumer product, the black-on-white shape that has become an icon of commodity, of buying and selling. The black square of feeling beat the red of the Russian Revolution to live on in the white space of the future.

Umberto Boccione, *Unique Forms of Continuity in Space* – a gleaming machinelike human form captured at speed.

Russolo builds noise-makers of his own design and hosts a concert of noise music. There is no recording, but there is a list of the instruments that were used: three buzzers, two bursters, one thunderer, one shriller, one shatterer and one snorter.

1914 There is a major impetus around this time in the europeanisation of the blues. Up until now the Blues form varied between 13.5 and 15 bars, to suit the lyrics or the mood of the performer. Eventually a 12 bar form based on the 1-4-5 chord progression (what we know as the blues today) will become standard. This occurred for three reasons. 1) It appealed to whites. 2) It solved problems understanding, playing and notating the blues. 3) It established harmonies and a form for band members to work with.

Charles Ives, *Concord Sonata*.

Cole Porter, 'I've a Shooting Box in Scotland'.

W. C. Handy, 'St Louis Blues'.

Jerome Kern invents the musical by integrating music, drama and ballet.

Edgar Rice Burroughs, *Tarzan of the Apes*.

1915 First transcontinental phone call.

Gustav Holst, *The Planets*.

Frank Sinatra born.

Orson Welles born; it does not take him long to realise he is Orson Welles, or Picasso.

Cabaret Voltaire opens in Zürich, and its participants adopt the name Dada. The movement doesn't advocate any ideology whatsoever, but the 'essence of spirit', freedom of expression, and an open opposition to the World War, middle-class conservatism and the moral degradation of humankind. Dada is a protest against everything. Dadaists advocate a transfer of ideas via sound rather than via words, considering sound more truthful. Their art consists of a mixture of languages, to help break through standard ethnic and social barriers. Dadaists create music based on newly formed industrial noises. They base their whole existence on randomness, a sampling of the world around them, a collaging of the bits and pieces of waste covering the planet, a confrontation of the arrogant existence of sense with a fracturing whirl of nonsense. At the heart of their fascination with the randomness of the universe is a love for machines – real machines, and unreal machines.

The 78 rpm record is introduced.

1916 Satie, 'Parade' – a collaboration with Cocteau, Picasso and Serge Diaghilev that employs a battery of sirens, car horns, typewriters, guns and blasting percussion. It outrages so many people on its opening night that there is a riot, and Satie, at last, after influencing Debussy and Ravel to no great acclaim, becomes a star. If his *Trois Gymnopedies* is, perhaps, a place where it could be said that ambient music began its seep, ebb and flow through the twentieth century, 'Parade' is a prime example of an early-twentieth-century modernist piece that launches the mechanical music that will clash, pulse and convulse all through the century – from *Musique concrète* and space rock via krautrock to industrial and techno.

Piet Mondrian's first Plus and Minus paintings.

1917   Czech dramatist Karel Capek invents the term 'robot' – in Czech, robot means 'worker'.

The Uncle Sam 'I Want You' poster brings thousands of recruits to the First World War.

The Original Dixieland Jazz Band (Back Home Again in Indiana).

Scott Joplin dies.

Thelonious Monk born.

Dean Martin born.

John Lee Hooker born.

Sergei Prokofiev, *Classical Symphony*.

Duchamp exhibits common urinal – *Fountain* – as art in New York.

Bobbed hair becomes fashionable.

1918   Claude Debussy dies.

Leonard Bernstein born.

Louis Armstrong, 'I Wish I Could Shimmy Like My Sister Kate'.

1919   Leon Thérémin develops the Theremin, which produces sounds using two oscillators which respond to the proximity of hands to antennae. The design makes use of electromagnetic waves, which means it can be played without any physical contact with the instrument.

Al Jolson, 'Swanee'.

First dial telephones.

Surrealism as a term coined by Guillaume Apollinaire after Nietzsche's '*sur homme*', superman, and Alfred Jarry's 'Surmale'.

The Bauhaus group is formed by Walter Gropius. This new school loves functional designs, and emphasises abstract geometry in its work. Their style wants to unite architecture, fine art and mass-produced technologies. They emphasise a machine-aesthetic optimism.

1920 Mamie Smith, 'Crazy Blues' – first blues recording.

Charlie Parker born; it does not take him long to realise that music has a poetry all of its own, and that poetry is called melody.

Max Wolf demonstrates structure of Milky Way through photography.

Guillaume Apollinaire, *Zone*, an ode to modernity. Apollinaire abandons punctuation as Schoenberg has abandoned the diatonic scale. Apollinaire is in love with technology.

> This morning I saw a pretty street whose name I forget
> New and clean it was the sun's trumpet
> Managers workers and lovely stenographers
> Pass by four times a day
> Monday morning to Saturday evening
> In the morning three times the siren moans
> A furious bell barks around noon
> Graffiti signs and billboards
> Posters notices shriek like parrots
> I love the grace of this industrial street

Dadaist Stephan Wolpe uses eight gramophones playing at different speeds.

1921 Fanny Brice, 'My Man'.

Charlie Chaplin, *The Kid*.

Darius Milhaud experiments with vocal transformation through phonograph speed changes.

Ludwig Wittgenstein publishes *Tractatus Logico-philosophicus*, which will become perhaps the most influential philosophical work of the twentieth century.

It is not a fact, and yet not as such a fiction, that Wittgenstein, in his time, is sat next to Kylie Minogue, in her time, as she drives at speed towards more speed, a city of speed made up of a mosaic of speeds that make themselves a world of speed that is going faster all the time, so fast it can seem still, unmoving, unmoved, a collision of speed and stillness, a juxtaposition of reality and non-reality, of image and word, of thought and dream. On the back seat there is, or there is not, a unicorn, in your time, as specified by these words as they appear in front of your eyes. Wittgenstein has very little to say, and Kylie cannot understand a word he does or does not say. She has never found a person's silence so perplexing, so disquieting. Playing on the radio in her car is an advert for some product, or a service, something to do with mobile phones. The voiceover is explaining, for those who might be interested, that 'What can be said at all can be said clearly, and whereof one cannot speak one must remain silent.' This is followed by a drumroll of sorts and a hiss of static. For no good reason at all she is suddenly eager to buy a mobile phone, although she already has one.

Much to her amusement, Kylie finds herself speaking. Wittgenstein professes to be neither amused nor unamused, and appears to be unconcerned with what Kylie is saying, this fast drive towards and around a city of pure momentum, and, indeed, with the unicorn in the back of the car, which is entirely outside his level of experience, or simply not sharing his time frame. Kylie is explaining that clarity of thought and expression are hard to obtain because we are always doing things with language. Uses of language have to be contextualised within living practice if they are to be understood, and there is all the difference in the world between the contexts of significant uses of sentences which *appear* relatively similar: 'Swifts fly very fast', 'How time flies', and 'The boat flew down the rapids'. Wittgenstein admits to an extent that he is sharing some experience or another with Kylie, and says without speaking that philosophy is a battle against the bewitchment of our intelligence by means of language.

'But,' says Kylie, while driving, while wondering deeply at the unicorn in the back seat of the car mythically leaning against time and reason, while amazing herself with her words, and her adventure, in this accelerating car, with this man, 'as it stands, this proposition is perhaps ambiguous. Does it mean that it is language itself that befuddles our intelligence? Or does it mean that we can combat philosophical confusions through particular clarificatory uses of language?'

'Both,' says Wittgenstein, or the unicorn, or both. 'Or not both.'

'Wouldn't it be funny,' says Kylie, 'if the important things in the world and in life – such as reality – exist in an eloquent silence where language cannot properly reach.'

She giggles, and wonders for a moment what is more mystical – the unicorn in the back seat, the landscape of events all around her, the city of speed piled up before her, or the fact that Ludwig Wittgenstein seems to exist, and is sat next to her, part of the view, and, indeed, all of the view, a view that is made up of words and beliefs and sensations and memories, and nothing while, what the hell, everything?

Wittgenstein is silent, and this means, in some ways, that he is travelling faster than reality, which is a speed beyond language, which is a fate approximately defined as near existence.

'Who is more human,' asks Kylie, 'Wittgenstein or the unicorn?'

There is no easy answer, and so Wittgenstein accepts in silence that once more he has reached the limits of his world.

Kylie feels herself thinking that the view she is racing from, through and towards is a model of reality that is made up of facts but which itself is not a fact. And then she thinks, *The twentieth century is some place to be.*

The unicorn is, quite naturally, tired, for it began life as a figment of the poet Gérard de Nerval's imagination many years before, and hasn't slept much since. The twentieth century is perhaps as much a figment of the unicorn's imagination as the unicorn is of Nerval's, but I don't at this stage want to make too big a deal of such a thought, because there's no saying where such a thought will lead – it could lead to the very breakdown of existence, some kind of metaphysical equivalent of the splitting of the atom, the end of conscious thought, of consciousness, of the reality of thought, of the thought of reality, because thought can only go so fast, so far.

Wittgenstein feels that what is happening to him is of supreme importance – clearly, as he is outside himself, his life, his time, his universe, his very context of being, and this is not something that happens in the everyday dream. But then the sense of the world must lie outside the world, and he is clearly, or murkily, outside the world, the world of himself, the world of his selves, so maybe he is dreaming that he is flying through sense, or orbiting nonsense, which means he is at the exact centre of his thoughts, which have no centre. But it cannot be put into words.

Which, Kylie thinks, is a relief. Kylie takes this opportunity – how often in life do you get such a chance? – to get Ludwig to admit that there is a unicorn in the car, but he won't. And is there a rhinoceros sat next to the unicorn that is or is not sitting in the car, fast asleep and dreaming something that cannot be reproduced in simple words? Wittgenstein thinks that he says nothing, because there is no answer, not now, anyway, not until there is, and to an extent he is very close to being more or less right. He also considers, on the side, very much to himself – because how can he be sure there is anything other than himself? – how difficult it is to see your own face without a mirror.

They flash by a billboard at the side of the road that points out that the world is everything that is the case. Kylie thinks she might get on Wittgenstein's case about such a proposition, but she notes, as quick as you like, that Wittgenstein has not brought a case with him. He is travelling light. Very light. He is taking unpackable nothing with him as he flies towards the city of happenings, through a landscape of events, at the edge of the mysteries of the mind, past a wasteland of connections that, you never know, make the world go round. 'Shit,' exclaims Kylie, to herself pretty much, as she decides, after all, that she is on her own in the car, which is racing towards a bridge, 'look at that bridge . . .'

It is a bridge of words spanning the highway in the shape of 1922, and Kylie can't help but wonder what on earth is on the other side.

1922   T. S. Eliot, *The Waste Land*.
James Joyce, *Ulysses*.

1923   Eddie Cantor, *Yes, We Have No Bananas*.
King Oliver, 'Dippermouth Blues'.
Bessie Smith, 'Downhearted Blues'.
Kurt Schwitters, *Ursonate* – 'Everything the artist spits at is art.' Schwitters in his Merz collages juxtaposed discarded remnants of contemporary commerce, with the aim of destroying rational, objective logic and celebrating the randomness and absurdity of life. *Ursonate* is somewhere between poetry and musical composition,

consisting of individual sounds, vowels and consonants which are recited with a special intonation and dynamic rhythm, like a piece of music. Its structure corresponds exactly to that of a classical sonata, four movements, an exposition, a recapitulation, and a cadence in the fourth movement. He uses the individual sounds pieced together in seeming nonsense in the same way that he uses found objects and materials in his collages. With both the collages and the spoken noise, there is meaning attached to, or buried beneath, or echoing the apparent nonsense or abstractness. Sense emerges out of the nonsense. In the lyrics to his songs Brian Eno will later be inspired by this way of choosing sound over meaning – meaning will emerge in the combination of seemingly unconnected words and sentences, meaning that can often contain more power and logic than conventional song lyrics tied to outmoded conventions. Samples from Schwitter's *Ursonate* will appear in Eno's song 'Kurt's Rejoinder'. The use of the voice to generate abstract text-sound, or, in a way, music, will find a way, via Cage and co., to *I am sitting in a room*, and the breaking up of words to create rhythm even sneaks into the Kylie 'la's.

Charles Le Corbusier, *Towards a New Architecture*. He declares that 'A house is a machine for living.'

György Ligeti born.

Experimental electrical recordings developed at Bell Labs.

The weekly magazine *Time* first published.

1924 George Gershwin, *Rhapsody in Blue*.

Man Ray, *Marcel Duchamp dressed as Rrose Sélavy*

35mm Leica camera first produced.

1925 Rodgers and Hart, *Manhattan*.

Franz Kafka, *The Trial*.

The foundations of quantum mechanics are conceived by Niels Bohr and Werner Heisenberg.

André Breton, first surrealist manifesto.

Satie dies.

a. In his one-room apartment, Satie had two pianos, one placed on top of the other, their pedals interconnected.

b. His room also contained a collection of more than 100 umbrellas.

c. He once bought twelve grey velvet suits at the same time.

He used one suit at a time until it was worn out, and then he put on a new one. When he died, there were six suits left in his room. Because of the suits, he was given the nickname the Velvet Gentleman.

d.   'Before writing a work I walk around it several times accompanied by myself.'

e.   'For a long time I have subscribed to a fashion magazine. I wear white socks and white vest along with a velvet coat, soft felt hat, and flowing tie – which is partially hidden by my beard – and on my nose I wear pince-nez, of course.'

f.   'My expression is very serious. When I laugh, it is unintentional, and I always apologise, very politely.'

Louis Armstrong, 'Heebie Jeebies'.

Buster Keaton, *Sherlock Jr.*

Pierre Boulez born; it does not take him long to realise that music is a labyrinth, with no beginning and no end, full of new paths to discover, where mystery remains eternal.

F. Scott Fitzgerald, *The Great Gatsby* – a novel about the tragedy of success.

Gertrude Stein, *The Making of Americans*.

Radio's *The Smith Family* introduces the soap-opera format.

1926   Béla Bartók, *Out of Doors Suite*.

Gershwin, 'Someone to Watch Over Me'.

Fritz Lang, *Metropolis*.

Rev. J. M. Gates, *Death's Black Train Is Coming*.

John Coltrane born.

Miles Davis born.

Ernest Hemingway, *The Sun Also Rises*.

Knee-length hemlines mark new high.

The first radio jingle, for Wheaties.

A new kind of microphone helps Bing Crosby to invent the crooning style.

1927   Ellington at the Cotton Club.

Schoenberg, *Variations for Orchestra*.

Kern and Hammerstein, *Showboat*.

The uncertainty principle, which says that electrons have no precise location but rather probability clouds of possible locations, is presented by Werner Heisenberg.

The Jazz Singer, with Al Jolson in black face, a mixture of silent film and musical, spells doom for the 'silent era'.

General Electric invent the modern flashbulb.

Meade Lux Lewis, 'Honky Tonk Train Blues'.

Louis Armstrong makes the greatest of the Hot Fives and Sevens. He is now setting whole phrases ahead or behind the beat, not just pulling single notes. This will set the stage for Swing. Armstrong is now a star, and because of him, New Orleans-style ensemble playing is disappearing and is being replaced by Chicago- and New York-style solos. In short, jazz is becoming a soloist art primarily because of Armstrong. A few songs of significance include 'Struttin' with Some Barbecue', 'Big Butter and Egg Man', and 'Hotter Than That'.

1928 Ravel, *Bolero*.

Eddie Cantor, 'Makin' Whoopee'.

Gershwin, *An American in Paris*.

Kurt Weill and Bertolt Brecht, *The Threepenny Opera* – which will lead ('How?' is the point and yet beside it) to the Doors, the Who's *Tommy* and Sting.

Maurice Martenot develops the Ondes Martenot, an electronic instrument that Olivier Messiaen will later write for.

Philo T. Farnsworth presents the world's first all-electronic television.

John Baird beams a television image from England to the United States.

The first television is sold – a Daven, for $75.

Dali and Luis Buñuel, *Un Chien Andalou*.

Walt Disney's *Steamboat Willie* introduces Mickey Mouse, and it is the first film with a fully synchronised soundtrack including music, dialogue and sound effects.

Karlheinz Stockhausen born; it will not take him long to press his ears to the back of a radio to listen to the hum of the transformers, and from there it will not take him long to penetrate the spiritual heart of the universe, and somewhere in between he will find that there is not long to travel between being shaman or showman.

Andy Warhol born; it will not take him long to realise that he is a deeply superficial person and that he likes boring things.

Rodchenko proclaims, 'Art has no place in modern life.'

1929 At the age of fourteen, Les Paul invents the electric guitar when he takes the needle from his record player and jams it into the wood beneath the strings of an acoustic guitar. The sound from his guitar comes out of his phonograph, giving birth to an amplification required for rock and roll.

Laurens Hammond develops the Hammond organ – based on the technical principles of the telharmonium.

George Crumb born.

Ellington, 'Mood Indigo'.

Maurice Chevalier, *Louise*.

Museum of Modern Art opens, New York.

1930 Cole Porter, 'Love for Sale'.

Aaron Copland, 'Piano Variations'.

Noel Coward, *Private Lives*.

Photo flashbulbs replace dangerous flash powder.

1931 Duke Ellington records the first extended jazz piece called *Creole Rhapsody* – this piece covers two full 78 sides. He will also record *Mood Indigo* and *Rockin' in Rhythm* (an early use of the word rock.) Duke is by now a celebrity.

Gracie Fields, 'Sally'.

Edgard Varese, *Ionisation*. A 37-piece showcase for thirteen percussionists, breaking up the sound and vision of Debussy, Stravinsky and Schoenberg into even more broken bits of rule breaking and experience.

Hawaiian lap steel guitar Frying Pan features the world's first successful electronic pick-up.

Dali, *The Persistence of Memory*.

1932 Schoenberg, *Moses and Aaron*.

The atom is split.

Aldous Huxley, *Brave New World*.

Shreve, Lamb and Harmon, Empire State Building, New York.

First freeway between Cologne and Bonn.

1933 Prokofiev, *Romeo and Juliet*.

The first men's magazine launched, *Esquire*.

1934 Gershwin, 'I Got Rhythm'.

Olivier Messiaen, *L'Ascension*.

Henry Miller, *Tropic of Cancer*.

Magritte, *The Human Condition*.

P. L. Travers, *Mary Poppins*.

1935 Bartók, *Music for Strings, Percussion and Celesta*.

Irving Berlin, *Top Hat*.

Invention of the first tape recorder – the Magnetophon.

IBM introduces the electric typewriter.

Gershwin, *Porgy and Bess*.

Swing music evolves from jazz.

Elvis Presley born; it does not take him long to realise that Elvis lives.

Terry Riley born; it does not take him long to realise that light can be heard.

1936 The British Broadcasting Corporation (BBC) debuts the world's first television service with three hours of programming a day.

Walter Benjamin, *The Work of Art in the Age of Mechanical Reproduction*. Benjamin argues that the modern ability to infinitely reproduce art robs works of art of their uniqueness, their magical aura. The end of the aura of art because of mechanical reproduction, he claims, will have a disintegrating effect on art.

Prokofiev, *Peter and the Wolf*.

Electronic speech synthesiser mimics human voice.

Carl Stalling creates Loony Tunes out of unpredictable sonic juxtaposition, wonky sound effects, and cut-up makeovers of pop, classical and folk songs.

Steve Reich born; it does not take him long to realise that his role as a composer is to sweep the listener away into a kind of very positive, ecstatic state.

1937 Picasso, *Guernica*.

Rodgers and Hart, *My Funny Valentine*.

Robert Johnson, *If I Had Possession Over Judgement Day*.

Ravel dies.

Gershwin dies.

The Glenn Miller Band debuts in New York.

War of the Worlds radio show directed by Welles.

Philip Glass born.

1938 Billie Holiday, 'Summertime'.

Ella Fitzgerald, 'A Tisket A Tasket'.

Jean-Paul Sartre, *Nausea*.

Robert Johnson dies.

Information Please quiz show debuts on radio – surprise hit.

Two brothers named Biro invent the ballpoint pen in Argentina.

1939 Joyce, *Finnegans Wake*.

John Cage, *Imaginary Landscapes*. Cage uses test tones from recordings which he plays on variable-speed turntables.

Glenn Miller, 'In the Mood'.

The Lion, 'Boo Boo La La'.

Coleman Hawkins, 'Body and Soul'.

Charlie Parker is in New York City working at Clarke Monroe's Uptown House. He'll be at Monroe's for about a year. One night during this year, Parker realises that by using the high notes of the chords of a song, he can 'play what's inside of him'. The rest is the history of Bop.

Charlie Christian's unique electric guitar phrasing allows the guitar to compete as a lead instrument head to head with the trumpet and the sax for the first time. Christian probably learned of the electric guitar from Floyd Smith whose 'Floyd Guitar Blues' made with Andy Kirk's Twelve Clouds of Joy is the first important use of the electric guitar.

Nathaniel West, *The Day of the Locust*.

Christopher Isherwood, *Goodbye to Berlin*.

Jean Renoir, *Rules of the Game*.

Regularly scheduled commercial flights begin crossing the Atlantic.

1940 Messiaen, *Quartet for the End of Time*.

Will Carter, 'You Are My Sunshine'.

The first Bugs Bunny cartoon.

Superman radio show debuts.

Howard Hawks, *His Girl Friday*.

Disney, *Fantasia*.

Chaplin, *The Great Dictator*.

1941 Ellington, 'Ko-Ko'.

Welles, *Citizen Kane*.

Bob Dylan born; it does not take him long to realise that people are crazy and times are strange.

1942 First computer developed.

Disney, *Bambi*.

Dorothy Parker, *Collected Stories*.

Albert Camus, *The Stranger* – 'Mother died today. Or maybe yesterday. I don't know.'

Cage writes: 'Many musicians have dreamed of compact musical technological boxes inside which all audible sounds, including noises, would be ready to come forth at the command of the composer.'

Dizzy Gillespie, 'Salt Peanuts'.

Bing Crosby, 'White Christmas'.

RCA Victor sprays gold over Glenn Miller's million-copy-seller *Chattanooga Choo Choo*, creating the first 'gold record'.

Jimi Hendrix born; it does not take him long to realise that the blues are easy to play but hard to feel, that craziness is heaven, that he hears sounds in his head and if he doesn't get them together no one will.

1943 Rodgers and Hammerstein, *Oklahoma!*

Ellington, 'Black Brown and Beige'.

Bartók, *Concerto for Orchestra*.

Jackson Pollock's first one-man show.

Mondrian, *Broadway Boogie Woogie*.

Vera Lynn, 'I'll Be Seeing You'.

Chagall, *Crucifixion*.

1944 Doris Day, *Sentimental Journey*.

1945 Charlie Parker and Dizzy Gillespie become known and co-founding partners of Be-bop. Dizzy and Bird and Miles Davis record a number of tunes in February, May and November, which establish Be-bop. These tunes, which are the most influential since the Hot Fives and Sevens, include 'Groovin' High', 'Salt Peanuts', 'Hot House', 'Billie's Bounce' and 'Now's the Time'.

Les Paul introduces close miking of instruments and echo delay into his recordings, as well as those of friends and collaborators like Bing Crosby and the Andrews Sisters.

Joe Liggins & His Honeydrippers, 'The Honey Dripper'.

Edith Piaf, 'La Vie en rose'.

George Orwell, *Animal Farm*.

Webern dies.

Arthur C. Clarke proposes geosynchronous satellite.

Modernism dies in Hiroshima with the dropping of the atom

bombs. Destruction of Hiroshima and Nagasaki suggests that the projects of modernism, science, reason and progress are seriously flawed. Beginning of postmodernism, which instantly involves a reprise of certain elements of modernism, or at least the suggestion that the past never really dies, it gains new life in new forms, is absorbed into the future, adopted, manipulated, referred to, re-created.

1946 John Hersey, *Hiroshima*.

Bill Monroe & His Bluegrass Boys, 'Blue Moon of Kentucky'.

Faraway Hill, the first American networked soap opera, debuts.

Arthur Crudup, 'That's Alright'.

Bertrand Russell, *History of Western Philosophy*.

Breton argues, in an essay entitled 'Silence is Golden', that music can be a powerful force for the achievment of 'incandescence' – that music can reveal an inner music of poetic language. He recognises music as independent of the social and moral obligations that limit spoken and written language.

1947 Bell Labs develop and produce the solid-state transistor.

Christian Dior re-establishes Paris as fashion centre after the war; introduces the New Look, an ultra-feminine antithesis to wartime austerity.

Tennessee Williams, *A Streetcar Named Desire*.

Thelonius Monk, 'Round Midnight'.

Les Paul Trio, 'Steel Guitar Rag'. The boogie-woogie bass lines on Paul's low E string offer an early glimpse of rock'n'roll.

Mahalia Jackson, 'Move On Up a Little Higher'.

Sartre, *No Exit* – hell is other people.

1948 Cage, *Sonatas and Interludes for Prepared Piano*. The piano is 'prepared' according to a detailed diagram by placing objects such as screws, rubber bands, coins or screwdrivers on and between its strings, producing a quite beautiful, muted, misted sound, like an imaginary oriental percussion instrument.

Pollock introduces his Action painting.

Truman Capote, *Other Rooms, Other Voices*.

The Broadcaster, marketed by Leo Fender, becomes the first commercially available solid-body electronic guitar.

Pierre Schaeffer, a sound technician working at Radio-diffusion-television-France, produces several short studies in what he calls the *Musique concrète*. They are broadcast as a 'concert of noises'. A favourite is 'Étude aux casseroles'.

The 33$^{1}/_{3}$ rpm long-player album is invented by Columbia, allowing up to twenty minutes of music per side, compared with the four minutes per side on the 78 rpm. RCA develops the 45 rpm single.

John Lee Hooker, 'Boogie Chillen'.

Norbert Weiner defines cybernetics as the science of transmitting messages between man and machine, or from machine to men.

The Big Bang Theory of the origin of the universe is developed.

1949 Simone de Beauvoir, *The Second Sex*.

Schoenberg, *Out of the Depths*.

Jean Cocteau, *Orphée*.

Miles Davis, *Birth of the Cool*.

Lucio Fontana, *Spatial Concepts*.

Jimmy Preston & His Prestonians, 'Rock the Joint'.

Joseph Schillinger publishes 'A Mathematical Theory of Music' in which he proposes that popular music can be composed by combining snippets of existing popular music.

George Orwell, *Nineteen Eighty-Four*.

Robert Strauss dies.

Charlie Parker meets Sartre in Paris when Sartre goes to see him play. Parker has already read some Sartre. Sartre says hello during a break. Sartre says: 'I like your music.' Parker replies: 'I like your music, too.'

Milton Berle hosts the first telethon.

1950 Messiaen, *Studies in Rhythm*.

Stravinsky, *The Rake's Progress*.

Pierre Boulez, *Polyphonie IX* and *Structures*.

Pollock, *Number 27*.

Muddy Waters, 'Rollin' and Tumblin''.

Radio programme *My Favorite Husband* moves to television as *I Love Lucy*.

In his paper 'Computing Machinery and Intelligence', Alan Turing presents the Turing Test, a means for determining whether a machine is intelligent.

Commercial colour television is first broadcast in the United States.

1951   Schoenberg dies.

In an effort to introduce rhythm and blues to a wider white audience reluctant to embrace 'black music', Alan Freed uses the term 'rock and roll' to describe R&B, or 'rocking music'.

Gunter Lee Carr, 'We're Gonna Rock'.

Flann O'Brien, *At Swim Two Birds*.

Theodore Sturgeon, *More Than Human*.

Elliot Carter, *String Quartet No. 1*.

Robert Rauschenberg, *White Painting*.

Deutsche Grammophon introduce the long-playing record.

Bing Crosby's company tests videotape recording.

Top 40 Radio invented by Todd Storz and Bill Stewart in Omaha, Nebraska. The idea of playing the same songs over and over again throughout the day is borrowed from the listening habits of restaurant patrons making selections on a jukebox.

Jackie Brenston with His Delta Cats, 'Rocket 88' – 'You've heard those jalopies and the noise they make/Well, you ain't heard nothing till you heard my 88.'

1952   The Cologne station Nordwestdeutscher Rundfunk is founded by Herbert Eimert. He is joined by Karlheinz Stockhausen, and they set out to create what they call 'Elektronische Musik'.

Pocket-size transistor radio introduced in Japan by Sony.

Albert Camus, *L'Homme révolté*.

Big Maybelle, 'Gabbin' Blues'.

Cage, *4'33"* – his silent piece; for piano, although it is unusually easy to transcribe for other instruments.

Gene Kelly/Stanley Donen, 'Singin' in the Rain'.

Sam Phillips forms Sun Records in Memphis, Tennessee.

Lloyd Price, 'Lawdy Miss Clawdy'.

RCA makes first three-speed record player for 78s, 45s and 33s.

Les Paul uses a custom-made Ampex tape recorder and begins experimenting with over-dubbing and other innovative recording techniques.

Varese receives Ampex tape recorder as a gift and begins work on *Deserts*, for orchestra and tape.

First sex-change operation.

Contraceptive pill developed.

1953   *Playboy* magazine launched.

The chemical structure of the DNA molecule is discovered by Watson and Crick.

Roland Barthes, *Writing Degree Zero*.

Samuel Beckett, *Waiting for Godot*.

Ray Bradbury, *Fahrenheit 451*.

Stockhausen, *Kontrapunkte*.

Big Mama Thornton, 'Hound Dog'.

The Crows, 'Gee'.

Elvis Presley walks into the Sun Studios to pay $4 and record 'That's When Your Heartache Begins' and 'My Happiness' for his mother. A dream begins, a dream about everything that has gone before, which will then affect everyone's dream about pop hereafter. One of Presley's heroes is Dean Martin, and his original intention is as much to sound like Dean Martin as it is to sound like Arthur Crudup; thus the first world-travelling voice of rock and roll is in fact a perverse cross between the clean-cut matinee-idol croon and the big-boy, bump-and-grind moan of lust – but then which, really, is the randiest? Dean Martin is the godfather of rock and roll like Stockhausen is the godfather of techno.

Japanese company Nintendo Playing Card Ltd becomes the first company to succeed in manufacturing mass-produced playing cards in Japan.

Horace Silver, 'Opus De Funk'.

1954 Elvis Presley, 'Milkcow Blues Boogie' – 'Let's get real, real gone for a change.'

Bill Haley & the Comets, 'Rock Around the Clock'.

The Chords, 'Sh-Boom'.

Fats Domino, 'Ain't That a Shame'.

Varese, *Deserts*. Like much of the new music of the time, it is totally tuneless. Varese dislikes the term 'music', preferring 'organised sound'. The piece includes a number of tape sounds, meant to be played back during the performance. The tape segments include factory noises, recorded in factories and sawmills in Philadelphia. This, in techno terms, is the first sample – avant-garde exploitation of sound before the existence of the youth movement in music.

Xenakis, *Metastasis*. Sounds like an aeroplane engine mutating into string orchestra, and sometimes even better than that.

Jasper Johns, *Flag*.

Hugh LeCaine, 'Dripsody'. The single sound source for this concrete piece is a drip of water.

Federico Fellini, *La Strada*.

William Golding, *The Lord of the Flies*.

J. R. R. Tolkien, *The Lord of the Rings*.

1955 Chuck Berry, 'Maybellene'.

Ray Charles, 'I Got a Woman'.

Julie London, 'Cry Me a River'.

Elvis Presley makes US TV debut on *Louisiana Hayride*.

Harry Olson and Herbert Belar, working for RCA, invent the Electronic Music Synthesiser – the Olson–Belar Sound Synthesiser.

RAI Studios established in Milan with Luciano Berio as its director. The studio philosophy emphasises texture, sonority and speech manipulation.

Start of ITV services in UK – to London area only. First UK television commercial broadcast, for Gibbs SR toothpaste.

Disney opens theme park in Anaheim, California.

Richard Brooks, *The Blackboard Jungle*.

Nicholas Ray, *Rebel Without a Cause*.

Death of James Dean in a car crash at the age of twenty-four.

Einstein dies.

Charlie Parker dies.

1956 Elvis Presley, 'Heartbreak Hotel'. *Billboard* call Elvis 'the most controversial entertainer since Liberace'. Elvis says: 'The coloured folks been playing it just like I'm doing now for more years than I know. They played it like that in their shanties and in their juke joints, and nobody paid it no mind till I goosed it up. I got it from them.'

James Brown, 'Please Please Please'.

Charlie Mingus, 'Pithecanthropus Erectus'.

Sonny Rollins, 'Saxophone Collosus'.

Allen Ginsberg, *Howl*.

Stockhausen, *Gesang der Junglinge*. Berio calls it the first great piece of electronic music. Against a backdrop of unearthly electronic sounds, the voice of a young boy comes across clearly and uncannily as 'an apple found on the moon', as Stockhausen explains.

An IBM team invent FORTRAN, the first scientific computer-programming language.

The term Artificial Intelligence is coined at a computer conference at Dartmouth College.

Alfred Bester, *The Stars My Destination*.

New World magazine publishes the first short story by J. G. Ballard, 'Escapement', about a couple locked in a time loop.

Roger Vadim, *And God Created Woman* – first sighting of Brigitte Bardot.

Hockney, Hamilton and Blake begin pop art in Britain. The first British pop art painting, *Just What Is It That Makes Today's Homes So Different, So Appealing?*, by Richard Hamilton shown at the Whitechapel Gallery.

Warhol, Lichtenstein and Rauschenberg begin pop art in America.

Eugene O'Neill, *Long Day's Journey Into Night*.

John Osborne, *Look Back in Anger*.

Louis and Bebe Baron write electronic score for *Forbidden Planet*. It is recorded using self-built analogue circuitry, and will remain more than just a primitive antique-synthesiser curio – more a resonant echo of a future that will almost be.

Pollock dies.

Screamin' Jay Hawkins, 'I Put a Spell on You'.

First Eurovision Song Contest, held in Switzerland and won by the Swiss.

1957 Milton Babbitt, *All Set*.

Jerry Lee Lewis, 'Whole Lotta Shakin' Going On'.

Buddy Holly, 'That'll Be the Day'.

Link Wray, 'Rumble'.

David Seville creates the Chipmunks by playing recordings of human speech at double speed. This kind of manipulation is not really used again in pop for about a decade.

Spike Jones, *Dinner Music for People Who Aren't Very Hungry*, which includes 'Duet for Violin' and 'Garbage Disposal.'

Jack Kerouac, *On the Road*.

Ingmar Bergman, *The Seventh Seal*.

Beckett, *Endgame*.

Yves Klein, *IKB 184*.

Soviet Union launches *Sputnik* – the space race begins.

1958   Varese, *Poème Électronique*. Played over 425 loudspeakers at the Brussels World Fair in the Phillips Pavilion, a building designed by Le Corbusier. At the other end of some scale or another, you could say that Alvin Lucier's *I am sitting in a room*, a room designed by no one in particular, is one speaker times 425 diffuse sounds.

La Monte Young, *Trio for Strings*. Young takes an interest in musical stasis to extremes.

BBC Radiophonic Workshop established.

The RCA Mark II synthesiser built at Columbia–Princeton Electronic Music Center. It is the first major voltage-controlled synthesiser.

Texas Instruments invents silicon chip.

Gibson Guitar Company patents the Flying V guitar design.

Jasper Johns, *Alley Oop*.

Chuck Berry, 'Johnny B Goode'.

Vladimir Nabokov, *Lolita*.

Elvis Presley drafted into US Army.

Captain Beefheart and Frank Zappa meet for the first time at high school.

NASA founded.

Broadcast is bounced off a rocket – pre-satellite communication.

First stereo records issued.

Physicist Willy Hinginbotham invents the first 'video game': this table-tennis-like game is played on an oscilloscope.

Alfred Hitchcock, *Vertigo*.

Harold Pinter, *The Birthday Party*.

Gerald Thomas, *Carry On Sergeant* – the first in the Carry On series.

1959   Miles Davis, 'Kind of Blue'.

Jean-Luc Godard, *Breathless*.

Ionesco, *The Rhinoceros*.

Xerox introduces first commercial copier.

Eddie Cochran, 'Summertime Blues'.

Richard Valens, the Big Bopper and Buddy Holly die in plane crash.

Raymond Scott invents the first sequencer, the 'wall of sound'.

Alain Robbe-Grillet, *Dans le labyrinthe*.

Bob Noyce of Fairchild Conductor US prints an entire electronic circuit on a single crystal or microchip of silicon. This breakthrough enables the computer revolution to begin.

BBC's *Jukebox Jury* produced in recognition of the growing importance of pop music.

Joe Meek, *I Hear a New World*. Working at the dawn of commercial stereo, tone-deaf non-musician Meek manipulates tape, splices loops, uses tape delay as an instrument, makes a steel guitar at home, blows bubbles through straws, bangs thumbtacks into the hammers of a piano, scrapes a comb across an ashtray, plays milk bottles with spoons, and finds ways to introduce motion into his mixes. Sounds speed up, spin around, move across an imaginary space between one place and another, in effect move through the brain between one ear and another. 'I've tried – and I've had to do it rather carefully – to create the impression of space, of things moving in front of you, of a picture of parts of the moon.'

Rauschenberg, *Broadcast* – a noisy abstract that conceals three radios. The radio knobs protrude through the canvas, allowing the viewer to manipulate the dials.

William Burroughs develops techniques of cut-up and fold-in with artist Bryon Gysin, the most significant contribution to the fragmentary, non-linear approach to modern narrative.

Introduction of the Barbie doll.

Nintendo start selling cards printed with Walt Disney characters.

1960 J. F. Kennedy elected president of US, the youngest ever.

Penguin Books is acquitted of publishing an obscene book, D. H. Lawrence's *Lady Chatterley's Lover*.

Ornette Coleman, *Free Jazz*. It is as if the musicians have blown apart the older forms of jazz (New Orleans, Swing and Bop) and represented them in a form that is musically analogous to the abstract art of Jackson Pollock – a Pollock painting was inevitably but aptly used as the cover art. It's all there – a whole history of feeling and sound, art and rhythm, power and thought, time and space, but taken apart, rethought, placed in a different time and space, so that the familiar and the known is made unfamiliar and unknown, so that the very idea of music that does this and that and then that and this in ways that had become comfortable is made fresh and challenging again. As the absolute essence of music as something that is always moving and changing, or how the best music comes out of the past and completely breaks free of the past, as an example of shocking newness in music to rival Stravinsky, Hendrix or Cage, as a sign of how music examines and transcends the way the past fuses with the present to suggest a future, *Free Jazz* is one of the greatest pieces of music of all time. It is thousands of years of musical ideas compressed into less than a real-time hour. Well inside a century, jazz has created its own turbulent history, breaking down and starting up again and again, with a parallel sense of rule establishing and rule breaking that classical music took centuries to develop. The recording era, the capitalist acceleration of consumer passion and fashion frenzy, has accelerated the evolution of jazz many times over. *Free Jazz* is as far as the rule breaking can go. It's the jazz atonality, and after this, there's nowhere to go, and yet everywhere else to go. *Free Jazz*, like all great musical masterpieces, says music always comes to an end, goes as far as it can, and then begins again, as something else, something the same and yet different.

John Coltrane, 'My Favourite Things'.

Chubby Checker, 'The Twist'.

First episode of ITV's *Coronation Street*.

Pinter, *The Caretaker*.

The Shadows, 'Apache'.

Bernard Herrmann, *Psycho Score*.

Leonard Bernstein, *West Side Story*.

Krzystof Penderecki, *Threnody to the Victims of Hiroshima*.

John Barth's *The Sot-Weed Factor* parodies historical novels.

Bryon Gysin, *No Poets Don't Own Words* – the words in the title are subjected to a gradually unfolding permutation, reordering the five words in a very systematic and mathemetical way.

Mattel's Chatty Cathy doll speaks eleven phrases in random order.

John Cage, *Cartridge Music*, an indeterminate score for several performers applying gramophone cartridges and contact microphones to various objects.

The word 'reggae' is coined in Jamaica to identify a ragged style of dance music.

1961 Ligeti, *Atmosphere*.

Robert Heinlein, *Stranger in a Strange Land*.

Blake Edwards, *Breakfast at Tiffany's*.

Berio, *Visage*.

La Monte Young, *Composition Number 1*. Musical instruction has shifted from the classical score notation to natural human language. The instruction for this piece is simply 'draw a straight line and follow it'.

Henry Flynt: 'Concept art is first of all an art of which the material is concepts as the material of, say, music is sound.'

The Shirelles, 'Will You Still Love Me Tomorrow?'

Ray Charles, 'Hit the Road Jack'.

Joseph Heller, *Catch 22*.

Robert Moog meets Herbert Deutsch, and together they create a voltage-controlled synthesiser.

Bill Evans, 'Waltz for Debby'.

La Monte Young, *Theatre of Eternal Music* – the beginning of a process, a process music, that will bridge the gap between the highly experimental and academic music of Varese, Stockhausen and Babbitt and the popular music of the time. Young reacts against a period of increasing complexity and sterility in classical music, he reacts against atonality and chromaticism, and the difficult rhythms and melodic ugliness that has developed since Schoenberg's twelve-note method. The musical trend Young helps to inspire, developed and enriched by Reich, Riley and Glass, will be labelled as systemic, repetitive, trance music, process music, acoustical art, meditative music, neo-primitive, solid state, cyclical, pulse, hypnopompic, and end up being known, perhaps in error, as minimalism.

James Tenney cuts up Elvis Presley's 'Blue Suede Shoes' and pieces it back together as *Collage #1 (Blue Suede)*.

La Monte Young creates the 'dream house', where the environment is part of the music.

Joe Meek dreams of a world where a needle-less gramophone might become a common household object.

John Lee Hooker tours Europe – opening act, the Rolling Stones.

Steve Russell creates the first interactive computer game: Spacewar.

Christo begins wrapping objects, including cars and architectural monuments.

TWA introduces regular in-flight movies in the first-class section of its New York–Los Angeles flights.

Hemingway commits suicide.

1962 The Beatles fail an audition at Decca Records.

Koerner, Ray and Glover, 'Blues, Rags and Hollers'.

The Tornados, 'Telstar'.

Iannis Xenakis composes *Bohor* for eight tracks of sound.

Little Eva, 'The Locomotion'.

The Beach Boys, *Surfin'*.

The Freewheelin' Bob Dylan.

Nabokov, *Pale Fire*.

GM introduces first robot on production line.

Andy Warhol, *Soup Cans*.

Beatles sign to EMI.

Terence Young, *Dr No*.

Marilyn Monroe dies.

Warhol paints Monroe diptych.

Sylvia Plath, *The Bell Jar*.

Philip K. Dick, *The Man in the High Castle*.

Anthony Burgess, *A Clockwork Orange*.

Berlin Wall erected.

First issue of the *Sunday Times* colour supplement magazine includes a James Bond story and cover pictures by David Bailey of Jean Shrimpton wearing Mary Quant clothes.

William Burroughs, *The Soft Machine*.

First Beatles hit, 'Love Me Do'.

1963 The Kingsmen, 'Louie Louie'.

The Ronettes, 'Be My Baby'.

The White Stripes, *Elephant*. Balancing white pop and black blues on the head of a mythical pin that pierced the cheating heart of time, loving the electric guitar like it is the only worthwhile modern invention apart from the 45 rps single, White Stripes, bunged up with bravado and baloney, pave the way for The Yardbirds to pave the way for Led Zeppelin, open the red velvet curtains of demented pop show business for Donny and Marie, The Plastic Ono Band, Ted Nugent, The Pixies, Sleater-Kinney, will grow up to become Fleetwood Mac, and go backwards in time to play rhythm for Louis Armstrong, bang tin cans for Robert Johnson and mix paint for Jackson Pollock. They look and almost sound like they belong to a 2003 where psychedelia, punk, new wave and grunge are as much the stuff of nostalgia as blues and rockabilly and their orthodox unorthodox wildly friendly sound would make comforting sense. A 2003 where bands the world over with the word 'The' punked and puked and popped and plained in front of their carefully styled one word names are coming out of garages and acting dumb like it was the godlike 1960s, or the godlike 1970s, any time there was godlike vinyl, any time there was godlike Iggy under the age of thirty, any time it was cool to wear thin ties, any time pop was black and white and in full colour. In 1963, *Elephant* is the greatest rock and roll album of all time. In 2003 some say that it still is, those that said that it was in 1973 and 1983 and 1993. They loved it for its sheer vinyl realness. Fanatics suggested the red of the sleeve predicted the bloody assassination of John F. Kennedy, when the kind of idealism and innocence White Stripes used riffs and ego to define and defile came to its savage end. Without The White Stripes, there would have been no Partridge Family, and no MC5, which makes you think.

The Surfaris, 'Wipe Out'.

Prince Buster, *Al Capone*.

Grant Green, *Idle Moments*.

Thomas Pynchon, *V*.

James Brown, *Live at the Apollo*.

Federico Fellini, $8\frac{1}{2}$

Babbitt, *Philomel*.

Roy Lichtenstein, *Whoom*.

Bridget Riley, *Fall*.

David Hockney, *Picture Emphasising Stillness*.

Welles, *The Trial*.

Joan Littlewood, *Oh, What A Lovely War!*

Betty Friedan, *The Feminine Mystique*.

A. M. Cassandre designs logotype for Yves Saint Laurent.

Philip K. Dick, *The Three Stigmata of Palmer Eldritch*.

First episode of the BBC's *Dr Who*.

Nintendo start producing games as well as cards.

1964 Marshall McLuhan, through his *Understanding Media*, predicts the potential for electronic media, especially television, to create a global village where the medium is the message.

Lichtenstein, *Good Morning Darling*.

Lee Morgan, 'The Sidewinder'.

The fully developed Moog is released. The modular idea comes from the miniaturisation of electronics.

Peyton Place premières on ABC and is the world's first prime-time soap.

Launch of BBC2. First night is blacked out by huge power failure in west London. First programme actually transmitted at eleven in the morning, *Play School*.

Dionne Warwick, 'Walk On By'.

Burroughs, *Nova Express* – it depicts a society addicted to 'millions of images'.

The last Bugs Bunny cartoon produced for theatrical release.

Eric Dolphy, *Out to Lunch*.

Terry Riley, 'In C'. A few bars of music are played by an increasing number of instruments until a wall of sound is created. It is rhythmical drone music without any classical connotations of melody. It seems to be an anti-music, in the way it steps outside the rules, clichés and standards that dominate classical music.

Stanley Kubrick, *Dr Strangelove*.

Richard Lester, *A Hard Day's Night*.

Cassius Clay becomes the heavyweight champion of the world.

Donald Barthelme, *See the Moon?*

The Supremes, 'Where Did Our Love Go?'

The Kinks, 'You Really Got Me'.

Millie Small, 'My Boy Lollipop'.

Ted Nelson coins the word 'hypertext' in 'A File Structure For The Complex, The Changing and the Indeterminate'.

1965 The Rolling Stones, 'Satisfaction'.

Steve Reich, 'It's Gonna Rain'.

John Coltrane, *A Love Supreme*. For all its revolutionary edge it is basically a modal jazz album, and with this jazz album Coltrane begins to gain a new audience of young rock fans who could relate to the music. (Rock is essentially modal.)

Autobiography of Malcolm X.

Varese dies.

Otis Redding, *Otis Blue*.

The Yardbirds, 'For Your Love'.

The Byrds, 'Eight Miles High'.

Herbie Hancock, 'Maiden Voyage'.

Hi-fi systems are commercially manufactured.

Karlheinz Stockhausen, *Solo*.

Harry Harrison, 'Make Room! Make Room!'.

Godard, *Alphaville*.

Joe Orton, *Loot*.

Cigarette advertising on UK television banned – the last one shown is for Rothman's International.

Critic Kenneth Tynan uses the word 'fuck' in a conversation with Robert Robinson on BBC TV.

Beatles awarded MBEs.

Robert Wise, *The Sound of Music*.

Bryon Gysin paints a large canvas with calligraphy while William Burroughs plays a tape cut-up of Burroughs' voice, radio static and Moroccan street sounds.

1966 The Velvet Underground and Nico.

Bob Dylan, *Blonde on Blonde*.

Warhol, *Chelsea Girls*.

The Monkees TV series begins.

Ligeti, *Lux aeterna*.

Legal production and distribution of LSD discontinues.

Michelangelo Antonioni, *Blow-Up*.

Thelonius Monk, 'Straight No Chaser'.

The Mothers of Invention, *Freak Out!*

Otis Redding and Carla Thomas, 'Tramp'.

François Truffaut, *Fahrenheit 451*.

Twiggy photographed.

The first episode of *Star Trek* is broadcast, featuring a creature that sucks salt from human bodies.

Introduction of fax machines.

1967 Jefferson Airplane, *Surrealistic Pillow*.

Walter Carlos, *Switched on Bach*.

Morton Subotnick, *Silver Apples of the Moon*.

Stockhausen mixes snatches of 137 radio transmitted national anthems with static and the sounds of crowds.

John Coltrane dies.

Jimi Hendrix, *Are You Experienced?*

The Doors, 'Light My Fire'.

Rolling Stone begins publication.

D. A. Pennebaker, *Don't Look Back*.

First floppy disk developed by IBM.

Dolby eliminates audio hiss.

Peter Nicholls, *A Day in the Death of Joe Egg*.

In order to appear on the *Ed Sullivan Show*, the Rolling Stones sing 'Let's spend some time together' instead of 'Let's spend the night together'.

1968   The United States of America, *The United States of America*.

The Velvet Underground, *White Light/White Heat*.

The Mothers of Invention, *We're Only in It for the Money*.

The Bonzo Dog Band, *The Doughnut in Granny's Greenhouse*.

Jimi Hendrix, 'All Along the Watchtower'.

Tammy Wynette, 'Stand By Your Man'.

Sly & the Family Stone, 'Dance to the Music'.

Gordon Moore and Robert Noyce found Intel (Integrated Electronic) Corporation.

Van Morrison, *Astral Weeks*.

Anthony Braxton, *For Alto*.

Tom Wolfe, *The Electric Kool-Aid Acid Test*.

Hippy musical *Hair* opens on Broadway.

Andrew Lloyd Webber and Tim Rice, *Joseph and the Amazing Technicolor Dream Coat*.

Elvis performs in a comeback special for NBC, his first live performance in seven years.

Calvin Klein and Ralph Lauren make names for themselves in fashion.

Ronald Sukenick, *Up*.

Walter Carlos, *Brandenburg Concertos*.

Holger Czukay, *Canaxis 5*. Samples Vietnamese boat women's song and creates two long pieces of environmental mood music incorporating various ethnic components from a number of sources. An early exploration in a rock context of the significance of world music on Western culture, and also, in the cut-and-paste techniques, sculpting together thousands of recordings dubbed from shortwave radio broadcasts, provides an early glimpse of a form of sampling and turntablism that feeds into the hip-hop continuum – from Stockhausen via Czukay to Public Enemy and DJ Shadow.

Sony develops the Trinitron colour-television tube.

The Monkees, *Head*. Beginning of a boy-band formula part 34x (mostly unused).

Photograph of earth from the moon.

Alvin Lucier, *North American Time Capsule 1967* – for voices and electronic systems vocoder.

Philip K. Dick, *Do Androids Dream Of Electric Sheep?*

A computer system including a keyboard, keypad, mouse and 'windows' is introduced.

Roger Vadim, *Barbarella*.

Ralf Hütter and Florian Schneider meet for the first time, as classical students at the Düsseldorf Conservatory. They are both taking a course in improvisational studies. They will form a group called Organisation. They will disband Organisation and form a group called Kraftwerk (German for 'power station').

Stanley Kubrick, *2001: A Space Odyssey*. The film presents HAL, a computer that can see, speak, hear and think.

Kylie Minogue born.

Part Two: The journey continues

30

And then, oddly enough, because history has told me that she is alive, I find myself sitting in the motoring car with Kylie Minogue. Her car is pale yellow, not a vulgar flame-yellow, more a subdued yellow, but an expensive yellow. Perhaps it's the yellow that's the colour of the centre of fame. You crack fame open, and this soft yellow would be the colour you find in the middle.

We are driving as fast as speed can allow without your brain melting, down a highway as high up as life, up and above a landscape of lunatic detail, out towards a city as silver as lust. Kylie is telling me about the life she has lived since 1968. It sounds like a good life, like a life a modern young girl would dream of having, a life that has involved ponies and mums and dads and sisters and brothers and swimming and sunshine and love and happiness and television and fame and singing and dancing and fashion and acting out all the possibilities in the world. A life of luck and confidence and ambition and image management and boys and sex and cinema and celebration and bliss and tears and smiles and wealth and cities and dancefloors.

She describes it all with such feeling and excitement you could almost believe that this young girl is real – at least that she's flesh and blood and not some mechanical bride connected by wires and convenience to the very soul of the machine she is driving. She seems as real as me, even though she is just made of words, of wires, and she is actually part of the car, part of the landscape she is driving through on the way to her very own future. She is part of the virtual sky that seems close enough to touch but would be dangerous if you did. The sky would burn you, singe your skin, eat into your bone.

She is pressed into everything that surrounds us, lighting up everything, an invention of some considerable ingenuity. Her memories seem real; they are certainly real to her, and I can tell that she believes them; I can tell just by being here, so close to her, so close I can smell her. She smells of metal and memory, of reality and time; she smells of herself, her own perfume, a perfume invented for her, a perfume you can buy in the best department stores in the city we're flying towards, a perfume named K, – for keep, for Kylie, for kangaroo, for kiss, for the k in sky, the k in skin, the k that splits .open sin, the K for Kraftwerk, the k for kinky, the way her eyebrows slide off her face into the world around her, the k for kinetic, the k in click, and her eyelids seem to slightly click when she blinks, the k for kick, which rhymes with lick, the k in luck, which rhymes with the beginning of everything. I am close enough to her to see that her nails are made of sculpted shapes of mirrored metal beautifully implanted into the clever flesh of her fake fingers. They are as curved and pointed as miniature rockets and as tough as nails, and yet seem as fragile as silver foil, as straight as the road we are hurtling down towards a city full of space-age buildings designed in honour of her strong, long metal nails. Nails that always point towards a future, a future full of space, rhythm and time and the sonic smell of K.

Sometimes her hair is long and sleek, a metal surface as light as air; sometimes it is a froth of bubble and squeak, as bouncy as sin. Sometimes she is wearing a neon bright white that seems projected in frozen flowing shapes on to her shape-shifting body, with a white-light hood that is draped loosely around her face, allowing her to glance across at me in a way that hides her thoughts yet, to a point, completely reveals them. Sometimes she is wearing a metal costume like an erotic armour that makes her skin seem almost real and wholesome. This close to her I decide that she was designed by a committee consisting of Pablo Picasso, Andy Warhol, Hugh Hefner, Giorgio Moroder and Isaac Asimov. She was cubed popped calculated curved sequenced manufactured out of emotional and mechanical bits of the morally crazed twentieth century and a blatant bit of the hyper-commercial twenty-first century.

'I was born,' she says, in a very prim and practised manner, like she's said these words many times before, 'on May the 28th 1968, in Melbourne.

The Bethlehem Hospital. I am a Gemini, and my mum and dad, Ron and Carol, named me Kylie Ann.'

I wonder aloud if, back in 1968, Ron and Carol could imagine the incredible, successful life that lay ahead for their very special little girl. But Kylie carries on with her story, like she was programmed to carry on, as if her story is now so stored in her memory that she likes to reproduce it in a certain way, in a certain order, with no interruptions. This is her story. It is everything she is. I am not yet meant to ask any questions. That, I presume, will come later.

'I have a brother, Brendan, and a sister, Danni.' She pauses, looks me straight in the eye, and her program seems to slip a section or two, because she tells me something that seems a little out of sequence. 'I have eyes of blue.' She smiles, and I can see, because I can see right into her eyes, which are subtle and strange constructs, made up of a kind of moist metal that glints like crystal, that this is almost true. I can see that everything about her is almost true.

31

What am I doing in the soft gold car with the obedient, upgraded Kylie FemBot model no. KX68Y, surrounded by an appearing-disappearing world of glass and liquid, driven towards city standard uncertainty at approximately the speed of truth? I'm in the car because Kylie asked to see me. She wants someone to ghostwrite her autobiography, a book that will tell her story through her eyes, or mouth, or thoughts, a book that will add to the commodity that is Kylie, that will tell the truth about who she is without revealing anything at all that might make people believe they have any idea who or what she might be. She wants to write a book without writing it, a book that will create more truths about her identity without admitting to anything real, so that people will be even more aware of the singer called Kylie while being even more removed from who she actually is, behind the scenes, under the skin, beyond the image. She wants a book that is full of facts that are tuned to a fictional pitch so that the story of her life rings true but adds to the levels of opaqueness she is folding around herself as her fame and fortune grow. A book that seems light and transparent and shadowless and fresh, but which is in fact a further little act of cunning in the construction of the reality of Kylie that is many times removed from the reality of the person behind the mask. The book, therefore, is to be a mask in the shape of a face, the face of Kylie, a face that exists only in the imaginations of people who believe in what they see and read, who believe in her smile, her voice, her performance, her body, who believe that she is real and always tells the truth. Who are convinced that she is sincere and faithful and loyal and their Kylie, the Kylie they want, the Kylie of their dreams. The girl Kylie, the TV Kylie, the star Kylie, the pop Kylie, the sex Kylie, the smiley Kylie, the gay Kylie, the cool Kylie, the new Kylie. The hit Kylie. The Kylie Kylie full of Kylie and yet more Kylie. The Kylie stretched to the limit with Kylies. (There are a number of Kylies, like there are a number of Elvis Presleys – hillbilly Elvis, king Elvis, movie Elvis, comeback Elvis, fat Elvis, Vegas Elvis, dead Elvis, resurrected Elvis, myth Elvis – and this signals how powerful Kylie has become as a pop icon: her name is legion, powerful enough to meet Elvis in his pop dream of heaven where song is sex and sex is song.)

She is interviewing me to see if I might be the person to write her book. She is auditioning me to judge my skills as a ghost, her ghost, the ghost of her career, which is to be told as if it bears some real relation to her life and her thoughts. She has her flesh-covered hand on the stupendously suggestive gear stick of her golden speed mobile as it slices through the landscape of a robot's imagination towards a city where she is queen. With a look in her eyes that implies she knows much more about life, love and evolution than her fans could ever really tolerate, she is asking me questions, and working out just how good I'll be at haunting her reality, at ghosting her strategies, at believing in her self-belief. At exposing her stardom while disguising her essence.

I tell her about myself. For the purposes of this assignment, I am a rock writer. A rock critic. A pop critic. A music writer. I haven't really written about rock or pop music regularly for twenty years, since back in the early eighties when I gave up writing full-time about pop music because, at twenty-five, I felt that I was too old to do such a thing. But, to be honest, I was so successful as a rock writer, so notorious, so distinctive that, decades after I stopped the regular writing, people still consider me to be a leading rock writer. For a while this annoyed me. It seemed to be pinning me down to being something that I wanted to grow out of. At twenty-five I felt that writing about rock music for the rest of my life would be a touch immature. It wouldn't be great enough.

For years I tried to escape the label of being a rock writer. More and more people started writing about music, labelling it, listing it, describing it, shelving it, and to be a rock writer became more and more debased and ordinary as an occupation. And the further I tried to escape being a rock critic, the more I seemed to be considered just that. It got more and more irritating, as exactly what I was worried about – being dismissed as a rock writer until I was in my eighties – seemed to be coming true even though I wasn't actually writing about music. I was hailed as an influential rock writer, and it was assumed I must have still been doing it, somewhere, even if no one knew where, and actually I wasn't. I eventually realised that it is a great compliment, and proof that I succeeded in what I set out to do when I started writing about pop music in the mid to late seventies.

Since the time I wanted to be anything, I always wanted to be a writer, and writing about music, which was what I knew most about, was the obvious way of becoming a writer. But it was writing, above all, that was of interest to me, and writing about music became the natural way forward because it would put me in close proximity to what I found was the most exciting force when I was a teenager. The writers who inspired me both to be a writer and to be a rock writer were American music writers such as Richard Meltzer and Lester Bangs, who seemed to be writers, with style and attitude, as much as they were rock critics. Their writing about music appeared to be influenced by great American writers such as Norman Mailer, Tom Wolfe, William Burroughs, Ernest Hemingway, spontaneous imaginative adventurers such as Jack Kerouac and Allen Ginsberg, and also wild-minded, paranoid reality-fuckers such as Philip K. Dick, Norman Spinrad and Harlan Ellison. Writers who wrote themselves into a history they made up as they went along, a history that changed the way that people thought, and wrote.

Meltzer and Bangs wanted their writing about the performance of others to be itself a performance. They wanted to reflect the fame of the people they were writing about by creating a kind of fame for themselves. They fancied themselves the equal of the musicians they were writing about, at least in terms of energy, vision, style, character and impact.

When I started writing about rock music, the idea was that you were entering a kind of championship. You were entering a competition. You weren't going to write about music and musicians and stay anonymous. This seemed entirely pointless, because as a writer – as a writer about anything but in this case about music – you needed to be noticed, to prove that what you were doing had some value, some individuality of its own. There was nothing interesting in the thought of staying hidden behind the things you were writing about. You were driven by your best, mad, beautiful predecessors into using the musical experiences you were writing about to create your own identity, as a writer, as a communicator of ideas and passion. You wanted to interpret other people's creative dreams into a form that respected and transformed those dreams.

In the British music papers, in the early seventies, provoked by the American model whereby new rock writers were twisting sixties New Journalist techniques for their own use, writers such as Nick Kent, Idris Walters, Ian MacDonald and Charles Shaar Murray were becoming, in their own way, in their own world, famous. They were wonderfully self-centred and intimate in the way they would write about the Stones, Roxy, Can or Bowie. They showed that a kind of writing that had value as writing and not just as dried-up guidance or wet, limp information. They told stories and made up myths and created energy in their writing that seemed to demonstrate that they knew they were in a competition, and the competition was to find out who the greatest rock-and-roll writer in the world was. In the seventies, it made boisterous sense that there was such an ambition. You could be close enough to the music and the stars, and you could report back from this new world with such closeness and understanding that you seemed as exotic, as important, as desirable as the worlds you were writing about.

In the seventies, to be the greatest rock-and-roll writer in the world was on more of an Ali level than it might be now. It was something to be. To be the Greatest. By 2003, being a rock writer was a nice career, sort of middle management, a way of organising a very chaotic world of music into nice patterns and packing them into a brightly lit supermarket. To be a rock critic in 2003 is to be a sort of clerk, a civil servant, a statistician. You give records marks like you are a geography teacher. You have a duty to discover new artists, but you perform this duty politely, with a corduroy reserve, a grey consistency. When I started, discovering new things, changing the entire shape and destiny of music because of some obscure record you had found that you wanted to ram down the entire galaxy's nose, ear and throat, it was a matter of existential urgency. You wanted to be a writer because you believed that writing changed the whole world, and you wanted to be a music writer because you knew that writing changed your own world, and your whole being was fused with this notion of change, and music, and writing, and change, and making people know that things could be better, stranger, darker, faster, newer.

When I started writing about music, the idea of being a rock critic was romantic, a thing of rebellion, it was an outsider thing to do, it contained madness, danger, you had to be a little foolhardy, it wasn't a particularly healthy pursuit, it didn't really have much of a track record, you were a pioneer into a new world that hadn't really sorted itself out. It did seem to be an opportunity to perhaps be the missing link between David Bowie and William Burroughs, a mixture of poet and pop star; this was a world where you could be part rock-and-roll hero and part avant-garde novelist, a world where, by mixing your two favourite things, words and music, you had the chance to be the very best at something, the best in the world.

I don't know if I started out with the sole intention of being the best rock-and-roll writer in the world; though, in an unformed way, because I believed in progress and beauty and the unknown, I did feel that I wanted to be better than anyone else at what I did. I wanted to burn the page like Lester Bangs, abstract the universe like Idris Walters, glamorise myself through association like Nick Kent, walk the talk, or talk the walk, or uncork the fork, or gawk the gawk, or whatever it was that Charles Shaar Murray did. I wanted to reshape the logic of the whole universe like Richard Meltzer did, build a civilisation of musical appreciation and interpretation in my own image. I wanted to play drum solos using language like Brian Case. I wanted to be as unpredictably knowledgeable as Angus Mackinnon and as obscurely funny as Ian MacDonald. I wanted to write with the beat of Bolan and Beefheart, with the soul of Coltrane, the brain of Eno, the body of Iggy, the politics of MC5, the otherness of Faust. I didn't want to just follow the usual history of rock music and add to it in an expected order; I wanted to make up new histories, new orders, and then resist falling into following those. I wanted to write about music in a way that didn't pin music down but that set it free. To write about music in ways that allowed it to keep moving, to keep changing, to keep being the thing that made it so mysterious and important to me in the first place.

And, of course, the thing that made it completely attractive to an adolescent locked into creating fantasy worlds about the imagination based on the fantasy worlds of maverick musicians, writing about music gave me a great opportunity to write about me, which was the thing I knew about the most, in a world full of things I didn't really understand. I didn't fully understand me, but I knew enough about me to make me a key figure in the writing about music. I relished this in the writing of Lester Bangs. As far as he was concerned he was the centre of the universe and everything had to relate to him in this position at the centre. If from this position his writing might coincide with an objective, more sensible reading of music and musical history, so be it, but what was most thrilling was his ability to read music as a series of signals that was all about him and how it related to his life. The sense Bangs made of all sorts of music from this point of view, from the centre he believed in the most, his centre, at the centre, was the greatest kind of writing about music. The kind of writing that connected directly with what he was writing about, the chaos of it, the strangeness of it, the reality of it that changed from moment to moment. It seemed more appropriate, more suited to the cultural context of the music, to the music itself, to write in this way, this extravagant, exuberant, introverted, extroverted, poetic, cracked, impatient way, than to write about rock in ways that seemed over-considered, and sober, and fussy, as if there was an absolute truth about the music, and not a series of lies that produced something to believe in that may or may not have been true but that was certainly sensational.

So writing about music from the point of view of me was making the best of the three worlds that meant the most to me: words, pop, me.

'But what about me,' murmurs Kylie slyly as we approach the city at a pace that makes me feel we're going to crash straight into it. The city seems to be just a surface, a painting of a city, a coloured photocopy pasted against the horizon rather than any kind of real city with real dimensions. Surely we're going to smash through a two-dimensional representation of a city and fall off the edge of the universe, turning upside-down as we plummet into oblivion? But Kylie has such a look of control on her face, a face that seems fixed into this position by someone at controls somewhere else in this universe, that I feel quite confident. Despite the speed we're travelling, and the unreality of our surroundings, I feel that it will all come good in the end. Soon, we will be in the city, the best place for Kylie's story to unfold.

But the auto-tone of her voice tells me she's not too sure I'm her kind of ghost, her choice of author. Clearly, as far as she's concerned,

I've been ranting and raving like a maniac, and she's not quite sure that any of it has anything to do with her life.

'I don't want a book full of you,' she explains, nicely feigning kindness, smiling as if she's saying exactly the right thing to me and it isn't going to hurt me, as if what's good for Kylie will be good for me. 'The book should be full of me and have no sign of you. The I will be me not you. I is Kylie. Kylie is I. You do not exist in my story. You have nothing to do with my story. You are just a machine I am using to feed my story into. You process it without any hint of you. You are no good to me if your writing is full of you. You must write it in the style of Kylie.'

If I wasn't so riled by her reference to me as a machine I might think of asking just what that style might be. It's funny that she thinks I'm a machine, though, when it's clear from the buzzing flicker around her physical presence, her ability to move so fluidly, and her lack of fear as she accelerates her car towards a speed beyond reason, that *she* is the machine.

32

On the edge of the city, just as we are about to cross the border between being outside the city and inside the city, we speed past a billboard. It is advertising the self, whatever kind of product that might be, and it says:

The more consciousness – the more self.
Søren Kierkegaard

33

Kylie looks at me out of the side of her face. She is in profile but she is looking at me. She uses one of her eyes to defy logic. Her face is not smiling, which is quite an event. She says, a little sternly, I think, 'And I don't want anything like that in my book.'

34

We're silent for a while as we drive into the city. I'm sure in her head Kylie is singing to herself. *La, la, la* . . . I'm sure. But, even if in some outside world everyone can hear Kylie sing, inside the car everything is quiet. For the moment, we are not speaking to each other. We pass another billboard. There is a huge amount of white space and a small line of black text.

35

Silence illuminates the soul.

Kahlil Gibran

36

'None of that, either,' says Kylie, but she's smiling this time, revealing a row of teeth that are a sculpture in themselves. Because Kylie is smiling I think perhaps she might let me analyse the meaning of her teeth. How much metaphor for the selling of her life resides in the complicated blank whiteness of those immaculate teeth! The glowing shapes of pure persuasion that she keeps half hidden behind her miraculously hinged lips . . . (Her lips, I notice, have little fine creases very sensitively etched into them, no doubt by a highly skilled craftsman, that are the letter K in different typefaces. I also notice that the lips are shaded with a near-human colour to make you believe that blood, perhaps a rush of blood, has something to do with the shape and appearance of the lips. I think that her lips, with these delicate branding marks of K and the slightly eerie colour, are perhaps the most artificial part of her face, which is mostly enriched with human quality. But you have to get very close to her to notice this.)

I think of starting to interpret her teeth. But she – or someone – switches off her smile very quickly, the luminous teeth are sealed from sight, and I realise that now isn't the time.

37

As if Kylie is aware that I've spotted the Ks on her lips and the lip colour somehow drained of humanity, she applies a fresh coat of lipstick. She has one hand on the steering wheel, and she looks into the driver's mirror, and she paints away the little Ks with a paste that is so smoothly pink and warmly human the whole sky turns lip-smacking pink in respect. As she applies the lipstick, the car goes even faster. I imagine that if she were to put on some eye-shadow, especially if it were verging on galactic green, we might end up going so fast we'd take off.

The city sucks us in, though. The city is moving towards us. The city is so alive we can hear it breathe. We can hear its stomach rumble.

38

I didn't mean to get carried away, I explain to Kylie. She looks at me as if she's highly dubious about my behaviour, as if I have been revealing a singular lack of self-control that is very definitely not the Kylie style. The thing is, I tell her, I knew you would ask me for some background, so I decided to do a bit of research into myself. I remember reading of a writer who, when it came to writing his autobiography, hired a private investigator to research his past, to look into his history. The writer felt that this would be one way to reconstruct a life that he had half forgotten.

I decided to do the modern equivalent, and punch my name into the Google search engine to see how I have been gathered, collected, framed, defined on the World Wide Web. Who am I on the Net? I figured that this would be a pretty good description of who I was, or who I have been. It would be accurate, neutral, and would sum up my achievements inside the media, as a writer, as a personality, as some kind of operator in arts and entertainments.

The Google search engine raked in versions of myself from across the virtual universe, and from the results you could piece together a version of me that is as good a biography as anything. What you could see straight away, from the very first mentions, is that I did become famous as a rock-and-roll writer – at least, as famous as you can become as a rock-and-roll writer. I did do the kind of thing I'd intended to do when I set out. I was clearly competitive enough as a pop critic, and keen on the contest I believed I was in, and I made quite a name for myself as a rock journalist. In fact, I was, occasionally, by some people, called the greatest rock-and-roll writer of all time. I say this without believing it, while knowing it to be fairly true, and would say that, on various occasions, during the late seventies and early eighties, while writing for the *New Musical Express*, I did materialise now and then as the greatest, but overall, in the list of greats, I would just about put myself inside the top twenty. Well, inside the top ten. About seventh. Or sixth. All in all, I think I was the fifth-greatest rock-and-roll writer of all time. Maybe the fourth. Actually, the third. The greatest non-American, anyway. And I could take on the top two Americans any day of the week.

Kylie rolls her eyes in Aussie annoyance, and arches her eyebrows in a way that suggests she doesn't believe it for a second. Second. Yes, perhaps I was the second-greatest rock-and-roll writer of all time. In fact, the greatest living rock-and-roll writer of all time. (Lester Bangs had died, in a final act of rock criticism that took the need to be commited to the cause a little too far.) And to think – I stopped writing about music full-time in 1983.

Part of the qualification to be the greatest rock-and-roll writer of all time is a complete lack of modesty. And having an utter lack of modesty as a rock critic is easy if you also have the other necessary qualifications – being shy, antisocial, awkward and desperately in love with your own company. All the things you repress in the real world – confidence, articulacy, charm – you could unleash from the privacy of your writing room (usually your bedroom) into your writing, creating a massively arrogant and charismatic persona for yourself in print that could be something you could only re-create in the real world when very drunk. It is with the arrogance and self-esteem still lingering in my mind and body after all these years, the adolescent sense of self-destiny, that I would now agree that I am the greatest rock writer of all time. Indeed, the adolescent rock-and-roll writer who still lives inside me after all these years, the kid writer who is supplying the energy for me to write this history of music in the shape of Kylie Minogue, would be absolutely convinced that I am the greatest, as long as he could say it in print, in secret, and not in public. In public, I would perhaps mention that I once wrote about rock music, and that one or two people said I was the best, and that actually I was an influence on pop writing over the last twenty years or so – as much as The Velvet Underground and Iggy were influences on a certain type of rock. I say this not saying that it is necessarily something to boast about, but simply as a fact. I was – and I would say this in public, perhaps a little more self-deprecatingly than I would in print, in private, with no one looking or hearing – as far as I can tell, the most influential of all rock-and-roll writers.

The one thing you notice as you gather up my name on the Web is that whole Websites have actually been built in the image of if not me then my writing – about pleasure, and excitement – and my philosophy – of music and meaning. (Freaky Trigger, London New York Paris Munich, the Church of Me, Oh, Manchester, So Much to Answer For,: the best places to go for writing about modern – past and present – music. But then, I would say that, because I appear to have helped supply these sites with their Ten Commandments, their basic principles.) I'm not boasting about this as much as my instincts actually compel me to, instincts from my teen years when I set out to be the greatest, the instincts that still make me . . . *quietly satisfied* to see how much what I did had an impact. (I would have expected nothing less, actually. I mean, I remember the moment I knocked out Nick Kent, with a flash of inspiration about Devo, and the moment I dismissed Charles Shaar Murray, with a double whammy of insight regarding Joy Division and U2. Admittedly Bangs was on an off day when I headbutted him unconscious with a quick sentence regarding The Cocteau Twins, followed by a great thought regarding Cabaret Voltaire, and he stayed down-faced when banged on the skull with my feelings about the Pop Group; but the fact was, I did it, I beat the King, I got the belt. At the time I had the belt, there were others who snatched the belt away from me. I had to grab it back. There was Ian Penman, the extreme rock writers' extreme rock writer, and we tussled for the belt, shared it, outdid each other with the thinking and the drinking and the writing, wanting the belt, treating it very seriously; we were Wolfe and Mailer, we were battling to be great, greater, greatest. There have been others since. I might, if pushed, acknowledge that they have taken over, pushed me back into the shadows, into history. There has been Simon Reynolds, who politely knows about everything, and his children, my grandchildren, bloggers who have taken the championship on to the Internet, the need to know, to define, debate, as part of a greater destiny leading to more knowledge about the point of pop, and I recognise their tussles with logic, their battles with meaning, the power of their passion for sound, the sound of sound, the noises inside sound, the surprise of sound . . . sound above all else, closely followed by image, closely followed by the relationship between sound and image, closely followed by their own individual relationship to the relationship between sound and image. I recognise the need to get to things first, to be the first to find and define the new sensation, to watch it develop, and then, as soon as everyone has caught up, to move on. The need to move with music because of how it can move you, because of what it can do for the soul, how it can make reality more than real and other than real.

There is, in the relentless Web writing, a reminder of the original sin and essence of rock writing as a kind of secretive discovery of secrets and new movements, an overwhelming need to find, again and again, new things. The great rock writer is caught between keeping those new things to himself – not letting the rest of the world ruin them with destructive demands and needs – and sharing them all with the rest of the world – for egotistical reasons, to show what fantastic taste they have. They want to show off about how they found the best new music before anyone else, and give the reasons why it's the best new music. It's the showing off that ultimately outranks the keeping of secrets. Though often, no matter how much showing off goes on, the music that's been discovered is so secretive it can never be anything other than a secret known only by the chosen few – in which case the writer can simply bemoan the idiotic lack of understanding in a world that just doesn't understand. From nowhere and everywhere, in secret places hidden behind real names and pseudonyms, Web writers continually update their excitement and disappointment with the fashions and obscurities of pop and rock. They do it purely for their own satisfaction – they'd do it if no one was reading – but they love it when they realise people *are* reading, are with them, following their obsessions with the constantly updated histories of music and, naturally, their intense self-obsessions. The anxious, self-important, show-off rock writing has found a home where it belongs, in the future, in front of and behind a screen, sharing the new fluid space of the Web with all the music that there ever was. Great rock writing has moved to where the music is moving. Somewhere out there.

But, whatever else is happening with the tradition of rock-writing exhibitionism, how public or private it has become, I was the greatest and, in the sense that the presidents of the USA are always called 'President' as long as they are alive, I am always the greatest, even as the world of rock and pop squirms beyond me, beyond anyone, because it is alive and dead and stopped and moving all at once, whereas in my day, when I was the reigning champion, it was just alive, it was always moving, more or less forwards, it hadn't become so overcrowded and stuffed with different time periods overlapping each other, muffled with revival and nostalgia and formula.

I am the greatest rock-and-roll writer in the world, for what it's worth. I have also been described as the worst rock writer ever, or the seventy-seventh best, or all pose and preen and no, you know, historical sense, or fucking annoying, or deeply pretentious, or beyond a joke, but where there is hatred there is, of course, something going on, there is a kind of love, and I have in my time been loved and hated – been hit, had songs written about my reviews, been copied, been parodied, been adored, been patronised – to the extent that I was, for a moment, for a while, the greatest-ever rock-and-roll writer.)

I'm stating this simply as something that seemed to happen, as these things do; simply pointing out to Kylie that I am not without the qualifications to write her book, the qualifications that might make her book a little more entertaining than it might otherwise be. I was the best, for a while, a moment, a week, a year, another two years, for a month here, a month there, but once, twice, three times, I was the best, I was the champion, the greatest. It's probably another reason why I gave up, why I retired. I'd done it all. More specifically, I'd said it all. There is only so much describing, glorifying, judging, exaggerating, dreaming you can do about music, week in, week out. Eventually, you can wear down your enthusiasm for music itself because you are having to find new ways to record your love and appreciation, to the extent that you begin to see music as a kind of fuel for your fantasies, mere fodder for your flights of fancy. I still believe that I was right to stop writing about pop at the age of twenty-five – there's a kind of stamina you need to really get inside the music, and inside the fashion of the music, ultimately just fashion, that deserts you after a while. Plus, you want the music, just the music, to take up your time, not the writing about it. I decided to write about music at my leisure, and to just let music lead me and follow me as it happened, naturally, without worrying about seeming in touch, on top. Then again, once it is in your system, the urge to keep up, to not drift off into the past, into the fleecy comfort of your favourite time and records, you find yourself skidding and slipping along with the currents of the current, anxious if you feel there is some shift in musical trends, commercial or avant-garde, that you are missing. If, once upon a time and space, you were so alert to newness and change in music, the whole damned flickering history of newness and change, because it was the basis for your original enthusiasm, then you will still have the need to see where things are heading, or not heading. And often things that I was interested in – a punk spirit, electronic music, the new pop dream of the early eighties – took time to make the mainstream, so that there was something fascinating about watching the music and styles I was interested in make it further and further into the centre of things. The early-eighties new pop philosophy, for instance, which was at the centre of many of my struggles for supremacy, was based on an idea of the smartness and surprise of pop that really started to make commercial sense at the beginning of the twenty-first century, with fantastic glamorous sonically saucy records by Missy Elliott, Destiny's Child, Sugababes,

Tweet, Britney Spears . . . and Kylie Minogue. I didn't write about it, much, as such, I just enjoyed it – enjoyed supporting the warped pop dream of Kylie against the revival straightness of Coldplay, even though, technically, I was twice – actually, three times – as old as I in some senses should have been to enjoy that music, as sound, as fashion.

Funnily enough, if you'll pardon the expression, I can follow my liking for the Kylie Minogue record 'Can't Get You Out of My Head' back to the days I wrote passionately about groups like Joy Division, Josef K, Cabaret Voltaire, Swell Maps, A Certain Ratio, The Pop Group, Subway Sect and the Fire Engines and said that this music should be in the charts because it is pop music, immediate, sexy, noisy, influenced by Captain Beefheart, Can and the Velvet Underground. I can take it back to when I loved listening to music by Carla Bley because it was like other things but totally unique. Kylie's song was pop music influenced by Joe Meek, Kraftwerk, Depeche Mode, Madonna, Air and New Order, but it transcended the influences, and this combination of spaced-out studio sound, rhythmic smartness and intimate human conversation was the kind of thing I loved to see in the charts – because it was such a surprise, it existed because of the commercial world of pop, but also in spite of it. And in the end, for me, the charts were merely a system where you saw music collected, and most of it just passed the time, but some of it made time, was all about time in the way that music should be, and because it was a place where there was a great battle between the value of ideas and the valueless ideas of the capitalist music industry. To see a piece of music exist inside this cold cynical system that had a value about it, connected to its musical uniqueness and the newness of the image and style wrapped around it, was always a great pleasure. Also, it was more and more a pleasure to have these moments of surprise the longer popular music continued in a more or less recognisable form – that such things could keep happening was a fabulous sign of creative vitality.

Kylie seems slightly stunned, maybe even a little scared, by my ranting. She isn't so sure that what I've been saying is relevant to her – if I was the best rock-and-roll writer in the world, 'So what?' as far as she's concerned. This means little to her. She just wants to hire a hot show-business writer who can wrap up her life story with a hint of mystery that is ultimately quite controlled.

And was I *really* the best rock-and-roll writer in the world, or even, reasonably speaking, one of them? Kylie's eyebrows are still arched terrifyingly high in shapely suspicion, and perhaps disbelief. I point out some billboards we are passing that feature some evidence taken from a review written a couple of years ago about books by Lester Bangs and me.

If the best criticism teaches you how to think, not what to think about, so it was the prose writers of the *NME*, especially Paul Morley, that changed everything in my adolescent universe.

Both writers seem to have made out of the fear and boredom of their teenage years an astonishing vision of what pop music could mean in the absence of much other meaning, and an awfully lucid sense of just how mean, reasonable and downright competent are the expectations and reactions that most people direct toward music (and, for that matter, just about any other art form).

If adolescence is a time for taking things far too seriously, the writing of Lester Bangs and Paul Morley teaches us (if that's not too serious a way to describe writers who, after all, have written little but record reviews) that, if we're lucky, the seriousness stays with us in all kinds of unexpected ways, and perhaps nowhere so much as in the way we hear (or fail to hear) words and music conspiring to infiltrate our psychic suburbs.

Kylie looks blank – oddly enough, this is one of the things I like best about her, the blankness, the way she disappears behind her appearance – so I take this as a sign that she's getting interested. (She just blanks out, but looks as though she might be paying absolute attention to your wants. She slips behind the business of her own thoughts and leaves behind an empty space, a blank canvas, on to which you can project whatever you feel like. She moves out of the picture and stays exactly where she is. She ghosts herself, which I suppose is why she is being so thorough in her interrogation of me. She knows what she wants. She knows all about ghosts. This must be the prime qualification of a classy entertainer – they know so much what they want that it all connects to what an audience wants. It all fits together. The perfecting of an image that will appeal to a wide audience without giving anything away other than the surface appeal of an image. She is all surface. You cannot look around her, beyond her, into her. She is all flat surface, a series of flat surfaces, spiralling off into fame eternity. She gives nothing away while giving the illusion that she is giving everything away. One day it might slip, she might slip, celebrities have been known to, and she could give something away, a little hint of her own reality, a possible reality, a sense of the realness there must be somewhere, and then it will all be out of control, out of her control; she will be crushed by the two realities of her fame coming together, the reality of the outside and the reality of her inside. But, for now, she is blank, beyond blank, full of blank, looking blank, being blank, and in all these pools and mirrors and images of blankness we can pretend that she is what we want her to be: the singer, the performer, the dream, the star. She is alive with her own stardom, her existence is just an extension of her celebrity. She breathes fame; there is nothing else. She is blanked out. There is nothing there apart from what the viewer, the listener, thinks there is. Kylie who might be alive has found a way to replace herself with a Kylie who has had no life, no past, just a present, just the moment. She is the wrinkle-free, smooth-skinned, tight-bodied moment: a vast emptiness embracing the moment she comes alive through a screen, a speaker, a headphone . . . An emptiness full of life for a moment and a series of moments that collide in time to create this illusion of permanence.)

But I'm thinking ahead of myself. I am already writing the book, her book, on the blankness of her presence, which is full of story, and I have yet to impress Kylie. I still have to win the commission. I'm about to say something else, something about my own wrinkled, rough, baggy great-ness, when Kylie notices a car a little way ahead of us. *Funny,* she thinks, *it always seems to be ahead of me, no matter how fast I go.* She thinks, because I'm doing the thinking for her, because I'm going to impress her with this skill, this technique of thinking for her, in her book, the book she will ask me to write because I will make her think it, I will persuade her to ask me by writing it down; I will think on her behalf that I am the perfect choice for the job of inventing her thoughts, I will think for her, *He is the perfect choice, he knows me, he can know me more* . . . Now, though, she's thinking, *I swear I overtook that car, somewhere, and it hasn't overtaken me since, and there it is, ahead of me.* It is a vivid supersonic car, a car of curves and material, a car from the future after the one after next, ice-blue, thought-green, infinity-red, softly silver, a mix of matter and fantasy, somewhere between toy and time machine. Something unexpected has appeared seemingly out of nowhere and out of nothing.

In the car there are four figures. They might be men. They might be machines. They might be ghosts in a machine. They are wearing luminous red shirts and immaculate black trousers. They are Kraftwerk.

Their car drives itself and they are as serene as time and they know everything. Their car makes a sound, the sound of the road, a sound as straight as motion, a sound that lightly smiles at space, and takes rhythm very seriously indeed.

They are Kraftwerk. They hear more, they hear less, they click with the switch, they travel in time, what you hear is what you get, they are in the car in front of the car full of Kylie's visual take on motion, in the car in front of the car fuelled by Four Tet's breathtaking breathing, in the car in front of the car flickering with Thomas Brinkmann's glistening cut-ups of time and space, in front of the car filled to the brim with DJ Hell's pounding clash of wire and fire smoke and beat body and bass, in the car in front of the car full of Air, in the car in front of nerd nihilists Radiohead, in front of scary snare master Dr Dre, in front of the bubble-garde avant-gum Neptunes, in front of Missy Elliott, in front of Moby, in front of LFI, in front of the car that is a computer-generated house, in front of the Ford Trance, the Mercedes Techno, the Toyota Ambient, in front of Derrick May, in front of Kevin Sanderson, in front of Joey Beltram, in front of Cybotron, in front of 808 State, in front of Depeche Mode, in front of the Pet Shop Boys, in front of the Human League, in front of Madonna, in front of Art Of Noise, in front of Front 242, in front of Einstürzende Neubauten, in front of New Order, in front of DAF, in front of the Silicon Teens, in front of Cabaret Voltaire, in front of David Bowie, in front of Throbbing Gristle, in front of Roxy Music, in front of Giorgio Moroder, in front of Cluster, in front of a history of atmosphere where Can, Lee Perry, George Clinton and Laurie Anderson free-flowed into each other . . . They drive past billboards advertising Japanese-produced drum machines spread out at precise regular intervals at the side of the highway . . . Roland 101, 202, 303, 404, 505, 606, 707, 808, 909, the magic numbers, the perfect sequence . . . They drive through a world where electricity is the basic essential element . . . They drive through a beautifully synthetic hyper-human landscape as Wendy Carlos becomes the first man and woman on the Moog . . . Kraftwerk glide on in front of a car as neat as destiny in front of the car in front of them which is filled with a liquid space and a literal place (mental and physical) where innovation can flourish . . . In front of the car in front of the car in front, which has Iggy Pop as a passenger, James Brown as an astronaut and Brian Eno as an alien . . . In front of the car driving to the coast of dreams that has a group of nodding Beach Boys underneath the rearview mirror . . . In front of the car in front of the car phasing in and out in and out in and out and in out in out and and in in in out out out and and and and aaaannnnd-dddddd driven with such severe, sensual simplicity by Reich, Riley and Young . . . In front of the car in front of the car riding through outer space out there beyond human grace driven by Sun Ra . . . In front of the car in another reality driven to the centre of the sonic planet by Miles Davis . . . In front of the car in front of the car on a moon that is in the shape of a silver apple . . . In front of the car in front of the car driven by a baby playing Raymond Scott's 'Soothing Sounds for Baby' . . . In front of the electric car beyond the electric car in front of the car in front being tinkered with by Stockhausen, Varese, Xenakis . . . Which occupies simultaneous space with a car Cage insists is made up of variable speed, chance, flowerpots and mushrooms . . . And Cage tells Duchamp his mind is percussion, Russolo his body is the flesh of noise, Satie to keep off the furniture, Schoenberg to count beyond twelve, and Busoni stands out on his own high in the sky and exclaims the hills are alive with the sounds of abstraction . . . And Debussy throws the chains off his car and harmony melts through his outstretched fingers . . . And Kraftwerk are in front of the car in front of the car in front of them and slip back and back as they move forward back and back to when humans used rocks as percussion, their bodies, voices and hands to make music, finding a way to make noise as a way to play, create, express . . . Slip back and forward into the heart and minds of humanity . . . Where the heart beats and the mind wonders . . . From the beginning of everything to the beginning of Kraftwerk time, when they discovered the abstract sophistication of simplicity and the precise ability to tell musical stories about technology and communication, when they began to make music that was an immediate response to everything they were in front of, and everything that was in front of them, and everything they were in front of that was in front of them. When they made music on machines in a room they had turned into a machine about a world that had turned into a machine that contained humans who loved machines and hated them like they loved and hated themselves.

They are Kraftwerk and pop music without them would lack the rhythm of breathing, would lack pulse, feeling, wires, art, source, history, strangeness, would lack the great ingredient that mixed with so much oddness to create so much newness. Twenty-first-century pop untouched by Kraftwerk, as flash and energetic or historically accurate as it might be, is going to be out of time, out of step, nostalgia, stuff, ordinary. To go back in time and steal from Love, Ramones, The Stooges, Sabbath, The Stones, the Kinks, from Wire, Gang of Four and Public Image – it will create pretty pastiche, it will send ripples of welcome energy out into a neutralised world, but artistically, which is a consideration, it will miss the point, it will be like making jazz now and ignoring everything Miles Davis did.

Kraftwerk drive past vast lit-up billboards that border the edge of the mighty city where Kraftwerk are king and that tell a story of Kraftwerk in ten modern parts. Modern parts that are metal and glass buildings on the liquid edge of the post-war, post-dream post-real city, beautifully designed buildings that merge with the city, that join every part of the city via underground tunnels and radio interference and wires and cables. This is the entrance to the city where time is lost and found at the same instant, the instant it takes for Kraftwerk to program a drum sound, and take on the moment, which is the moment before next, and we're right up against the view of a city that takes our breath away, that takes physical space away and replaces it with mental space, a mental space full of buildings and sound built for fun and purpose by a group whose music is all about the city, the city of sound, and ultimate experience.

1. Firstly, there was nothing wooden about Kraftwerk. For Kraftwerk, if it didn't have a button, it wasn't worth pushing. Wooden instruments with crude string fixtures and an obvious lack of buttons and switches did not feature for long in the way Kraftwerk made their music. Frankly, the music you could make using wood, string and brass would not be capable of achieving the level of soul Kraftwerk were after, let alone the level of precision. They were interested in understanding the quirks and quality of the modern technological age, and they used synthesisers to construct their music in a way that would: a) be part of their understanding of the modern technological age; b) create the most appropriate soundtrack to the modern technological age; c) be an influence on the modern technological age itself; d) predict how the modern technological age would surround us with machinery that would start

to control our lives and dominate our immediate surroundings; e) be extremely electric, because anything else is far too rustic, and cannot possibly communicate the correct things about the beauty and the ruins of the present world.

2. Secondly, Kraftwerk were sad. Sad about some things. Sad about other things. It was the sadness of life, the sadness that life goes, in ways that are beyond reason, very much more nowhere than somewhere. It was the sadness of knowing that you must try hard to head somewhere knowing that really we are nowhere. The sadness of doing something knowing that it all comes to nothing. The sadness that the excitement of experience dissolves into an eternity beyond experience.

They clicked and crackled with sadness. There was a strict sadness in Kraftwerk's music. This came from the way their music was based around a poignant pointless longing for a new version of the past that would never be brutalised by the Nazis, for a past that looked forward to a utopian future and tried to make it happen, for a past that was a perfect midway point between a history that moved life and society forward and a future that accepted this history with smart, thoughtful grace. The sadness was also because Kraftwerk believed in this utopian future and they knew it could never come true, ruined by historical pressure, and political corruption, and the failure of dreams to come anywhere near true. Their music was an echo from an unsullied past and a shadow of a dreamlike future – an echo and a shadow placed so deliberately and so bravely between the melancholy drum rhythm of a present that disappeared instantly the drum was synthetically hit. Their music was lost in the spaces between the past, the present and the future, spaces that show us that we are adrift, we are not fixed, we are constantly rootless, never settled. We float through space. Kraftwerk attached this floatation and this space to a rhythm of such cracking fragility, a rhythm that steadily represented a muted longing for truth, for stability, for certainty. They used machinery to mark out space and time amid awesome chaos; they used eerie, emphatic electronic noises to mark out minute human territory amid the monstrous drama of the universe. The electronic noises symbolised the chemical impulses that make us human.

Kraftwerk were sad because we cannot remain innocent for long. Kraftwerk were sad, ultimately, because their music, as active, composed, definite as it was, as it is, as complete as it seemed, lacked something. Something was missing. Something like the answers to all the questions we ask ourselves about life, love, death and what is happening at this moment. Kraftwerk created a kind of perfection that hinted, extravagantly, that there are answers to all the most difficult questions, and that they might yet come because of the relationship between man and machine, but actually, we don't know what they are, not quite; they are outside of our thinking, of our feeling, just beyond. The sadness in their music came from the way that they reduced everything to a combination of heartbeat and absence, of meaning and the ghost of meaning, of belonging and not belonging.

And then there was the way they used the human voice – voices that sounded like the recently departed heard on an answer machine, voices that reminded us how strange it was that increasingly we hear each other across space, over phones, through screens, at an electric distance. The new world looked truly fantastic, above our wildest dreams, but it sounded fantastic as well, human but ghostly, separated from our natural ways. They used voices that sounded somewhere between the way we talk and the way we think.

3. Thirdly, they were artists, above all else. Artists first, musicians second, perhaps third, even fourth. They were classically trained, they knew their way around composition and theory, but they developed their music by slipping around the back of this training, by treating their learning as an advantage but not completely essential. Their musical technique ensured that they understood enough about structure and melody to achieve musical quality even when they abstracted sound and manipulated noise, and their musical education meant that their avant-garde sensibility was both moderated and liberated by a sensualist instinct, with a need to please the senses even as they explored the limits of sound. They began as artists, not as rock musicians; as experimentalists, not as entertainers. They began with serious intent to remake reality, to remake history, to create new kinds of myths about their country, their surroundings, their feelings. To build new myths about music, and where it came from, and where it was going in the technological era.

They treated sound as part of the material of their art – and art was their way of marshalling their thoughts about history, and progress, and the relationship of the individual to history and progress. Sound was the canvas on to which they applied their images; sound was the surface on which they positioned sound, and themselves; their image was the substance they manipulated using sound that communicated their consideration of what communication was; and sound was their way of communicating how astonishing existence was, in part because sound was a better medium by which to communicate astonishment than were words, or images, or shape. Kraftwerk put everything together – sound, image, word, shape – to produce their art, an art which sounded just like art should sound if it made a sound, alive with mysterious clarity.

They began with very straight faces, the straight faces of artistic intent, and they never totally lost the straight faces, the inscrutability. If they did smile, they did it in private, or behind straight-faced masks, or they used robots to represent to the world their straight faces. They ended up as possibly the funniest Germans of all time, as comedians, as satirists. Sometimes, especially when their music was so irresistibly a combination of aloofness, catchiness and beat and the off-beat that it sauntered over into the pop charts, there was a hint of novelty about the group. They were at times dismissed, oddly, as one-hit wonders – but in a way this fitted in with the nature of their art, which was to demonstrate the ways and means of the modern world in all its transience and desperate newness. They needed to involve the immediacy and deliberateness of pop music into what they did, as pop music was the representation through sound of their obsession with a modern life that was driven by freeways, radio communication, TV, telephones, computer technology. Pop music was modern life, and so good were they at mocking up a pop music as part of their vision of modern living that it now and then became real pop music. It crossed over into the alternative reality of the pop charts, and was a temporary blip on the temporary pop landscape. A communication about the magical temporariness of modern life became itself a part of that culture. They were commenting on it and becoming part of what they were commenting on, which was part of the perfection of Kraftwerk. They were all at once object and subject.

Occasionally, their obsession with the rhythm of image and the image of rhythm, with the way that rhythm articulates all the parameters of music, their fascination with myth-making and mass-marketing, meant that they accidentally coincided with fashionable movements – they started out randomly progressive, edged with psychedelia, breaking the sound barrier, Floyd-ish; they were Krautrock, cosmic nutters travelling beyond musical gravity through the space of sound, Can-ish; they were a little bit theatrical glam, sci-fi, made up and artificial, their life was their performance, Bowie-ish; they were vaguely punk, fiercely independent, DIY Wire-ish; they were post-punk edgy, uncompromising and unclassifiable, Front 242-ish; they were comic situationists, wrapped in cryptic visual and aural warp, Devo-ish; they were electropoppy electronic, synthed and scanned, Human League-ish; they were new-romantic dreamy, severely flamboyant, Soft Cell-ish; they were acid-dance anonymous, fascinated with the movement of brain and body, 808 State-ish; they were post-rock, in a slow time of their own, Tortoise-ish; they were intelligent dance music, mapped logorhythmical strangers, Thomas Brinkmann-ish – but they were never fixed inside any particular genre. A claim could always be made that they belonged somewhere, that they could be pinned down, because what they did created a lot of the vocabulary of modern pop music, a lot of new pop and abstract dance music was created in their image, and their artistic interest in their appearance mapped on to pop music's need to move fashion forward. You could see traces of them everywhere, so they never seemed as far out as Neu!, as far-fetched as Faust, as far gone as Tangerine Dream. But they slipped across genres, they crept around them, they escaped classification. They never belonged anywhere but where they wanted to belong, in their own space; they never fitted in with what was happening around them. Even their clothes were different – they looked like they were from the open past, or the closed future, like eccentric professors who seemed to never really worry about their clothes and yet actually worried about them greatly. Clothes were a burden, and yet very important, and Kraftwerk no doubt took great care to appear so removed from the fashions of the day.

They were so outside the world of pop and rock, because of the way they followed their own history, their own musical set of references, that when they did visit the mainstream world they truly seemed like aliens. Charming, almost childlike aliens, clever at disguising whatever subversive purpose was at work. They were never (directly) scary. They were always friendly, if a little stern. They never seemed to want to abduct anybody. They would visit, and then they would depart. They would subtly alter the DNA of popular music with their visits, but they never performed complicated bloody surgery. Their influence was by osmosis, by some form of extrasensory perception. They hovered above the surface of planet pop, looked a little strange, seemed a bit peculiar, left sweet, stimulating messages in a language that was other than pop yet part pop, and then departed with no fuss, as modestly and as discreetly as they had arrived. They were kind, even quite cute, but distant. Pop changed, often because of them, so that when they visited they could seem somehow familiar, but essentially they were not of this world, they were outsiders, perhaps the most avant-garde group, the most experimental outfit to ever have hit songs, as if Marcel Duchamp was creating a sound-track to his bicycle wheel and dominating a quaint Hit Parade, as if La Monte Young was squeezing all his eternal monotony into pop brief-ness and storming the charts. They were artists using sound in such a simple, smart way that their sound became commercially successful pop music. As artists their interest was in making songs that reflected progress and the way they reflected progress itself created progress, and they described progress so sublimely that it occasionally sounded like – could be recognised as – blissful pop music. Kraftwerk made pop music where the definition of pop music is that it creates a distinct tension between representing for a moment in time the sensation of progress and main-taining for all time, through highly organised repetition, simple comfort levels. Or they made pop music where the definition of such is that it is about the clashing in sound and rhythm, between the past and progress, between the mental and the physical, between the sentimental and the metaphysical, and between this moment and the next – which is, for now, the rest of time. Or they made pop music if the definition of pop music is that it is something produced as a temporary thing but that at its very best ends up achieving a kind of permanence. (Kraftwerk's pop is the most permanent of all – if the time ever comes to look back on the last fifty years from a real distance, sometime in the thirty-first century, it will be the music of Kraftwerk that best symbolises how music at the end of the twentieth century broke experience into bits to show how experience itself was beginning to break into bits.)

Kraftwerk found a musical place where the mixing and matching of the predictable and the unpredictable was at its most uncanny and moving. They were on the outside of everything, and simultaneously they were on the inside of it all. They kept their distance, a million light years away from making commercial sense, and they were right in front of our eyes and ears.

4. Fourthly, if you cut Kraftwerk, they pretty serenely bled the words *Music is careful attention paid to ongoing experience*.

5. Fifthly, they avoided, with their straight faces and their art deter-mination, their documentary approach and their presence of mind, the

rock-and-blues Anglo-American pressure that was, in the late sixties, dominating the sound of non-classical new music. Committed to carrying on German culture from where it had been violently amputated in the thirties by the Nazis, determined to find a new German identity in a country just recovering from the carnage and guilt of the Second World War, they looked towards the purity and beauty of the German Bauhaus movement and the extreme rigorous experimental curiosity and technological power of leading German avant-garde composer Stockhausen. From Bauhaus, they took the philosophy that the work of artists should not be a simple reflection of individual creativity but should be inseparable from the surrounding technology and community. They carried forward Stockhausen's work in developing the technological means for producing electronic music, and a sensitivity to how sounds from the new environment could be involved in the music. By taking Germanic sources from the thirties and the fifties, they were commenting on the book-ends to either side of the demonised role of the Germans in the forties.

The source of their pop, then, was not blues, soul, America, beat, sex, love, cliché − it was art, noise, technology, ideas. Their music was a completely new model, based on a fantasy of what pop music might have sounded like had it not begun in the blues, in wood, in anger, in lust, in sexual frenzy, in poverty. What if it began in the avant-garde, in metal, in celebration, in abstract art, in universal awe, in modern comfort laced with psychological anxiety?

Because Kraftwerk did not exist in a vacuum, could not separate themselves totally from what was happening around them, were not the types to be flatly nostalgic, and they did not want to be obscure; they combined their visionary art urges with a kind of academic appreciation for what was happening in other areas of rock and music. From rock, along with German contemporaries such as Can and Tangerine Dream, they were interested in the way early Pink Floyd were stretching rock, breaking beyond the conventional song structure, using free-jazz ideas in the blending of time signatures and texture. As if they were appraising an enigmatic ancient artefact, they viewed The Beach Boys as massively exotic. In their eyes, The Beach Boys' stories were not as interesting as the way those stories were being told, the precision of the structures and the complicated compactness of the rhythms. They admired the way the Beach Boys could concentrate a maximum of fundamental ideas into a three-minute pop song and could capture such richness of location, atmosphere and mood. They were taken by the intelligence of their thoughts, and how they placed this intelligence regarding American reality into their songs. The Beach Boys compressed American experience into their music and did it in such a way that they became part of the American experience. Kraftwerk wanted to do this as a German band: make an ethnic German music using the tools, culture, experience and influences that were relevant to them in the late sixties and early seventies. In that sense their music was native German blues, country, pop music, influenced by absurd Dada, rich Schubert, electric shocking Stockhausen and idea-activist Joseph Beuys. Kraftwerk blended the pop literacy and sonic sensitivity of The Beach Boys with the ancient and modern Bauhaus belief in the spiritual fusing of form and function.

As they started to create their rhythms using drum machines, for convenience and for economic and aesthetic reasons, Kraftwerk aimed to create streamlined shape. Their contemporaries in Germany were deviating from the Anglo-American tradition by using machines to free themselves from form, or to extend form, to elongate songs, to break things up, to turn things inside out. Kraftwerk, meanwhile, devoted themselves to producing a much more conventionally appealing abstract electronic music, mimicking and artificially re-creating the regularity of pop rhythm, splicing this with rhythmical cues taken from the ruthless grace of Satie, the trippy clapping of Reich and the metaphysical beating of Riley. While the likes of Can, Faust and Tangerine Dream pursued their energy inside inner and outer space, Kraftwerk ventured out on their own down a completely new and different highway, an earth-bound highway, where their music was itself the sound of the highway. It captured the rhythms of the modern world, a world where the new and the old were deliriously intertwined, and it kept faith, through the reliance on steady rhythm, on the beat of travel, talk, telecommunication, with the sound of pop, which is the sound of today. Because the source material was so different from other pop music, so unusual, and because it was created in a completely new way, fashioned from machines, filtered, manipulated, treated, tricked, it was without cliché, as fresh and as shocking as great art, yet perversely some kind of twentieth-century relation to pop and rock. It had pretty much emerged outside of any of the normal black influences on rock and pop – the African and Asian influences on Cage, Reich and Riley reached Kraftwerk many times removed from their original lifetime – but one of the great ironies of a group whose machines sometimes seemed fuelled by irony was that the Kraftwerk influence would feed into black music, taking with it the influences of avant-garde music, many times removed from its original lifetime, but in enough of a way to completely revitalise black-American popular music that, oddly, had not been inspired by the black adventures of free jazz. Kraftwerk's non-blues application of repetition in music, their natural Germanic avoidance of black music's usual terms of engagement, the sophistication of their connection of form and content, their love of sound for its own sake, their belief in the electricity of the future, was eventually more of a turn-on to modern American blacks for whom the blues was too ancient, woody and ransacked a form.

6. Sixthly, black musicians in turn replaced the lust, chaos, disenfranchisement and anger, certainly the sex and intoxication, into the middle-class and deeply, artfully strange Kraftwerk model, and made it very clear that what Kraftwerk had done by mixing art with technology, simplicity with machinery, wit with seriousness, soul with precision, sadness with happiness, coldness with heat, celebration with organisation, calmness with action, spirit with intellect, was to create a fabulous dance music, a body music for the mind, a mind music for the body.

Against the usual grain for white rock music, Kraftwerk stole nothing from black music – at least not crudely, not directly – and they gave loads back. Most Anglo-American rock and pop was next to useless for new black musicians to raid for influences because it merely bastardised black music. Kraftwerk offered up a whole new untouched universe of sound and rhythmical opportunities.

7. Seventhly, were a member of Kraftwerk to appear in the car with Kylie – which is unlikely, being realistic, as they don't often leave their own car, because they like to keep their secrets in their own car, but . . . If, say, one of the original members of Kraftwerk – say, Ralf Hütter – was to suddenly be in the car with Kylie, and if he was to say something, which is really pushing the levels of plausibility, but just say, for the sake of this fantasy, that Ralf popped up in Kylie's car to escort her into the city that is now upon us, let's imagine that he has sent over a robot replacement to fill in for him, then robot Ralf might like to say to Kylie, and yet not really to her, more to himself, in a voice you'd swear was quite real:

'On stage we operate electronic control panels, circuit switches, and keyboards. And we turn knobs, switches, regulators and sound filters. I have singing fingers, speaking fingers, which communicate by technique. It goes along with this most highly sensible technique that one can only perform with minimal mobility. One has to visualise like the captain of a spaceship. Only a few millimetres displaced, and the sound is already away.'

Kylie can think of nothing to say in reply, so she just keeps driving. Ralf keeps talking, and does something with his mouth that you'd swear was almost a smile:

'Without a loudspeaker no one could ever experience Kraftwerk. You cannot play our music on a piano. That does not work. Notes have no value for our music. A piano is simply old. We have long ago lost from our gaze this archaic musical instrument.'

Kylie has no idea what a piano is. She asks Ralf how he would describe his music – she thought it might help her describe what her music is. There is no smile on Ralf face, there is no expression at all, as he replies:

'The mechanical universe of Kraftwerk has been cloned or copied in Detriot, Brussels, Milan, Manchester, and even psychedelicised by the delirium of house music. You can define it as you want – sci-fi music, techno disco, cybernetic rock – but the term I prefer is robot pop. It fits in with an objective which consists of working without respite to the construction of the perfect pop single for the tribes of the global village.'

It is Kylie's turn to almost smile, as she thinks that perhaps, as a robot-pop superstar, she has constructed the perfect pop single.

8. Eighthly, when you drive listening to *Autobahn*, you realise how your car is a musical instrument. Outside, the landscape, as it changes and stays the same, as it turns into itself framed by the windows of the car, is a perpetual work of art. 'Everything is art!' said Duchamp the myth machine as he turned on his laptop and hooked up to himself.

9. Ninthly, at a party in Paris in 1977, hosted by Iggy Pop and David Bowie, Kraftwerk were given a five-minute standing ovation when they entered the room. I am going to suggest, for the sake of the numbers, and the list in this part of the book, the list that is like an address on the edge of the city Kylie has cleverly reached, that this was in fact a nine-minute ovation.

I want to know a number of things in relation to this story, but mostly:

What were Bowie and Iggy thinking as they applauded? What were the members of Kraftwerk thinking as they were applauded? It would be great if there was a tape of the applause – it would be a wonderful souvenir of a moment that should be commemorated with a street name or a plaque on the wall.

I think that Iggy was thinking that dreaming about machines really meant dreaming about the genitals. He was thinking about genitals and wires and noise and sex. He was thinking – clap clap clap, smile smile smile – that the repetition of machines is the repetition of our sexual acts with their duplication of eggs, sperm and blood. The neural processes that machines mimic are our deepest desires and meticulous obsessions. He was thinking, 'I could do with a drink, a fuck, a slap on the back, a knife to twist, a dream to dream, some food, some drugs, give me danger, give me strength God fuck God', and for some reason in his head his mind his body his place in the universe he found himself in a fierce fast car driven by a young Australian girl with flirty blonde hair and a crisp but shimmering online look like she'd lived all her life in an electric dream, and the wheels of the car made a provocative circular rhythm, and he said to her, 'I am a passenger', and she said, 'Boy, it's more than I dare to think about', and he said, 'And I ride and I ride and I ride', and she said, 'La la la, la la . . .'

David Bowie had the strangest smile on his face, like he was about to disappear in a puff of lemon smoke, like he was the ghost of a dead future haunting a dying present, and he didn't move a muscle as he clapped and clapped, clapping the Kraftwerk beings just for being in Paris, just for being an artistic embodiment of their own ideas. He was thinking: 'Kraftwerk perceive everyday events and transform them into dramatic situations. Just as poets and writers play with words and phrases, painters play with colours and perspectives, and sculptors play with shapes and forms, so Kraftwerk play with sounds and rhythms. The qualities attributable to the arts are equally applicable to their music. It is shaped, phrased, coloured, moulded, mixed and modified into a unified experience. The music is fundamentally just sketched out, creating an abstract framework, leaving the filling in of narrative and meaning, the setting and the time frame, to a great extent, to the listener. With such vague and ethereal music, Kraftwerk excel in transforming the commonplace sounds of daily life into a stirring and spiritual experience. They see all but participate in nothing.'

He clapped even louder and his smile crossed over into the land of the lost and yellow smoke started to surround him.

Kraftwerk entered the room, spotting Iggy Pop sat with a very young, almost transparent girl on his lively lap, and David Bowie glowing at the centre of some golden smoke pretending to know where he was. The corners of their mouths moved up a millimetre in the direction of some kind of smile. If they smiled too much, they would have to apologise. They precisely thought:

Ralf: 'We also kind of dance when we perform. It's not that we actually move our bodies but it's this awareness of your whole body. You feel like a dancer.'

Florian: 'Your brain is dancing. The electronics are dancing around the speaker.'

Ralf: 'We've had this idea for a long time but it has only been in the past year that we have been able to create what we feel is a loudspeaker orchestra. That is what we consider Kraftwerk to be. A non-acoustic, electronic loudspeaker orchestra. The whole thing is one instrument. We play mixers, we play tapes, we play phasers, we play the whole apparatus of Kraftwerk. That's the instrument. Including the lights and the atmosphere.'

Florian: 'Sometimes I can taste the sounds. There are a lot more feelings than just the feelings going through the ears. The whole body can feel the sounds.'

Ralf: 'You have to face yourself to come to the point where you really think about what it is that you want to do. Not to hide behind too many notes or behind . . .'

Florian: '. . . the speaker cabinets . . .'

Ralf: 'To open up the simplest sounds . . .'

Florian: 'We don't like bombastic sounds. We prefer more refined sounds.'

The whole room stood and cheered. Iggy looked like he was full of, you know, energy. Bowie didn't look like he knew how to disappear after all. Kylie drove off as fast as she could, finding the future with a quick lick of her fully functioning lips, not sure she understood completely what had just happened.

'We are the robots,' said Kraftwerk, and the applause was loud enough to waken a dead Dadaist who was dreaming that he was sitting in a room, a room not like the one you are sitting in.

10. Tenthly, first the image reflects reality. Then it masks it. Then it

hides the absence. And then, as if by magic, it bears no relation to reality whatsoever.

Meanwhile, the real masked absent Kraftwerk drive in front of the exquisitely photogenic Kylie, leading the way for her and anyone else who's interested in the future; and, just before she drives into the time of the city, she gets out of her car and dances. A halo of white light lightly fizzes around her image-smoothed body, and she moves in time that moves in her, and time seems to slow down and move faster, to stop, and go, to stop, and go, to go into space, the space of the music she is dancing to.

She offers up her sacrifice, commits to the cause, gives her equivalent of the Iggy/Bowie standing ovation. Her applause is in the way that she moves, and the way her song switches on, and off, and on, and off, and la la la, and the way the movement of body and mind across the surface of machinery pays homage to the limitless possibilities of digitally manipulated sound and vision. Her eyes slant in ecstasy, her body sways in thanks, her automatic friends automatically join in, they march in unison, they dance in harmony, their bodies touch, they process temptation, they give their bodies to the mouth of a TV screen, the screen devours them, adores them, their brains embrace, their hearts beat together as one, la la la, their wires connect, they're in the church of Kraftwerk, machines inside a machine inside a machine dream of human ecstasy, a machine wrapped in a machine wrapped in the riddle of humanity. Kylie glows in the dark because Kraftwerk built an *autobahn* to the future, because they planned the future.

They drive along the *autobahn* through the bright day and the lonely night. Time changes shape, space refreshes itself, the landscape reflects their neon genius. The numbers on the electric clock rising up above and beyond the mechanical city tell us straight that we are at the centre of the universe, the universe which is a city, which is nowhere to be found but technologically ubiquitous.

We are the centre of everything, because they are Kraftwerk and they connect us from here to there and everywhere.

39
Now, sat in the car built in the image of Kraftwerk, we do as we are told, and we turn on the radio. Spilling from the speakers, some voices

talk to us, making up a history for us, helping design the way the outskirts of the city change in dimension and density to become the city on the edge of forever. We are behind Kraftwerk and we are ahead of the past, and we travel through the voices, which travel through us, which drive us forward, which keep us company. The talk on the radio is a mixture of buildings and thinking, feeling and concrete, music and mind, dreaming and metal. The talk is the road that takes us into the city, and it begins to tell us how the city will be a maze of nothing that makes sense and everything that does, an A to Z of surface and surfaces where you can find the meaning of some things out in the open, and find the meaning of other things hidden in shadows.

The first voice is saying:

'Noise. Unwanted sound. In engineering, it's information that interferes with the transmission of a signal. Noise is sound without order, chaotic order. We're surrounded by it – the thundering of machines in the street outside, the noise of machines in our houses and the places where we work.

'Noise is the opposite of music. Music, we like. Noise, we don't. Who would want to combine the two? But that's just what lots of new popular music does. Industrial music copies the cacophonous noises of factories and puts them to a beat.

'Techno music, the music of synthesisers, is a collage of sound effects copied – sometimes directly recorded by sampler machines – from the racket of technological life. Techno music erases the boundary between noise and music. Why?

'Tonight we show how today's noisy and dissonant popular music is part of a serious tradition of twentieth-century art. Poetic modernism, Italian futurism, English vorticism, French Dadaism, American precisionism – all the avant-gardisms of the early century – were obsessed with representation of noise. They were the precursors of contemporary techno pop – heard in dance clubs, at raves and in the headsets of kids on the subway – music that is preoccupied with repetition, and with the drama and euphoria of machinery.'

MUSIC PLAYS: 'THE AGE OF LOVE' BY THE AGE OF LOVE.
This is the modern landscape and a modern drama; this is modern music. It's called techno; this particular piece is by a group who are not a group but who are, anyway, called The Age of Love. This piece is also called 'The Age of Love',

released on a vinyl record for disc jockeys to use as dance music in discotheques in the early 1990s. As far as I know, it's the only track recorded by the Age of Love, who may just have been one teenage guy in a basement with a computer and a keyboard and a sampler, recording his music as digital bits directly onto his hard-drive; he may call himself something new for every record he makes.

The world of techno music is anonymous, the music home-made; there are few star groups. Black futurist Derrick May, who may have started the thing we call techno, in Detroit in the eighties, with his friends Juan Atkins and Kevin Sanderson, said that techno was George Clinton meeting Kraftwerk in an elevator. It was a mix of Eurostyle conceptual music and the black conceptual art of Funkadelic, a fusion of precise electronic music with the fluid urban soul of black music. It was the bright, smooth Motown fed through the wired, warped lens of Kraftwerk, a splicing of the mechnical and the soulful. The beats were familiar from house or electro, but they were harder, sharper, colder, infinitely more complex, and they resurrected the pure mean strength of funk that disco had whitewashed in the name of a simple good time. Melancholy strings coated the stripped-down beats, strings that echoed the classic, yearning disco strings, and that reminded you of how disco hurtled into the future once electronics replaced the orchestra. The techno strings were from sparse outer space, and helped to create a sound that was neither acoustic nor electric, that was just itself, dead on the moment, dead on the pleasure, dead on the rhythm, dead on life, deadly. Techno lost most of the melodic content of disco, emphasising the rhythmical elements and experimenting with the quality and stress of sound – the light, loose sound of disco was darkened with harder beats and tightened with harder feeling, and funk, after its frivolous disco detour and the strange romantically scientific affair of two or four Germans with a studio-bound drum machine, became techno.

May, Atkins and Sanderson were basically taking primitive Japanese electronic equipment on the verge of obsolescence to slam together a mixture of European electronic pop, post-bebop Gil Evans melancholy cool, nasty, up-against-the-wall funk and the emptied magnetism of Detroit. To be more basic, Detroit techno is highly syncopated – there is a lot of bebop in there – and it often features triplets over quarter notes. In the world of electronic dance music, Detroit is a name that carries as much aesthetic baggage as Memphis does to the genre of soul and Chicago does to the blues. A hint, though, of the difference of this American music city, and something that separated it from the Detroit of Motown, was that it would be soul-twinned with the techno city of Berlin.

With the growth of affordable midi-encoded technology and desktop digital audio, there was greater sophistication of arrangement, and the development of *new forms of techno that used the essential mechanical versus technical feel as part of new explorations, that led to new genres, and splitting of genres, genres within genres. Listening to techno is like taking a stroll through an art gallery. There are many painters who claim to have their own unique style. It goes from the rock techno of The Chemical Brothers and The Prodigy to the pop techno of Daft Punk; there's the twisted techno of Aphex Twin, and there is even the MOR techno of Enigma.*

This is a style of techno called trance. Some people say that, if you dance to it long enough and take some hallucinogenic drugs at the same time, you'll have a religious experience.

Maybe you find it hard to believe that simple machine noise, repeated in patterns, can lead to a spiritual experience. Unlike most popular music, which comes in the form of songs with a more or less understandable narrative, this music is cold and abstract. Trance builds tension to which there is no climax and no release. Through minimal rhythmical shifts, remote synth patterns and uncompromising exploitation of repetition, trance producers devise structures that aim to disengage the mind while the body exhausts itself. When you return to the mind, it's fresh and ready for the next stimulation. The young people who listen to it see themselves as a kind of intellectual avant-garde in the world of pop.

I'm in Pit Records, a literally underground techno record shop on Toronto's Queen Street West, talking to the owner.

SHOP OWNER: Right now what we're listening to is a straight-up trance.

INTERVIEWER: What does trance mean to you?

SHOP OWNER: There's a couple of different kinds of trance, hard trance or like this one would be sort of . . . Practically there are three different: there's uplifting trance, hard trance, and sort of straight-up trance, which this particular tune would qualify itself to. There's also psychedelic trance, which is harder and faster and whatever.

INTERVIEWER: What is hard trance?

SHOP OWNER: Hard trance would be primarily like a heartbeat with heavy build-ups, rising and going down, rising and going down, with a heartbeat, maybe about 135, 145 bpm.

INTERVIEWER: What's bpm?

SHOP OWNER: Beats per minute. You know, you've got 0 to 70 bpm in ambient, you've got about 140 in trance, in Goa, 220 in hardcore . . .

INTERVIEWER: What is Goa?

SHOP OWNER: Goa is psychedelic trance. It's sort of 140, 150 bpm, quite busy, very, very intensely layered. On any particular track you might have anywhere between 16 or maybe even a lot closer to 20, 25 different samples simultaneously at the same time. It's fairly complex, in terms of production. Trance would be chillout, fast but soothing, but there'd be a little wibble in Goa trance that would make it just that little bit more trippy.

INTERVIEWER: How fast does techno get?

SHOP OWNER: It depends. It could get anywhere from 130 to 145 . . . Not very fast, but sometimes, because of the way the drums are being set, there may be a layer of four different drum machines, and some-times, because of the way it's being chopped up, different drums are getting different tempo. The bpm it basically lays down with the main drum pattern that lies underneath and that's based on that one, the very first beat that goes on the track, that's where the bpms are being counted for the track . . . Techno is like an abstract variation of house. Whereas house grooves smoothly, techno kicks furiously. Techno is a harder-edge-driven dance music that has the same rhythmic patterns as other house genres but uses a harder synthesiser and a harder sample. It doesn't really feature the hand-clap; it's not as obviously derived from disco as house. House was disco's revenge on those who had said, at the end of the seventies, 'disco sucks'.

INTERVIEWER: What is hardcore?

SHOP OWNER: Hardcore is pretty fast beat, anywhere between 150, 160, up to 180 bpm, maybe even 220; it's frenzy, it's chaos.

INTERVIEWER: How do you dance to it?

SHOP OWNER: How do you . . .? You just express yourself in a different way. Some people jump up, some people just shake their bodies and throw their hands, some people just will nod and some people will jerk. It depends. Gabber is the hardest and fastest style. The number of beats per minute can go up to 400 . . . But in general it's around 200. Gabber means 'mate' in Dutch, which is where it originated, at the end of the eighties in Rotterdam.

A few doors away, a similar shop, also below ground, called Speed Records. This shop is hard-edged, concrete painted white. In the front of the shop, clothing: the plain, genderless workwear of the techno fan – nylon weaves with rubber and plastic snaps, velcro closures and zippers. In the back, two turntables, speakers the size of houses, and racks of vinyl records in plain white wrappers. They offer no guidance to the outsider. No album photos, no blurbs. Just inscriptions like: 'Reptile Mix – Plasma Team Reboot'. Some of the records are marked 'progressive' or 'forward-thinking' – the rhetoric of avant-gardists everywhere. I talk to the owner of this shop.

MUSIC PLAYS: PLASTIKMAN CD.

INTERVIEWER: What's the kind of music we're listening to now? How would you describe it?

SECOND SHOP OWNER: I'd describe it as German minimalist techno, probably. And I don't know if this particular track is the Basic Channel Guys, but it's off the Basic Channel record label. They're pretty experimental and pretty cutting edge, these guys.

INTERVIEWER: For about the last three minutes we've heard maybe two notes in this piece. Is that minimalism common to a lot of techno music?

SECOND SHOP OWNER: Yeah. It's what's between the notes that's really important.

INTERVIEWER: Slight variations in sounds?

SECOND SHOP OWNER: Yeah. The subtlety. The sounds you hear between the sounds are really what's important.

INTERVIEWER: Is this music mostly for dancing, or do you just listen to it?

SECOND SHOP OWNER: It's for both.

This is really the essence of minimal music, I think. It's just so, like, spacious. I mean, people will say that minimal music is about space. I have a different feeling. It is about space, and it's about what's in between the notes, but it's also about ideas of weight and, like, concentration and about, like, movement. And this is a good example: something that's got very few elements.

It's very strange how it makes you feel. I've played this track for people and put it on tapes, and even though you can't skip through it because it's so minimal, when it's in the mix – and that's, like, an important part of techno, it has to be in the mix; it's a constant flow, that's the whole idea of the music – when it's in the mix it literally freaks people out. It brings them to a point where they feel like their heart is racing, and then it just drops. It can just stop. It's a very strange feeling.

INTERVIEWER: Is this made in America, this music?

SECOND SHOP OWNER: This is actually made in Canada. It's a little-known fact that one of – well, it's not a little-known fact, but it's strange because we were talking about Germany and Europe, and the person who made this song, Richie Hawtin – Plastikman – he's well-known in Europe. He goes to Europe probably every couple of months to play, but in Canada he's not as well-known. He's pretty much anonymous. And he's one of the fathers of minimalism. He's very conceptual with his work, too, so that's kind of fun. I think a lot of the fun of music is, you know, being conceptual and seeing how far you can push the envelope and seeing, like, how silly you can be within the context of creativity.

MUSIC PLAYS: 'ELECTRONIC BIRTH' BY DJ BONE.
This rather numbing music tends to attract intellectuals. The Canadian poet Christopher Dewdney is the author of Last Flesh: Life in the Transhuman Era. *He listens to techno music.*

CHRISTOPHER DEWDNEY: For me, it's a pure source of energy. I listen to techno strictly as a source of energy. It's food for me. It's also a little bit of . . . I guess I'm a futurist, in a sense. So techno also maybe has that edge to it. It's quite modern. It's modern music. It's about looking forward. But I primarily use it as an energy source.
INTERVIEWER: You like the regularity – the monotony – of it?
CHRISTOPHER DEWDNEY: Curiously, I don't find it monotonous. The rhythm, for me, is simply a structure that I'm comfortable inside of. And once I'm inside of that rhythm, I want to be stimulated by the various reflections and textures. It is a minimalist kind of structure, too. So, in a sense, I find it very clean and pure; very easy to listen to.
INTERVIEWER: Do you work with it in the background?
CHRISTOPHER DEWDNEY: I don't work with techno, with really heavy, hardcore dance techno on. I do work with rave and trance rave on, which is more ambient; particularly ambient rave. That is music I can easily work with. In fact, I prefer to work with it.
INTERVIEWER: Describe the sound of ambient music for me.
CHRISTOPHER DEWDNEY: Ambient is a little *still* – a lot of synthesisers. There are rhythms, but it's a little bit more . . . It's lower key, in the sense that it's not quite as quick a rhythm. It deals with sort of shifting fields of sound that change over longer periods of time than straight techno or dance, I guess. It can now be many things – in the seventies,

there wasn't a beat, a pulse, or melody, it was much more atmospheric, pretty passive, whereas now ambient can be quite active. Ambient like a lot of other genres broke up into other genres, split off into ambient industrial, ambient noise, dark ambient, which became known as isolationism, perhaps in an attempt to get away from the word ambient, which is often thought to be a close relation to muzak, which is deemed a bad thing, a terrible thing. There was ambient dub, ambient space, ambient world, ambient pop, ambient electronic and ambient techno. What it all has in common, whether soft and new age-y, or hard and dissonant, is that the sound kind of floats; it's in space, it creates space, the stillness of space that somehow still moves . . . It's a moving stillness. A moving lack of forward motion.

MUSIC PLAYS: 'BASSCADET' BY AUTECHRE.
Techno music wouldn't exist without the synthesiser, a simple electric organ with a variety of sound effects, invented by RCA Laboratories in 1959.

The synthesiser gained widespread use as an instrument in the 1960s – but only as an imitation of other instruments, for use in recording sessions. It can imitate trumpets, pianos, even the human voice. And it's cheap. But the first use of synthesisers in classical music was by the intellectual avant-garde.

MUSIC PLAYS: *COMPOSITION FOR SYNTHESIZER* BY MILTON BABBITT.
This is American composer Babbitt's Composition for Synthesizer, *from 1961.*

In pop music, it was an intellectual German band who began using synthesisers that just sounded like synthesisers. Fuzzy. Electronic. They didn't sound like any instruments anybody had ever heard. The band's name was Kraftwerk, which means 'powerplant', and they were the fathers of modern techno.

MUSIC PLAYS: 'AUTOBAHN' BY KRAFTWERK.
In the all-natural, ecologically conscious seventies, Kraftwerk were provocative, to say the least. They were futurists. They sang the praises of prosperous Europe. They loved the smoothness of high-speed trains. They wrote paeans to radioactivity, odes on the beauty of highways. Their biggest hit was a twenty-six-minute reflection on the German autobahn.

Perhaps because Germany is so technologically advanced, it has produced the most music about technology.

Germany was also the breeding ground for the edgy counteraction to Kraftwerk's optimism. If we admired the beauty of machines, why couldn't we admire their ugliness too, their frightening power? The German underground of the 1980s was dominated by music called simply 'industrial'. It was made by jackhammers and drills, by pounding mallets on steel chemical drums. The pioneering industrial group had the apocalyptic name of Einstürzende Neubauten, which means 'collapsing new buildings'. And it was apocalypse they were after, all right.

MUSIC PLAYS: 'WOMB' BY EINSTÜRZENDE NEUBAUTEN.
Industrial groups arose all over Europe and North America, making threatening music. The words to the songs were generally grim – dire warnings about the future of mankind in a toxic wasteland. But the musicians were obviously as much in love with industry as they were in fear of it. Apocalypse, as Hollywood has long known, is glamorous.

The industrial sound has haunted techno music for a decade now. And industrial has split into two directions: popular dance music with a hard edge, like the so-called Rotterdam school, and an artier, even more minimalist school which makes roaring white noise untainted by music. Japan, that science-fiction writer's dream of a technological fantasy world, is a centre for these experimental noise bands, bands who often attach shocking sexual performances to their painful concerts. The idea here, as it was with the Dadaists of 1915, is mayhem and scandal. Art, if it exists according to Dada, and this isn't entirely clear-cut, is made up out of everything and nothing, of water heaters, tufts of hair, and drinking fountains. For Kurt Schwitters, Dada daddy, it lauds the absurd music of words, the hijacking and poetic arrangement of junk and torn newspapers. The children of Dada are constantly disassembling and reassembling in their own way. Sampling the world.

MUSIC PLAYS: 'MORBID ANGELFISH' BY MERZBOW.
This is a Japanese band called Merzbow, mainly the work of a Japanese artist born in Tokyo in 1956 called Masami Akita. He formed Merzbow in 1981, and they have released more than fifty records and CDs, although in truth the amount of music Merzbow have made is known to no one. Akita named the project Merzbow after a great work by the German collage artist Schwitters that he called The Cathedral of Erotic Misery. Schwitters made art from oddments he picked up from the street, just as Akita makes music, as he says, from the scum that surrounds his life. Akita was particularly taken by the surrealist idea that everything is erotic, everywhere is erotic – for him, noise is the most erotic form of sound, and all of his works relate to the erotic. He took the noise in rock that there was in the feedback of Hendrix, the smashed guitars of The Who,

the noise at the end of King Crimson's '21st Century Schizoid Man', and extracted what he saw as the gimmickry in the music, the stupid playfulness. He mixed what he called the sick part of rock with a sick sense of noise, and attempted to violate sound unemotionally, and to overload sound with feedback, torture his equipment, rip apart sound, and create a 'death scream of electronics'. Noise, he said, is the unconsciousness of music in the way that pornography is the unconsciousness of sex.

Japanese noise bands are the purists, the intellectual hardcore. They relish the ecstasy of sound itself. They have international followings, magazines, Websites. Two Toronto followers of this music are radio hosts on the University of Toronto's campus radio station. Ted Phillips spins experimental music of all kinds; Margaret English spins improvisational 'free jazz' and is involved in an annual festival of noise music in, of all places, London, Ontario. Our conversation was pretty noisy.

TED PHILLIPS: Right now we're listening to a Japanese group called – what are they called?

MARGARET ENGLISH: Haijodaiken. Which is led by a guitarist named Jojo Hiroshiga who runs a Japanese label called Alchemy that is fairly important in the Japanese noise movement. It's solid noise. I mean, there's . . . I have three categories for noise. And that's noise in music, noise as music, noise for noise's sake. And this is definitely noise for noise's sake.

There's a lot of discussion about why the Japanese in particular like this kind of music. It might be a dietary thing – new foods transforming the young of Japan into different sorts of beings. It might be something spiritual – this is sort of like a bloodletting, or something like that; I don't think it's meditation, but some release of evil spirits, purging of something. It might be that they use the noise as a soundtrack for the busy technological life of metropolis. It might have been something to do with the dropping of the atom bomb . . . Their revenge, or simply their reaction to the ultimate nightmare.

40

In a sudden spurt of white noise and a gush of red nerves, Masami Akita – the craven dark lord of Merzbow, the man with the sex of death in his eyes – breaks out of the radio and into the car, and Masami Akita meets Kylie Minogue and Kylie Minogue meets Masami Akita. The car quivers with anticipation. Of all the people Kylie meets in the car, Akita is the most difficult for her to read. He is the most alien thing she has come across on her journey into the unknown.

His avowed attempt to destroy all conventional music makes him not a little creepy. He seems a little . . . *primitive*, sort of broken, with an anger Kylie cannot begin to comprehend. What Kylie adored about Kraftwerk was the way they loved music, even as they turned it into something else. She adored their sense of play, even as they pretended to be disciplined workers. Masami, as far as she can tell, although she might not be doing the thinking, replaces music with, pretty much, nothing, and doesn't seem to be playing at anything. He replaces music with pain, pressure, distortion, disturbance, scratches, scrapes, bleeps, bleaks, mangles, tangles . . . sickness . . . great chasms of rupture, miniature piercings of dread, loaded lumps of laceration, pensive hunks of density, drips of death, loss of life, hectic listlessness . . . the universe sliced and smashed and ripped and torn into noxious bits and then transplanted into the sound of noise and then packaged in a way that vaguely relates to the twentieth century. Kylie is worried, now that he is so close, that he might turn her into noise. Grab her and crunch her up into groove and gasp, gas and motion, grind her down into dust and spasm. She thinks, to some extent all by herself, that he is someone who would want to take sound, bury it alive in a satin-lined coffin loosely tied at the ankles and wrists with silk rope, blow it up into little scorched pieces, then stick it all together in the shape of a razor blade. She's worried that he might use that razor blade on her. He seems to be on the side of death, his favourite sort of life is decomposing life. He is the master of decomposition, whereas Kylie is very much on the side of life. Life is for living. It's all about composure.

Her melodious life and his brutal death are sat side by side in the startling car of destiny hurtling furiously towards the city of love and hate. She knows enough, to her surprise and fear, to worry that, sat in a speeding car with someone who thinks that pain is foreplay, who thinks that death is deeply erotic, she might be heading for a car crash of Mansfieldian proportions, ending with his semen mixing with the crunched glass of the windscreen splashed all over her headless body . . . her immortality slashed across the surface of celebrity time at the exact moment she screams as the car turns upside-down and over and over and the roof caves in and time moves still and the last thing she sees is his raging grimace of pleasure a furious moan of triumph as he witnesses the light-ning glass flash of fame exploding in a Diana techno-mess of blood and metal. Kylie thinks to herself, faced with such danger, the danger of extinction, of losing her head, that it is time for a change of image. There is nothing Kylie does better, or likes better, when faced with the possibility of disappearing from sight, than changing who she is, what she looks like, how she feels.

Not even in this story of music, where everything meets everything some place or another, do these two have that much to talk about. Eventually, after a period of tense silence broken only by the pure sound of Kylie breathing as she changes her look and the actual noise of Masami bleeding as he stares into the sun, they do find common ground. They find common ground in the list. The list is what brings a world of chaos into some kind of pattern. The list fixes a broken world floating out into the outer space of emptiness. The list links us to ourselves, places us together, puts us in order. The list soothes us in the way it organises memory and shapes the consciousness. Everybody loves a list for making sense of the awesome nature of all the stuff that surrounds us. The list is at the heart of everything. Everything is part of a list. Humanity is one long list linking nothing with something.

The list links Kylie with Masami: the model entertainer with the morbid artist. Masami is, for all the black sex, metaphorical bleeding and literal depravity, just a performer, and he has tools he uses to create his performance, just like Kylie has her tools. They are both makers of myth – one myth is illuminated by the money, fame and sex of the world; the other is blackened by the chaos, pornography and menace of the world. Both, oddly enough, mean well.

Masami politely supplies his list:

Porta two four-track cassette recorder
DAT recorders
Cassette recorders
Filter Bank FB3 Mk 2
Maxon DM 1000
Korg DRV 1000 reverb unit
Roland SDE 1000 delay unit
EMS Synthi 'A' synthesiser
Moog Rogue synthesiser

Therematic Theremin
Ishimashi Theremin
Novation Bass Station synthesiser
Various contact mic units
Ring modulator
Various junk metallic tools
Various effect pedals
Leader high-and-low frequency generator
Relaxation alphawave generator
Stargazer mind-expansion sound visualiser
Novation synth rack

Kylie has a representative supply her list:

Kylie Minogue's hair and make-up products by L'Oreal
Hair styled with FX toss lotion
On her face, Translucide Lasting Luminous Make-Up in Nude
   Beige
On her eyes, Wear Infinite Eye-Shadow Duos in Sand Painting
   with Wear Infinite Eye-Liner in Brown Suede and Voluminous
   Mascara in Blackest Black
On her cheeks, Cheek-to-Cheek Sculpting Blush duet in Desert
   Rose
On her lips, Shine Delice Sheer Shimmering Lipcolour in Copper
   Canyon

This breaks the ice. Masami offers Kylie some of his metal tools. Kylie gives him a gift of some Nude Beige. Their hands accidentally touch, and stay touching just a little longer than maybe they should. Masami is warmer than Kylie might have thought. Kylie is colder than he imagined, which he likes. As he reluctantly pulls away his hand he notices the sharp metal glint of her fingernails, which matches the metal and shine of the tools he has given her. 'Call me Masami,' he says quietly. 'Call me Kylie,' she answers.

They look into each other's eyes. Masami's seem surprisingly dreamy and distant, while Kylie's eyes are, to Masami's deep delight, the syringed shape of * with a ~ etched around the edges. Kylie's not concentrating on the road, just on the blood that is now pumping through Masami, but not out of him, changing his shape; but the car knows what it's doing, has been fed enough information by Kylie's determination to know where to go next. Parts of Kylie turn as soft as spiral honey. Other parts light up, a rainbow of electronics. He reaches across her, into her, through her, and feels the blessed contours of her serial number, tenderly caresses the KX68Y, the number of the FemBot, the number that opens up infinity.

The hi-tech life of Kylie takes hold of the lo-tech death of Masami and they touch each other as if there are no such things as life or death, only their two selves, minds slammed together amid all the need and speed in the universe. The hardcore Masami defects into the softcore Kylie with ravaged tenderness. Software embraces hardware and ecstasy ensues. Masami loves the way she smells, like metal petals embedded at the centre of the moon. He can't believe she's real. Kylie loves the way Masami feels, like velvet at the centre of an electric butterfly. He's so real it's frightening.

They kiss mysteriously and their softness and hardness come together, liquid molecules spill from one mouth to another, codes are modified, matter is transported, he drags her under, spins her around, the film of life bursts open, and in Kylie's head she hears the sound of for ever and ever and ever, and in Masami's head he hears a haiku committing hari kari. The rhythms of the pair combine supernaturally, the digital rhythm of Kylie that comes out of dreamtime radio and nighttime disco, the tactile rhythm of Masami that unfolds from fury and pain, and their embrace symbolises the emotional strength of the couple, and the logo of the embrace is the singable smile of Kylie that can make the earth move, the torrential tears of Masami that can make the stars fall from the sky. The earth moves, it quakes and buzzes and ripples and melts, as the noise god and the robot-pop goddess disappear into the trance of sex, the drone of love, the beat of surrender.

Their kiss is remixed – for him, by Autechre; for her, by the Pet Shop Boys – but they each love both mixes, one pure emotion frozen in time, the other pure libido in motion, both mixes tied down to an endless floor of pounding rhythm, both mixes liberating them from the prison of their own flesh.

They kiss the car as well, they kiss the car until the volume of the world is turned up to obliterating maximum; and, because of this kiss, this wired and writhing three-way kiss on the highway to the incandescent city split between heaven and hell . . .

. . . . there is a last-minute swerve or two, a kink in the road, a few bumps, a thrilling skid, some shudders of pleasure, an acceleration of lust, a few glitches of rhythm and light, and Kylie ultimately reaches the dream city in a cut-up climax of audiovisual perfection. Kylie's face fills the screen, a long gaze of longing, a sigh of experience, establishing an emotional reference point amid all this frantic, frankly unbelievable change, creating, you might hope, a powerful bond of identification for any audience that could be viewing this dance in wonderland. We believe in her face, we believe the identity, we trust the brand, we follow her where she is going, we want to understand where she has been.

An edit from facial to long shot of body. The hormonal camera glides up her exposed thigh as she turns away from the world while turning towards the future, and the white of her costume stands for freedom of movement, the purity of motion.

Kraftwerk's 'Trans-Europe Express' glides past, sweeping the future along with it. The road swerves past party-hungry clubs with names like Sanctuary, Studio 54, Paradise Garage, Warehouse, past the sound of Donna Summer's 'Love to Love You Baby' and 'I Feel Love', Bobby O, past disco, Disco8, Disco Magic, Hi-NRG, 'Blue Monday', house, Derrick May, techno, 'The Strings of Life', pleasure will be sensual in the afterlife, Chicago, four to the floor, thanks to you, Todd Terry, Frankie Knuckles, 'I Like to Do It in Fast Cars', you're the one for me, synthetic Kraftwerk strings, a Eurobeat bassline, sparse insistent drum-machine pattern, Juan Atkins, 'Beyond the Dance', 'Slave to the Rhythm', Electrica Salsa, Hacienda, garage, acid, Spectrum, Shoom, summer of love, 'Pump Up the Volume', Berlin, Manchester, Rotterdam, rave, energy flash, hardcore, trance, big beat, chemical beat, 'Little Fluffy Clouds', kinky disco, neo-disco, no-disco, Warp, speed garage, DJ Hell and his wedding party from hell, just outside Munich, where electro opens up the house, Compost, Tru Thoughts . . . the DJ the high priest of engineered pleasure performs the continuous live mixing of hundreds of samples of music information collected into rhythm after rhythm, with an audience that is participating and thus interacting with the flows and rhythms of energy . . . You've got to dance like no one else is watching, dream like you will live for ever, live like you're going to die tomorrow, love like it's never going to hurt . . . The car moves through the rhythm . . . moves through movement and movements . . . through the heat of the moment

. . . through the radiant liquid of fashion . . . through rhythm changing into rhythm . . . rhythm escaping rhythm rhythm capturing rhythm rhythm possessing rhythm . . . rhythm turned into variations of rhythm . . . dream rhythms insane rhythms . . . impossible rhythms . . . rhythm as simple and as complicated as the body itself . . . rhythm is rhythm . . . The moving body in the moving car . . . moves . . . through the dance of time . . . right on the edge of the dancing city . . . the city that repeats itself and repeats itself and is never the same always different . . . the city forever in motion changing into itself responding to the sound of the moment . . . the city that gives birth to rhythm, the rhythm that gives birth to the city.

42

Kylie puts her foot down and the car responds to the specific demands of her body and before you can say 'la' Kylie has entered the city. Kylie has arrived to meet her maker. She has arrived in her future. She is connected to a new operational configuration. She feels the bliss whispering beneath her electronic cells.

The sky above changes colour, changes shape, changes material, is soft, blue, then hard, metal, white, dark, then seems like a screen dense with racing clouds in the shape of facts, theories and opinions. Then the sky is lost behind the city as concrete, glass and brick crowd around the car, cutting it off from the past, the sky, the landscape, drawing the car into its body, its mind, its whole being. The car has pushed its way through the twentieth-century dream and landed right in the centre of a city made up of invention and happening. The city is a list like the landscape was a list like everything is a list, listing itself, counting itself down, and up, and on. The city is broken up into shapes and movement, chaos and order, time and timelessness, art and showbusiness, people and machines, sex and food, love and loss, action and perception, fame and shame, hype and commodity, syncopation and monotony, money and power, mind and body, rhythm and noise, wares and waste, dreams and desires, zones and drones, reality and non-reality, production and reproduction, geography and psychology, information and privacy, shopping and weightlessness, memory and paranoia, nerves and systems, loneliness and intimacy, abstraction and anxiety, form and formlessness, stability and infinity, content and discontent, links and hyperlinks, paradise lost and paradise found, romance and nihilism, poetry and technology, surface and more surface, deep surface, and deeper surface, surface beyond any doubt. The city is fact and fiction. The city is a reflection of its own subconscious and everything just happens and is made to happen. The city renews itself as it goes along, sifting sands in a fixed tumult. The city is inside Kylie and Kylie is inside the city. The city is a list beginning and ending with itself.

As Kylie drives further into the city, into the sensation of herself, into a sea of blue concentrate lit by pulsing flickering blue globes, listening to brass drums, white noise and bass heart, it becomes everything that there is to see, and feel, and want. The city is as strange as a melancholy chorus in a hypnotic modern pop song sung by a version of a human being, as strange as the dark side of the moon.

They can do incredible things these days.

43

1969   USA lands two men on the moon.

Woodstock festival.

Led Zeppelin, *Led Zeppelin* and *Led Zeppelin II* – the beginning of time.

The Band, *The Band* – the beginning of time 2.

The Velvet Underground, *The Velvet Underground* – the beginning of time 3.

Captain Beefheart & His Magic Band, *Trout Mask Replica* – the beginning of time 4.

The Stooges, *The Stooges* – the beginning of time 5a.

MC5, *Kick Out the Jams* – the beginning of time 5b.

Jackson 5, 'I Want You Back' – the beginning of the boy-band formula part 2a, b and c.

James Brown, 'Funky Drummer' – the beginning of time 6x.

Kool Herc – raps over popular songs and extended short breaks by using identical records and looping the required segments using an audio mixer – the beginning of time 6y.

Brian Jones dies.

Rupert Murdoch buys the *Sun*, which is relaunched in a tabloid format.

Allen Jones designs 'fetish' furniture.

Angela Carter, *Heroes and Villains*.

Manfred Eicher establishes ECM label – Editions of Contemporary Music. Fights with Factory, Tamla Motown, Decca, Warp, Leaf, Nonesuch, Island, Parlophone, SYR, Compost, Sub Pop, Sire, Kranky, Domino, Obscure, Harvest, Rough Trade, Mute, Ninjatune, RCA, Lo Recordings, City Rockers, Sun and Apple to be the greatest label of all time.

King Crimson, *In the Court of the Crimson King*.

Ursula le Guin, *The Left Hand of Darkness*.

Children's Television Workshop introduces *Sesame Street*.

Monty Python's Flying Circus debuts.

Dennis Hopper, *Easy Rider*.

Advanced Research Projects Agency goes online connecting four major US universities – the beginning of the Internet.

1970 The deaths of Jimi Hendrix and Janis Joplin within a month of each other. Rock and roll, the sixties phenomenon that has blown up out of the fifties compression of underground black rhythms and commercialised white neuroses, falls to bits, only to recover, then fall to bits, only to sort of recover, then shatter into fragments, only to disappear up its own history of appearances.

Barthes, *The Death of the Author*.

The Mary Tyler Moore Show premières.

The Grateful Dead, *American Beauty*.

Free, 'All Right Now'.

The Kinks, 'Lola'.

The Velvet Underground, *Loaded*.

Tim Buckley, *Starsailor*.

Soft Machine, *Third*.

The Last Poets, *The Last Poets*.

Black Sabbath, 'Paranoid'.

James Brown, 'Sex Machine'.

Germaine Greer, *The Female Eunuch*.

The floppy disc is introduced for storing data in computers.

First jumbo jet.

Alvin Toffler, *Future Shock*.

J. G. Ballard, *The Atrocity Exhibition*.

Nic Roeg, *Performance*.

Alvin Lucier, *I am sitting in a room*

1. 'So one night I got a couple of Nagra tape recorders – they

were the best you could find at the time – an ordinary Beyer microphone and a single LKH loudspeaker. I went into the living room in my rented apartment. It had a shag rug on the floor and drapes on the wall, kind of dry acoustic. I thought I would experiment by putting sounds into the room, tape recording them, playing the tape recording back into the room through a loudspeaker, recording that, playing the copy back in, to see what would happen. We all know about room resonances, don't we? The length, width and height of a room, plus whatever the room's made of, imply certain frequencies because of their wavelength. Every sound has a wavelength. So that if you have a room where, say, frequency X fits that room, it'll sound louder than a frequency that doesn't fit that room. Now, in a concert hall you don't find that. You want all the frequencies to sound equally. So, it was a way to explore the resonant frequencies of a room.

'I sat in a chair in front of the microphone and asked myself, "What can I put into this room?" I could use a poem. And then I thought, "I don't want to use a poem, I don't want to use anything aesthetic. I don't want anything artistic." I thought, "Poetry: grandiose." I didn't want something large. I didn't want to evoke anything. The thing maybe we don't like so much about opera is that it is grandiose. It doesn't feel right any more.

'So I sat down and wrote a text right that night. I decided to say, in the text, what I was going to do. So, the content of my text was an explanation of the compositional process. There was a genre of pieces in the sixties in the United States in which you told the audience what the structure of the piece was. You didn't try to hide it. So I began. "I am sitting in a room different from the one you are in now." (I knew the tape was going to be played somewhere else.) "I am recording the sound of my speaking voice. I am going to play it back into the room again and again until the frequencies of the room reinforce themselves, so that any semblance of my speech . . . is destroyed.' And so forth. I practised a little, so the pacing would be right. I wanted time for the speech to go into the room. The reason I used speech was because it has so much in it. I could have used clarinet or piano or something. It has all this wonderful noise – shh, click, ph, th, all those noisy sounds.

'It seems to be that in those days we invented a new little form in music – composers such as Steve Reich, Bob Ashley and me. I guess it came out of electronics, where you could get something started and it would just go by itself. But the formal idea that interested me was that there just isn't any form. There's just one gesture, one thing that goes in a straight line. It doesn't side, it doesn't fall, it doesn't go backwards. It's just one thing. I just repeated the same procedure. I didn't do anything else. I didn't make any changes except to make sure that the volume was the same. But I didn't make any changes to improve it. I didn't do anything to make it more interesting. This is my basic idea – It might be a bad idea, but it's my basic idea – that you let one thing go without intruding on it. And then something happens unexpectedly. So that it's not just one thing after all.'

2. Steve Reich tells Lucier that he should just redecorate his Room for the rest of his career, that he should make a business out of it, move it into the mainstream, make it a brand, turn it into a kind of sonic circus, fill arenas, make stadia the 'room' that he is sitting in not like the one you are sitting in, with thousands of people sitting in the room, hearing one voice turn into a universe. *I am sitting in a room* is Lucier's *Dark Side of the Moon*, his *Thriller*, his *Sergeant Pepper*. Instead, he tries many other things, exploring the physical properties of sounds and the sonic elements of natural processes in constantly changing ways. He pushed forward to find ways to make you believe the room you were in listening to music was changing shape because of the sounds you were hearing. He used brainwaves to generate music. He used plug-in toys that made noises to make music. He amplified clocks. 'I wanted to make a work in which the performer could slow down time, stopping it, if possible, simply by thinking.' He wired up skin to produce sound. He inserted microphones into the mouths of various vessels, including a small milk bottle, a sea shell, a vase and an empty ostrich egg, and recorded the reading of a poem by John Ashbery as the words passed through these vessels. He recorded the sounds of tape recorders, radios, mechanical toys inside paper bags, shoe-boxes, kettles and small suitcases, and then played the recordings inside concert halls, football stadia and cisterns, and then

recorded the sounds, so that sounds are first altered by a small room and are then altered by a larger room. He uses conventional instruments unconventionally. He experiments with sound just below the level of human audibility. He writes music with titles such as 'Music for Piano with Slow Sweep Pure Wave Oscillators' and 'On the Carpet of Leaves Illuminated by the Moon'. His work pitching acoustic instrumentation against electronic oscillation and his general pursuits of sonic studies predates much of the minimalist electronics, the laptop toytronic, folktronic hyper-editing and rhythmical deconstruction of the late-twentieth-century mouse music and avant pop art. Similar effects – X-rays of sound that break through rhythm and break up space – different means. It is, though, all music connected to a room, and other rooms, one room where the piece is first thought of, and other rooms where the music is played, and listened to. 'Me and my room,' says Alvin, smiling, and a few people hear him say it.

Kylie says, 'I can hear you.'

Alvin replies, 'And I can hear you.'

Oddly, he cannot see her. And, as far as she can tell, she cannot see him. 'Goodbye,' she murmurs.

1971 Isaac Hayes, 'Shaft'.

Marvin Gaye, 'What's Goin' On'.

Funkadelic, *Maggot Brain*.

Betty Wright, 'Clean Up Woman'.

The Chi-Lites, 'Have You Seen Her?'

Sly & the Family Stone, 'Family Affair'. This and the Kraftwerk track 'Klingklang' feature the first recorded drum machines in pop.

Louis Armstrong dies.

Faust, *Faust*.

Can, *Tago Mago*

Carla Bley, *Escalator Over the Hill*.

Stanley Kubrick, *A Clockwork Orange*.

Carole King, *Tapestry*.

T. Rex, *Electric Warrior*.

Jim Morrison dies.

The Intel 4004, the first microprocessor, is introduced by Intel.

Nolan Bushnell and Ted Dabney, the future founders of Atari, begin their attempt to create an arcade version of Spacewar, calling it Computer Space.

Weather Report, *Weather Report*.

Disneyland opens in Orlando, Florida.

WANG 1200 is the world's first word processor.

Jerzy Kosinski, *Being There*.

Caroline Davidson designs the 'swoosh' logo for Nike. She is asked by owner Phil Knight to come up with a logo for the side of a shoe; she comes up with the swoosh. Knight pays her $35.

1972 Roxy Music, *Roxy Music*.

David Bowie, *The Rise and Fall of Ziggy Stardust and the Spiders from Mars*.

Gary Glitter, *Rock and Roll Part 2*.

Rolling Stones, *Exile on Main Street*.

Lou Reed, *Transformer*.

Stevie Wonder, 'Superstition'.

Nuggets (Original Artyfacts from the First Psychadelic Era 1965–1968). Garage rock ground zero.

Lee 'Scratch' Perry, 'Rhythm Shower'.

1. The architect of dub, taking Jamaican music into the outer limits, the missing link between Meek and wild, between Brown and Marley, between Marley and Pole, between sound and space, between sea and land, between toast and trance, between tree and house, between arrival and delay, between steady and unsteady, between distance and vision, between comparison and uniqueness, between centigrade and Fahrenheit, between drum and bass, between the devil and the deep blue sea. The greatest showman on whatever his planet is called demonstrates that sound isn't real, except when it's as real as you make it, mixes noise, space, dust, art, science, magic, black, gravity, speed . . . and names . . . He's switched names as much as he has changed sounds and minds: the Upsetter, Lord God Muzick, Super Chin from the Castle Grey Bed, King Perry, President Abraham Perry, the Last Dustbinmen, the Gong, Westminster Bank Perry, Inspector Gadget, Daniel Dandelion the Lion, the Super Ape, Paul Getty, Kojak, Kimble the Nimble, Duppy Air Ace Marshall, William Shakespeare, King of the Jews, the King of Mess, the Hebrew King, Gabriel the Archangel, Pipecock Jackxon, Santa, the Red

Ninja, Lord Thunder Black, Dr On The Go, Doctor Dick, the Firmament Computer, Mr P. the Weather B, the Ghost of King Arthur, Jesus H. Christ, the Cheshire Cat.

2. 'But I don't want to go among mad people,' Kylie remarks.

'Oh, you can't help that,' says Scratch. 'We're all mad here. I'm mad. You're mad.'

'How do you know I'm mad?' says Kylie.

'You must be,' says Scratch, 'or you wouldn't come here.'

3. 'My mama told me Lee Perry/Was my Daddy' – 'Lee Perry' by Dubcheck.

Harrison Schmitt and Eugene Cerman are the last men to walk on the moon – in the twentieth century at least.

Andrei Tarkovsky, *Solaris*.

Bob Fosse, *Cabaret*.

Francis Ford Coppola, *The Godfather*.

The first digital watches.

Bushnell and Dabney found Atari, after a term from the Japanese game Go. Atari is the equivalent of 'check' in chess. The first game they create is called Pong.

Electronic mail is introduced by computer scientist Ray Tomlinson. He uses the @ symbol to distinguish between the sender's name and the network name in the email address.

Robert Moog patents his electronic synthesiser intended to make any sound available through electronic synthesis.

Tom Verlaine and Richard Hell form The Neon Boys

Suicide describe their show at the Mercer Arts Center in New York as Punk, Funk and Sewer music.

1973 Perry Henzel, *The Harder They Come*. The film introduces reggae to the West.

Pink Floyd, *Dark Side of the Moon*.

Mike Oldfield, *Tubular Bells*. Avant garde m.o.r. masterpiece, the missing link between Elgar and Prince, between Bert Jansch and the Orb, which bizarrely gives birth to Richard Branson.

Iggy & the Stooges, *Raw Power*.

John Martyn, *Solid Air*.

Faust, *The Faust Tapes*.

Stevie Wonder, 'Living in the City'.

Todd Rundgren, *A Wizard, a True Star*.

New York Dolls, 'Trash'.

Incredible Bongo Band, *Apache*.

Picasso dies.

George Lucas, *American Graffiti*.

William Friedkin, *The Exorcist*.

Thomas Pynchon, *Gravity's Rainbow*.

Herbie Hancock, *Headhunters*.

A calf is produced from a frozen embryo.

Erica Jong, *Fear of Flying*.

Kurt Vonnegut, *Breakfast of Champions*.

J. G. Ballard, *Crash*.

Barcodes introduced in supermarkets.

1974 Kraftwerk, *Autobahn*. Apart from a flute and a guitar it is totally electronic.

Bob Marley, 'Natty Dread'.

Gil Scott-Heron, *The Revolution Will Not Be Televised*.

Tangerine Dream, *Phaedra*.

Love Unlimited Orchestra, 'Love's Theme'.

Robert Wyatt, *Rock Bottom*.

Sparks, 'This Town Ain't Big Enough For Both of Us'.

Patti Smith, 'Hey Joe'.

Joni Mitchell, *Court and Spark*.

The Meters, *Rejuvenation*.

Electronic pocket calculator first marketed.

Keith Jarrett, *Köln Concert*.

Nintendo develop image-projection system employing 16mm film projector for amusement arcades.

Giorgio Armani creates his first men's-wear line.

Vivienne Westwood and Malcolm McLaren change the name of their shop on the King's Road to Sex.

Tobe Hooper, *The Texas Chainsaw Massacre*.

Stephen King, *Carrie*.

Robert Pirsig, *Zen and the Art of Motorcycle Maintenance*.

Coum Transmissions, an early version of Throbbing Gristle, perform alongside twelve replicas of Duchamp's *Bicycle Wheel*.

The word 'Internet' first enters the vocabulary.

1975 Patti Smith, *Horses*.

Television, 'Little Johnny Jewel'.

Donna Summer, 'Love to Love You Baby'.

Brian Eno, *Another Green World*.

Bob Dylan *Blood On the Tracks*.

Kiss, *Kiss Alive*.

Michael Nyman, *Decay Music*.

Bill Gates and Paul Allen form Microsoft.

Altair, the first personal computer, introduced.

Atari's Pong the hottest-selling Christmas present.

J. G. Ballard, *High Rise*.

Tom Wolfe, *The Right Stuff*.

Welles, *F For Fake*.

Milos Foreman, *One Flew Over the Cuckoo's Nest*.

Trevor Griffiths, *Comedians*.

Samuel R. Delany, *Dhalgren*.

Van McCoy, *The Hustle*.

Rubik's Cube patented.

Brian Eno and Peter Schmidt create Oblique Strategies, a set of cards with instructions and suggestions that might be applied to a variety of creative activities. While recording in the studio, Eno would place the cards face down around the room. When faced with a creative problem, one of several cards could be consulted for inspiration and direction. More than 100 cards offered a variety of suggestions:

> Give way to your worst impulse
> Emphasise the flaws
> Use 'unqualified people'
> The most important thing is the thing
>   most easily forgotten

First commercial supersonic flight with Concorde.

John Lydon walks into Malcolm McLaren's Sex shop wearing an 'I Hate Pink Floyd' T-shirt.

Brian Eno is knocked over by a taxi as he crosses a street on a rainy day. He lies in a hospital bed, heavily medicated. A friend had brought him a record of harp music to listen to. Eno plays the music on a record player that isn't working very well. The volume is barely above the threshold of hearing – one speaker is silent and the other is pointing away from him. The wind and rain outside mix with the harp sounds he can barely hear. Eno is too weak to get up and alter things. At first, the fact that he cannot hear the music frustrates him. But then he starts to relax. He surrenders. 'I drifted into this kind of fitful sleep, a mixture of painkillers and tiredness. And I started hearing this music as if I'd never heard music before. It was a really beautiful experience. I got the feeling of icebergs. I would occasionally just hear the loudest parts of the music, get a little flurry of notes coming out above the sound of the rain . . . and then it would drift away again . . .'

1976 Philip Glass, *Einstein on the Beach*.

Augustus Pablo, *King Tubby Meets Roots Rockers Uptown*.

Patti Smith, *Radio Ethiopia*.

The Ramones, *The Ramones*. The beginning of time.

Abba, 'Dancing Queen'.

Martin Scorsese, *Taxi Driver*.

Roeg, *The Man Who Fell to Earth*.

Queen Elizabeth becomes the first state leader to send an email.

Sony's Betamax and JVC's VHS battle for home-video recording market. Sony will lose.

1977 Kraftwerk, 'Trans-Europe Express'. The beginning of time 2.

The Buzzcocks, *Spiral Scratch*. The beginning of time 3.

Having shown Kraftwerk some of the tools and techniques necessary to develop the texture and humour of their music, and having prepared the way for pop techniques of interacting with media, in a world that is rediscovering the three-minute single and the dynamics of immediacy, Stockhausen rediscovers the four-hour opera.

The Sex Pistols, *Never Mind the Bollocks*. The beginning of time 4a.

The Clash, *The Clash*. The beginning of time 4b.

Mike Leigh, *Abigail's Party*.

Gilbert and George, the *Dirty Words* pictures.

Suicide, *Suicide*. The beginning of time 5a.

Donna Summer, 'I Feel Love'.

David Bowie, *Low*.

Cindy Sherman, *Untitled Film Still # 3*.

Chairman Mao dies.

Nintendo develop home-use video games in association with Mitsubishi.

JVC place two-page advertisement in *Asahi Shimbun* newspaper to launch VHS video format in Japan; the format is introduced elsewhere under the name Vidstar.

John Badham, *Saturday Night Fever*.

George Lucas, *Star Wars*.

Elvis Presley dies; it does not take him long to realise that he lives.

Marc Bolan dies. It does not take him long to realise that he'll dance himself right out of the grave.

Man Ray dies. It does not take him long to realise that death is more surreal than life.

1978 Sony introduces the Walkman, the TPS-L2 – the first portable stereo.

Midway introduces Space Invaders into arcades, the first game that tracks and displays high scores.

First test-tube baby born in Britain.

Pere Ubu, *The Modern Dance*. The beginning of time 5b.

Kate Bush, *The Kick Inside*.

Funkadelic, *One Nation Under a Groove*.

Magazine, 'Shot By Both Sides'.

Public Image Ltd, *Public Image Ltd*.

Nick Logan launches *Smash Hits*, a pop magazine aimed at young teens.

Dallas premières.

Carl Andre, *Equivalent VIII* (the bricks).

Brian Eno, *Music for Airports*.

1979 Joy Division, *Unknown Pleasures*.

The Fall, *Live at the Witch Trials*.

Neil Young, *Rust Never Sleeps*.

This Heat, *This Heat*.

Swell Maps, *A Trip to Marineville*.

Francis Ford Coppola, *Apocalypse Now*.

Blondie, 'Heart of Glass'.

Margaret Thatcher becomes Britain's first female prime minister.

Charlie Mingus dies.

Sid Vicious dies.

Italo Calvino, *If on a Winter's Night a Traveller.*

Holger Czukay, *Movies.* Czukay's first solo album after Can split in 1979, a sublime refinement of his shortwave sonic-collage techniques.

Jean-François Lyotard, *The Postmodern Condition: A Report on Knowledge.* The 'postmodern condition' rejects any claim to absolute truth in favour of relativist interpretations of the world, which results in metanarratives collapsing into meaninglessness.

1980   John Lennon murdered.

Who shot JR?

Joy Division, 'Love Will Tear Us Apart'.

Former movie star Ronald Reagan elected US President.

Talking Heads, *Remain in Light.*

Marshall Jefferson, 'Move Your Body'.

Blondie, 'Rapture'.

Nick Logan launches *The Face*, a glossy style magazine for the new decade.

Ted Turner launches CNN, the first all-news network.

Norman Mailer, *The Executioner's Song.*

Sony introduce the consumer camcorder.

Tim Berners-Lee, a graduate of Oxford University, becomes frustrated while working for CERN – the European Particle Physics Laboratory in Geneva – because his daily schedule, list of phone numbers and his documents are stored in different databases on different machines, making it impossible for him to access them simultaneously. He writes a program entitled Enquire-Within-About-Everything which enables him to access his private data across multiple machines and databases.

1981   MTV goes on the air, starting with the Buggles' 'Video Killed the Radio Star'.

Nintendo develop and begin distribution of the coin-operated video game Donkey Kong.

Jean Baudrillard, *Simulcra and Simulation.*

Human League, *Dare* – a new pop mixture of localised punk self-expression, international pop obsession, lust for life, Kraftwerk machine-kinkiness, nightclub thrills, studio fun, fame fascination, and A for Abba meets, somewhere over a rainbow on Mars, Z for Zappa. Human League, after a start that was more Krautrock than glam pop, become part of an eighties thing that is seen to be about style above content – in fact, there is a lot of content, it's just that the content is all style.

David Byrne and Brian Eno, *My Life in the Bush of Ghosts*. Sampling radio voices and singers from around the world.

Grace Jones, *Nightclubbing*.

D.A.F., *Alles Ist Gut*.

George Miller, *Mad Max*.

Grandmaster Flash, 'The Adventures of Grandmaster Flash on the Wheels of Steel' – stitching together Queen, Chic, the Sugar Hill Gang, Sponnie Gee, Blondie and a children's story; the first rap record to feature live DJ scratching on to vinyl.

Laurie Anderson, 'O, Superman'.

Yoko Ono, 'Walking on Thin Ice'.

Raymond Carver, 'What We Talk About When We Talk About Love'.

Charles marries Diana.

The mouse pointer is attached to computers.

IBM introduces its Personal Computer.

1982 Ridley Scott, *Bladerunner*.

Steven Spielberg, *E.T.*

George Clinton, 'Atomic Dog'.

Thelonius Monk dies.

The Sugar Hill Gang, 'Rapper's Delight'. Three MCs rhyme over a house band playing the break from 'Good Times' by Chic. Because the technology of the day does not allow the Sugar Hill Gang to sample the song, they hire the band to play the same section over and over again.

ABC, *The Lexicon of Love*.

Grandmaster Flash, 'The Message'.

Michael Jackson, *Thriller* – will eventually sell 25 million copies.

Barbara Kruger, *I Shop Therefore I Am*.

Pac-Man named *Time*'s Man of the Year.

AIDS officially identified in US.

Japanese school of designers, including Issey Miyake and Rei Kawakubo, enjoy major couture success.

Roland introduce the TB-303 Bass Line. While never sounding like an actual bass guitar, it helps to create the warped, driven bass sounds at the off-centre of every mutation of house, techno, big beat, jungle.

Arthur Baker and Afrika Bambaataa used the discontinued Roland TR-808 drum machine to help record 'Planet Rock'. The 808 doesn't do what it's meant to do – or what it should do according to Roland. It sounds a little too mechanical, it slips and skips a bit, it's never exact, so there's a kind of technically estranged swing to its rhythm, and you can get inside it and literally fiddle with its soul, wire its heart, and ultimately it finds a place in all great post-punk post-soul post-Kraftwerk electronic music, the slips in time and microskips in rhythm opening up whole new worlds of static flow-motion where the precise beat of art meets the accidental science of beat or vice versa.

Laurie Anderson, *Big Science*.

1983   Compact disc introduced, a new format developed jointly by Sony and Phillips, with a recording length of seventy-four minutes – long enough to accommodate Beethoven's *Symphony No. 9* on one CD.

New Order, 'Blue Monday' – rock, as such, goes dance, as such, and things, as such, are never, as such, the same, as such, again, again, again, as such. In one history of popular music, a line drawn from the La Monte Young, via the Velvet Underground, all the way to Daft Punk and Missy Elliott, passes right through the drum-tender centre of 'Blue Monday'. A line from Roxy Music to Röyksopp, from, as such, one form of beauty to another, as such, takes on beauty, passes right through the beautiful essence of 'Blue Monday', which, as such, the greatest example of how pop music, as such, can distil such, as such, beauty into its combination of melody, texture, rhythm and repetition. 'Blue Monday' was a sort of mistake, an experiment with a new drum machine that ended up with the rhythm that, as such, linked punctual rock that was with a punctuated dance that wasn't quite yet, and in that sense is part of a history of rock that is a series of mistakes, of misreads, that begins a whole new detour, a brand-new direction, and these mistaken directions, these accidental turnings, tend to lead to the strangest and most beautiful part of the city of music. As such, such, such . . .

The Smiths, 'This Charming Man' – some singers just want to carry on telling stories.

Frankie Goes to Hollywood, 'Relax' – some singers just want to be stars.

Cyndi Lauper, 'Girls Just Want to Have Fun' – some girls know more than the boys.

Herbie Hancock, 'Rockit' – some old jazz experts recognise how mistakes lead to the best rhythms, because all music starts with improvisation.

Afrika Bambaataa, 'Looking for the Perfect Beat' – some explorers treated rhythm as mystical. For the sake of argument, this is the first recorded use of digital sampling known to historians.

Sonic Youth, *Confusion is Sex*.

David Cronenberg, *Videodrome*.

Michael Jackson performs his moonwalk for the first time on MTV's celebration of Motown's twenty-fifth anniversary.

Katherine Hamnett, 'Stop Acid Rain' T-shirts.

Madonna shows her navel.

Launch of the *Now That's What I Call Music . . .* series. Another date that might mark the end of something – something possibly positive – and the beginning of something else – something possibly negative. It might, for instance, have heralded the end of the seven-inch single as we knew it. It might have just framed the single in such a brutally marketed way that it contributed to its makeover, enabling the idea of the pop song to actually last longer than it might have done otherwise. It was destined to happen, and the generic name for the series was slightly ahead of its time – an odd, friendly, corporate title for something that milked pop music for all it was worth and was aimed at maximising revenue for the featured singles during the period just after their peak, when people are prepared to buy with a less critical eye. Or ear. This recycling trend began in Britain, where initial reluctance to the idea was quickly removed when *Now . . . 1* sold 900,000 copies – record companies' fears that it might interfere with their main artists' sales were removed, and the size of the sales meant that they ignored criticism about this format stifling new talent and not helping to develop the product life-cycle of the featured artists. Prior to this series, it was rare a thing for various-artists compilations to feature original music – previously, the closest you could get to buying a souvenir of recent chart music was to buy compilations on which hit songs were cheaply covered in a spirit of spirited semiprofessionalism.

The rest of the world soon followed, and if we perceive that one of the histories of rock that can be told is the history of rock as a history of hits, then the *Now . . .* series is the biggest 'act' of the last twenty years. Initially launched by EMI and Virgin, it has since been copied by other labels, and the market has been widened to include dance-, jazz-, classical- and ethnic-based music – eventually evolving into the chillout albums. The person responsible for the series anticipated that it might last to about *Now . . .* 5. If you have the entire series – and if you do you are very sad and yet very happy – then you have a history of the way pop music changed imperceptibly and massively, always resembling itself and the trends it was following or setting, over a long, short twenty-year period. For some reason, the series was represented graphically by a cheerful pig – this might have symbolised the record industry; it might have symbolised an audience greedy for the same old stuff instantly repackaged; it might have been a subtle way of suggesting that if this cash cow works, pigs will grin inanely. The pig was pictured listening to a chicken singing. This confuses the issue further – perhaps this was a comment on the absurd, in some ways wonderful mixing and matching of songs that had nothing to do with each other apart from the fact that they were hits and they then settled next to each other on compilations like this.

The track listing for *Now That's What I Call Music . . . 1*:
  Phil Collins, 'You Can't Hurry Love'
  Duran Duran, 'Is There Something I Should Know?'
  UB40, 'Red Red Wine'
  Limahl, 'Only for Love'
  Heaven 17, 'Temptation'
  K.C. & the Sunshine Band, 'Give It Up'
  Malcom McLaren, 'DoubleDutch'
  Bonnie Tyler, 'Total Eclipse of the Heart'
  Culture Club, 'Karma Chameleon'

Men Without Hats, 'Safety Dance'

Kajagoogoo, 'Too Shy'

Mike Oldfield, 'Moonlight Shadow'

Men at Work, 'Down Under'

The Rock Steady Crew, '(Hey You) The Rock Steady Crew'

Rod Stewart, 'Baby Jane'

Paul Young, 'Wherever I Lay My Hat'

New Edition, 'Candy Girl'

Kajagoogoo, 'Big Apple'

Tina Turner, 'Let's Stay Together'

The Human League, '(Keep Feeling) Fascination'

Howard Jones, 'New Song'

UB40, 'Please Don't Make Me Cry'

Roberta Flack and Peabo Bryson, 'Tonight I Celebrate My Love'

Tracey Ullman, 'They Don't Know'

Will Powers, 'Kissing With Confidence'

Genesis, 'That's All'

The Cure, 'Love Cats'

Simple Minds, 'Waterfront'

Madness, 'The Sun and the Rain'

Culture Club, 'Victims'

1984 Rupert Murdoch's Satellite Television relaunched as Sky Television.

Band Aid, 'Do They Know It's Christmas?'

William Gibson uses the term 'cyberspace' in his book *Neuromancer*.

Rob Reiner, *This Is Spinal Tap*.

Prince, *Purple Rain*.

Hüsker Du, *Zen Arcade*.

The Smiths, *The Smiths*.

Frankie Knuckles, *Your Love*.

Milos Foreman, *Amadeus*.

James Cameron, *The Terminator*.

Jay McInerney, *Bright Lights, Big City*.

Kate Moss discovered by Storm model agency when boarding a plane at JFK airport aged fourteen.

Front 242 inscribe the words 'Electronic Body Music' on the sleeve of their debut 12".

Talla2XLC, the first ever techno club, opens in Frankfurt.

Domain Name System is established, with network addresses established such as .com, .org and .edu.

First portable mobile phone; weighs two pounds.

Ronald Reagan re-elected.

Pete Waterman, the Jeffrey Archer of the music business, sets up his record-production company Pete Waterman Limited. Waterman spent most of the late 1960s as a club DJ and joined Magnet Records in the early seventies as an A&R assistant, breaking records such as Alvin Stardust's 'My Coo Ca Choo'. Signs Chris Rea and claims responsibility for starting disco craze with Silver Convention, a band who feature Donna Summer as their lead singer. Creates hits in the early eighties for Nik Kershaw, Tracey Ullman, the Belle Stars and Musical Youth. Just after starting PWL Waterman meets Mike Stock and Matt Aitken, who have written 'The Upstroke', a female Hi-NRG version of Frankie Goes to Hollywood's 'Relax'. The song, released by two-girl band Agents Aren't Aeroplanes, is not a hit, but is, oddly, championed by John Peel. Stock, Aitken and Waterman, not yet known as Stock, Aitken & Waterman, also write and produce the 1984 Greek entry for the Eurovision Song Contest. It comes last. For a couple of years Stock, Aitken & Waterman are tireless, tasteless, neo-trendy, proto-gimmicky producers, working on everything from Divine to Roland Rat, Bananarama to Georgie Fame, working their way inexorably to becoming ruthless overground un-trendy hit-makers.

1985   David Lynch, *Blue Velvet*.

Double D and Steinski, 'Lesson Three'.

Madonna, 'Material Girl' – her least favourite of her hits.

Jean Paul Gaultier uses Madonna's underwear as her outerwear. In the car at the edge of the universe of style, which is deep with surface, Madonna is wearing this corset, breasts pointing midway on the compass of sensation between the north of pain and the south of pleasure, bra worn as shield and weapon. Or is she draped in the Gothic black of self-knowledge, the exact opposite of Kylie's kiss-and-sigh white, as she sits next to Kylie in the car that is so close to the laser-cut city you can feel the electricity flicker through your optical nerve?

Madonna is now driving, taking the wheel that she has known since she was a young girl absolutely belongs to her, the wheel she uses to steer herself towards her dream of total control, of personal power, her wheel of fortune. Madonna, of course, is a great driver. She drives for America, she drives around the world, she drives across this tele-landscape, she takes us to the edge of the city, the digi-city of light and noise, the graphic city we can now say, thanks to William Gibson, who we've just passed, is under a sky the colour of television tuned to a dead channel.

Madonna is suddenly wearing a T-shirt. At first, written across the T-shirt are the words 'What was postmodernism?' The letters then change to supply answers as she drives along. A change of gear, a change of wording, a change of image.

a. A menu
b. Dispersal
c. Mutant forms of play
d. Decentrement
e. Polymorphous metanarratives full of themselves
f. Clever misreadings
g. Demystification of the self (whose identity became plural and perverse)

Madonna's T-shirt sticks with the words 'plural and perverse'. Little does she know that, in fifteen years, when postmodernism has warped into post-reality, which is instantly post-itself, she will be wearing a Kylie Minogue T-shirt. As she drives, right now, made-up, dressed with skill, strangely apart, sexually certain, drives across surface, the utter matter of surface, towards the skin and circuits of a city made up of flesh and pixels, she hasn't got a clue who Kylie Minogue is.

As she drives, she gets a hard-on. The road, the view, the sex and the city ahead, it's all so tantalising. Kylie notices the hardness, the soft hardness pointing straight towards the sin and tones of the city, but doesn't say anything.

Madonna's T-shirt now reads: 'I was born a woman (sex)'.

Now it reads: 'I was made into a woman (gender)'.

She strikes a pose – there's nothing to it.

Madonna is driving the car like she's driving through MTV, through the relentless speed of the pop video, the promo, the cut-up and haste shattering of image, past, present, now, then, when, what, who. Video helped turn the pop star into something more and more artificial, more and more fake, false, distant, machine-like. Madonna raced through MTV with the quickest changes, the biggest smile, the sneakiest looks (back to Fritz Lang, to Marlene, Marilyn, Rita, forward to herself, her own exploitation of pretence, her own manufacturing of her own manufacturing, her own ironic take on her own sincere sense of irony). She crossed boundaries of sex, style, identity, taste, time, space, she was not who she said she was, she changed her mind, sound, look, clothes, hair, eyes, career, existence, changed herself into herself a hundred times, switched masks, switched personalities, cancelled out herself, sped through herself, looked again, blinked, posed, played, smiled, gave nothing away, but herself, which didn't exist outside the video, which was positioned inside quotation marks, inside brackets, inside MTV, which moved fast, but Madonna moved the fastest of them all, changing before anyone knew she needed to change, changing as soon as she changed. She exploited the way the video disposed of truth and authenticity, and left behind pure surface, the pure appeal of pure appearance. She was first, in many ways, to understand that the video meant she didn't need to represent anything other than Madonna, the name, the brand name. She could change at the speed of MTV as long as the name remained the same. Madonna was Madonna however she looked and sounded, because it was Madonna, doing what comes naturally, changing with the weather, changing during the ad break, a change is as good as a rest. She played the new game, this new visual game, where she could make a new thing, this new hybrid of song and image, where you weren't releasing singles any more, you were releasing signals, coded outbursts packed with signs that referred to themselves, or, if they referred outside themselves, always ended up being beamed back into a place that belonged to Madonna. Madonna used her image and the moving image of the video to reproduce herself in a flurry of Madonnas that confirmed the idea that there was only one Madonna.

She took it from Bowie, who might have got it from Dylan, or even from Brando, or Liz Taylor, or Jean Cocteau, this need and ability to swap and change identities, to protect yourself from your own boredom with yourself by becoming someone else while not really changing. Acting out, but not in fiction – a sort of non-fiction acting, a theatrical manipulation of reality. Bowie made up characters loosely connected to who he was, who he wanted to be. He wrote himself into the future with a series of stylistic and visual changes. Sometimes he changed the name of the character he was playing. Madonna did the same, but never changed her name. But, like Bowie, like Dylan, she made herself up, and made herself up fully prepared for a new MTV-broken world that was about to suck up image and spit it out again. Madonna changed before she was sucked in so there was no chance of being spat out again. She never stayed still long enough.

Madonna changed her image as fast as a viewer can channel-zap. You could channel-zap through Madonna. She was multi-channelled, here a virgin, there a get-up-and-go girl, here a total tease, there a superstar, porn star, vamp, model, actress, singer . . . Then an artist, then a queen, and such are queens that your laughter is sucked in their brain. Now she's having you on, turning you on, always ahead of you, changing gear, changing views, playing at being an appearance, stealing, taking, moving, speeding, recycling, revising, revisiting, an artist working in business, a business woman working in art. She played at being all-woman, but never really let on that this was truly the case. She played at sexy, her videos were sexy plays, but never really suggested she was hot, or actually horny, or even slightly moist. She was a woman imitating a man imitating a woman. A simulation of a consumer's expectation of a sexy, objectified media female. She was after power – the power over a male world that was demanding things from her that she was never going to give. She was going to *pretend* to give them. This might be a very fine line, but Madonna turned it into a very broad line. She controlled herself and her images, she parodied her role as female pop star, she made off with all the clichés and spun them around and wore them down, she did what she told herself to do. She created her image as an image of star by herself with her own instinct for what was right and what was wrong. She escaped being imprisoned in a male-manufactured image, escaped being possessed by her audience, frozen in one position, in one personality, by slipping from image to image, skipping outside the reality imposed upon her by an outside world, and stripping away the conventional meanings attached to the female superstar. She controlled the way she became one of the most famous women in the world by following her rules, pursuing her representation and exaggeration of the clichés of female pop stardom.

She gained her power. 'It's a great feeling to be powerful. I've been striving for it all my life.' And, just in case you thought it was all too good to be true, she did little with that power other than make herself more powerful, more famous. But that was the point – she wanted to show that as a woman she could be just as selfish, just as self-obsessed, as any man. She achieved this at great speed; and, although you wouldn't want to listen to her music in a contemplative, musical way, it was a hell of a sound-track to her rise. Her music was the perfect music to play while pondering her rise as superstar – cool, calculating, always pouncing at the right time in the right way, sounding perfectly modern, for a moment, and then even another one, remixable, with the allure of fashion, and none of the depth, although occasionally this lack of depth, this careful sound, this perfectionism conspired to give us a version of a pop classic. And now the best thing about Madonna, what made her so ahead of her time, knowing it and not knowing it, is that you can use her, colourise her, mix her, remix her, as part of your own narrative of meaning, as the world turns into another kind of world. Add a drum track. Place her somewhere strange. She has given herself such power she is way beyond being bothered if we use her as a character in our own dream of what the world means.

Kylie has been watching Madonna with great interest. She thinks it is all very healthy, the way Madonna has this simultan-eous existence as Madonna and not Madonna, as a reality and an illusion. She wonders what place, what space, Madonna occupies where she lives any kind of life, or if her life is all about main-taining image through changing what and where and when and why and who she is. Is she all that she seems to be, all image? Is she nothing but a name? Is she nothing but what she has persuaded us, and therefore herself, she is? Did she disappear behind her changing image so many times there was truly eventually no one left? Do we just see ghosts of Madonna, echoes of her image, is it just the after effect of her image that we see change, is there nothing of her *but* the change, the changing from one thing to another, the change from one change to another change? If she stops changing does she totally cease to exist – or does she *start* to exist, to live an ordinary life?

Kylie is endlessly fascinated. Meeting Madonna, even though she didn't really say much to her, has made this strange journey very worthwhile. She looks across at the driving, driven Madonna, like she is looking at some great tourist attraction, surrounded by onlookers and photographers – Madonna is the Eiffel Tower, the Statue of Liberty, the Taj Mahal, the Christ at Rio de Janeiro, Times Square – and has what she can only describe as a feeling of religious intensity. Madonna seems to be saying 'I love you' to Kylie but, of course, Kylie knows that she doesn't mean it, and Madonna knows that Kylie knows she doesn't mean it, but the atmosphere somehow is charged with emotion. Something is going on, even if it isn't love as we know it. And then . . .

Madonna's gone. She was never really there. She has turned herself, with such trickery and determination, into a figment of the imagination. She is part of the view, a feature of the city, an address at the centre, a part of the world inside us, the world in here, where the world really matters, inside our imagination. She is not driving the car. She is not in the car. She's part of that building ahead of us, she's the mirrored glass, the seventy-seventh floor, she's that bridge, that neon sign, she's that cloud in the sky that's changing shape, she's that river that bends just the way it wants to, she's the rain racing fast and certain across the windscreen of the car. 'Goodbye,' Kylie murmurs.

Kylie is driving the virtual vehicle once more, across a million minds at play, driving through a fast thick ocean of white noise. Don DeLillo, *White Noise*.

The Jesus & Mary Chain, *Psychocandy*.

The Fall, *This Nation's Saving Grace*.

Kate Bush, 'Running Up That Hill'.

Grace Jones, 'Slave to the Rhythm'.

Terry Gilliam, *Brazil*.

Miucci Prada designs black, unlabelled, hard-wearing, finely woven nylon handbag.

Dolce & Gabbana first make their name. They once admitted that they wouldn't mind if their only contribution to fashion history was a black bra.

Russian programmer Alex Pajitnov develops the game Tetris to be played on a PC.

Images can be broken into digital bits.

Digital audio recording and playback expands greatly, sample time gets longer and longer, and more bands experiment with the technique. The industry is baffled by this new art form, and by whether sampling actually constitutes copyright infringement. Early samples neither credit nor split royalties with the original artist.

1986 Run DMC, 'Walk This Way'.

The Smiths, *The Queen Is Dead*.

Janet Jackson, *Control*.

The Beastie Boys, *Licensed to Ill*.

Oprah Winfrey goes into national syndication.

Launch of Fox, the fourth American television network.

BBC begins daytime television. Included in the first programming is the Australian soap *Neighbours*. Set in Ramsay Street, in the mythical suburb of Erinsborough, *Neighbours* is a virtual matrix for the differences of white Australia.

Kylie Minogue joins cast of *Neighbours*, playing Charlene Mitchell.

Launch of Q magazine.

Jeff Koons, *Rabbit*.

1987 Andy Warhol dies; bored forever.

Eric B & Rakim, 'Paid in Full'.

Coldcut sample Yemenite singer Ofra Haza on 'Seven Minutes of Madness', their remake of Eric B & Rakim's 'Paid in Full'.

Public Enemy, *Yo! Bumrush the Show*.

Sonic Youth, *Sister*.

Prince, *Sign 'o' the Times*.

thirtysomething begins broadcasting.

Pete Waterman sets up his PWL label to release the debut single by Mandy Smith, who is tabloid-known for being the teenage bride of the Stones' Bill Wyman. Working as a teaboy at PWL, Rick Astley becomes the first real Stock, Aitken & Waterman plaything with the release of 'Never Gonna Give You Up'.

1988 CDs outsell vinyl LPs for the first time.

Negativland, 'Escape from Noise'.

NWA, *Straight Outta Compton*.

Bret Easton Ellis, *American Psycho*.

The Pet Shop Boys, *Introspective*.

The Pixies, *Surfer Rosa*.

D Mob, 'We Call it Aciiieeed'.

Derrick May/Rhythm Is Rhythm, 'Strings of Life'. May gives Frankie Knuckles a demo tape to play in his club, Knuckles gives it its name, techno begins in the city of Ford and Barry Gordy's Motown, Detroit. May says, 'Today the automobile plants use robots and computers to make their cars. I'm more interested in Ford's robots than Gordy's music.'

Computer memory costs 100 millionth of what it did in 1950.

Parents complain that children are staying away from school to watch the daytime showing of *Neighbours*, so the BBC move the programme to 17.30, repeated the following lunchtime.

Stock, Aitken & Waterman establish themselves as super-producers with the creation of Kylie Minogue's 'I Should Be So Lucky'. 'Our songs do all sound the same,' Waterman says, responding to criticism that their songs, whether acid knock-offs, football songs, disco dramas, big pop hits or wet ballads, are all alike. 'They sound successful. They don't actually sound the same, but if someone says to me they all sound the same, I shake their hand and say, "Thank you very much." It means I've done my job properly.' Kylie's 'Lucky' is number one for five weeks. SAW have hits falling out of their ears all year. Many of them should have stayed in their ears. Furious with such condescension, the group construct a track they claim is an original funk song from the early seventies, 'Roadblock'. It sounds convincing, proving that SAW are indeed convincing men, in the same way that they are confidence men. Pete Waterman, when asked what it's like having so many hits, quotes what the Beatles said when they were asked the same

question: 'You're too busy to know.' His thoughts on his role in the creation of Kylie: 'History will show that "I Should Be So Lucky" turned the key to the number-one television show of all time [*Neighbours*, in case you were wondering] and the number-one female artist of all time.'
Stephen Hawking, *A Brief History of Time*.
Launch of *Hello* magazine.

Celebrity is making itself up as it goes along.

Celebrity is invented by the media. (As if you didn't know that.)

Celebrity is made up out of boredom and disappointment.

Celebrity is considering itself. It is coming to very little conclusion. It doesn't have to.

When I consider the made-up colour of Cher's stretched skin, or look at the fake new hairdo of Victoria Beckham, or wonder about the brain power of the nearly real Naomi Campbell, or stagger under the weight of Elizabeth Taylor's decaying mystique, I can't help but think a number of things about the tricky notion of celebrity. These things include the thought that celebrity culture is empty and dehumanising; but, luckily, some juicier, less literal-minded things come to mind as well.

Celebrity is representing how the manipulation of perception is replacing reality, or easing us, uneasily, forward into a new post-real reality, where celebrity takes the biscuit, and sells its soul, and gets a nose job.

Celebrity is dramatising one's own life with a video camera. Celebrity is *Big Brother*, the Internet chat line, the karaoke machine, persuading us that we too can look like a star. We can even be one.

Celebrity is sitting top-right, back row on *Blankety Blank*. I'm a celebrity – get me out of here!

Celebrity is growing up as a celebrity and losing its virginity in tabloid public.

Celebrity: because sex sells better than politics.

To be a celebrity is widely regarded as the most exalted state of human existence.

Celebrity used to have a little but now it's got a lot.

Celebrities are great, or at least they're OK, and not doing anyone any harm, except perhaps themselves, and maybe us.

Nothing escapes celebrity, not the local Lotto winner, or the most powerful man in the world. Celebrity seeks out everything, even failure.

Celebrity is not itself but is a photograph of itself.

Celebrity is what happens when you pass the audition or when your smile can be seen through the crowd or when your dress is less than a dress or when your life is nothing but an audition and celebrity can be what happens when you fail the audition.

We can take it out on celebrities and they have to put up with it because they are nothing if not targets for our pent-up frustration as well as our loose love.

God, the very original celebrity, dies, and his place is taken by Nietzsche, whose place is taken by Freud, whose place is taken by Einstein, whose place is taken by Monroe, whose place is taken by Presley, whose place is taken by the Beatles, whose place is taken by the Sex Pistols, whose place is taken by the Spice Girls, whose place is taken by Britney Spears, whose place is taken by a processed idol, whose place is taken by a process.

Celebrity is hiding behind dark glasses, peering out on a world of its own making.

Celebrity has got its eye on you.

Victoria might die terribly; she might lose her looks, which would be careless of her; she might fade away; she might stick around like a celebrity stick-insect permanently camouflaging herself as gloss on the glossy pages of the celebrity magazine. She might be the consumer world's Vera Lynn and end up a dame. She'll manipulate us some more. She'll be manipulated some more. We'll victimise her. She'll victimise us. We care, up to a point. The point being that we don't really care.

Celebrity opens its mouth and says what we want it to say.

Celebrity is as fake as fuck and as real as anything.

Celebrity is being one of Charlie's Angels, whether in the twentieth or twenty-first century.

Celebrity is not responding to the allegations.

Celebrity is actually raping itself, but not reporting the rape. Celebrity is thinking that you know you want it and impatiently wanting you to agree whether you agree or not.

Celebrity is coming down in flames.

Celebrity is not reading its autobiography.

Celebrity is writing only two words of its autobiography. A signature on the title page.

Without celebrity we'd all be as anonymous as each other – and how boring is that?

Celebrity is the titillating balance between everybody being as famous as each other and everybody being as anonymous as each other.

Celebrity has children and the children of celebrities are themselves celebrities because they are the children of celebrities.

'Celebrity is the pox of success.' Harrison Ford said that, so we can ignore it. Far more interesting than what he has to say is the style of his latest haircut.

Celebrity is like the religion we are all in control of in an out-of-control way.

Celebrity marries itself.

Celebrity renews its vows in the total privacy of a completely deserted desert island on which no tourists ever step, with only luggage carriers in attendance. And a whole editorial and photographic team from *Hello* magazine.

Celebrity is the face of meaninglessness in a meaningless time, which is a kind of meaning. Perhaps celebrity is the search for meaning translated in front of our very eyes into a search for pleasure.

Celebrity is singing 'If I stop lying I'll disappoint you.'

To get to the bottom of what celebrity means in early twenty-first-century Britain you would have to pay careful attention to Kylie Minogue's bottom.

From Malcolm Muggeridge to Madonna, from Andy Warhol to one of his subjects, from the cover of *The National Enquirer* to the cover of *Time*. To put it another way, celebrity is Liberace's surname, it's Engelbert Humperdinck's middle name. To put it another way, it's selling your house, which used to be owned by Jayne Mansfield, on QVC. To put it another way, celebrity is in the imagination for ever.

Inside, celebrity is crumbling. It can't cope.

The celebrity uses the television interview to break down and intimately confess in the hope that you might forgive their sins or grant them martyrdom or buy their book or let them back in.

Celebrity is our frenzied desire to know who fucks who and who fails and who fights.

Celebrity is our way of making sense of what we did during the day.

Celebrity is mystery maintained and mystery destroyed.

Celebrity is allowing the cameras total access to their lives.

Celebrity is nothing more than a collection of cosmetics.

Celebrity is shooting dead someone you've just met because you haven't had a hit for thirty-seven years.

Celebrity is trying not to get old so it will never die.

Celebrity is never growing up.

The celebrity takes over from where we begin and where we end. They are a part of us, a version of ourselves, a figment of our imagination, an episode in our dreams. It may even help us, more than any book, bible or novel, to process our own experiences.

What does a celebrity know?

What does an intellectual know?

Celebrity has replaced class as the determining factor of status.

Celebrity is remixed a thousand times.
Celebrity is listed.

If Jesus came back he would have to come back as a celebrity, and he would wear the crucifix of the celebrity, the Nike swoosh, on the peak of his baseball hat.

Celebrities, being the fussiest people on the planet, cause the most fuss, and are the most fussed-over.

Celebrity changes its appearance using knife, chemicals, computer and sleight of hand.

Celebrities are great. Well, they're OK. I wouldn't want to be one, not unless you're seriously offering, but they help make the world a different place. And, if you like, an indifferent place.

Being a celebrity is having the kidnap attempt on you foiled by a tabloid newspaper.

Celebrity is posting on your unofficial website: 'I would request that as I no longer seek to be a famous person and instead wish to live a normal life could people please afford me my privacy.'

If I saw Brad Pitt and Jennifer Aniston walking down the street, I would ask them for their autographs. Actually, I probably wouldn't. But then, I wouldn't go up to them and say, 'Celebrity sucks.' I wouldn't ask them if they recognise themselves. I wouldn't ask them if celebrity represents the triumph of entertainment over life itself. I wouldn't ask them who they felt was the maddest – them, their fans, their stalkers, those who didn't care about them, the media. I wouldn't shoot them. I suppose I would look at them for as long as I could before they called for help.

Celebrity is demanding that your dressing-room is all white – repainted white, decorated with white sofas, filled with white lilies, candles and cushions.

Celebrity is having to ask for help because all of the attention has got out of hand.

Celebrity is a bubble that bursts.

But it still manages to make a comeback.

Celebrity is a rumour about itself.

Celebrity sells itself.

Celebrity is a copy of something else that we then copy.

Celebrity is never satisfied with what it's got.

And the world goes on, famous for being there, famous for turning up, famous for the very fact it exists, famous because it spins round and round.

Donna Karan launches the DKNY label in an attempt to dress her daughter.
Naomi Campbell becomes the first black model on the cover of French *Vogue*.
1989 Lucille Ball dies.
Salvador Dali dies.
Jaron Lanier coins the term 'virtual reality'.
Nintendo releases the handheld GameBoy.
The Berlin Wall falls.
De La Soul, *3 Feet High and Rising*.
New Order, *Technique*.
The Stone Roses, 'Fools Gold'.
The Orb, 'A Huge Ever Growing Pulsating Brain that Rules from the Centre of the Ultraworld'. Discovering a late-night calm-down club music based on playing Eno-type ambient music accidentally drizzled with house beats coming in from another part of the club, the Orb's blend of ambient and house sends ambient music off in a number of directions, from the ocean to the sampler, from the mind to the body, from the ears to the feet, leading to the likes of the ambient techno of Aphex Twin and the experimental ambient of Mouse on Mars. The minimalism of ambient gets less, and the mixing of relaxation music and relaxed beats gently advances towards 'chillout' music, perhaps the most successful new commercial genre of the early twenty-first

century. The word 'ambient', coined by Eno in a derived moment of aptness, initially derided from all sides for its lack of authenticity, intellectually for its second-handedness, in the rock world for its sentimentalist softness, eventually becomes, along with the sound it describes, utterly ubiquitous. A relaxed Eno, relaxed to the point of meek, pretty much inherits the earth.

A Guy Called Gerald, 'Voodoo Ray'.

Steven Soderbergh, *sex, lies and videotape*.

Nintendo makes annual profit of $1 billion.

TV Guide puts Oprah Winfrey's head on Ann-Margret's body.

The dark prince of Sydney rock, Michael Hutchence, meets the white princess of Melbourne pop, Kylie Minogue. He shows her the intoxicating arts of the night, she introduces him to a little glitter. The legend has it that Hutchence introduces Kylie to her own body, which she then places at the centre of her performance.

1990   *The Simpsons* premières. The animated series grew out of short items included in the *Tracey Ullman Show* since 1987.

Milli Vanilli admit to lip-synching their hits, and have their Grammy withdrawn.

Vanilla Ice samples the most identifiable parts of David Bowie and Queen's song 'Under Pressure' for his hit 'Ice Ice Baby'. Unlike, say, MC Hammer, who sampled Rick James' 'Superfreak' but credited it, Vanilla Ice neither licenses nor credits the steal. The case never goes to trial, but it is later thought that the copyright holders threatened to sue and the case was settled out of court.

Seinfeld premières.

John Zorn, *Naked City*.

The KLF, *Chill Out*.

Depeche Mode, *Violator*.

Public Enemy, *Fear of a Black Planet*.

John McNaughton, *Henry: Portrait of a Serial Killer*.

Tom Ford joins Gucci as chief women's ready-to-wear designer.

Tim Berners-Lee returns to CERN Laboratories and sees that no one has done anything with his 1980 Enquire Within program and that data at the laboratory is even more distributed than before. He proposes the use of a Hypertext-based system to access the data stored across multiple machines and databases. While working on a project to enable information sharing within internationally dispersed teams and the dissemination of information by support groups, he proposes a Web concept.

1991 The first Web application is ready for use by the scientists at the CERN Laboratories – 'We are forming cells within a global brain, a place where the whim of a human being and the reasoning of a machine coexist.' For Berners-Lee, the World Wide Web, as he calls it, is 'the universe of accessible information, the point about it being a universe is that there is one space'.

Nirvana, *Smells Like Teen Spirit*.

Damien Hirst, *Physical Impossibility of Death in the Mind of Someone Living*.

Slint, *Spiderland*.

Public Enemy/Anthrax, 'Bring the Noise'.

Douglas Coupland, *Generation X*.

Miles Davis dies.

Massive Attack, *Blue Lines*.

Primal Scream, *Screamadelica*.

My Bloody Valentine, *Loveless*.

James Cameron, *Terminator 2 Judgment Day*.

Richard Linklater, *Slacker*.

Cell phones and email are increasing in popularity as personal and business communication tools.

Biz Markie samples Gilbert O'Sullivan's 'Alone Again Naturally' for his song 'Along Again'. This sampling case becomes the first to be settled by a court. The presiding judge begins his judgement by quoting the Seventh Commandment: Thou shalt not steal. He concludes by referring the case to the US Attorney's Office for consideration of criminal charges. The case sets the standard for viewing unlicensed sampling as a crime. To legally sample a song a performer must obtain permission from the copyright holder of the sound recording (the record company) and the copyright holder of the composition (usually the song publisher, sometimes the original artist, or the record company).

Tom Cruise marries Nicole Kidman.

1992 World Wide Web demonstrated and distributed beyond CERN Laboratories.

Bill Clinton elected US President.

New Web terms – HTTP and URL.

AOL announces that it has 200,000 subscribers.

Kate Moss becomes the face of Calvin Klein.

First edition of ProTools. It begins as a simple editing system and evolves fast into combination mixing desk/sampler/computer, the musical box that musical dreamers – Bacon, Cage, Meek – had been dreaming of for centuries. It will eventually change the way music is made, a sort of cross between a digital razor blade, a time machine, a studio, a dream and sound library. Every instrument in the world can now exist in software, every sound known and unknown can now be produced with the click of a mouse. ProTools synthesises pop music completely, and ensures that it will travel into the future, eat itself, beat itself, treat itself, repeat itself, compete with itself, delete itself, reboot itself. Within a matter of years, ProTools will give birth to Britney Spears, rebirth Madonna, feed wires into Kylie's flesh and voice, reheat heavy metal, live a life with Elvis, Pink will fight back against its digital ruthlessness, and electro-wired avant-gardists will slip and slide deep inside the texture of a piece of music, manipulate the atoms of sound, slip between the finest cracks of existence, shred-fibred beats and distant tones into a list as long and mysterious as a list of DNA that makes up a human being.

Aphex Twin, 'Didgeridoo'.

DJ Shadow, 'In/Flux'.

Radiohead, 'Creep'.

Pavement, *Slanted and Enchanted*.

Arrested Development, *3 Years, 5 Months and 2 Days in the Life of . . .*

Dr Dre, *The Chronic*.

Ice T, 'Cop Killer'.

CDs surpass cassettes in sales.

W. H. Smith announces it will stop selling vinyl LPs.

Launch of the Cartoon Network, which shows cartoons around the clock.

Vivienne Westwood awarded OBE in recognition of her services to British fashion.

1993 Marc Anderson creates new user-friendly Web browser called

Mosaic. Interest in Web explodes.

Rumours fly that mobile phones cause cancer; sales continue to soar.

Nokia sends text messages between mobile phones.

Intel launch the Pentium chip.

Björk, *Debut*.

Beck, 'Loser'.

New Order, 'Regret'.

X-Files debuts.

Launch of *OK* magazine.

1994 The World Wide Web becomes stronger and stronger. The first retail transactions take place on the Internet: Pizza Hut takes orders.

Wired magazine debuts.

E.R. and *Friends* begin broadcasting.

Quentin Tarantino, *Pulp Fiction*.

The Beastie Boys, *Ill Communication*.

Dust Brothers, *Chemical Beats*.

Oval, *Systemisch*.

Nirvana, *Unplugged*.

Kurt Cobain commits suicide.

In Japan, the debut of the Sega Saturn and the Sony PlayStation.

Simon Fuller, the Spice Girls.

Launch of *Loaded* magazine.

Liz Hurley photographed in a Versace dress.

Mathew Barney, *Cremaster 4*.

Michael Jackson marries Lisa Marie Presley – the strangest thing that has ever happened, outside the birth of Christ, the self-consciousness of Kafka, and the debut album by Van Der Graaf Generator, is the end of the twentieth century in a news-generating, soundbiting, sense-busting nutshell, pulling together fame, pop culture, TV, hype, religion, myth, money, reality, fantasy, the avant-garde, plastic surgery . . . The collaboration is somewhere la la, or Dada, or wow, between work of art and science fiction – in fact, it is both the last great work of art of the twentieth century, the last great piece of twentieth-century science fiction, and there-fore the end of science fiction; and for $300 million you would be able to buy the marriage, frame it, and hang it on your wall.

Or you could use the $300 million to turn the whole thing into a science-fiction movie about the end of reality, a reality which is replaced by an exact copy of itself, except that Michael Jackson is now a small boy called Harry Potter. Two years later, in one reality or another, Jackson and Presley divorce – the strangest thing that has ever happened in the world until the daughter of Eminem marries the son of Michael Jackson (the daughter was born a boy, and the son was born a girl, and, at the time they marry, Elvis Presley is starring in a film about an imagined marriage between Kafka and Marlene Dietrich. Presley plays Dietrich. Nicolas Cage is Kafka. A critic describes the film as the strangest thing that has ever happened outside the concept album *In Search of Amelia Earhart* by Plainsong, soon to be turned into a TV mini-series starring Lisa Marie Presley as Amelia Earhart and Michael Jackson as the clouds over the Atlantic Ocean).

Tom Ford becomes creative director of Gucci.

1995 O. J. Simpson trial; an estimated US audience of 150 million watch the not-guilty verdict being read.

Tricky, *Maxinquaye*.

Fatboy Slim, *Everybody Needs a 303*. The DJ reborn as cult cheerleader, making from scratch the sounds he thinks are missing from his record collection.

Leftfield, *Leftism*.

Underworld, 'Born Slippy'.

Edwyn Collins, 'A Girl Like You'. When Elvis makes his next record, this will be one of the songs he does, and it will be followed on the album by his version of 'Can't Get You Out of My Head', followed by a little Eminem.

Eminem's debut album, *Infinite*, is greeted with little acclaim, and some mirth at the out-of-date anti-Gulf War songs. No one knows what his name is, but then once upon a time no one knew Elvis.

David Fincher, *Seven*. When Elvis makes movies again, they will be directed by the likes of David Fincher.

David Foster Wallace, *Infinite Jest*. Elvis's next movie will be scripted by Foster Wallace from an orignal story by me based on a story by Philip K. Dick called 'How to Build a Universe That Doesn't Fall Apart Two Days Later'.

Windows 95 is released – the soundtrack to the next Elvis film is by Brian Eno, who produced the sound you hear when Windows 95 starts up. Elvis's love interest will be played by Kylie Minogue. David Fincher has now pulled out of the movie, and it is being directed by David Cronenberg, because Elvis will only work with a director called David, as he is comfortable with the name. Kylie is delighted with the choice, having been intrigued when Cronenberg said, 'As humans, we try to transcend the body by transforming it.' Cronenberg explains to Elvis and Kylie that they are going to make a film about sex. 'What is sex? Is it art? Is it just pleasure? Is it politics? Is it war? It's probably all those things.' Elvis says: 'Sex is sex.'

Kylie says: 'Sex is reality.'

David asks: 'What is reality?'

And Elvis and Kylie sing together: 'Reality is that which When you stop believing it Doesn't go away' – although they don't actually sing those words, they just sort of sing, 'La la la, la la . . .' *Wow*, thinks David, *this is going to be a great film.*

John Lasseter, *Toy Story*.

Sony demonstrates flat TV set.

Sony brings the PlayStation to America.

Amazon.com opens an Internet bookshop.

The Spice Girls sign with Virgin.

Tracey Emin, *Everyone I Have Ever Slept With, 1963–1995*.

Panorama interview with Princess Diana receives biggest-ever audience for a non-entertainment programme – more than 22 million.

1996 Rapper Tupac Shakur murdered.

Charles and Diana divorce.

DJ Shadow, *Endtroducing* – the record collection of Josh Davis, a few thousand hours of textures, hooks, delays, echoes, shadows, beats, twists, sounds, songs, likes, unlikes, loops, wants, guesses, specifications, technical misreads, springs, quotes, lies, phases, phrases, drips, trips, hips, hops, smears, grains, dreams, memories, predictions, shouts, fades, hisses, notes, tones, drones, tapes, trips, rips, slips, signatures, forgeries, sonically compressed into an hour of approximate certainty.

Underworld, *Second Toughest in the Infants*.

Tortoise, *Millions Now Living Will Never Die*. Approximately, vaguely, distantly, remotely, possible, ethereally, Tortoise are the Miles, the Berry, the Beatles, the Can, the Pistols, the Pixies of one of those movement moments in rock's history, when something happens that sounds like the new sound, that sounds like it needs to be called something new, and rock, which is spiralling into control, which has burst into bits and pieces (and the beats and peaces of dance and ambient), has a little spasm of something else, an appropriately jerkless jerk of inactive action, with what became known, quietly, as post-rock, which it isn't, any more or less than anything else since 1953, or '65, or '77, or '89, or next year – it is the knowing sound of a music that knows its past and knows where it is and knows how to move into the future, the academic, fused, measured development of decades of spontaneity, a final gasp of shock, a last glance at the likelihood that rock can transcend its influences, a place where Ry Cooder could be fed through a Soft Machine and turned into something dubbly Neu!, a place where the ocean of rock, connected to an ocean of blues, minimalism, jazz, country, funk and soul, gets washed up on an island all of its own, a place in the middle of everywhere but along way from home – rock has been shipwrecked. If one story of rock is the story that has nothing to do with hits, then that story reaches its glorious anticlimax with Tortoise, who can do strange new things with the idea of the climax. But even as they isolate themselves from the mainstream on their desert island of contemplation and experimentation, the ocean around them washes their ideas vaguely back around the planet, but not so you'd really notice, and somehow this saps their strength.

Tortoise make a big play to be a part of a rock history that was certainly very much in the thoughts and dreams of boy rock writers, but ultimately it remains a kind of fantasy of how mainstream twenty-first-century rock might have been if it had followed the golden route from Neu!, Funkadelic, Steve Reich and Henry Cow via the Pop Group and The Pixies under an Ornette Coleman sky and a Lee Perry sun and a Sun Ra moon, with a hint of the storm of the Stooges, John Coltrane and Faust, to the all-dreaming future. It might have been the progressive rock or the jazz fusion or even the easy listening of its era, but it offers tantalising glimpses of a world where Barclay James

Harvest were influenced by Steve Reich, or where Return to Forever were struck numb by Aphex Twin and Burt Bacharach worked with Jim O'Rourke rather than Elvis Costello.

Commercial rock doesn't really take up the various challenges issued by Tortoise. Instead, rock follows the obvious usual route, gets all super-melodic, hyper-nostalgic and pre-itself by referring back to The Beatles, The Who and The Jam or X.T.C. and Wire, or it takes only the Black Sabbath from Nirvana and not the Raincoat part, or it takes from Radiohead only the melancholy sugar, and none of the vicious sour, and Tortoise are left on their desert island, washed-out if not washed away. Meanwhile, pop carries on as always, blasting the past into the present, caring only about the thrill of sound and the speed of fashion.

The Prodigy, 'Firestarter' – but what sound, pretty much.

The Spice Girls, 'Wannabe' – and what fashion, pretty much.

Tamagotchi virtual pet becomes an instant sensation in Japan.

Julian Opie, *You See an Office Building*.

David Cronenberg, *Crash*.

AOL has 5,000,000 subscribers.

1997 Sheep successfully cloned.

DVD players and movies instant are instant success after cautious launch.

Survivor shown in Sweden; the rest of the world soon follows. A researcher working on the show begins developing a new idea, eventually called *Big Brother*.

Fatboy Slim, *Better Living Through Chemistry*. Norman Cook, the animator of the sonic cartoon Slim, just wants everyone to be friends, and, like a science-fiction Tony Blackburn, a MOR DJ on crack, spins dance music to a programmed processed point midway between funk and fun, blows up a bubblegum big-beat teenybop techno that bounces between Monkee headfuck glee and Chemical Brothers smash and spice, and makes pop art out of mutating happy hooks with demented repetition.

Radiohead, *OK Computer*. The worlds of Wire, *Wired*, the Wire and the World Wide Web all wrapped up in a universe of everything for the boy fan who knows everything, the missing link between a fraud and a masterpiece, between deathly and deathless, between Can and muzak, between the graphic and the non-linear, between the post-rock of Peter Hammill and the rock of Tortoise, between glam and glitch, and, for those of you who really do know everything, between Lard Free and Coldplay, or between Yes' *Relayer* and Porcupine Tree, or between Blodwyn Pig and Aqualung, or between Don McLean and Don Caballero. In a Robbie Williams sense, the missing link between U2 and Aphex Twin.

Spiritualized, *Ladies and Gentlemen We Are Floating in Space*.

Amon Tobin, *Bricolage*.

Daft Punk, 'Around the World'.

Blur, 'Song 2'.

Missy Elliott, 'Supa Dupa Fly'.

Louise Bourgeois, *Spider*.

George Armitage, *Grosse Point Blank*.

James Cameron, *Titanic*.

Don DeLillo, *Underworld*.

Allen Ginsberg dies.

The Verve, 'Bitter Sweet Symphony'. Proving how far the use of sampling has moved outside the world of hip hop and electronic music, the Verve include as a major part of the composition a sample of Andrew Loog Oldham's orchestral instrumental version of the Rolling Stones' 'The Last Time'. The band credit the Stones, but are denied permission to use the sample. When they go ahead, Allen Klein, the sixties manager of the Stones, who owns the copyright, demands and receives 100 per cent of the publishing royalties for 'Bitter Sweet Symphony'.

Launch of British Channel 5; the Spice Girls perform the opening. Princess Diana dies in a car accident. The recording of a rewritten version of 'Candle in the Wind' by Elton John, sung at her funeral, becomes the biggest-selling record of all time.

Palm produces the first hand-held device.

AOL boasts 10,000,000 subscribers.

Eminem performs at the LA Rap Olympics, and finishes second. Dr Dre hears his demo, and signs him to his Aftermath label.

1998 Frank Sinatra dies.

Air, *Moon Safari*.

Mercury Rev, *Deserters' Songs*.

Cher, 'Believe'.

Tracey Emin, *My Bed*.

Geri Halliwell leaves the Spice Girls.

Sol LeWitt, *Progression*.

Last episode of *Seinfeld*.

BSKY launches Sky Digital, its satellite digital television service.

The Coen Brothers, *The Big Lebowski*.

Darren Aronofsky, π.

Apple iMac is launched, becoming the fastest-selling PC in history.

Estimated number of World Wide Web pages: 300 million; 1.5 million added each day.

1999 TLC, *Fanmail*.

Magnetic Fields, *69 Love Songs*.

Add N To X, *Avant Hard*.

Aphex Twin, 'Windowlicker'.

The Cinematic Orchestra, *Motion*.

Madonna, 'Beautiful Stranger'.

Steve Reich, *Reich Remixed*.

Robbie Williams, 'Angels' – the missing link between Benny Hill and George Michael, between wink and wank, between the middle of the road and the end of the pier, between tears and treacle, between Andrew Lloyd Webber and the Who, between the Rubettes and Oasis.

Britney Spears, '. . . Baby One More Time' – originally written with Ritchie Blackmore's Rainbow in mind, but Blackmore, who once played guitar on records made by Joe Meek, didn't look so good in a schoolgirl uniform and Rainbow's singer wasn't so good at twisting every syllable into a fake orgasm. Britney is the missing link between Madonna's navel and Nabokov's most famous novel, between the Madonna who existed just before she didn't exist and the Kylie who existed and didn't exist in much the same way, between a world of pop and a world of suggestion, between virginity and virtuality, between this book about Kylie Minogue and Alvin Lucier and another book about herself and John Cage, between a one-hit wonder and a one-phenomenon wonder, between fame and money, between sex and the city, between fame and loneliness, between Pepsi and Coke, between the meaning of it all and the meaning of her next video.

Moby, *Play* – a classic example of 'innovative, unconventional codes gradually being adopted by the majority'. After Holger Czukay's *Canaxis and Movies* album, after Byrne and Eno's *Bush of Ghosts* album, after different versions of the same idea from Public Enemy to Radiohead and DJ Food, Richard 'Moby' Hall drags the idea of making a fake ethnic record as dreamed by an imaginary culture right into the mainstream. Moby uses more than 200 samples from Alan Lomax's *Sounds of the South* CD box set; he builds compositions around the recordings of field hands and prisoners and eases some borrowed soul into his wishful washed-out electronic music. 'I'm glad there weren't any problems sampling this stuff,' states Moby, sweetly. A buy-out is negotiated with the Alan Lomax foundation, and a flat fee set for royalties. 'Although I'd like to be able to sing like an Afro-American woman, I can't. I found the voices first, and then wrote around them. The sampled voices were the inspiration for the songs in which they're used. The fact that the lyrics were great was sort of a happy accident.' Moby has no doubt he has not stripped the voices of their soul and cultural significance by placing them in the middle of flat-packed modern beats and plumped-up postmodern soundscapes. Initial indifference to the record is replaced with rampant commercial success as every track on the record is licensed for use in commercials and films – in a twisted, time-travelling adventure coordinated by Moby, poor, neglected, uncredited 1930s blues singers end up crooning for American Express, Volkswagen, Reebok, Motorola, Adidas and Audi. 'We said yes to everything because we didn't think the record would sell. It was a way to promote the album after everyone at radio and MTV intitially didn't want to play it.' The music ends up advertising Moby, who becomes a brand just like the ones his music was bought to sell. This example of corporately sponsored, fake-ethnic, ambient business blues ends up selling ten million copies – Moby should give a cut to Eno and Byrne, who should give a cut to Czukay, who should give a cut to Stockhausen, who should give a cut to the spiritual centre of the universe, in the hope that some of that reaches the souls of the singers who originally sang the songs that Moby stole.

Basement Jaxx, *Remedy*.

David Sylvian, *Dead Bees On A Cake*.

Fila Brazilia, *Touch of Cloth*.

Daniel Myrick and Eduardo Sanchez, *The Blair Witch Project*.

Spike Jonze, *Being John Malkovich*.

Jim Jarmusch, *Ghost Dog*.

David Cronenberg, *existenz*.

The Wachowski Brothers, *The Matrix* – 'The Matrix is everywhere. It is all around us, even now in this very room. You can see it when you look out your window, or you turn on your television. You can feel it when you go to work, when you go to church, when you pay your taxes. It is the world that has been pulled over your eyes to blind you from the truth.' The Matrix is designed, like Huxley's brave new world, to oppress you not through totalitarian force but through totalitarian pleasure.

Simon Fuller, S Club 7. What is S Club 7? S is for semi-reality; S is for Simon, who is the group's sovereign source of truth, their manager, their maker, their marker; S is for simulations of the real, for that which never hides the truth but hides the fact that there is none; S is for Simon, who is Agent Smith in *The Matrix*, Simon who aims to take over reality with entertainment, as understood by the S that is his self, Simon who sees songs as cans in a shop, Simon who renders artistic criticism profoundly irrelevant, Simon who pushes MTV back into an old-fashioned past where it began, Simon who breaks pop music into a series of ads for itself, who breaks pop music into a series of fads; S is for the satisfaction that is soon over and must be replaced, by the S for new series, the S for sell sell sell, for the sale of selling, for Simon's shop, full of canned songs, and singers with barcodes stamped into their bodies; S is for Simon says with evangelical indifference.

David Beckham marries Victoria Adams.

Build-up of fear around Y2K.

'Everything has to end – even the twentieth century.'

2000 'The year 2000 will not take place.'

Big Brother begins fully fledged mass reality-TV hysteria. Along with *The Weakest Link*, supplies image addicts with voyeuristic dramatisations of interpersonal betrayal. In the distorting mirror of the camcorder everyone is a star. The revolution might have been televised; the audition certainly is being.

Sony PlayStation 2 launched; uses DVD.

Nintendo sells its 100-millionth GameBoy unit.

Eminem, *The Marshall Mathers LP*. Everyone knows his name, or at least one of his names, and he is the latest greatest figure living in the dream Elvis started having nearly fifty years ago, the latest greatest fictional character acting out the idea of being controversial pop star with something to say, MTV-friendly in an unfriendly kind of way, a funny drummed-up mixture of the fucking pen and, fuck it, the sword. He is, in the Elvis dream, the missing link between the elusive Dean Martin and the post-elusive Dr Dre, which makes him the ultimate American link between Bing Crosby and fucking fuck you.

Clint Mansell, *Soundtrack to Requiem for a Dream*.

Outkast, *Stankonia*.

Yo La Tengo, *And Then Nothing Turned Itself Inside Out*.

Múm, *Yesterday Was Dramatic – Today is OK*.

Common, *Like Water for Chocolate*.

Destiny's Child, 'Say My Name'.

Thomas Grunfeld, *Misfit-Giraffe*.

Barbara Kruger, *Untitled – everything will be okay/everything will work out/everything is fine*.

Lars von Trier, *Dancer in the Dark*.

Christopher Nolan, *Memento*.

In British *Vogue* Kate Moss plays muse to modern British artists, including Tracey Emin, Sarah Morris, the Chapman Brothers and Sam Taylor-Wood; advertising and art merges once and for all just in time for the twenty-first century.

Simon Fuller, Hear'Say. 'Pop music is about celebrity and not just about music any more and people haven't quite figured it out yet.' Brutal realist, greedy egomaniac, ultracamp showbiz amoralist, anti-thought menace, Fuller enlivens decaying music industry by creating an instant powder pop music that does not have to rely on original creative talent to generate the music – music being the least important element in the formula to create stars with addictive qualities and absolutely no complicated, complicating depth. The most important parts of the formula: a low-octane, low-level prettiness, of face, melody and attitude; a ferociously fresh cleanness, of face, hair, teeth, mind, feet, genitals; combined with allusions to sex that are a mixture of corny, discreet and vaguely blatant. Fuller's projects create a union between those who totally believe in the circus, in the fiasco of entertainment, and those who cannot believe that so many young people, volunteering for a new form of national service, wish to make music without any reference to Cochran, Dylan, Reed, Smith, Bowie, Pop, Cobain, Curtis, Eminem. But then Fuller doesn't want talent that shows any sign of thinking – no independent minds, thank you. He wants cheap labour. This isn't even a contemporary version of the Hollywood dream factory. He's sending children up the filthy chimney of dreams and if they're lucky they'll emerge out of the other end not too covered in the soot of disappointment. Most of his talent will get stuck in the chimney.

Fuller viciously mixes exploitative and effectively imprisoning fifties star-processing and deal-making with highly developed twenty-first-century multimedia accessing. He completely bypasses forty years of pop-music development in a slippery move of reductionist genius. There is no sign in his fantasy world of those pop moments – the surprise moments that bring sprinkles of surrealism, radical sensuality, puzzling mind games into everyday homes, that enliven pop, making it more than just business, business as usual, business-minded, business only. Fuller wipes out half a century of instant madness and flash hybrids, of twist and bliss, he reverses, undoes, destroys the hip gyration of Elvis, the highs of Hendrix, the nights together of the Stones, the blows of Iggy, the love of Buzzcocks, the hate of the Sex Pistols, the reinventions of Madonna, the moods of Nirvana, the danger of Dre. Just a drop of the madness of Jackson, Janet or Michael, would be appreciated, a hint of the neediness of a Gallagher or even a Britney. A young Bowie would want to be Aladdin Sane, Ziggy Stardust, other, out there; a Fuller conscript wants to be on time, obedient, groomed, grateful, Cliff, Doris Day. Fuller intends to spoil the fun of pop by determining that pop is simply about fun. He suggests people take pop too seriously by grimly, fearlessly taking out all the wit and imagination channelled into pop since the early part of the twentieth century.

He uses the power pop music has created over the years in feeding into the dreams of young people by denying that such a power ever really existed, and his conclusion seems to be that pop music is about nothing other than money, and money-making, and a few people controlling dreams with no consideration for the value, or the meaning, of the product. The product is just the product. Which is just the product – the singer delivering the product is merely stocking the shelves with the product, and can be replaced at any time with other stockers, if that's not too anti-stockist an attitude. Fuller has in turn twisted to the point of awful honesty the cheating idea of the hit parade – and to him it will always be a hit parade – by attempting to turn it into an endless contest where people vote to create acts who then take up an instant place in the chart. The illusion of choice the charts always represented is taken many deceitful stages further, as consumers are given the feeling that they are choosing the stars, although they are in fact allowed to choose from only a very small set of carefully selected options. Fuller has reduced the charts to its absolute essence in order to feed his insatiable appetite to produce celebrities.

Since the charts always were an industry construct bearing no real relation to any notion of fair play, what he has done, while crude and cynical, is effectively just a radical revision, with an in-built censorship for the troublesome elements of surprise and unpredictability, of the overall scam of pop music. He has performed a kind of hyperreal updating of a system that was getting a little tired, a little quaint, a little unreliable, for a new world where the market's role is to convince us that little exists in the world but the market. The market as defined and designed by the likes of Simon Fuller. He takes MTV a few stages further: not even bothering to pretend to rock-and-roll notions of cool or rebellion or integrity, not even bothering to simulate them, or echo them, or even act as if they ever happened – in fact, they are just an irritation, an obstacle in the way of his processing. He confirms the audience's actual muteness, their true helplessness faced with his scheming, by simulating audience response, with viewers' polls, voting, studio audiences and other forms of bogus interaction. The idea of any diversity of voices or interests is completely eradicated. He has advanced the way that capitalism has exploited oppositional point of view for its own growth, its absorption of pop otherness, of other ideas, of other ways, by getting rid of even a scrap of originality in performance or expression, and pushed us close to the point where any communication is only allowed to happen in order to benefit corporate and institutional profit.

Fuller manufactures a pop endgame – dissolving in a televised instant the fascinating tension between art and commerce, the battle that has played out for fifty years between money and dreams and has thrown up such songs, such worlds, such power. Commerce wins, money takes over; it is a victory for the pop right, the pop straight faces, the pop meanies, the pop spoilsports.

He makes pop seem important by parading it all over live TV, but he has taken away its real importance, as agent of change and missionary of sensation, and turned it into mere TV, just stuff, soap, teen drama, game-show fodder, a perpetual audition, a permanent celebrity factory. Warhol without the framework, or the skeleton, or the distance, or the weightlessness, or the strategy, or the invention, not even the blank expression. Possibly, then, pure Warhol, the anti-art charlatan dust of Warhol, just add water, just add logo, jingle and pose, art with the art taken out, entertainment with the entertainment turned into a tightly formatted eternity of repetition. For Warhol, fifteen minutes of fame was an aphorism, a part of the joke of himself against himself. For Fuller, fifteen minutes of fame is the basis of a business plan, with a veritable Van Gogh of value.

He has developed a plan to conquer a world full of voluntary victims with disposable pop stars carefully stripped of all human texture and edginess – to produce pure image, pure brand, pure digital emptiness, fulfilling William Burroughs' prediction that even more 'sophisticated images' will ultimately 'control you gooks right down to the molecule' by sedating whole populations with easily accessed image fixes. In this sense, Simon Fuller is Burroughs 'death dwarf' blasting out grainless, painless images and manipulating a cosmos of passive voyeurs with simple-minded but devious entertainment. He is the definitive virtual James Bond villain, and may have Cyborg elements implanted into his body – sort of Colonel Tom Parker meets Ed Sullivan, Alan Freed, the Terminator and Rupert Murdoch in a story by Philip K. Dick where the population of the world is lulled by machine-programmed lullabies into believing that everything is all right while the real world rots around them. At this point in time, the world needs a superhero to rescue us from the evil clutches of the maddest person in pop. On the other hand, Fuller might just be destiny, the ultimate shadowy figurehead for the point of pop as a perpetual turnover of repetitive images that simplify grand extravagant impulses into a set of very narrow signals – the faceless face of pop creating images in the image of themselves that are used and discarded like tissue paper. Pop ends not with a bang nor a even a whimper but with an ultimate formula master-minded by the ultimate control freak.

Napster file sharing unnerves music industry.

More than three million blank, recordable CDs are sold monthly. Pop ends not with a bang nor even a whimper but quietly, or loudly, homeless, in the home. It's from 'the home', which is nowhere in sight, unless it's your own, that the art of the bootleg mix appears, whereby anonynmous raiders of the twentieth century, or 'bastards', armed with a decent hard drive, a lust for life, a love of music that borders on the diseased, and a warped sense of humour mash up tracks taken off the Internet, twist genres across themselves, and rewrite musical history in a way musicians would never think of. Access on the Internet to acapella vocals and instrumental backing tracks means that homebodies, who are all in the mind, can ignore legalities and logic and all manner of niceties and splice together any music that takes their fancy. Destiny's Child's horny 'Bootylicious' is mashed in with Nirvana's holy 'Smells Like Teen Spirit' to create 'Smells Like Booty'. Nirvana's Dave Grohl thinks it sounds like 'a fucking mess'. It does and it doesn't. It's a collision of idealistic rock-writing idiocy, nostalgia for musical moments that seem beyond time and place, that aren't about then or then but are about now and here, and non-musical musical passion for the unexpected. It's a hybrid of technological possibility and intimate, mental excitement. Technology can be used to put anything together, within reason, or not – heavy metal gets to meet bubble pop, hip hop gets to meet everything, naturally, this branch of electro sneaks into that branch of electro, sparks fly, sheep are cloned, mated with chickens, country is set in *Musique concrète*, soul mates with illbient, has kittens, the kittens file themselves under Dada, that superstar meets that avant-garde dementia, and in a few far-fetched ways pop completes itself. Pop ends not with a bang nor a whimper but with everything happening at once. It happens in twenty-second bursts of hook and bang, in snatches and scratches of voice and lust, in slaps and slabs of time and space.

In a room, not like the room you are in, using their heads and a sense of where music connects and disconnects, ProTooled-up laptop artists make their contribution to the way music is splitting up into a billion available bits of sound and feeling, fragmenting into the dust of eternity, spiralling into infinity. The craze is swiftly tamed, turned into a commercial promotional add-on, but, for a while, the mating of one song with entirely another, for reasons of sound, seriousness and silliness, creates the true sound of the twenty-first century – pop has been everything for fifty years, and now it can be all this, mixed up to hell, mixed up in heaven, found in the air and remade as lunatic loops of near reality. Some bootleggers, who are actually more librarians of lunacy, cram 100 intros from songs into 12 minutes, recognising that no one has the time to listen to everything unless it is processed into an abbreviated form of excitement that performs its nostalgia fast, so you don't have to leave the present for too long, which is never a particularly good idea. Eminem's 'Without Me' is stuck up and under numerous songs – Led Zeppelin's 'The Wanton Song', Genesis' 'Land of Confusion', Moby's 'Porcelain', the Smiths' 'This Charming Man', Daft Punk's 'Aerodynamic', the Human League's 'Don't You Want Me?' – for reasons that are satirical, musical, historical, hysterical and pointless.

Exponents of the mashing of smashes, the clipping of hits, the mutating of song, the maiming of melody, the fucking of beats, the pummelling of memory – Soulwax, Osymoso, Freelance Hellraisers, Richard X, Ted Shred, Dsisco, themselves a mash-slash mix-up of masked DJs, hackers, surrealists, theorists, imagineers, nerds, historians, comedians, crackpots, futurists and terrorists – are perhaps at the ragtime stage, the race music stage, the skiffle stage of something that will eventually shape the way music is produced and listened to in the twenty-first century. Or they are simply the sonic set's equivalent of trainspotters, laptop fetishists, culture nomads, pop obsessives, introspective exhibitionists, techno aficinados collecting sounds and organising them for a dwindling bunch of fanatics. On the other hand, they are contemporary Dadaists; the Dadaists used their feet or an occasional tram or railway to get them out into the street scenes they wished to testify to, whereas the modem version of transport is the mouse, the keyboard, the modem, the remote control – chrome-wheeled, fuel-injected data-access systems they've learned to skilfully manipulate through the exotic multidimensional virtual passage-ways of the macro-mediascape at full tilt. Meanwhile . . .

Melody Maker folds.

The most-performed song of the twentieth century: 'Happy Birthday'.

Concorde crashes near Paris.

2001 Puff Daddy changes name to P. Diddy.

The Strokes, *Is This It* – rock and stunted growth, rock as stunt, a toy for the boys, the missing link between Television and mastur-bation, between privilege and sacrilege,

Prefuse 73, Vocal Studies and Uprock Narratives. Meanwhile, in another sample of a universe, pop, known for the occasion as sort of hip hop, has a new life inside the laptop, where it will connect with everything, and be known as nothing. Madonna, inciden-tally, has moved into the laptop, at fifty megabytes a second, she's got into the laptop in the way she once got into the groove, and she knows that, inside the laptop, which is the doorway to every-thing, there lie the secrets of all the things she has been inter-ested in – the formulas for fame, self-preservation and immortality using the sound, the body and just the right processed hint of the next big underground thing just as it slips to be the last next big thing. She has evolved in twenty years from the smash-and-flash, pre-AIDS gay underground into the commercial mass of the mainstream and then out there into the digital universe, the image machine reflecting the end of the century and the begin-ning of another by changing as much as the times do, which is all the time. The only apparent flaw in the workings of the image machine of Madonna is that her husband, Guy Ritchie, is not

207

much of a laptop guy, and will not be the right person to direct the right kind of film for Madonna, where she plays a post-gender machine, Misx Symbolic, freshly formed out of a cyber pod, perhaps in the Elvis film after 'How to Build a Universe That Doesn't Fall Apart in Two Days'. This film, *Flux Loopy*, is to be directed by Spike Jonze, with a soundtrack by Chicks on Speed. Elvis plays Flux and songs he sings in the film include John Cale's 'Hello There', The Fall's 'Solicitor in Studio', Boredom's 'Super You', Robert Wyatt's 'Muddy Mouth', Lee Hazlewood's 'Must Have Been Something I Loved', Cat Power's 'Come on in My Kitchen', Swan's 'Children of God', Nick Cave's 'Stranger Than Kindness', Blackalicious' 'It's Going Down', the Jesus & Mary Chain's 'Vegetable Man', Hüsker Du's 'Recurring Dreams', Pavement's 'Shoot the Singer', the Beastie Boys' 'Heart Attack Man', Slade's 'Coz I Luv You', The Butthole Surfers' 'Moving to Florida', Ass Baboon of Venus's '4 AM Coffee Song' and Carl Perkins' 'Let the Juke Box Keep on Playing', which I think gives you a good idea of the plot.

Mario is twenty years old.

Albert Einstein named *Time*'s Man of the Twentieth Century. Annoyingly, he prefers the Strokes to Prefuse 73.

Simon Fuller, *Pop Idol*. The death dwarf's glow continues to grow, an early candidate for man of the twenty-first century as he continues his plot to turn the whole world into an audience surrounded by a screen full of nothing but a smile. Of course, he does not really exist, and by 2004 no one can remember his name, although he runs most of the world even if the universe is beyond him.

Felix da Housecat, *Kittenz and Thee Glitz*. Taking hard house and electronic body music, the unhinged fringe sounds of the early eighties, and editing them into the twenty-first century as if the late eighties and nineties rave and slow dancing had never happened, as if guitars never made a comeback, this creates another genre to name. Rumours abound that those responsible for the lumpy resultant name 'electro-clash' are in fact business consultants, the kind who call mobile-phone companies O2, doing a bit of off-duty brand advising. DJ Hell, the celebrated leader of this nu movement, a German hybrid of high-life playboy and lowlife avant-garde hedonist, likes the name, and it sort of sticks. (A rival consortium attempts to call the music 'synth-core', although 'hard-sizer' might be just as appropriate. Someone suggested 'ghetto tech', but no one was really listening.) No one knows what 'electro-clash' really means, except in the obvious sense of a clash of suicidal new-wave punk NY sensibilities with the electro-strangeness of Cabaret Voltaire and Front 242. It's not that the music suffers from having such a crap name, although the public perspective of it is not helped – the contrived name makes the whole movement seem contrived, when really at its best it's just great crazed, sexed-up tits and bass hyper-power pop with agony and ecstasy knobs on, and when it's better than that – say, with Detroit's Adult – it's just the kind of fucked pop you hoped might have happened in a world where there has been the Human League, Nitzer Ebb, Iggy Pop, Prince and Throbbing Gristle. Fischerspooner – who wetted themselves at the hyped end of the movement, signed up as if they might be the Sex Pistols of the movement, if not the Clash, or at least the Damned, or perhaps Spandau Ballet, if not Duran Duran – are the missing link between Cirque du Soleil and the Tubes, if not the missing link between very early Roxy Music and a very late Jobriath. For the way Fischerspooner mix Kylie, though, tangling her up in boasts of bass and braids of shimmer, they can be forgiven most things.

Röyksopp, *Melody AM*.

Fennesz, *Endless Summer*.

Missy Elliott, 'Get Ur Freak On'. The missing loop between Bessie Smith and Xenakis, between Brown and Beefheart, between Labelle and the lust chord, between ravishing sixteenth-note syncopation and the bending shaking repetition of time, between funk and the future, between disco and saliva, between love and fuck you, too, between the minimal and the maximum, between the Cheshire Cat and Pluto, between sexual tension and the Space Race, between labour and laughter, between focus and restraint, between everything stops, everything goes and everything comes around, between snare and space, between the mute and the note, between random and pattern, between going down and down-tempo, between copyright and copywrong, between the animal and the magical, between post-this and post-that, between genre 002 and genre 342, between the mixing desk and the clitoris, between the body of Prince and the mind of John Cage or vice versa. Pop as art is the sum of its parts plus the sum of its past less the weight of the obvious times the electronic mystery plus the tricking and matching of hormones and tones plus the square root of rhythm and electrics out of the mouth of the future as it plugs into itself, and Missy Elliott responds to 100 years of post-technological music like Picasso responded to centuries of art, by trading in tradition for the imagination, by disintegrating the familiar. She's pro-progress while all the while the Fuller is anti-progress, and she shows how music is a massive library of ideas that can be passed on by methods that are the modern techno-logical equivalent of ancient aural traditions. 'Get Ur Freak On' becomes its own library of music, as it is shared around the world as the basis for a thousand bootleg tributes, creating tributary after tributary of beats and breaks, a dream stream of sonic perversion and sordid sifting, a world of pop of its own, its own genre, its own journey into the future.

Sticky featuring Ms Dynamite, *Boo*.

Wes Anderson, *The Royal Tenenbaums*.

Peter Jackson, *The Lord of the Rings*.

The Coen Brothers, *The Man Who Wasn't There*.

Microsoft's Xbox versus Nintendo's Game Cube.

Tom Cruise divorces Nicole Kidman.

Baz Luhrmann, *Moulin Rouge*. Possibly, at least in the context of the story, the story of stories, the cities of cities, as told in this book, this is the greatest film ever made. The love song turned into movie myth. Kylie Minogue makes an appearance as the Absinthe Fairy: a postmodern, post-hyperreal, post-ordinary, post-this, post-that, post-famous Tinkerbell.

Now That's What I Call Music . . . reaches number 50. The series started back at the tail end of the vinyl years, but thrived in the brand-new era of the compact disc and by the 40s the *Now . . .* albums were often among their respective years' bestsellers.

Now . . . 50 is, despite the world going to hell in a Simon Fuller-designed hand basket, a pop classic containing numerous sophisti-cated pop classics, as well as bundles of trash, showing that, if *Now . . .* has been representative of the death of the old-fashioned 7" single that warped and crackled with sudden life, it has also been responsible for showcasing the rebirth of the single as a compact signal of packaged modern excitement in a world crowded with packaged modern excitement. The single has transformed itself – it's not what it was, it's everything that it is, it's the same as it ever was, it's the world that's got bigger, the technology that's got stronger, the business that's got louder, it's stupid, rubbish, disposable, cynical, glorious, sensational, it's a contradiction in terms, and, whether your point of view is Waterman or Dre, The Beatles or Kraftwerk, Osmonds or T. Rex, Engelbert or Iggy, Lulu or Madonna, Teletubbies or Jilted John, The Stone Roses or The Tremeloes, *Now . . . 50* will remind you why the pop single, three and a bit minutes of commercially organised, deeply flirtatious sound, play and rhyme, has been one of the more successful entertainment forms of the past fifty years.

The track listing for *Now . . . 50*, in reverse order:
Afroman, 'Because I Got High'
The So Solid Crew, '21 Seconds'
Jean Jacques Smoothie, '2 People'
Groove Armada, 'Superstylin''
Daft Punk, 'Digital Love'
The Ones, 'Flawless'
N-Trance, 'Set You Free'
The All Stars, 'Things That Go Bump in the Night'
Geri Halliwell, 'Scream If You Want to Go Faster'
Louise, 'Stuck in the Middle With You'
Victoria Beckham, 'Not Such an Innocent Girl'
Kate Winslet, 'What If'
The Lighthouse Family, 'I Wish I Knew How It Would Be to Feel Free'
Gabrielle, 'Don't Need the Sun to Shine'
Emma Bunton, 'Take My Breath Away'
Jennifer Lopez, 'Ain't It Funny'
Travis, 'Sing'
Wheatus, 'A Little Respect'
Sum 41, 'Fat Lip'
Alien Ant Farm, 'Smooth Criminal'

The Dandy Warhols, 'Bohemian Like You'

OPM, 'Heaven Is a Halfpipe'

Liberty X, 'Think It Over'

Samantha Mumba, 'Baby Come On Over'

Mary J. Blige, 'Family Affair'

Mis-Teeq, 'One Night Stand'

Britney Spears, 'I'm a Slave 4 U'

Eve featuring Gwen Stefani, 'Let Me Blow Ya Mind'

D12, 'Purple Hills'

Destiny's Child, 'Bootylicious'

Jamiroquai, 'Little L'

Superman Lovers, 'Starlight'

Iio, 'Rapture'

Nelly Furtado, 'Turn Out the Light'

Blue, 'If You Come Back'

City High, 'What Would You Do?'

Wyclef Jean, 'Perfect Gentleman'

Sophie Ellis Bextor, 'Take Me Home'

Five, 'Let's Dance'

Steps, 'Chain Reaction'

Bob the Builder, 'Mambo No. 5'

DJ Otzi, 'Hey Baby'

Westlife, 'Uptown Girl'

Kylie Minogue, 'Can't Get You Out of My Head'

Part Three: The journey continues

44

'Oh,' says Kylie, with more than a hint of sarcasm. Her sarcasm seems a little dangerous when you remember that her mind is directly connected to her driving. We are now deep into the city broken up into bits and noise, edited into a fury of beat, commerce and commotion, and I think she needs to keep her senses very much on the road, and the twists and turns she's navigating.

'You finally get to mention me.' She says this in the way only a star, full of herself, full of broken bits of stars, can say it. With such aggressive emphasis on the word 'me' as to suggest that she loves herself, with an intensity that could easily become hate.

'I've been mentioning you a lot,' I gently reply, careful not to say anything that might provoke her further. I need to get her back with me, back on my side. 'And think of everyone who hasn't been mentioned, all the sights and sounds and scenes and happenings that we haven't got space for.'

'Yes,' says Kylie, her voice brimming with fame, fortune and petulance, 'but this book is meant to be all about me.' 'Me' is surely her favourite word. She says it this time in a way that says her favourite sentence is 'Me, me, me'.

'It's my book. My story. My journey.'

'I'm placing you in some kind of context.'

'But what about my life?'

'I'm making your life fit into the story of everything. That should flatter you.'

She blinks with a crisp trace of a click, with a tough distant look space-dusted all over her face that suggests here is a girl who knows what it is to be flattered, and she doesn't feel flattered right now. I defend myself some more, for what it's worth.

'I've put you,' I say, 'in a list along with Picasso, Duchamp, Welles, Kraftwerk, Berners-Lee . . . Musically, you come after Erik Satie, Steve Reich and New Order . . . pop, disco, house, Monroe, Madonna, Blondie, Princess Diana, it all leads to you.'

She is silent. The colour in her cheeks, a smart special effect floating millimetres above her flash face, seems to fade a little, as does the yellow of the car. She seems sad, like the sadness there is in her ballads, even in 'Can't Get You Out of My Head', but without the sense of happiness that there is in the background, round the edges, etched into the rhythm.

'There just doesn't seem to be much information about me, about who I am.'

'What, that you're the missing link between Olivia Newton John and Natalie Imbruglia? That you were turned into the girl next door by the Stock, Aitken & Waterman factory, more a dumb mannequin than a highly sophisticated entertainment womandroid with the physical and mental capacity to achieve image immortality? That you used to be known as the singing budgie? That your first hit was a cover of "The Locomotion"? That Michael Hutchence used to say that his hobby was "corrupting Kylie"? That Madame Tussaud's had to ask people to behave towards your wax model as they would behave towards you in person because the underwear on the dummy was being groped too much?'

I'm being a little snide, and she is obviously hurt by the fact that I've suddenly turned on her. Her skin colour is turning a little too silver, the car's yellow is becoming sour cream. Her showbusiness smile tightens and seems a long way off from ever appearing again.

'Don't forget,' she warns me, showing that she's in complete control of the situation, 'that I haven't yet decided whether you should write the book for me.'

She's right. I've been writing it in my head, but being an advanced FemBot model with special new experimental skills – you should check out the specifications of her powers of persuasion – she has been able to get inside my mind and scan a fantasy printout of what doesn't, as yet, even exist. She is, of course, totally in control of the situation – as of yet, I haven't got the commission. And reminding her of some of the cheap recycled clichés about her life and career is not the right way of going about getting her to give me the commission.

Trying to convince her that I'm the right person to write her book because I am genuinely interested in following a cultural journey that might go from Dali via *Barbarella*, Microsoft and *Vogue* to Kylie, from Debussy to Minogue, isn't really going to work either. What she wants to read is a book that tells the story of Kylie as a mix of the truth and the fantasy, that balances the early reality of her life with the later unreality of her fame, and that manages somehow to perform the trick of making her early life seem unreal and the fame seem real.

She wants to read a story that talks about how she transformed herself from being an exploited, lightweight pop creation, the crude invention of a male-run industry keen on mixing cheap pop sounds with her eager cuteness and mindless optimism, into a pop creator, someone who dreamed up her own version of her own self, exploiting the pop industry around her to create the space that would produce fame on her terms. She wants to read a story that talks about how her mid-nineties song 'Confide in Me' drew the line between the two parts of her pop life – the A B C bland, smiling, clean, innocent, simple old Kylie, appealing to a straightforward quite forgetful audience of teenage girls and a few boys, now replaced with the semi-E'd-up, playful, seductive, knowing, body-conscious new Kylie. A Kylie who appeals to a more sophisticated audience, one constantly searching for different and witty ways of processing pleasure.

A gay audience, who really know their way around pleasure, quickly responded to playful Kylie, high on life and love, and this suggested that she was tapping into something a little more enduring than before. She was making her whole life a performance, and her commitment to this ultimate cause managed to lift her out of the ex-soap-actress pop box and into a new world where the intensity of her self-belief, attached to an inevitable vulnerability connected to the possibility of failure, would transform itself into the flickering magic of pure fame.

Kylie had found her image, an image she could play with, an image her audience could play with, an image based on ideas of desire and mystery, the mystery of desire. She was beginning to develop a look and a sound that suggested she could lead people into a different world, another world, a world of possibility. This is the ultimate thing a pop star does for their audience: to create alternate realities full of enticing, beautiful energies that are very different from any everyday reality.

The businessman wishing to make money out of pop never really understands this – it is always going to be the creative individual who appreciates this, who identifies enough with loneliness and the monotony of everyday reality to be able to slip into a new reality and take people with them. It is always going to be the dreamer who dreams; and some time in the nineties, after the soapy start, the empty teenybop years, Kylie started to dream. She dreamed with her body, she dreamed of ultimate fame, a fame beyond words, and slowly she began to change her reality, with such force that the reality around her started to change.

The dream of the celebrity, the dream of themselves changing the world simply through their fame, can be so strong that sometimes it can actually work. Kylie, once a little bit of air and fluff in the vague, merchandised shape of Madonna, became a substantial commercial-art merging of image and innuendo, with her own shape and her own look based around her own self-determination. Eventually, after songs that were more energy than enigma, more formula than content, she even got her own individual sound. The machine-tooled rhythm and techno-transcendent sound of 'Can't Get You Out of My Head' was borrowed from certain other sources, but blended with remnants of her voice, and stretched around the look in her eyes, it belonged to no one but her, and her dream became electronic, it became digital, able to travel across the world into the mind of everyone, and stay there, glued to the memory, the way stars are stuck to the sky. The virgin princess in an always-diminishing minor celebrity's world became the turned-on, tuned-in virtual queen of the new and endless renewable world of fame, as much a landmark, a cybertourist attraction, as Madonna.

Kylie looks a little happier now. This is the sort of stuff she wants to have in her book. She wants the warm, friendly little details – that her father was fifth-generation Australian and her mother moved to Australia from Wales as a young girl. As a young teenager, Kylie was a fan of Adam Ant – 'I still kind of shudder at his name' – and Siouxsie & the Banshees. The first boy she ever kissed was called David. 'It was a good kiss. He was a bit of a rebel and I thought he was quite exotic with his crazy, curly black hair.'

The light is returning to her eyes, and her skin is becoming more recognisably human. The memory of her first kiss is something she wants in her book more than she wants old news about a four-hour opera by Stockhausen or stories about celebrities and musicians other than her. She doesn't want me to get carried away with writing.

While she is in a better mood, looking at me now from the corners of her eyes as if I might not necessarily be as mad as a writer, I think it would be a good time to mention how you might chart the rise, and fall, and rise of Kylie through her albums, even just the titles of her albums – her debut album was called *Kylie – The Album*, and this was bouncy-bouncy Kylie with a blowdried smile and the hard-working neediness of all ex-child stars, the hope that the success might be maintained by clinging on to the childlike demeanour, the innocence, the life-loving eagerness to please. The big hit was 'I Should Be So Lucky', a song from an imaginary musical about a girl whose whole life had led to fame and success, a fairytale of singing and dancing and acting, and this was the big opening song, and the big closing song, and there wasn't much in between, and there wasn't much to come, but it cheered you up for a while, this part-exuberant blast of sub-sassy tailored noise that announced that here was the girl next door living the life she had only dreamed about.

If this had been the hit in Kylie's one-hit wonder adventure, the novelty song that spun out of her *Neighbours* life, then it would have been remembered quite fondly – a canny attempt to create the sound of Australian sunshine in the damp north of England, a canned-pop fantasy of the goody-goody good life. With hindsight, it might be noticed that, although ninety-nine per cent of the song was sugar-based and greased with artificial flavouring, there was a fugitive one per cent that hinted at the possibility that life could be a little odder, stranger and darker for Kylie, that there could be disappointment in life, and that all might not go well forever. When tucked into her repertoire later in life, and rearranged as a sad slow song sung by someone now bruised by the realities of love, sex and fame, the implication was that the young girl singing her heart out for love and fame had not necessarily been as happy as she seemed. The song fitted into *Kylie!* the upbeat musical, where all that matters is happiness, and it also fitted into the later, odd-beat story of Kylie (!) as the girl who won control of her own destiny but where loneliness is a fact of life.

Her second album was called *Enjoy Yourself*, and that's an order. It was a completely airtight hearty and heartless Stock, Aitken & Waterman production job, so she was trapped in a highly calculating, deeply dull fantasy of what great pop was, and it was all about fun, and then some; a fun that is presented a little too frenetically, a little too fearfully, a fun that celebrates the nowness of fun, a fun that must be changed as quickly as possible into money. The recording of fun that panics because time is running out, and youth doesn't last, and memories fade, and fashion moves on, and replacements are waiting in the wings, and we're not actually sure she can really sing.

It was the cash-in album, the exploitation of Kylie's late-eighties fame that seemed at the time to be about to burn up, leaving just the ashes always left behind by cashing in on temporary fame. If it had all ended here, it would have been a classic end-of-career compilation of professional material made by an ambitious actress who wasn't quite jill of all trades but was superskilled at play-acting versatility and who was never really up to it as singer, celebrity or pop sensation.

Then she met Michael Hutchence, and she was older, and it was the nineties, and the album title was *Rhythm of Love*, and the biggest song from it was 'Better the Devil You Know'. It was still Stock, Aitken & Waterman, waterered-down soul pop with a shopping-centre beat, a seaside-pier sensualism, but it was a little edgier, a little darker than the earlier girl-next-door stuff – Doris Day mixed with the little girl in *The Partridge Family* was now a bit more Lulu, a shade more Bangley. There was a kind of progress to things, there were changes in the way Kylie presented herself, secrets were being kept, sex was being snatched, and savoured, and if the whole Kylie thing had collapsed at this point, then she would have been remembered as more singer than actress, but more Stock, Aitken & Waterman puppet, their Woolie's Madonna, totally connected to their fiercely competent but plastic vision of pop as soundtrack to everyday life.

She had to escape Stock, Aitken & Waterman, and the fourth album, *Let's Get To It*, was half SAW, half-independent Kylie, a hybrid of the cheap plastic and a frustrated emotion, a tense mix of exhilaration and exhaustion – it was the girl leaving home, pulling away from a family who never wanted to believe that she was actually having sex and getting drunk. She was staying out late, and there were one-night stands, and she knew more positions – culturally, musically, emotionally – than her old pop family, the Stock, Aitken & Waterman beast that made music that didn't really stay out after midnight, and they had never actually heard of Kraftwerk, just the Hi-NRG knock-offs, and things had to change.

The fifth album was called *Greatest Hits* – and she'd had quite a few, so it was a good title, and it was a title that announced that Kylie had quite a past, a bit plastic, a bit anonymous, considering how famous she was, and it was a title that said 'There might not necessarily be a future; this might be it'. Had her pop life been over at this point, and it could easily have finished there and then, once the formula of secondhand pop, careful studio contrivance, eighties fame and gentle image-shifting had broken down, then she would have been sort of a Kim Wilde Bananarama Sheena Easton object of remembrance, fixed in time, sexlessly sexy, soullessly soulful, beaten to the back of the mind by the demands of an industry for fresh talent, new beats and younger youngsters. Something – a pretty face, a song to go with it – to be nostalgic about. She would have spent the rest of her life making comebacks, touring on behalf of the good old days, or returning to soap – the hits, and there were plenty of them, but most of them dissolved like sugar, and the ones you remembered were just too sticky to completely dissolve, might not have completely rescued her from a life of playing Charlene. It is worth noting that although some Australian actors who appeared in *Neighbours* went on to have names we might recognise, like Russell Crowe and Guy Pearce, and act out in a big wide world, other ones went on to have names like Jason Donovan, and become the kind of celebrities who eventually have nothing but their past to rely on, a past that was a long time ago, a past that essentially consisted of a part in *Neighbours* and a couple of hits on the back of it.

Kylie as an actress in fiction is more Donovan than Crowe. More TV than film. More pantomime than theatre. What she now had to do was demonstrate that as an actress in non-fiction she was more Madonna and Cher than Sheena or Kim. Of course, she had a go. She kept going. Even after *Neighbours*, after Stock, Aitken & Waterman, after passing through two factories whose attitude towards talent is that you use it up and then dispose of it, she had the energy. The fact that she did have the energy, the mysterious energy of ultimate ambition, is perhaps the clue to why she didn't disappear into the past, but moved into the future, the ever-present of fame.

The *Greatest Hits* album wasn't the end. It wasn't the beginning, either.

It was sort of the end of the beginning. The aim for all female pop singers who have an aim in sight is to create a situation where they are known by just their Christian name. Where that one name is enough for everyone to know who is being talked about. Cher. Madonna. Janet. Kylie had begun her pop life with an album titled *Kylie*. There had been more than twenty hits. But she wasn't really Kylie. Not in an iconic way. She knew it, as well as anyone. Her next album was called *Kylie Minogue* – the statement was: 'I am beginning again, this is my name, and I will try a different way to become just Kylie.'

If we think that perhaps a series of people have played Kylie in the way that different actors play James Bond, Dr Who or Batman, then it is with the *Kylie Minogue* album that the second person appeared to play Kylie. The first person went through *Neighbours*, Stock, Aitken & Waterman, and Hutchence. Now there was a replacement. She was born again. She was on a cooler label, the Deconstruction dance label engineered by Mancunian Hacienda DJ/M People mastermind Mike Pickering, and there was a hipper appreciation of how the Minogue phenomenon could be better exploited in clubs – not as disco music, in the seedy SAW sense, but as dance music, in the abstract, gay-meets-world, rave-meets-night, light-meets-dark way.

After the SAW times of daylight song and dance, Kylie willingly slipped out of the big time, into the night, fell between the grooves, got lost in rhythm, was trying hard for credibility hounded by her previous appearance as the girl next door who needed Michael Hutchence to rough her up a little, and he was hardly Prince, or Bono, he was probably more of a wannabe than she was. She sang a duet with Nick Cave, a very specific act of anti-Waterman rebellion – 'Where the Wild Roses Grow', a tortured, grinding, melodramatic ballad for Cave's *Murder Ballads* album, and she even let Cave kill her in the video. 'Even great beauty,' said Cave, with a degraded seriousness the likes of Pete Waterman would say is the devil's work, 'must die. Look, I am killing Australia's golden girl. I am murdering SAW's pretty pop tart, I am letting the snake of the real world crawl all over her, I am letting the blood of Kylie's optimism leak into the sewer.'

Kylie had embraced the world Waterman loathes, a world where what matters is not success, but art. A world where what counts is originality, not imitation. Content, not form. Meaning, not money. She had broken free of the pop parents who spoiled her with a love that was really a kind of controlling hate. If it had all ended here, in the water where Cave killed her, killed her to preserve for all time her naked beauty, killed her out of a kind of love Pete Waterman could never understand, killed her to release her from the torments of soap fame, then it would have been a perverse end to a quite lightweight pop career, but more strange fun than anything SAW managed to trap with their broad-shouldered machines and their narrow minds.

For a moment it did seem that Cave had killed off Kylie, or at least the career of Kylie. In 1996, for the first time in eight years, Kylie released no records. It did seem that it was all over now, and that Kylie in the future would be just a memory, the girl next door who was all pop, then handed from Waterman to Hutchence to Cave, from one male world to another and then to her final resting place, in the dark cavern of Cave's imagination, where there are cobwebs even Masami Akita would be impressed by. Audiences seemed to want Kylie the life-loving pop girl, the girl who sang straightforward songs slapped and tickled on top of a big and bouncy 4/4 beat, who sang ballads soaked to the skin in preserved sentiment and sweetened shine. This new Kylie was a little tricky, a secondhand Madonna, a little lost, and, if she did live next door, she played music too loud, and kept really late hours, and sometimes looked as if she hadn't slept for a couple of days. Sometimes, like when she had been playing with her unsavoury friend Nick Cave, she looked like death warmed up.

There is always a new Kylie, though. We know that now. Kylie Minogue playing at being Kylie Minogue sheds her skin, and a new Kylie appears, another actress plays Kylie being Kylie, with new skin, a new set of limbs, a new catalogue of poses, a new hungry look in the eyes. She might have been written off after the Cave incident, towards the end of the nineties, as she went all mock-indie and fake-real, but she was just growing new skin, absorbing new information, accepting new programmes.

There was an album to be released in 1997 with the title *Impossible Princess*, featuring a track written by her new indie friend James Dean Bradfield from the Manic Street Preachers called 'Some Kind of Bliss'. This was intended to help launch the ironic, post-pop, post-pap, post-lost Kylie, the girl who had found her feet and her art, the girl who was more moody art-pop Pet Shop Boys happening than grinning Pete Waterman mannequin.

It didn't quite go according to whatever plan was in place. The title of the album was changed after the crash that killed Princess Diana. There could only be one impossible princess in town, and Diana was really dead, really an impossible princess, whereas Kylie had only flirted with a fictional death, and from inside the Kylie camp it looked a little distasteful to be using the word 'princess' at a time when the word had been permanently reserved by the dead Diana. The album, at least in the UK, became the more prosaic *Kylie Minogue*, as plain as the former star now seemed to be, and her song with James Dean Bradfield didn't communicate the basic celebratory bliss generally associated with Kylie. It was a development of the Nick Cave application − serious boy rock singer thinks, in a private moment on his own in his bedroom, 'Wouldn't it be great if cute and malleable pop kitten Kylie was actually a slightly deranged diva with dark dreams and troubled urges? Wouldn't it be something if angelic Kylie was really immense temptress?'

'Some Kind of Bliss' wasn't a SAW-type smash. It wasn't even any kind of Manic Street Preachers-type smash. It was an indie-pop minor hit. And Kylie without smash hits is like Kylie without skin. The hits she has are the flesh on her bones.

By 1998, some writers would mention Kylie and write 'remember her?' in brackets. Her time had come and gone and the hits had dried up and surely there was no more new skin. A song she made with one third of kitsch designers Deee-Lite, Towa Tei, seemed to confirm that Kylie was now out of skin, and well out of the limelight. With hindsight, another way of looking at it was that this collaboration was the ultimate moment of change, and indeed it might well be that the second Kylie playing Kylie who made the *Impossible Princess* album that wasn't and who became known as indie-Kylie was now replaced by a third Kylie playing Kylie, and that the stardom that was ahead began when, with the help of the dotty Tei, she became a font. A font with real front.

Kylie and Tei's song was called 'GBI', and it used the same sample as the Deee-Lite greatest hit 'Groove Is in the Heart', which was either genius or desperation, and in it Kylie played a typeface. She played a typeface called German Bold Italic. As the typeface, she sang the song, about the joys of being a newly invented typeface, as if it was almost a relation of Alvin Lucier's *I am sitting in a room*. In fact, if she had done a version of *I am sitting in a room* it would not have been as far removed from Ramsay Street and the top of the charts as this fractured hybrid of hip-happy techno and post-fashionable experimental absurdism.

45

Hello
My name is German Bold Italic
I am a typeface
Which you have never seen before
Which you have never seen before
I can compliment you well
Especially in red
Extremely in green
Maybe in blue blue blue

You will like my sense of style
You will like my sense of style

I fit like a glove – ooh!

Gut ja!
Gut ja!

46

It was the exact mechanical moment at which the otherworldly actress
Kylie Minogue who was playing a character who just happened to be
called Kylie Minogue found herself in a car on a road not like the road
you are on where she could hear the wheels on a car driven by Kraftwerk
and they were driving towards a city where she could be anything she
wanted to be. A typeface. A superstar. A star-type. A super-face.

47

It looked very strange to the outside world, as if Kylie, who had already
lost her skin, had now lost her marbles, too, and had run away to join
an avant-garde circus. How rebellious was she going to become in order
to get as far away from Pete Waterman as humanly possible? She'd stopped
having hits, she'd allowed Nick Cave to kill her, James Dean Bradfield
to turn her into a bore, she'd stripped away her skin, perhaps the very
essence of her art, the skin that gave her shape and meaning, and now
she was acting like she'd rather be Laurie Anderson than Shirley Bassey.
Pete Waterman's act of revenge on his wayward child star was to form

Steps, sort of five smiling neighbourly Kylie's in one group, a group formed with the understanding that the centre of the pop universe is filled with Abba, with Swedish Motown, with white prepacked soul pop, and to spite Kylie he made damned sure that this new invention had heaps of smash hits, each one a nail in the satin-lined coffin Kylie had been placed in by silly boys who thought that pop should have meaning. When Waterman had his stupidly wonderful Steps cover Kylie's 'Better the Devil You Know', and turned it into their song, their gay anthem, their number one, he was slamming the coffin lid down on Kylie's face once and for all, jumping up and down on it with terrifying glee, stomping out the 4/4 beat of dumb-down disco melodrama on the metal plate on top of the coffin that announced, in German Bold Italic, that Kylie Minogue should be so lucky, lucky, lucky, lucky, she should be so lucky in love. And death.

In the end, it's obvious, but it's true. In the end, as Eno would tell you, you just have to follow where the evidence leads. It wasn't Masami Akita or Nick Cave or James Dean Bradfield (or Zappa, or Eminem, or Bert Jansch, or Madonna, or Ringo Starr, or Courtney Love) who, in this story – which, as you know, is made up, but then, what isn't? – killed Kylie Minogue. It was Pete Waterman. The murder weapon? Steps. He didn't push her down them, he just threw them at her. Cunning bastard. Motive? He felt betrayed by the brazen way in which she turned herself from a fabulous pop star, a living doll, into a fucking piece of fucking typeface. He couldn't stand it any more. He snapped. There's only so much a man can take. He gave her the very skin she danced around in. And she tore it off and flung it in his face and stomped off as the lower-case letter y.

The funny thing was, though, that even as the Steps smashed holes in the charts in ruthless, thrilling, bland point harmony, even as Waterman shrieked at the moon as self-styled mastermind of pop and bounced up and down in a crazed frenzy on top of her coffin, Kylie was still breathing.

48

The warm, frozen I-want-something-if-not-exactly-you-but-you-never-know smile Kylie uses to light up a song, a video, a CD sleeve, a magazine cover, has nearly returned. She's a little concerned that she has almost died – who wouldn't be? – but despite that she's happy that she was being mentioned a lot, which obviously made sense to her, that there will be a lot written about what she was and what she did in what is, after all, her autobiography. She also likes the fact that, actually, she wasn't dead at all. She was about to pull off that most amazing of celebrity tricks: brilliantly enact a successful comeback that produced a fame even bigger and shapelier than the original fame. Pete Waterman might have thought he had performed a great act of revenge on the girl who ran off to be weird, but the girl whom we thought had no skin in fact had more skin than you could ever believe, and, more than that, it was tough skin. She was about to show Pete Waterman what pop superstardom is really all about, and the fact is that true pop stardom, the pop stardom that makes culture-changing history, always relies on a really great piece of music. Not a well-programmed, or well-conceived, or carefully targeted, or efficiently organised piece of music, but a really great piece of music.

I am dying to get to this next part of the story, the story where Kylie – who, in some kind of real world, is not that much more than 150 centimetres tall – grows in size until she is as big, virtually, as a city, a city of fame, under a cloudless sky of success; but I still have to convince Kylie that I'm the right person to tell her story.

I've been saying nice things about her. But is that enough?

One thing I had noticed as I searched my name and my history on the Web, so as to find out who and what I am in order to explain to Kylie why I am qualified to write her book, was the number of mentions that some of my previous books were getting. I've decided to show Kylie some of my previous work. This also means I'll be showing it to you – in the car, you, me, Kylie, we are in the city now where, without really even thinking about it, you can find anything you want, any sound, any opinion, any piece of information, any person. Perhaps we are driving along a street in the city, and this street is in the shape of three extracts from a book I published which was a collection of all the sleevenotes I have written over the past twenty-five years.

I have written more than fifty sleevenotes, for acts such as The Kinks, Magazine, Depeche Mode, The Modern Lovers, Blue Orchids, Josef K, Billy Mackenzie, Pere Ubu, Grace Jones, Comus, Yellow Magic Orchestra, Japan, Art of Noise, Z'Ev, New Order, Joy Division, 23 Skidoo, Ultravox, Cabaret Voltaire, Teenage Jesus and The Jerks, and they were all compiled in a book entitled *Reborn, Relived, Reissued and Rewritten*.

The extracts I want to show Kylie, which form this particular section of the city on the edge of forever, open up on to three of my favourite pop groups, Sparks, the Human League and Fad Gadget; and, as is the way with the city we are inside, the essays are a part of one city that can open up on to other cities, in other worlds, all connected together, all within easy reach. In fact, once you're in the city, the city Kylie has driven us into, everything is within view – the shape of the city is the shape of the mind is the shape of the universe.

I explain to Kylie that I think the pop music of Sparks, The Human League and Fad Gadget supplies clues as to what it is that is so exciting, so alien and glamorous, about her music, and also how her music fits into a map of popular music that is like a map of the city we find ourselves in, surrounded by buildings and words and songs and images and faces and thoughts, and other things that are out of sight, but that can eventually be found with the help of the dream world and the electronic world.

49

SLEEVENOTES: Reborn, Relived, Reissued and Rewritten

Sparks – It's a Mael Mael Mael World

SPARKS TWENTY FLYING FACTS:

'WHO WERE THOSE MARXED MEN?'

1. *Really, it was just Ron and Russell, ex-models, ex-icecream salesmen, ex-anglophile teen nuts, extreme, exactly. Really, it was Ron and Russell. You just had to look, look, look.*
2. *The song titles alone made Sparks* **one of the greatest pop groups of all time***. You just had to laugh. Achoo! (Bless you.)*
3. *It is a mael, mael, mael world. You just have to love it.*
4. *'heartbeatincreasingheartbeat' – you just had to listen.*
5. *What are we talking here? Ha! Between you and me, something somewhere mad soft and shifting that was so hard to describe that it ended up easy to describe. Between you and me, we're in a dream, and so are Sparks. We're sparkling at an elastic point on a sparking line between Walt Disney and David Lynch, between Roxy Music and Stephen Sondheim, between The Bonzo Dog Doo-Dah Band*

and sort of Rundgren at his toddest, between the Monkees and One Flew Over the Cuckoo's Nest, between Scaffold and Salvador Dali, between 1974 and 1976, between Monty Python and Rolf Harris' Cartoon Club, between Gary Glitter and Frank Zappa, between Abbot & Costello and Kurt Vonnegut Junior, between 'This Town Ain't Big Enough for the Both of Us' and 'Looks, Looks, Looks', between po-faced and m for mania, between cheers and tears, between 'Kimono My House' and 'Indiscreet', between Mael and Mael, between meals, between you and me.

POP ART

6. *Todd at his Toddest produced their first record, when they were called Halfnelson. The fact is that the name didn't fly. Sparks do, so Sparks did. 'Their music is so obviously and totally different from anything we've heard before,' said Todd at his fondest. 'Their music is like a pop-art cartoon.' Fast/slow, push/pull, static/active, warm/cold, acid/sweet, and* **nature is so glorious***.*

CAKE

7. *The guy who sang 'I Had Too Much to Dream Last Night' for The Electric Prunes produced their second LP. The first two albums became sort of curious collectors' items, something somewhere between Lothar & the Hand People and 'In the Year 2525'. Ron and Russell were thinking of taking early retirement. Ron would have designed cars, and Russell would have eaten cake.*

TRIP

8. *And then, as these things happen, they came to Britain, where madness is often cherished. It's called the Hendrix Syndrome – you get sold back to your home country, who ignored you as peculiar, as something alien and suspect. And Sparks became known as the best British group ever to come out of America. All Ray Davies, Roy Wood, Pete Townshend and Baby Bowie slipping on a trip through misted B-movie cheap Spectorised psychedelia-ish boom! Thump and tripping on a slip through an artoon comicscape factually spaced-out some-*

where between the jolly Sgt Pepper and the cruel Marquis de Sade. Get the funny picture?

INZANY

9. In 1974, they made 'Kimono My House' – the title being a Mael reference to Rosemary Clooney's 'Come On-a My House'. The opening song, also the opening song of this compilation, is in fact the ideal way to open any compilation of the greatest pop songs of all time. 'This Town Ain't Big Enough for the Both of Us' a startled, shiny/matt, smooth/rough, opaque/translucent, thick/thin, collision-and-bruise song, a crammed scram through the imagined Mael world of inzany pressure and emotional crack. 'heartbeatincreasingheartbeat'. It was a bit of a heart-beating shock to a tamed pop system, and shot Sparks into the charts, just like that.

PRETTY

10. So there they were, all of a sudden, as wonky as the Mothers, as pretty as David Cassidy, and having hit singles that were stained and sprayed with surprise.

CURIOUS

11. This was how the critics tended to write about them when they were turned up all funny and furious and swift and symbolic during '74/'75: '. . . sharp, witty lyrics, intricate tunes and arrangements so tight they are rigid, all served up in the distinctive, rather manic style the band has made its own . . . The high-pitched and high-speed delivery has a curious appeal . . .' Well, that scratched the surface.

THE 1970s

12. In '74/'75 Sparks were teen idols; imagine a group being screamed at like Blue, who sang about a weird world as madly and sadly as The Flaming Lips. Fans were turning away from the Osmonds and Mud to spanky bop-beat to songs about tacky tigers, suicide, stampeding elephants, Yehudi Menuhin and betrayal.

13. *Ron had to tell the* Daily Express *that he was in fact not related to Charlie Chaplin. Of more than 3,000 articles written about the group during '74/'75, only two failed to mention Adolf Hitler. I wonder why Hitler was ever mentioned? It's a mael, mael world.*

14. *They were voted brightest hopes for 1975 in* Melody Maker. *Cockney Rebel were third. Magma were equal eighth with 10cc.*

15. *A popular headline to describe the group at the time was 'RON AND RUSSELL ARE A COUPLE OF BRIGHT SPARKS'. Ron would be compared to a child-molester or an accountant. Russell was the Shirley Temple. The Pretty and the Witty. They explained that their parents were Doris Day and Albert Einstein, and that they would be appearing in Jacques Tati's next film,* Confusion.

16. *Angelic Russell was given his own column in teeny magazine* Mirabelle *and* Valentine*: 'SPARKLING RUSS WRITES TO YOU'.*

   'I really like postcards of dogs, and Lassie is an all-time favourite of mine. Once, I received an autographed photo from him, it had a little black paw print on it, and it said, "Lassie wishes you love and licks." That says it all.'

   You know, it probably did.

17. *If there's a history of pop to be written that is accurate and exciting, Sparks will be in there, cheating and heart-beating near enough to Eno's Roxy, Bolan's Boogie, Barratt's Floyd, Bowie's Pretty Thing, Harley's ego, just over the rainbow from Garland and Piaf and closer than you'd think to The Incredible String Band and The Doors; and as a matter of fact the thing was that they were, in a word,* **electric***. And they were the kind of group who positively influenced plenty of pop to come, from early Queen ('Bohemian Rhapsody' is Sparks without the sparks) to latter-day Depeche Mode.*

18. *Here's what Russell had to say to those people who said that his vocals were unintelligible, just as they were having hits, and selling out concerts, and gazing out from magazine covers . . .*

   'I deit slivijd mdbub fuus idoiala loodoosi fy idildoa aoso slso dodada nosthinj how is the tirghth dnowonv.'

   Said Ron, as close to his brother as he looked far away, 'I echo these sentiments.'

   You know, he probably did.

19. *And then that was that, just about just like that. The tracks on this compilation, made up when they were Islanders, trick up and tick out to us from a moment when everything clicked in time and space, when it was just so the right year or two and the right place for these grand garbled and clear-thinking pop starts to kick in the imagination. As everything rock switched about in a blur of satin and tat from post-Woodstock dizziness to pained punk purpose, from the glitter crazy to the pinned half-crazed, from the brightly lit to the mainly real, Sparks fitted in just right, exactly, extremely, a good time, a good thing, a wonderful freak accident, an anti-bland blast of sarcastic optimism. This was their moment, when a little bit of ambiguous this and uncertain that was just what was needed. They had a few more moments, and they may yet have more. Sparks have never been totally extinguished, because the way they played during the songs presented here meant that there will always be a little space in our pop hearts for their slapsticky wisecracking rave-ups, we'll always be ready for that 'heartbeatincreasingheartbeat'.*

20. *'heartbeatincreasingheartbeat' – I guess you could say that I loved them like brothers.*

The Human League's Greatest Hits

H

H is for human. H is for him and her. H is for heart, hug, honey, here, home, handbag, handsome, hyperreal, hand, hue, history. H is for hundred and hundreds of words beginning with H that tell us so much more than something about the not-happy but not-unhappy world of the hip gloss pop group the Human League. H is for hip: the Human League were hip, and then not hip, and then hip, and then not, and then again, and then hardly, and yet again, and finally beyond hip, virtually iconic, almost heroic, deliriously tragicomic, a moderne European classic.

Put your hand on your heart and hail the gorgeously plugged Human League and love in the privacy of your own head their drugged-on-romance, slightly hurt hits. Music that we listen to in vague order to experience our own desires. The most self-possessed and self-obsessed and image-processed and true-confessed software that you could ever hope to slip into your hardware.

Honestly.

U

U is the first U in the Human League, the U that isn't silent, the U that there is in future, trust, unlikely and beauty.

M

M is for machines have really taken over, but the melodies go on for ever, and a new mix made on new multi-versatile machines can't put a good melody down, and the Human League at their modulated-motive best are the sweetest, sharpest celebration of the coolly late-twentieth-century man-mixed mix of machines and melodies.

And me – and this is Paul writing – I've always felt that Phil Oakey is a little mad, in a positive, enchanting sort of way.

A

. . . and I remember when the Human League began, so late seventies, sullenly fringed and very pre-Tarantino nerdy, all wired up with every-where and nowhere to go, a vulnerable nostalgically futurist model whose boyish crow-baby songs were the stark result of a socket-and-see atti-tude, Yorkshire science fiction with a tacky techy beat and an unkempt vitality, avant-garde fiddling and diddling that was so timid it was fun and catchy, glam rock versus glum rock. They were the sort of lo-lite lowlife Kraftwerk, maimed electro-rock with Northern new-romantic hi-lites, an obscure, accidental charm.

So how come, within three years, so early eighties, they were like a gauzy, cubist, humanised Abba, extrovert rather than introvert, as female as male, quite kempt if not completely chic, so fetching it was far-fetched, and fabulously commercial?

How did this happen?

What on earth did the girls have in those handbags?

Well, what else was going to happen to the Human League?

Thinking about it, there was no other way it could go.

They just became more themselves,

Built in Phil's wonky perfectionist image, based on his belief that addiction to pop songs is a dream thing, the best thing, the only thing.

They just got more Human League. More sophisticated, more plastic, more made-up, more real life, more tarty, more science fiction, more vulnerable, more romantic, more melodramatic, more special effects, more tantalising and titillating nonchalance. Yet, more Yorkshire. And because this was the early eighties, there was more money to spend, more money to borrow. More electronics. More sockets. More plugs. More wires.

The Human League change with the times (adorably, they embody fluctuation), but they are always themselves. So seventies, so eighties, so nineties.

So late-twentieth-century. So pop. (A liquid fantasy world rooted in some kind of hard fact).

So A, aptly, is for apt. The aptness of pop music. (The human mind at play.) Pop music: advertising itself. Augmented in instant instances by the dreamy past, the sudden present and the fatal future. In the charts.

And the Human League, measured by those terms and a few others, are pop artists.

N

N is for so when I'm alone at night, I look out of my window, and it comes to me: we don't have to live great lives, we just have to understand and survive the ones we've got.

Not that this begins with an N, but 'not' does, so there you have it.

Not that this has anything to do with the Human League, but then again, it actually does, so there you have it.

L

L, naturally, is for 'The Lebanon', and this and the zentrally mental 'Being Boiled' are the only two songs on this smart selection that aren't about real love and soapy life. They're about unreal hate and dirty death, sung with deadpan incongruity, reproduced with flashes of Sheffield steel, and they show that there are more things that make our human Phil mad than loss, lies and loneliness.

But then again, love is all that matters.

Love and a slice of lemon. Loosely speaking.

E

E is for the Human League warning us quite early on: ecstasy takes some getting used to.

A

. . . and the answer is: love is a nervous habit.

Another answer: a sort of hungover tenderness.

Another answer: the irony is, everything is synthetic.

Another answer: a promiscuity of image sources and style sources.

G

G is for guys and girls.

1. The glossy Human League are one of the greatest of those great groups who have this poised and flirty male-female combination . . . The Velvet Underground, Talking Heads, New Order, The Pet Shop Boys, Throwing Muses, The Cardigans, The White Stripes, Adult.
2. The guys had heart-to-heart talks and the girls tried on their earrings. Or vice versa.
3. Boy meets girl and love is a dangerous thing.

U

U is for the second U in Human League, the silent U, the secret U, the poignant U, the real U. It is worth sleevenoting that, again, the greatness of the Human League is emphasised by thinking of those other great groups that have two Us in their name . . . Hüsker Du, Pere Ubu, Durutti Column, Culture Club, Ludus, the Sugarcubes, Lulu & the Luvvers (they've got three but who's counting) and U2 (they count, if you think about it).

That the Human League are the only pop group to have two Us, two Es and two As in their name somehow helps seal their greatness.

E

E is for the last letter in the Human League, and E is for an element of technological suavity, and E is for the emotions that these songs give character to – or do our emotions give character to the songs? – and E is for each human being is a world that's peopled, and E for the entertainment of promise, and E is for elegant solutions, and E is for easy complications, and E is for the essence of the Human League that is 'Don't You Want Me', and E is for the end, or, more accurately, E is for the end of part one. Surely the Human League will sing for ever and ever, always entering the future, always ending to begin again, always escaping into themselves, into the spaces and places that exist between people, between lovers, between lives.

See you in eighteen years' time. The end of part two: The Human League, the Las Vegas Years.

The Best of Fad Gadget

Before Fad Gadget, the pop group who lived somewhere sometime between the 1870s and the 2080s, there was a sentence floating in space that both neatly defined the meaning of marvellous and explained something about this marvellous group: 'Beyond entertainment, beyond curiosity, beyond all the emotions such narratives and legends afford, beyond the need to divert, to forget, or to achieve delightful or terrifying sensations, the real goal of the marvellous journey is the total exploration of universal reality.'

Before Fad Gadget, who were formed in the late 1970s, and reformed ever since, there was, at a pinch, Artaud, Bolan and Cale (John). There was Arp, Ballard and Cluster. There was art, the body and causality. There was, clearly, Kraftwerk, and, less clearly, Kafka: Fad Gadget operated at a pace in a place where the most fantastic object in the universe is man, closely followed by machine, closely followed by everything else. There was Wire and wires. There was Pop and Poe. There was Moroder and Marx. There was Suicide and suicide. There was Iggy and the interpretation of dreams. There was Exultation and exhaustion. Hormones and hidden rhythms. There was Cabaret and Calvino. Smirk and smack. Joke and Jung. Gristle and Garland. Seamy and Sparks. McLuhan and Marinetti. Todd and tragedy. Pere Ubu and Pere Ubu. There was, perhaps, Black Sabbath and Burroughs. Abstract concepts. Bizarre phenomena and curious fact and macabre fancy. Emotional impulses.

There was devil as desire.

A nose for trouble.

A head for heights.

A world to consume.

Secrets to uncover.

Blood and shaving foam.

Before Fad Gadget there wasn't really the Beatles, or the Stones, or even the Kinks. There was the Pretty Things. And Scott Walker. (Fad

Gadget, who wore a mask to unmask his true feelings, is the missing link between the Scott Walker of *Scott*, *2*, *3* and *4* and the Scott Walker of *Tilt*.) And Ziggy Stardust. And then there was Lou Reed and the creative imagination as a parasite of reality.

Before Fad Gadget, the man, machine, movement, mentality, mission, there was a world before Fad Gadget. A world he could only imagine adding to, altering, aiding and abetting. It would be lovely to say that the world was never the same after the antics of Fad Gadget precisely because of the antics of Fad Gadget, but that wouldn't be correct. But it wouldn't be entirely incorrect, either, for reasons that are too complicated to go into here, but that hold up well to strong analysis. For most people, Fad Gadget is no one who is nowhere who did nothing. There is some truth in this. There is also no truth whatsoever.

It is where there is no truth whatsoever that the story begins.

Before Fad Gadget, there was the East End of London, teenage years, St Martin's School of Art, Leeds Polytechnic, 1973, 1974, 1975 and 1976. There was glam rock and punk rock, posing, drum machines, tape recorders, Brian Eno and Rough Trade. There was Mark P and the *NME*. There was Monochrome Set and Daniel Miller. There was 1977. Rotten and great.

Then there was Mute Records. Fad Gadget were Mute's first signing. You can guess the rest.

There was Foxx and folk – the Fad Gadget LP *Under The Flag* is strangely a strange English folk masterpiece that conjures up a world where the Incredible String Band influenced the Human League. No one guessed that was coming. Nor indeed the moment when Fad Gadget supported Gary Numan, and the Fad Gadget singer, who may or may not have been party to all the important information about the mood and manner of the group, ripped pubic hairs from his groin and scattered them among the audience. How disconnected was that, incidentally. And yet how political . . . it also didn't happen.[1]

There was Amon Duul, Beuys and Cage . . . and D is for Duchamp, who was a kind of dancer. And Fad danced too, because he was, in a manner of speaking, asked to.

---

[1] I don't know how this fits into the scheme of things, but the last thing Frank ever said to me, a few weeks before he died, suddenly, from heart failure, was that this never happened.

Before Fad Gadget, the one man and his double, there was no need to label and categorise Fad Gadget. If there is a need to do such a thing now, how might we do it? Where do we place this obscure elusive man and his group of minds in a world that likes to put things in their place? Fad Gadget never knew their place – that was part of the charm and challenge of the outfit. But is there a place for them? Where do they fit into the history of things and groups and pop and art and all that?

The fact is, Fad Gadget are so unfittable – not unfit, because that is an entirely different matter – that they seem to fit everywhere. They're pop, avant-pop, electropop, punktronic, folktronic rock'n'roll, cult, pioneer, industrial, ambient, sleaze . . . He's everywhere and nowhere . . . They're all over the list of lists that twist all over the place that there might not be for them . . .

He and they never belonged anywhere in particular but they're embedded into the history of pop music. They're in it up to their necks: all mouth and submerged glory.

For instance: a history of great eccentric-outsider British male performers who sang their own songs that leave behind an important history of post-war feelings and overall human obsessions. They pulled such great faces, too, at established ways, and the establishment. A Top Ten list of suchlike would have to include Roy Harper, Syd Barrett, Kevin Ayers, Robert Wyatt, Peter Hammill, Vic Godard, Howard Devoto, Morrissey, Luke Haines – and Frank Tovey, whose real name, for those of you new to the theatre, is Fad Gadget.[2]

A list of definitive original British electropop pioneers, who pressed the buttons of pop in ways that were simultaneously familiar and unfamiliar, would have to include OMD, The Human League, The Normal, Cabaret Voltaire – and Fad Gadget. And then there was Depeche Mode, who, as you probably guessed, began their pop life supporting Fad Gadget in tiny venues in the middle of nowhere.

A list of post-punk heroes – and villains – would include Siouxsie & the Banshees, The Cure, Joy Division, Echo & the Bunnymen, The Teardrop Explodes – and Fad Gadget.

Sometimes Fad seemed quite Scottish, and you felt they moved through the circle of Josef K and the Fire Engines. They seemed as mad as Spizz, as lonely as Vinni Reilly – whose real name was Durutti Column

---

[2] There he is falling off the stage in the space between birth and death.

– and as shattered as David Sylvian. Sometimes they seemed in the same camp as Soft Cell and other times as happening as The Flying Lizards. They seemed as deft as XTC and then as deviant as The Virgin Prunes. Once or twice you got the vague feeling that a lamb had lied down on broadway and that another name for the group might be The The The.

And all the while they were being themselves.

Then there was Fad Gadget, who you could say is pretty Aronofosky, sweetly Lynch, with a glee of Gilliam. There is a world where Fad Gadget composed the soundtracks for *Lost Highway*, *The Matrix*, *Brazil*, *Natural Born Killers*, *Crash*, *The Wicker Man*. A world where he won an Oscar for his music to the *Shadow of the Vampire* film, and was nominated for something not yet made by Mike Leigh.

Then there were the Pet Shop Boys, who were as cosmically English and as locally artful as Fad Gadget. Then there was Madonna. I'm not going to stretch the point, because it doesn't really need stretching, but it's quite easy to plot a move from Fad Gadget to Madonna. You go from Fad to Mad via Dimitri From Paris and Mirwais. Knowing your Fad Gadget you could hear Daft Punk coming a kilometre away.

You can also travel in nighttime luxury from Fad Gadget to Moby. The route that takes you there passes through Daf, Front 242 and Plaid. You can move from Fad Gadget to DJ Shadow easily enough, as long as you stay in the shadows, and Fad Gadget is an Aphex Twin in shifting body and masticating mind as much as Richard James; he's also a second cousin to a Cocteau Twin in nonsense terms. He's left of the field, he's under the world, he's a twisted firestarter. Fad felt himself, he was just as likely to scrape foetus off the wheel as anyone, he was as tricky as they come, he could make money disappear as quickly as KLF, and there were times when he could go as low as Nick Cave.

And then as low as Leonard Cohen.

And then, stranger, as lowdown as Leadbelly.

As a female entity – talk about issues of identity! – Fad Gadget are as spaced as Laurie Anderson, as cubed as Björk and as batty as Bush. As a monster, Fad cut the ribbon to open the road that led to the Thrill Kill Kult and Velvet Acid Christ, as a dreamer, he saw Legendary Pink Dots before his eyes, and as a cartoon he ripped out the heart of Marilyn Manson. As a pop scientist he was one of the first to add N to X and as an adult pop artist he was a member of the sonic youth controlling his bleeding in the test department. He was a potential Dr Who as much as Dr John or Dr Dre. He's Charlie to the Angels, who are Britney, Missy Elliot and Cat Power. He loved penetration as much as Autechre, the dark as much as Haujobb, the light as much as Air, and nailing space to time as much as Trent Rezner. He fished with spoons, he snared for Venus, and all his clothes were fastened with velcro.

He loved intervals as much as Steve Reich.

There he is in the interval between nowhere and everywhere.

And then there was the big booming hammer of the eighties, and lots of money, and not a lot of money, and there were big heads and small minds, consumer giants and commercial midgets. There was 1984. Designer dreams and new brands of chaos. There was success and failure. Supply and demand. Triumph and disaster. Acceptance and rejection. Expensive habits. Moral decline. Fad Gadget manipulated his body, sometimes he broke his body – he could turn it into a song, sometimes even a musical. He changed his music, the way a man who changed his name often does, and he was – 1985 – deadly serious, quite nervous and quietly hilarious. There was 1986, 1987, 1988, 1989, fools and gold, and Frank started protesting, about you and me and himself and our surroundings, and he never felt more like singing the blues. What was he and they now? The missing link between Lonnie Donegan and Squarepusher? Don't just dance with your body, he implied, dance with your mind as well. The world cracked up like Frank always predicted it would, in his songs, the sound of his songs, the beats to his songs, the pulse and the pain and the mystery.

He hated the cracking up as much as he loved it. He'd been cracking up himself ever since he noticed the cracking up, all those years, and changes, ago.

There he is in the crack between how and why.

And then there were the nineties, and all those technological shifts, with messages and mediums blending and smashing. Frank, so good he named himself a few times, mixed silence and some sound while a pop world busied and bothered itself adding to the images and beats and ways and meanings that Fad Gadget had helped think up all those years, and exploitations, and corruptions, ago.

Before Fad Gadget, the question was: where was Fad Gadget? He was in the hints of things to come. After Fad Gadget, the question is: who is Fad Gadget? The answer is: someone who is in the gaps between everything that has happened in pop music since Kraftwerk, since glam, since punk, since himself. He's the gadget in the machine. He's the fad that never was that's all around us.

Whoever he is, whatever he was, wherever he may be, he's always about to open his mouth again, and play with art, and work at entertainment, and move, marvellously, from a world that is before him, to one that is different.

50

Kylie and I have coffee in a café between Madonna and Monk called Between Life and Death. We are in a city unrooted to any definite spot on the surface of the earth, a city shaped by connectivity and bandwidth rather than by accessibility and land values. The city is largely asynchronous in its operation, and is inhabited by disembodied and fragmented subjects who exist as a collection of aliases and agents. Its places and spaces, the walls and the foundations, were constructed virtually by software instead of physically from stones and timbers, and the places and landmarks are connected by logical linkages rather than by doors, passageways and streets. The city renews itself each day through exchanges of public image and private gestures.

In such a city Kylie could be any size and shape she wants. For now, because she had felt like she might be on show, because she had felt like she might be in the pages of a book written about her life and style, she wants to be the exact size and shape she is in the imagination of her biggest fan. This is how she looks as we chat, as designed and coordinated as she appears in one of her videos, say the one for 'Spinning Around', which was a single released in the year 2000, a song that seemed to seal a kind of comeback, a new kind of Kylie fame, a fame which surely couldn't get any bigger. It was a bit hit, the kind of big hit that covered her with skin, the skin she revealed in the video, the skin of stardom and confidence, the skin of the future.

In a way, with 'Spinning Around' she had come full circle – the song was an echo of the kind of teasing pleasing energy once constructed for her by Stock, Aitken & Waterman, and it expressed a kind of sexual heat and charged enthusiasm that people loved getting from Kylie. But there was an added bonus for this new Kylie: because of what she had gone through since she had fled the Stock, Aitken & Waterman prison, because of the chances she had taken with her image and fortune, because of the way she had shed skin and fame and certainty, because of the fact that she had managed to relight her fame, set herself on fire again, recover herself with the skin of achievement, the skin of success, it all seemed that much more dramatic and satisfying. She was still no Madonna, or, at least, she was just the lightweight Australian version, and her music was still really just a collection of moves and actions crudely cribbed from other movements and acts. But this kind of comeback, from the depths of hasbeen hell, from the obscurity of typeface playacting, had a poignancy about it, certainly for those who pay attention to the fragility of celebrity. It was an act of some kind of courage to begin again her pop career, having broken so many rules, and having broken the ultimate music-industry rule of being a female pop singer relying on the signification of sex to sell herself and actually being over thirty. Ultimately, she had escaped the clammy clutches of the idiotically evil Pete Waterman, and her new success was a brand-new start based on her love for pop, not his.

There might have been elements her love for pop shared with his – the glamour, the beat, the sex, the brightness – but this was a less corrupt kind of pop, a less flat-packed pop. This was the sound of pop alive with the energy and self-belief of someone who had committed themselves to the fantastic transforming power of entertainment. For years, it looked as if Kylie had come to an end, as if it was all over. In fact, it was leading, apparantly, to this moment. The comeback number one, the anti-Waterman exuberance, the Kylie smile that could stretch around the MTV world. We weren't now wondering how the Kylie phenomenon might end, how sadly, or oddly, but were wondering how the Kylie fame might now extend into the middle-of-the-road future. Kylie was breathing again. It wasn't the greatest thing in the world, but there was a certain enjoyment to be had in watching someone rebuild a life of fame, a certain interest to be had in watching someone negotiate the speed and hustle of pop fashion and find a way back in. Kylie now wasn't consigned to the eighties, she hadn't disappeared into the kaleidoscopic nineties, she had made it into the twenty-first century. It was quite an achievement, even if some people suggested that it was merely down to the way she wore a pair a gold hotpants in the 'Spinning Around' video. Kylie, squeezed into a pair of hotpants revealing as much of her brand-new skin as possible, certainly reminded people that Kylie's body pop art was second to none, and that the Kylie comeback had taken a supersonic amount of cheek. Whether it was down to the celebrity skintight hotpants and the way they revealed her innermost secrets of drive and ambition, or whether people were just happy to have happy Kylie back celebrating happiness in exhibitionistic pop form in the way Madonna wasn't doing any more, she was back. She had made it, again. If this had been the extent of her comeback, if it had all just gone this far, that would have been enough. The fact that around the corner she was about to climb into a digital automobile and drive into a digital city broken up into entertainment, retail, social and sexual sectors – the red-light glow above the city was as golden as Kylie's hotpants – had not really occurred to anyone. She had re-established the image of Kylie as pop mistress of zest, against all the odds, and all she had to do now was maintain the energy.

Kylie is sipping coffee in a quiet moment that is almost off-duty, give or take the fact that she's appearing in these very pages and has to keep up a certain level of appearance. She is very close to letting me write her showbiz autobiography. We are having quite a grown-up conversation about it. She quite likes the three pieces about Sparks, The Human League and Fad Gadget, but she has issued me a challenge. She wants me to write a sleevenote for one of her favourite bands.

I ask her who she had in mind.

'The Manic Street Preachers,' she says.

I say, 'I hadn't really thought of putting them in the book.'

She says, 'If you want to write my life story, you're going to have to.'

I say, 'I don't like their music.'

She says, 'It's not necessarily about the music.'

I say, 'What is it about, then?'

She says, 'Just write something about them. I'm not interested in your opinion; that's irrelevant.'

I say, 'My opinion is all I have, as a writer.'

She says, 'There's no real reason why you like, say, the Human League and not the Manic Street Preachers, apart from some strange snobbery, which is completely out of date anyway, because it's much cooler to like the Manics than to like The Human League. The Human League are old. The Manics are new.'

I say, 'There are thousands of reasons why that is just not true.'

She looks at me with two blue eyes that shine out loud with the hardcore persuasion that success brings, and she says, 'Don't be difficult, just write me something about one of my favourite groups. If you like me you'll do it; if you write something nice, think of the bonus points you'll get.'

I say, 'You win.'

She says, 'I always do.'

I'll write about the Manic Street Preachers. I don't really like them, but Kylie is right: I should forget my snobbery, I should do it for her, for her comeback, it'll be my little gift, she likes them, there must be a good story in there somewhere. They're just as much a part of the city as anything else, and even though they might be in a part of the city I don't often go to, I should be able to travel to where they are, and write about the view, a view that contains things of interest, if only because of where they came from, who they wanted to be like, and because their original lead singer went missing, presumed dead, as if the only way he could get to be the rock-and-roll legend he wanted to be was by just not being around any more.

'I'll do it.'

'I knew you would.'

'How did you know?'

'I know what you're thinking.'

'How do you know?'

'That's my secret.'

51
As Welsh as a Title for Some Text in a Book

As Welsh as a photograph.

As Welsh as floating in space.

As Welsh as rain as Welsh as dust as Welsh as sadness as Welsh as sea as Welsh as grass as Welsh as shadows as Welsh as sense as Welsh as mountains as Welsh as views as Welsh as air as Welsh as eyes as Welsh as thought as Welsh as cold as Welsh as the rust that never sleeps as Welsh as the Sunday of life.

As Welsh as 'I would like to say that central to my work is the feeling of awkwardness and self-consciousness that one experiences in the face of profound emotional events in one's life. These experiences, such as death, loss, or sexuality, cannot be supported by a lifestyle that has sought so arduously to deny their meaningfulness, nor by a culture whose fabric is so worn out that its public rituals and attendant symbols do not make for adequate clothing. One, truly, does not know how to act! Each new event is a crisis, and each crisis is a confrontation that fills us with much the same anxiety that we feel, when in a dream, we discover ourselves naked in public.'

As Welsh as morbid associations.

As Welsh as a willingness to use an eclectic range of clashing imagery and subtly ill-matched stylistic conventions; as Welsh as the way different thoughts and images, some erotic, some not, jostle for position in the male psyche.

As Welsh as worry.

As Welsh as truth.

As Welsh as an attention to the activity of sounds.

As Welsh as the dead dead calm.

As Welsh as a pop group.

As Welsh as seeming.

As Welsh as the machine presence in contemporary life.

As Welsh as we are all vulnerable.

As Welsh as a song.

As Welsh as a welcome.

As Welsh as Warhol's Marilyn.

As Welsh as a liking for the complex, the sick, the tatty, the bizarre, the shoddy, the vicious, the overtly or covertly sexual.

As Welsh as somehow his body was intermittent.

As Welsh as naïve imitation.

As Welsh as first thing in the morning.

As Welsh as a world of advertising that cares more for the container than the thing contained.

As Welsh as love.

As Welsh as accepting the glorified legend in preference to the actuality of our immediate experience so much that the legend becomes commonplace and, finally, devoid of the very qualities that first interested us.

As Welsh as disappearance.

As Welsh as the way your gaze hits the side of my face, etc.

As Welsh as life.

As Welsh as mascara.

As Welsh as death.

As Welsh as life and death as Welsh as leftover life to live as Welsh as having no patience to wait for tomorrow.

As Welsh as the bleeding to death of time in slow heartbeats.

As Welsh as 'I want to be your toy'.

As Welsh as a boy's presumption.

As Welsh as junk/television sets/unsold magazines/a dressmaker's dummy wearing a wedding dress/wallpaper showing a pattern of male and female sexual organs.

As Welsh as Jesus Christ and Joseph Beuys and Jayne Mansfield and Jobriath and you sounded so sad on the phone so sad.

As Welsh as something somehow stupid.

As Welsh as transcendence.

As Welsh as a sceptical shy mouth.

As Welsh as 'Come on, baby, light my fire'.

As Welsh as a lifetime's understanding.

As Welsh as coming.

As Welsh as 'Do you think she still loves you?'

As Welsh as Michael Jackson and Bubbles.

As Welsh as an explosion of emotion.

As Welsh as wanting to be loved.

As Welsh as an inside joke.

As Welsh as the middle of the day.

As Welsh as 'Here's the tradition, and we should know about it, but we should also know how we're going to go beyond it'.

As Welsh as an empty room.

As Welsh as the vein-fucked death of Sid Vicious as Welsh as his real name as Welsh as his way as Welsh as the car James Dean drove into fiction as Welsh as the bullet and the car and the plane that kill the famous as Welsh as nothing much happens around here.

As Welsh as a sign of the times.

As Welsh as a word that rhymes.

As Welsh as your secret is safe with me.

As Welsh as the scream as diamond-dust shoes as Exile on Main Street as the rapidity of sleep as raw power as Berlin Alexanderplatz as self-portrait in the nuclear age as The Magic Roundabout as pisschrist as The Naked Lunch as this is England this is how we feel as time takes a cigarette as she is beyond good and evil as we're vacant pretty vacant as a working-class hero is something to be as in every dreamhouse a heartache as Jesus died for somebody's sins but not mine as a surrounded sister.

As Welsh as John Cale.

As Welsh as a scene from a dream.

As Welsh as the sheep arranged romantically in the usual manner on a bleak background of bald stone.

As Welsh as a kind of Kylie clone.

As Welsh as a gang of four.

As Welsh as being stranded.

As Welsh as the soul of an angel.

As Welsh as the candid chronicler of a degraded culture.

As Welsh as selling your soul so utterly you forget it was yours.

As Welsh as a black mirror.

As Welsh as a love–hate relationship.

As Welsh as he lost his mind, undressed, ran away naked.

As Welsh as 'I was loneliness'.

As Welsh as a world bounded by TV and movies and rock and roll.

As Welsh as the use of familiar objects in the light that is not quite.

As Welsh as taking humour seriously.

As Welsh as 'And I could go on as though nothing was wrong'.

As Welsh as looking as Welsh as being looked at as Welsh as wanting to be looked at but not wanting to be looked at as Welsh as posing and supposing as Welsh as 'Are you looking at me?'

As Welsh as a wish.

As Welsh as his bruised limbs his numbered bones his empty head.

As Welsh as 'Boring, isn't it?' as Welsh as this and that thing being the same because they must be.

As Welsh as the 'dead theatre of death'.

As Welsh as a destination for which their whole lives were a preparation.

As Welsh as an urgent dilemma.

As Welsh as a scene from a film.

As Welsh as a slashed wrist.

As Welsh as Shirley Bassey.

As Welsh as a procession of grey shades as a sparse haze as another corner to turn.

As Welsh as being caught in your own mind.

As Welsh as pain.

As Welsh as Marx saying that the commodity appears at first sight a very trivial thing.

As Welsh as 'They all look so pale'.

As Welsh as confession.

As Welsh as myth.

As Welsh as Elvis, The Beatles, Led Zeppelin, The Monkees, The Brady Bunch, Nick Drake, Kung Fu, The Flintstones, *Sonic Youth, Pop Quiz, the Nolans, Salvador Dali, Siouxsie Sioux, The Mothers of Invention, Marie Osmond, The Jesus and Mary Chain, Drew Barrymore, Peter Cook, Phil Spector,* Star Trek, *Dolly Parton, Lenny Bruce, Rita Hayworth, The Pixies, Sweet, Diana Ross, P. J. Proby, Sun Ra, Sonny and Cher, Pere Ubu, River Phoenix, Marvin Gaye,* Smash Hits, Charlie's Angels, *X.*

As Welsh as juxtaposition.

As Welsh as a dream of tremendous statements.

As Welsh as disappearing into a photograph.

As Welsh as meanwhile, the rumours accumulate.

As Welsh as a neat lawn.

As Welsh as a wall.

As Welsh as a pierced whisper.

As Welsh as Top of the Pops *as Welsh as making it as Welsh as hair and rhythm and self-love and tales of melancholy love, revenge, half-seen smiles, misery and stilled confusion, etc.*

As Welsh as change.

As Welsh as resignation.

As Welsh as Robert Smith's 'Wednesday'.

As Welsh as the straight man and the clown.

As Welsh as 'Sell your soul to the company / Who are waiting there / To sell plasticware / And in a week or two / If you make the charts / The girls will tear you apart'.

As Welsh as where you want to go today.

As Welsh as witchcraft.

As Welsh as another photograph.

As Welsh as obviousness or obscurity.

As Welsh as a leopardskin pillbox hat.

As Welsh as pleasure.

As Welsh as the dream images of a collective.

As Welsh as a photographed thought.

As Welsh as 'The movement towards the negation of meaning was exactly what meaning deserved'.

As Welsh as parts of the face.

As Welsh as slipping the reins of my harness.

As Welsh as an array of resemblances.

As Welsh as 'Just what is it that makes today's homes so different, so appealing?'

As Welsh as lies.

As Welsh as kidnap, exile, torture, self-mutilation, and death.

As Welsh as being.

As Welsh as Sylvia Plath (1932–1963).

As Welsh as a pin-up as Welsh as being dead on a wall as Welsh as being trapped in a book of photographs of the present that must become the past however hard you try/smile/sulk.

As Welsh as the space between you and yourself.

As Welsh as the fluid line of Le Corbusier.

As Welsh as Catherine Zeta Jones.

As Welsh as 'I know what it's like to be dead'.

As Welsh as worship.

As Welsh as the youth who has rejected all words that could ever be spoken.

As Welsh as 'They are perfectly safe, this is a photograph'.

As Welsh as fun, fun, fun.

As Welsh as an ever-changing chorus of manic-shaman-rebels promising existential freedom – sex! ecstasy! liberation! – from the endless trudge.

As Welsh as an unlikely world.

As Welsh as the last line of Don DeLillo's Great Jones Street.

As Welsh as appearance.

As Welsh as protest.

As Welsh as the confusion surrounding Brian Jones' death.

As Welsh as keeping in touch.

As Welsh as our days being numbered.

As Welsh as the bare drab rubble of the place.

As Welsh as doom and glamour.

As Welsh as a savage god.

As Welsh as hoping.

As Welsh as the miracle of matter.

As Welsh as a blaze of supernovas.

As Welsh as a sighting.

As Welsh as the man who fell to earth as Welsh as your mind being blown as Welsh as a drive-in Saturday as Welsh as the boys keep swinging.

As Welsh as 'I was interested in endings, in how to survive a dead idea'.

As Welsh as a nostalgia for the present.

As Welsh as going.

As Welsh as a little existential joke about a spot of time.

As Welsh as hate.

As Welsh as Berlin as Welsh as sweet Jane as Welsh as a walk on the wild side as Welsh as a transformation.

As Welsh as a dream of triumphing in collaboration with your friends.

As Welsh as chaotic cool and pseudo revolution.

As Welsh as a postcard from nowhere.

As Welsh as 'Somehow his eyes were the wrong way in'.

As Welsh as a fantasy of fame.

As Welsh as 'We are all pretenders. Don't we all live double lives?' as Welsh as a transparent mask as Welsh as an expression that doesn't yet belong.

As Welsh as Damien Hirst (b. 1965).

As Welsh as a game of hide-and-seek.

As Welsh as very private random little possibilities.

As Welsh as brushing up against ghosts without even knowing it.

As Welsh as 'Dying is nothing, you have to know how to disappear'.

As Welsh as the overflowing of a dream into real life.

As Welsh as last thing at night.

As Welsh as the beginning of time.

As Welsh as the end of innocence.

As Welsh as a blank space.

52

In the centre of a city that is pure comeback, Kylie is suddenly very busy, busy replacing herself with herself faster than she can change her mind, her clothes, her hair, but she manages to get a message to me that she loves the Manic Street Preachers piece, and I have succeeded in whatever challenge it was that she had set me. Apparently, I'm one beat off being chosen to write her book.

I'm a little jumpy. Elsewhere, she has been collaborating with many other artists, writers and entertainers, all of them doing exctly what it is that I want to do: dreaming up interpretations on a variation of Kylie, working out just what it is that makes Kylie – the mind, the body, the performer – tick, and then tock, at just the right moment, with just the right smile, and just the right movement of the hip. A great part of her comeback was a song she sang with the Pet Shop Boys. I can't help feeling that it was the conversations I had been having that led to this collaboration, the way I had been persuading her that it would be better to work with witty electronic art pop rather than with the witless half-bland half-punk of the Manics.

While she was working with the Pet Shop Boys, the singer Neil Tennant had recommended she try their label, Parlophone, as the latest stage on her journey of commercial sponsors. After the freakish factory of PWL, Peter Waterman's label, and the friendly but faddy DeConstruction, it would be a more mature, even more protective and nurturing place to be. Neil, being a gentleman as well as one of the greatest songwriters of his generation, would not mislead her. She took his advice, and Parlophone were interested – it must be said, to their credit, at a time when everyone thought Kylie would never have the right kind of skin again, that she had been consigned to the past, and that she'd already had a second act with no chance of a third. Signing to Parlophone on the advice of Neil Tennant would eventually lead to 'Can't Get You Out of My Head', the flesh of Kylie turned to song, and being the author of this book, and therefore, in this story, the biggest ego in the world, give or take Eno and Dre, I take a small bit of credit for steering her spiritually towards the Pet Shop Boys, who then guided her into their home, a home which had enabled them to flourish as artists and entertainers for twenty years.

Surely this will swing it when it comes to ghostwriting her autobiography.

She is somewhere fluid and free in the city of fame, communicating in little bursts of static, flirt and beat, but I manage to interpret a message I receive from her – sent as she performed live in front of a worldwide audience of four billion at the closing ceremony of the 2000 Sydney Olympic Games, as if she was the biggest pop star in the world – that there is one last challenge.

She wants me to write something, maybe an interview with somebody she likes, where I wasn't so, as she put it, up front, where I manage to communicate intimate, revealing details about the person I'm profiling, and don't reveal anything as such about me.

She wants to see if, in fact, I can be responsible, and not play games, and not pretend I am as important, if not more so, than the subject I'm writing about. Can I make myself more or less invisible, put the spotlight on someone else, when all is said and done do what she wants me to do, get rid of the I of me, and get into the I of another?

In the early eighties I wrote a book called *Ask: The Chatter of Pop*. *Ask* was a selection of interviews with such pop performers as Sting, Iggy Pop, Meatloaf, Peter Gabriel, Grace Jones and Ted Nugent. I like to think I revealed as much about the people I was interviewing as I did about me. I like to think, actually, that I'm a pretty good interviewer, and, even though I don't hide myself, I don't pour myself through the profiles either.

In the nineties, I published a follow-up to *Ask*, *Ask Again: The Splinter of Pop*, another collection of interviews. I get a copy to Kylie while she's filming her cameo for the *Moulin Rouge* film, while she's celebrating joining U2 and Madonna as one of only three entertainers to have hits in the eighties, the nineties and the zeroes. I ask her to read one of the pieces, one about someone she likes.

She chooses Jarvis Cocker.

53
Jarvis on hearing the first question
'Well, I'm just going to have to light a cigarette and think about that, aren't I?'

Jarvis on making an entrance
Jarvis Cocker, the ribald, cerebral entertainer from Sheffield in Yorkshire who once shook something pretty fundamental in the shaky face of Michael

Jackson, makes a deadpan entrance into the wine bar, sort of across himself, looking as if he wants everyone to notice him but no one to make any sort of fuss. He contrives, as is his wont, to look like a cross between a listless terrorist and an ancient puppet, cruel and cuddly all at once. It isn't pushing things too far to suggest, looking at him as he struggles into the wine bar out of the early-evening chill, that he acts as if the native hue of his resolution has long been sicklied over with the pale cast of thought. He's carrying two bulging carrier bags stuffed with books and papers. He might well have just found these in the road.

Jarvis Cocker, the peculiar bugger, looking vaguely harassed, vaguely startled and an absolute expert at finding the more human ways to cope with ennui, has produced yet another successful entrance. No one in the wine bar stares or anything, everyone is very skilled at pretending not to notice him, just as he would want. But in a way, they're all applauding. Applauding Mr Beanpole.

And, in an indifferent way, he is taking a bow, without looking anybody in the eye. Then he finds a table where he can take off his extraordinary costume – there are no two ways about it, he is going to have to disrobe – and settle down to have a glass of red wine and a low-tar cigarette.

Jarvis on being Jarvis

'I've always been Jarvis. I don't know why me mother thought it up. I should ask her, really. It was a terrible cross to bear when I was at school, 'cause our school was pretty normal. Everyone was called John or Andrew. But then, that's part of what you do if you want to become a pop star. You have to take things that are potentially a handicap and exaggerate them so much that in the end they become a selling point. Look at Prince. He's just a little shortarse really. And I'm just a Jarvis.'

Jarvis on his mother

'My father left home when I was seven, so I can't remember much about him. My mother was quite a forceful person and was always trying to get me to come out of my shell. She got married young because I was on the way and I think she felt that she'd missed out on lots of things that she wanted me to experience . . . She would always say, "Why don't you go hitchhiking across France. Go on . . ." She got me a job in the fish market 'cause she thought I was too much of a shrinking violet. She thought it would be good for me to be with the rough market boys. I quite liked it actually. We used to go on this annual fish-market trip to Blackpool and stuff like that and just be really stupid. I never did go hitchhiking across France, though.'

Jarvis on his father (1)

'This is a theory that I've come up with over the past few weeks . . . Maybe because of my father leaving when I was young – and all the fathers round my way did a similar thing; it was as if they were all sat in the pub one night and they all decided to fuck off at once – with my father leaving, maybe that made me think that I didn't want to travel in a straight line or anything. I decided to act in a more exaggerated kind of way because I didn't want to take life seriously. It seemed to me that if you took your life too seriously, like me father, then you ended up in the kind of mess that I wasn't prepared to be involved in. The rigmarole of day-to-day life seemed to go nowhere. Which is kind of a contradiction in terms, considering as I've ended up writing about that kind of everyday life. Maybe I'm fascinated with the everyday because I've never been able to do it. I'm not very everyday. Living a normal life, you know, normal as in just routine, doesn't appeal to me. So in a way it's exotic for me. It's strange and it's that strangeness I'm drawn to writing about.'

Jarvis on dreams and The Monkees

'I've wanted to be in a pop group since I was nine. Maybe I thought it would be like being in a gang. I was always hankering after it. I suppose I thought that if I was in a pop group, I wouldn't have to make an effort getting girls. They would just flock around me. Which is stupid. I used to think lots of stupid things. Like, when I was twelve I thought that when I was famous – this was before video – I would pay somebody to project episodes of *The Monkees* so that I could watch it wherever I went. And then, you see, in a strange way that became true, because a couple of years ago when we were in America they released all the episodes of *The Monkees* in a boxed set and I bought it. So in a way I achieved one of my main ambitions. Of course, I never got around to watching them.'

Jarvis on lifestyle (1)

'I remember seeing a *World in Action* on the Playboy Empire in the early seventies, and it had a marked effect on me. There was this bloke flying around the world playing chess surrounded by shagpile carpets. I thought, "Yeah, that looks all right." The reality of it is something far darker and much more self-deluding. You don't see that when you're young, though, do you?'

Jarvis on trauma

'It's much more traumatic for me to have to go to the supermarket and pick out the food for a week than it is for me to go on a stage. Because I know how it works to go on a stage. I know what you do. It's what I've done the most in my life. That's another thing that occurred to me the other day. I've been doing this pop thing for half my life. Seventeen years. I'm bloody thirty-four . . .'

Jarvis on time

Jarvis Cocker, the thin man who looks as if he's spent a lot of his life kicking his heels and shrugging and assessing and adding up and muttering and stooping and rummaging around and getting nowhere and reckoning and camouflaging and noting and sorting and sighing, is a little late for this appointment, and he'll be a little late for the next one. It's safe to say that, in many ways – and it takes many forms – Jarvis Cocker, the light pessimist, the dark optimist, who's as blunt as he is sharp, has an unusual sense of timing. He's just behind time. And just beyond it. You'd conclude that it is time that has so angled his body and rounded his shoulders.

Jarvis on being thirty-four

'I'm still doing what I'm doing now and I'm thirty-four. By that age me father had married me mother, got divorced and fucked off. I'm still doing this essentially adolescent thing. And sometimes I think I should have just knuckled down and got old in the everyday way and some-times I think, you know, I'm part of some new kind of adulthood. I bloody hope there's a new kind of way of growing old without just sinking away . . .'

Jarvis on punk

'The thing about punk was it got you to question everything. It showed you that you didn't have to go along with the everyday rigmarole. You could stick two fingers up at ever having to fit in. I was too young to ever get properly involved in it at thirteen, fourteen, but I remember that it was a big thing to decide whether you were on the side of punk or whether you were going to stay on the other side and still listen to Lynyrd Skynyrd and stuff like that. Once you'd made that decision, it was for life. It's maybe hard for people now to get their heads around this 'cause there are so many different movements all going on at the same time, giving you these easy opportunities to be different. But back then it wasn't just about what music you were listening to but what path your life was going to take. Once you'd decided to go with punk there was no going back. It influenced everything you did, your whole attitude towards life. And it was exactly the right thing at the right time for me, 'cause I was so awkward that I couldn't hack it in the straight world. And even if I wore normal clothes they didn't look right on me 'cause I was so tall and had glasses and my teeth were all over the place. I was always a figure of fun at school; I felt ugly. So when this thing came along where people were making themselves ugly on purpose it was really liberating. Being a bit of a mess was OK.'

Jarvis on TV (1)

'I could never understand how it worked. Like my mother, I understood how she worked. Because she was obviously a human being, like myself. I could see that. I wasn't that stupid. But a box that you turned on and pictures came on, I just couldn't understand how the pictures got into the box. So it seemed like you should take a lot of notice of this thing. It was almost like a magical thing.'

Jarvis on TV (2)

'The small moments, the small details, the small things of life, they've been important to me from very early on. From a very early age I took a lot of notice of TV, and of songs on the radio, and the way they sort of avoid the small things in life. I built a lot of my expectations about life from the TV and silly love songs. This was a really stupid thing to do. I knew loads of love songs before I even tried to go out with a girl. So comparing a picture of what I thought it would be like to what it actually was like, well, I thought I'd been conned. Considerably conned by pop songs. So my intention has always been to put across what love and girls and all that is actually all about. A bit of grim reality, if you like. I don't know how useful that is in the long run. Perhaps it's nicer for everyone to go along with the illusion. Am I just being a party pooper? I wonder about that. But I can't help it. I like to show up reality.'

Jarvis on TV (3)
'Television always lets you down, doesn't it? It's like when you go to a party, about two o'clock, everyone starts talking about *The Double Deckers* or something like that. But then if you ever see one of those programmes again they're really disappointing. You spend all that time all your youth thinking it was all rather good and it's a bit crushing, really, when they're repeated and you see how crap they actually were. What a waste of time.'

Jarvis on TV (4)
'I'm hoping to move into like a post-television period.'

Jarvis on TV (5)
'I used to think that it was impossible to imagine life without television, but I'm trying to watch less now. It's getting worse, isn't it? I know people always say that when they get older, but as you get older you do realise how TV shows you things but it doesn't give you any understanding of things. It just passes the surface of experience in front of you. And you end up getting people like myself who are jaded without having any real reason to be jaded. You feel that you've seen everything. Seen it all. Of course you haven't. I think I've now learned that real life is more interesting than television. Well, it's summat, innit? Another statement of the bleeding obvious.'

Jarvis on the blindingly obvious
'I'm very good at stating the blindingly obvious. A lot of what I sing about, and talk about in interviews, they're really obvious things. But then, the obvious can often be overlooked.'

Jarvis on the dole
'I always assume that I'll live to be pretty old. Seventy, eighty. Then you're allowed to be really crotchety. I haven't got much excuse now. I can remember feeling really old when I was about twenty-one or twenty-two. I was stuck in this relationship that just refused to die and all of my

friends had gone to university and the bloke I was living with had gone on holiday and I was just stuck in Sheffield for, like, a fortnight and then I realised that I couldn't think of anyone I could go around and visit. So I spent a fortnight in this house on my own and I'm on the dole and I thought to myself, "Well, I'll be on the dole and then the dole will turn into the pension and that will be my life. Then I'll die." Actually, I'm hoping that the dole experience will be good preparation for old age. Eking out an existence with not much money and fuck all to do with your time. Except watch the television.'

Jarvis on who, or what, or why he is (1)

'I mean, I'm a born spectator. I just love to watch. It's safe, innit? And you get to pretend ironic distance from something. As long as you don't get terribly cynical. You have to stay interested in things or you'll never muster up the enthusiasm to get involved.'

Jarvis on form

The wine bar looks a little too good, too French, to be true considering that it's down a sidestreet just a 100 yards from London's Cambridge Circus. The atmosphere of the place, the clutter, the music, the customers, the fact that there are people inside speaking French, that the waitress is palpably pissed off that you cannot correctly pronounce the name of the wine you order, fixes the place as somewhere in the south of France, possibly sometime in the early seventies. Jarvis Cocker, the well-known individual, has chosen the Beaujolais wine bar as a rendezvous, acting as if it makes perfect eccentric sense that this French tourist trap set in the heart of London is the kind of unlikely place he prefers to meet. In some ways, the place, with all its wonky charm and hustly bustle, seems to have tumbled right out of Jarvis's fantasy, out of some crummy sex'n'spy film he saw in the early seventies. It's so old-fashioned and insouciant and stuck in time, but it has its own ingrained sense of dusty, aloof style. Just like Jarvis, the suave, cultured overgrown cad who's always working hard and with such self-consciousness to be sensitive to the civilising influences of the day, or the day before.

Jarvis on his father (2)

'It's hard to work out why I wanted to be so famous in the first place, and what that need has been compensating for. I think if you aspire to fame you are trying to compensate for something that is missing in your life. Or you're trying to prove a point to someone. Maybe now I'm beginning to realise that you don't have to spend your time overcompensating all the time. You can have your faults and maybe you're not that bad after all. You know what I mean? I always felt that I was inferior. Not very worthwhile. I didn't think I had much to give. I've got no practical skills. I can't do any magic tricks or anything.'

Jarvis on girlfriends

'I remember that it took me ages to get a girlfriend and when I finally got one I couldn't handle it 'cause I thought, in a stupid way, "That's it, no problems now, I've got a girlfriend." But the actual hard work comes with trying to keep it together and make it interesting. And it's the same thing with fame, even though I should have learned my lesson by the time fame finally came. But I still thought, "Great, all my problems are over, everything starts now." But in the end I was still left with my shitty personality, but in a new context.'

Jarvis on his feminine side

'That was just an accident, really; because of my father leaving and my uncle dying there was just no father figure around when I grew up. I happened to learn everything about sex and relationships from eavesdropping on my mother and her friends. Everything I discovered was the feminine take on things. Which is no help at all, really, when you start to go out with girls. You're too sensitive. I'd rather have been a brute and ignorant than realising what a cunt I was being.'

Jarvis on his twenty-nine-inch waist

'It's not twenty-nine inches any more.'

Jarvis on men

'I like them when they're skinny. I think men are better-looking when they're thin. Perhaps it's because they look like girls then. I've never had a homosexual relationship. It just never appealed. Maybe homosexuality is something I'll get into in my middle ages. I've just never had the inclination. Maybe I should have done.'

Jarvis on idiocy
'I think you have to run the risk of looking an idiot, otherwise life just wouldn't be interesting.'

Jarvis on being asked if he's a weakly, hypochondriacal kind of guy
'Naah, I'm hard as, me . . .'

Jarvis on who, or what, or why he is (2)
Jarvis Cocker, Hamlet times Bottom, lolls into this faux French plot, this theatrical prop of his, acting as if he is faintly preposterous wearing a floor-length houndstooth check coat buttoned up to the neck and a woollen balaclava. He attempts to discreetly take off this mammoth piece of inexpensive material, and reveals, on the quiet, a brilliant red-satin lining that momentarily lights up the dingy wine bar. Previous owners of this coat, for it is immediately clear that such a coat has a history, might include a 1980s tin-pot dictator, a 1970s Jobriath, a 1960s Dr Who, a 1950s George Melly, a 1940s Jerry Lewis, a 1930s Cab Calloway, a 1920s Harry Houdini, and so on, all the way back to the late 1880s when this coat, this coat that thinly embraces the comedy and tragedy of the entire century, began its existence in the fictional pages of Arthur Conan Doyle or Robert Louis Stevenson. Thick fog seems to seep out from its collar and sleeves.

'It cost me three hundred dollars,' Jarvis, the raving necromantic, admits. 'There's a hat, scarf and pair of trousers that go with it.' The thought of this renders Jarvis and anyone who might be listening speechless for a few seconds. He slumps in his chair. He's a great slumper. His pupils are sad dots floating in watery grey a million melancholy miles the other side of the fat lenses of his chunky, carefully-couldn't-care-less glasses. Look at his feet, if you care to. Even they seem sad. Perhaps it has been arranged to seem that way.

Jarvis on shoes (1)
'Shoes are my favourite item of clothing. I love shoes. Today I'm wearing my geography-master shoes.'

Jarvis on shoes (2)
'They're the hardest thing for a man to buy and for them to look good. Shoes are getting a bit more outlandish now, which is good, but then

they always spoil them by putting big wide toes on them that make you look like a Mr Man or something. There has got to be a middle ground between dire conformity and the "Oh yes, I'm Timmy Mallett" look. In shoes, in everything. There has to be that middle ground.

Jarvis on clothes

'I got a bit disillusioned with punk as fashion after I went to this Stranglers gig in Sheffield and I had a little jacket on and this tie that me mother had knitted and all these fucking stupid Strangler fans in their mohicans were chasing me, going, "Oh you fucking mod", and stuff like that. I was taking punk at face value, that it didn't matter what you looked like as long as you made it up yourself. That you hadn't bought it new off the peg. I think that you can have some really good fun with clothes. You should never take it too seriously, but I never wear clothes as a joke. I like to wear things and think, "Can I get away with this?"'

Jarvis on making it

Jarvis Cocker, the dysfunctional family entertainer with a fringe on top and a cheery sneer down below, takes off his balaclava to reveal dung-coloured hair that creeps in different directions to his body, and a quite-famous head, the kind of head that makes heads turn in not-so-polite society. The head of Jarvis Cocker wasn't always so famous, and it does, famously, have the look of a head that had a long time to wait to be famous. It's full of features but looks as if the features might soon have worn away if fame hadn't surprisingly swooped along to frame this head as oddly appealing. His face looks as though it was suddenly stopped in the middle of a slow, anonymous change. Fame caught him vaguely awares. He spent all of the eighties and half of the nineties as an amateur outsider, a marginal tinkerer, a lush outcast. A bit of a loser. There's still a bit of that bit of a loser in him now. It's difficult to shake off. Thatcher's Britain had defeated his dreams. The same sort of flat-packed change in the air that has led us to New Labour and Cool Britannia, the need for newness, however secondhand, and freshness, however tightly packaged, sort of swept him into power. The dotty trouble-making qualities, arch hedonism, topsy-turvy chic, social interest, working-class wariness and ropy intellectual frankness that had previously doomed him to obscurity – too much meaning, man – were, in a sudden, gradual kind of a way, exactly what made him a flawed and self-deprecating icon for the new world. The new world where everyone under the age of fifty, or fifty-five, and over the age of ten, or five, knew what it was to be hip in a comfortable sort of way, and where a new set of generations fancied a bit of punk spirit but without the, you know, spit and wildness. A new world that needed a few new heroes to tell them where they were, where they'd been, if not quite where they were going. Jarvis Cocker, the un-hoity-toity wit who knows a few things about passionate boredom, a character formed by TV, radio, film and magazines, a culture fanatic steeped in the camp and warped lore of the sixties and seventies as if they really happened, a raving autodidact, a lonely, freakish boy who just wanted some friends, a classic English oddball, became a new hero for the knowing nineties by doing exactly the kind of retroactive, subtle and cantankerous things that not long before had exiled him.

In the end it took a couple of songs, a few gestures, some drunken action, his cranky zeal, the combination of a literal representation of his smart arse and the bizarre participation of Michael Jackson, and an exhausted gaze. And, now that he is famous, as famous as a fantasy, surface calm hides deep qualm about the whole rigmarole.

Jarvis on fame (1)
'Yeah, it was exciting becoming famous and all that stuff, in a way. I would have thought that I would have been quite prepared for it, having waited such a long time. But that made it worse because I'd had plenty of time to build up the illusion of what I thought it would be like. And then, you know, it wasn't like the illusion that I'd had. I wanted the illusion, not the reality. Oh, you know what it's like, and this is the bugger, but when anyone gets famous all they do is start to moan about it. They say things like, "Oh, I can't go to the chippy any more."'

Jarvis on fame (2)
'You think it'll be great going to clubs and everyone knowing you and being really cool – "Yeah, nice one, Jarvis, see ya later" – but in reality it's going into pubs and people saying things like, "How's your mate Michael Jackson getting on, then?" I found it hard to go out. It's a bit of a contradiction because obviously I'm an attention-seeker because

I'm in a band and I go on stage saying, "Oi, listen to me", and I've got the lowdown on what's going on today, but then the way I write or do things is to get into situations and not be the centre of attention. To be invisible. Which is pretty impossible now when I go into a pub and everyone notices. Now I go into a situation and change it immediately, which ain't the point as far as I'm concerned. I've found that a bit hard to get used to.'

Jarvis on fame (3)
'And I still wanted to write songs like I used to, observing things around me. But what was around me was my fame. And I didn't want to start writing whiney songs about the pressure of fame.'

Jarvis on fame (4)
'It's like I always say: "If you do something long enough, you'll eventually be in sync." It's like the watch that's right twice a day. Eventually, I was right. And then I guess I'll be wrong again.'

Jarvis on fame (5)
'You have to resist the thought that you are something because of it. You are, in the end, just saying the kind of things you would be saying anyway. The things you've been saying all along. You've not suddenly become this fabulous sexy aesthetic being or anything.'

Jarvis on fame (6)
'It was always a big thing to be a mainstream success, even when we were on an independent label. I never really wanted to be on an independent label. When I was on the dole I felt that I was one of the invisible mass of people who advertisers never targeted. I always felt that my kind of thing should be in the mainstream. So when all that started to happen, in 1995, it was like some kind of revolution. Punk had finally caught up, or everything had caught up with punk, you know; things could be different. Instead of Phil Collins playing at the Sheffield Arena there was us supporting Oasis and it was exciting . . . But the trouble is, I've felt since that the mainstream has a debilitating effect on everything, a diluting effect. Maybe if things appeal to a lot of people it blands things out. What I wanted, like it said on the back of our last record, was, "We don't want no trouble we just want the

right to be different." That's all. That's what I thought the mainstream could be. Lots of people doing their own thing and being allowed to say their piece, in the mainstream. But the mainstream can never be a wide band of different things. It must by its very nature be homogenous. It brings everything down to its level. It claims you.'

Jarvis on being claimed by the mainstream

'It tries to control you. It's like a thing with its own power. The press is part of it, the way it exhumes your previous life and tries to create your personality for you by the way it covers you. I ended up wanting to lie all the time, to resist the attempt to clean me up and reduce me to, like, this monstrous shorthand. Over time, the same stuff gets written again and again, the same stories and stuff, and it becomes less and less yourself as you know it, that they're talking about this creation, this other thing. I don't even recognise it. What you are becomes dictated to by the media. I thought this might be fun, but it's not. You become a product. The whole thing starts to turn into a series of amusing anecdotes, as if that's my whole life, you know – the time I fell out of a window and ended up in a wheelchair, the time me mother sent me to school in lederhosen, the time I was kidnapped by two blokes, and, oh yes, the time I got on the stage in front of Michael Jackson . . . And soon, there's nothing left of me. In a way, by following the rules like a good boy in the search for fame, you realise that you cheat your own life by turning it into some kind of cheap marketing device.'

Jarvis on fame (7)

'When I ended up in all the tabloids, it was so galling. Because really I'm a very secretive person. And it was just so embarrassing more than anything else. All this personal stuff that was coming out.'

Jarvis on lifestyle (2)

'The problem is that the lifestyle you were aspiring to was art directed, and photographically retouched, and there were models in it, not real people, and you were aspiring to something that never really existed.'

Jarvis on image

'I never subscribed to the David Bowie *Aladdin Sane* split-persona kind of thing. I always wanted the on-stage me to be pretty much as I am –

and it *is* aspects of me, slightly more amplified, but then, well, because more people know that louder, on-stage version of me, then I have to make it a bit louder, so it doesn't get boring, and then that's the one people know, that's the version that's on TV and in the magazines, and in a way it becomes more real than the actual real me. And that version of me is now embodied in the wax figure of myself standing in the Rock Circus in London.'

Jarvis on Jesus

'This bloke asked me how old I was and I said I was going to be thirty-three in a couple of weeks and he said, "Oh you're going to have total trouble." And he laid on me this whole Jesus-age thing. Men are supposed to have some midlife crisis when they get to thirty-three because Jesus was crucified at thirty-three. And you're supposed to look back over your life and measure your achievements and find them wanting in relation to Jesus. Which is pretty obvious, really, because not many people parted the Red Sea or fed the five thousand or whatever. And that got me thinking . . . there's that thing when you're young, you think that you're the only one who has any kind of insight into things, why the fuck can't people see how things are, like me . . . you set yourself up as a bit of a Christlike figure. You think the whole world revolves around you. And I was thinking about that and I decided that I wouldn't like to be Jesus. Because I wouldn't want to be crucified. 'Cause I bet it hurt. I bet it was really painful. And then there was that whole Michael Jackson thing, where I got annoyed because you know it was like he was thinking he was Jesus. I wouldn't like to be Michael Jackson, either.'

Jarvis on Mickey Mouse

'That's the joke of it all. We're getting to the crux of it now. You imagine when you're young that becoming famous will make you completely free. And in a way it actually makes you less free. If you fuck somebody, for instance, the chances are it's going to be in the paper the next day. So, even though you have more opportunities to fuck around like you dreamed of when you were young, you're best advised not to do it. And if people do want to fuck you, well, how do you know it's you, the actual you, who they want to fuck? They might just want to fuck your image. They're not fucking you. They're fucking Mickey Mouse. And then they're making money out of selling the story that they've fucked Mickey Mouse. I don't want to be fucking Mickey Mouse.'

Jarvis on song
Jarvis Cocker, the anxious master of self-absorption, the solipsistic lounge singer who has brought a valiant new torpidity to showbusiness, has finally made a new album with his group, his gang, who were called Pulp long before that made any kind of fashionable sense. He finds himself, with warmth and reluctance, spending the day, and the week, even the month, perhaps the whole year, doing some interviews to think aloud and maybe find out, as he talks, what this new album, *This is Hardcore*, is actually all about. He says that he finds interviews an interesting way to dredge up what the songs are saying, because when they were written, he wasn't really sure. He was just involved in the writing of them, not necessarily the meaning. So as he talks, he finds out whether the album is strong and coherent, and maybe finds out whether other people like it. This worries him much more than he lets on, and he lets on a little. Is it still Pulp time? Is it still Jarvis Cocker time? Or has the Sony retro white-cube digital clock of time, and style, flipped on?

He lights another cigarette and anybody sitting nearby would see how long and narrow his fingers are. Which makes you consider his disconcertingly cute nostrils and his timid yet fruity little mouth. But only for a moment.

The songs Jarvis wrote in the eighties were just about his more smashed Northern self, the bloodless sound of underprivilege. The songs he wrote in the nineties were about losing his self in the lost city of London. And quite enjoying it, what with one craven thing and another. The spy had earned a whole new bunch of privileges. The new set of songs is about how he lost himself to fame and then how he found himself out, and then found himself again, as lost as ever, but on his own terms. It's the soundtrack to a kind of nervous breakdown, and a kind of recovery. It's a phobic extravaganza.

If you've never been a Pulp fan, this album won't particularly change that. If you've toyed with Pulp, then this album will invite further toying. If you like, indeed, love Pulp, then this album won't end the affair. No one tells pop stories as stoically and funnily, as defiantly and casually, as

Jarvis Cocker. Not many pop singers are as maundering and meandering, and who else can be as blissful as when noting the remissions of coping? There's a great deal of fun to be had hearing how he mixes the edgy and the tranquil as he reports back to the real world how hot and cold it is to plunge, overnight after fifteen years, from total obscurity to popular adoration. And, of course, there's the wistful, twisted sex. The subtext – the rub-text – of everything that Jarvis has written, of all the moves he's ever made, is that we are such sexual animals, so driven by sex, and lurking even deeper down is this throbbing notion that life is a sexually transmitted disease that leads, sooner or later, to death. Jarvis Cocker is an orgasm addict – he's always at it, in mind, body or spirit – and he's not afraid to admit it. If he was told that he only had five minutes to live, he'd have a quick wank while thinking such seamy, creamy thoughts. Let's face it, he always looks so damp and, well, depleted. In the end, *This is Hardcore* demonstrates with such awkward smoothness that Jarvis Cocker has had quite a time of it in the past few years. You can hear the screaming and you can hear the chuckling. You fully understand that Jarvis Cocker has nerves of plastic.

Jarvis on This is Hardcore, *which is as ramshackle as ever but somehow also beautifully organised*
'I didn't want to make a mean-spirited album. Obviously, I felt that there were parts of fame that I found distasteful but I thought there would be something very mean about me saying, "Oh, you don't want to aspire to fame, it's shit, you stay in your job at Sainsbury's stacking shelves. Be content with that. It's horrible here being famous." So even though, on a selfish level, there was a lot I had to get out of my system, on a basic therapeutic level, I hope I've managed to do it without being too negative and cynical. It starts out very dark with 'The Fear', which is about these panic attacks you've no doubt read that I was getting. I would think that I was going to die. But then it lightens up.'

Jarvis on This is Hardcore, *which, in the alphabet of what it's all about, as usual has D for doldrums, E for exhibitionism and F for the fluff you pick out of your navel*
'It's saved a lot of analysis. And talking about it I find that it means more to me now than it did at the time. It's starting to make sense. Basically, it's about somebody digging a tunnel out of a prison camp.'

Jarvis on This is Hardcore *answering a question about whether he is digging a tunnel out of the prison camp of fame*

'Well, that's a bit dramatic. But it has been a problem for me, because I wasn't sure that I actually had a life any more to write about that wasn't just a cliché. I want it to be that people can hear the songs and relate them to their own lives. That's very important to me. And the life I've been leading over the past two and a half years has not been the kind most people experience. But most people will quite rightly think, "Well, what's the problem? So you stay in hotels all the time. Great. I wish I could! Shut up, you little git." So not only did I have to deal with this different world but I also had to try and find a way to write about how I was dealing with this different world without it being irrelevant and distant. So, you know, I explored this new world. And I made mistakes. I went to a few celebrity parties, and it might have looked like I was completely in control, but I wasn't. I was losing control. But, you know, I had to experience it. It was offered to me. I couldn't turn into an anorak person and say, "Nope, I'm not interested." So I tried it and became one of those people with the red shiny nose you see in the press in party photographs. I could have gone all the way quite easily. Luckily I had some friends who weren't involved in the music press who gave me some perspective on it all. So I was saved, but then I didn't really know whether I wanted to write about all that shit. So I wasn't sure that I even wanted to make another record.'

Jarvis on This is Hardcore, *which features a drummer with a sense of timing even more intriguing than Jarvis Cocker's*

'I'm glad I made it now that it's out of the way, even though it was very painful. Only time will tell if it's our masterpiece or anything. It would do me in if it didn't do well. But then I have to think of the records that I really treasure, like *Scott 4*, which basically finished off Scott Walker's career. It sold fuck all. I'm sure it must irritate the fuck out of him now to be told that it was his masterpiece. He went through hell for the next fifteen years.'

Jarvis on failure

'Well, if it doesn't do well I'd have to go back on the dole, I suppose. We haven't got that much money because of bad business deals in the past. I'm not a millionaire. I'm not even half a millionaire.'

Jarvis on being told that Pulp's music does have this tendency to sound like a Northern Boomtown Rats or a posh Sham 69 or a scruffy Tin Machine *or all the albums David Bowie ever made, except* Tin Machine, *smeared together*
'Get out of here . . .'

Jarvis on being told that it sounds like he's got a dose of irony fatigue; that, like a lot of great comedians, he's realised that irony is not enough but that what's beyond irony is scary
'You might be on to something there.'

Jarvis on the thing he's enjoyed the most about This is Hardcore *up to now*
'I keep my mouth shut for up to a minute at a time.'

Jarvis on the music
'We're not musicians. It's all about the mood. The mood of the music is more important than what's actually being played. We don't want any muso thing or anything. To me the music should be transparent, in that you cannot imagine it in any other setting. It can only exist to frame those lyrics. Lots of people seem to concentrate on the lyrical part of the songs, but the thing is the lyrics always come after the music has been written. 'Cause I don't sing words when we're writing the songs. I just sort of moan in tune.'

Jarvis on the vinyl age
'I suppose we sound like we belong more to the vinyl age than anything else. It's funny to think that the vinyl age is all over, and to see it so plundered. I wonder what's going to happen once the vinyl age is all used up. Then again, it might take the rest of time to recycle everything that went on during the vinyl age.'

Jarvis on why the song 'Seductive Barry' is nearly nine minutes long
'Well, it's a song about sex, innit, so it had to be long. Sex can some-times last up to nine minutes. Sometimes even longer.'

Jarvis on the last ever Pulp album
'I think you have to treat every album as if it is the last album you'll ever make, otherwise you just can't raise yourself up to the required emotional pitch to actually get the stuff up out of you. I'm not going

to say definitively that this is the last Pulp album ever. It's just a relief to get it out of the way and for it not to be sour or anything. Let's just say it's the last Pulp album of the century.'

Jarvis on who, or what, or why he is (3)
Jarvis Cocker, the woeful, congenial pop star who sure knows how to mar the surface of plausibility, who's gladly soiled the whole convention of glamour in pop and replaced it with a certain pell-mell energy and yet also a cunning kind of deadness, takes another sip of red wine. A man who can quite easily plunge into the intimacy of conversation and talk about himself with a mind that's both absent and present, he knows the value of red wine, even this cheap red wine in this far-fetched wine bar, to help the talk skip merrily and jerkily along. Under his exceptional coat, he's wearing a naturally undersized black mock-velvet jacket, a scratchy-looking sweater the colour of dung, and a pair of black skintight trousers made out of some material that was probably very space age in the year 1961. He doesn't look like someone who has now and then been known to want to nail modern British life down. Then again, he looks exactly as if he is such a fantasy.

Jarvis on marriage
'For obvious reasons, I've always thought that I'll never get married.'

Jarvis on children
'It's something I've thought about recently but it's not something I'll do while I'm still in a group. You might end up writing a song like "Beautiful Boy", which I could never live with.'

Jarvis on New Labour
'When it was coming up to the election I was getting all these calls from New Labour asking me to rock the vote and that kind of shit. I've always voted Labour and wanted them to get in, even though they're pretty dismal now, but I couldn't do it. It just didn't seem appropriate for someone who deals in what I deal with to get up and stand behind that. They even tracked me down to America. I went away to America to get away from things and to think about whether I even wanted to make another record or whether I just wanted to piss off out of it and do something else. And I was staying under an assumed name in the

middle of nowhere and I got this phone call at ten in the morning. It was Olivia from New Labour. "Can we count on your support?" No fucking way.'

Jarvis on DJ-ing

'I like to play new records and all that, and great old stuff. But I love to play Europe's "The Final Countdown". Just for a bit of light relief. I just like the start of that record, and the fact that it's made by these dumb Scandinavian poodle rockers trying to sing this song about going to Venus and maybe you've seen us. Venus and seen us. Great rhyme.'

Jarvis on football

'I'm not that into football. I can get excited when it's the World Cup and all that, and you find yourself succumbing in the strangest ways. But I think that patriotism often manifests itself in the most horrible kind of fascistic way and you don't want to think that you've got any of that inside you. But then if England are 2–1 down in a semifinal you find yourself shouting at the top of your voice. There's something buried deep within you that comes out in those types of situation. If I'd have done the English World Cup song, and in the end you can't resist such a great, corny challenge, I'd have got the whole squad to do a bit of mass singing like on "Back Home". But really I can't imagine me singing on a football song. I suppose stranger things have happened.'

Jarvis on Britpop (1962–1998)

'The only theory I can come up with as to why we have the best music here is because among creative people there is this natural distaste for the establishment and because the establishment in this country is so pukey people here have to invent something for themselves that is positive. If things were more interesting and children got on with their parents and it was a nicer society to live in, people wouldn't need to invent these little subcultures for themselves. The only good things about Britain are all the alternatives to the established society. The subcultures are something to be proud of in this country. The mainstream stuff is pretty atrocious.'

Jarvis Cocker being blindingly obvious (again)

'I used to like Nic Roeg and I like Mike Leigh.'

Jarvis on becoming a film director

'I aspire to it. It's something that I think would be appropriate for me to do in the new millennium. Because a lot of things in my life have been put on old while I'm in a pop group. Like having kids, you know, getting on with the rest of my life.'

Jarvis on Englishness (bad)

'Peter Greenaway is the most horrible example of Englishness 'cause his films are completely passionless. That dry and . . . castrated . . . preciseness. Which is how a lot of foreigners characterise us. And there is that cold thing in us . . . I can be like that. I try and counter it.'

Jarvis on Englishness (good)

'I like the World Service. I really despise the fact that they've put a soap opera onto the World Service.'

Jarvis on The Full Monty

'I've not seen *The Full Monty*. I want to see it. There's a bit of our music in it. Obviously I want to see it to see how Sheffield comes across on celluloid. I'd be interested to see if dumb Americans come over and take a holiday in South Yorkshire expecting to see cheeky characters taking their kecks off and stuff like that.'

Jarvis on Damien Hirst

'I think his interviews are very good. His art is impressive in its scale but I find myself really getting into traditional things. Like I went to that Sensations exhibition and the things I found myself really liking were the paintings. A lot of that other stuff, it's like being told the same joke over and over again. You laugh once and that's kind of it. Whereas painting releases its meaning over a long period of time.'

Jarvis on the year 2000

'Well, we'll have used the old century up, and it will be time to start looking forward. We've all tried to have the last word this century, which has made it an interesting time, but then it's all going to have to change. It will be no good looking back. It will be no good repeating the same mistakes of the past thirty or forty years. As to what the form that things will take after the year 2000, I have no idea. I imagine that there will be a sense of anticlimax. You'll wake up on the first day of 2000 and you won't be wearing a white-nylon spacesuit with a zip up the side and you'll have a hell of a hangover.'

Jarvis on his girlfriend

'She works in mental health. I guess she brings her work home with her. She's not interested in music, so that's really good. I don't bother playing her our music. She's not impressed with what I do. She doesn't like me being famous because she thinks that unsavoury people get involved. And she's right. I can't tell you her name. I've got to keep some things private. I have though, haven't I?'

Jarvis on getting the joke

Jarvis Cocker, the experimental entertainer, the philosopher of misfortune, a man enthralled by his ridiculous memory, who's struggled to feel at ease with his own streaky ill-at-ease-ness, very rarely smiles, and laughs even less. Certainly in public smiles are kept to a tight minimum. He doesn't want to give too much away. The straight face is at the heart of his pop art. When he does smile, or even laugh, it's a choice sight. It's like rock bending. Or is he about to sneeze? It's almost as much a shock as if Buster Keaton was in front of you, forced to smile by circumstances more than politeness. I think it's safe to say that Jarvis Cocker, the pop singer with the appetite for the grits and quiddities of human psychology, smiles more inwardly than he does externally. When he does smile it's as if he has to turn his face inside out, and you can almost hear him creak.

Jarvis on what's it all about, Jarvis?

'Without wanting to sound trite, I would say that the basic message of *This is Hardcore* is: be careful what you hanker after, it may come true. And it won't be quite what you expected. And what the hardcore is, it's the hardcore of who you are, because in the end that's all you've got. And after everything that's happened to me, the life before fame, and then the fame, what's left of me, what carries on after the fun and games, is the hardcore of who I actually am. And there's not a lot I can do about this hardcore. Even if I don't particularly like what's left. I have to get used to it.'

Jarvis on spending an hour and a half in a delightfully seedy wine bar with another journalist

The creaky Jarvis sits opposite me, knowing what's about to come next but not knowing. We try like grown-ups to achieve regular eye contact, and fail like ex-punk misfits. In one of the overstuffed carrier bags that Jarvis has with him there is a copy of a book I wrote a dozen or so years ago called *Ask: The Chatter of Pop*. He says he's just doing his research. Damn – now he knows all my secrets.

In the book, written even before this recent deluge of print and TV and radio locations where people can talk and talk about pop, I pointed out how there was an awful lot of chatter in pop. Even when there was just a handful of music magazines and style glossies and when the mainstream press rarely covered pop, the chatter of pop was ceaseless. A lot of sales talk and self-centring. A lot of hype and hysteria. A lot of lazy lightweight analysis. A lot of useless information. This wasn't necessarily a bad thing. It was just a fact of pop life. Since then, the chatter has got even louder and louder, and more dense, and it's all over the place, and everyone's at it, pop chattering, feeling hip, feeling groovy, saying more and more about less and less. And there among all the chatter, in many ways head and shoulders above it, is Jarvis Cocker, worried to a media sickness that he might be just saying the same old things over and over again. But the media needs chatterers like Jarvis. There's so much space to fill. No one chatters better than Jarvis Cocker, who's got a bit of a twinkle in his throat even as he speaks with broken robotic evenness. He tries not to repeat himself, but there's only so much he can say, only so many things he can make up, only so much personality to project, even for Jarvis. Sometimes, as he's telling one of his stories, you can see he's thinking, 'Oh, I've told this story so many times before. I'm eating myself up. All this talk is making me decay.' But he can't stop. He is a willing victim of the chatter of pop. Up to and including now. After all, even if you do get crucified by the chatter, it doesn't really hurt as much as being crucified on a cross. Does it?

The interview begins. Jarvis Cocker, the crooked pop star with a crooked smile and a crooked outlook, prepares to light up, inhale, and, of course, pose.

I ask the first question.

54

Kylie is singing 'I Should Be So Lucky' like she's eighteen again. She is singing 'Better the Devil You Know' as if she can now think of a kind word or two about her evil pop-father Pete Waterman, as if she has forgiven him, forgiven everyone who has doubted her, dismissed her, ignored her. Including, in a way, herself.

She is singing 'Can't Get You Out of My Head', a pop song that came out of some of the greatest pop songs of all time, out of New Order's 'Blue Monday', out of everything by Kraftwerk, out of Donna Summer's 'I Feel Love', which she is singing as well, because she feels love, because she is inside the love of the world, the love that is reserved for the truly famous, the true stars. She is changing her costumes, new skin is rushing in by the minute, her face is changing, her body is changing, a new Kylie is drafted in to play the new Kylie at the exact moment the video for 'Can't Get You Out of My Head' is first played on MTV; she is surrounded by screens, so many screens there is nowhere for her to go; outside the screen she doesn't exist . . . She is gazing into a void, somewhere between the past and the present, where she is turned into pure light and sound and projected out to the far side of the universe, she is calling her new album *Fever*, a code word for the name of her fame, her name is Kylie, she is a showgirl, she is the top of everybody's wish list, she's everybody's, she's nobody's, she's manipulated, she's manipulator, she's in a dream, she's in everyone's dream, she's everywhere, she's nowhere.

From somewhere – where is vague, as it is bound to be, because Kylie has turned into electronic waves that flow randomly around the outside world – I get a message from Kylie. It comes to me at the exact moment I first hear 'Can't Get You Out of My Head' blended in with New Order's 'Blue Monday', which is, a lot of the time, my favourite piece of pop music by my favourite group. Some of my books have been about the history of New Order, how they were previously Joy Division, my favourite rock group, and how their singer Ian Curtis killed himself. New Order emerged from the crashes of Joy Division playing a music that was the missing link between Kraftwerk and everything electronically great that came afterwards, and overcame the loss of their lead singer by, in a way, replacing him with space, and time, the time and space you find, beautifully, between electronic beats.

Somehow, as I hear Kylie virtually sing her happy song of loss – she's lost her youth, but she must keep going, until the end of time, where there is relief – mixed in with New Order's electrically charged song of loss – they've lost their past but they must keep going, until the end of time, where there is space to breathe – it is as if the the new lead singer of Joy Division is Kylie Minogue, and for private reasons there is something fabulous and irresistible about that. To see and hear the ghost of Joy Division shimmer through the illusion of Kylie Minogue into entertainment immortality is a moment that makes me realise that pop music – call it what you will – creates some of the most magical moments in life, and those moments can be so magical that all you want to do, sometimes, is write about them, hold them in place. You want to explain to yourself just what it is that is so enchanting about music, and the way that music combines with image, and the way that music and image take their places in the city of bits, the bits of our life turned into signals flashed on to screens. Screens that are filled with dreams, dreams screened off from real life.

There is a message from Kylie in the musical merging of 'Can't Get You Out of My Head' and 'Blue Monday'. It is a message sent to me, which is fair enough, because this is my book, and a message to anyone else might have gone astray. The message says: 'You can write my book.' The message says: 'You can come and join me in my car.' As busy as Kylie is, though, as she turns herself into a million blank surfaces for people to project themselves on to – and such transformation takes a lot of work – she finds time to issue instructions: to make sure the book is about her; to make sure it is full of the me of Kylie.

I join her in the car that is about to drive into the city where everything happens at once. She looks at me with a look that means she doesn't have to say anything. Now that I am writing her book, I can read her thoughts.

I answer the question she doesn't even need to ask.

'Yes, the book will be all about you. If I can find you.'

We drive off in silence.

Part Four: The journey continues

55

I've decided to call the book *The History of Popular Music as It Should be Told, from Erik Satie to Kylie Minogue.*

Listen.[a]

Listen to silence. It is the first thing on the soundtrack that goes with this book. A measure of silence.

In that sense we might say that the first piece of music on the soundtrack to this book is *4'33"* by John Cage.[b] This composition suggested that you sit at a piano and play nothing for four minutes and thirty-

---

[a] 'Listen' is an anagram of 'silent'. And so everything is an anagram of everything.

[b] John Cage (born 1912), inspired by the anti-past determination of Claude Debussy, the Dada deeds of the dead-droll Marcel Duchamp, the dramatic sensitivity of the extreme tenderist Erik Satie and the pushy, radical wisdom of the reality-shifting Arnold Schoenberg, thought about sound and music and noise more than anyone you can think of in the twentieth century. What was music? What wasn't music? Therefore he thought about silence more than anyone else in the twentieth century. Thinking about music, about how loud you could get, and about how quiet you could get, how stupid and how serious, meant that his compositions, and his non-compositions, consisted of experiments in the creation of sound and meaning that would liberate what music could be. In some sense, he finished off, rounded off, thoughts and feelings begun around the end of the nineteenth century by Claude Debussy, who had set to demolishing the vast cathedrals of Wagner and the thick blocks of Mahler. Debussy's music was made up out of the sea, the wind, the sky, the sounds in the air. The sounds between the things of life.

Debussy withdrew into music, and let music seep into his being. Cage continued

three seconds – which is in a way sane, and also quite insane, but it is also beautiful and full of bravado, so it's got all the elements of a great piece of popular music. Anything is possible, and at the entreme end of possibility is silence. Silence measured out in time, silence performed,

---

this drift. He searched for sounds that were so natural they seemed unnatural, and moved towards a state of being where there would be no difference between himself and his music. He would be his music; his music would be him. He grew to think that music was thought about thought, that it was a mental consideration of the mental and of the physical. A chance to make the reality of the outside world come closer to the unreality of the inner world: music for the mind, of the mind, where objective sensation melted into subjective reasoning, where the solidness of the environment evaporated into the vagueness of feeling. Where forms of uncertainty dissolved into a certain formlessness. Starting with Debussy, music began to float. It began to melt. It followed the curve of the horizon. It took leaps of faith across time and space and anticipated the edits and the cuts into which the twentieth century – internally and externally – would be broken up.

Cage felt, after Debussy, and then Stravinsky, and then Schoenberg, that music could be anything. It could be about anything. So it could be something. Then it could be nothing. It could be as clear as light. As beautiful as breath. As thoughtful as thought. As accidental as life. As specific as death.

Mostly, and least of all, music could be very loud, very active, very quiet, and very inactive. It happened, because you thought about it. It didn't happen, unless you thought about it. And when you come to think about it, once you have thought enough about the bigness of sound, and then the ever-so smallness, once you have contemplated to an infinite degree the absurdity of sound, and the specialness, then the logical conclusion to all this noise and thinking and preparing, the ultimate conclusion to the problems and solutions of noise, is silence. Cage thought, randomised and composed himself until he found a freedom where he could make as much noise as he wanted to, in whatever way he wanted to, and he could make as little noise as he wanted to. Cage took the silences in the air around us, as sensed by Mozart, as located and distributed by Debussy, and then Satie, and then Ravel – the sultans of quiet, the princes of fuss-lessness – and spread them through his music. The silences got larger. Eventually there was more silence than sound. On 29 August 1952, after Cage had reduced the movement in his music to next to nothing, where his compositions were becoming just a combination of title and leap into the unknown, the pianist David Tudor performed for the first time, in Woodstock, New York, Cage's *4'33"*. The performance, at Black Mountain College, is widely regarded as the first 'happening'. Some listeners at this première were unaware they had heard anything at all, let alone the piece of music that ended music for all time and started it up again.

4'33" is mostly played at the piano, although the score calls for any number of people playing any number of instruments. It is divided into three movements. All of the notes are silent. The composition takes its name from the fact that it requires

silence not taken for granted. Silence counting down to . . . the very thought that you can think of a piece of music that consists of silence.

As you read this book, there might be silence for more than four minutes and thirty-three seconds. Perhaps for you the whole soundtrack

---

four minutes, thirty-three seconds to perform the piece. The pianist uses a stopwatch to control the tempo. They use their own private means to keep a straight face, or whatever type of expression they deem appropriate.

Why is it *four minutes and thirty-three* seconds of silence? Cage said it was just a random length. It might have something to do with the speed of the planet, or the beats of a heart per minute. It might have something to do with the temperature of -273 degrees Fahrenheit, where all motion must stop. Perhaps it has to be this long for everything to resolve. Any longer, it's too serious, or not funny enough. Any shorter, it's too funny, or not serious enough. It is, in the end, exactly the length it should be, because it is the length it is, because this is how long David Tudor read in the score that it should last.

On stage, Tudor happened to lower the lid of his piano. The audience waited. Tudor wasn't waiting. He had begun. As soon as he had lowered the lid of his piano, he had begun. The audience still waited, but Tudor was thirty, forty, fifty seconds into the piece. After thirty seconds, Tudor in fact raised the lid of the piano to signal the end of the first movement. The audience knew they weren't waiting any more, but they weren't sure what had arrived to make them stop waiting. The piano was not being played. Tudor was barely moving. What was he hesitating for? He turned the pages of his score, he lowered the lid of the piano to signal the beginning of the second movement, he raised the lid and lowered it again for the final movement, and he played nothing at all. Raindrops pitter-pattered on the roof of the building. There was a little whispering and muttering from the audience.

Were the audience meant to be listening to Tudor's concentration, or the sound of his breathing? Were they meant to be listening to their own breathing? Or to their own thoughts? Were there ghosts in the room humming with unlikely persistence? Perhaps the sounds to hear were the occasional cough, the murmur of a confused onlooker? Or a door creaking? A snigger? A sigh? Did the piece actually consist of the sound a piece of paper made as it floated gently from the piano to the floor? Had Cage organised that plane passing overhead? What sound, what dreadful, wonderful sound, was about to happen? What was the silence building up to? What enormous climax?

Four minutes and thirty-three seconds later, using a stopwatch to measure the length of each silent movement, Tudor raised the lid of his piano. He had finished. The climax was the most enormous thing of all. It was a hint of infinity, where everything is waiting for everything. Tudor looked a little like he thought he might be shot, but mostly as if he believed he had achieved something. The audience, to an extent, went some way to believing it as well. Some were alert enough to respond with the sound of one-hand clapping. Some, angry and bewildered, simply didn't clap. They didn't like being roped in as collaborators in this empty sham. Some of

to this book will be made up of silence. Perhaps you need peace to read.

But, as you read this true story of popular music from the beginning of time to the end of the world, or from 1903 to 2003, or from this morning to this afternoon, the silence will be invaded. Even if you don't

---

them, somewhere between polite and understanding, clapped in the conventional manner, and thus sealed the notion that a performance is anything you say it is. Everything else is just interpretation. The audience, nonplussed, applauded, and a circuit was completed. Silence existed as art, as entertainment. As history. As a change of mind. An intended lack of intention. Meanwhile, elsewhere, rock and roll, which was very intended, was just beginning to come together in some other areas of the body and mind of America. (The liberating intended lack of intention of Cage and the all-round intoxicating intention of rock and roll would dog each other's steps for a few decades until they came together in a looped copulation of glee planted inside something or other by Missy Elliott.)

Music had gone as far as it could go before it began again. Cage had described silence and suggested that there was no such thing as silence. Cage had written silence, and claimed it was musical. It was a hard thing to do, to write. He knew that people would think it was foolish, but he also knew that it could be the most important thing he ever did. It would be seen as anti-art, anti-music, anti-life – in fact, it was the ultimate celebration of art, music and life.

By exploring silence, and by discovering that the silence of the sky was the limit, Cage became, as a twentieth-century artist, something like the missing link between Claude Debussy and Dr Dre. (This takes some explanation: how do we get from a bad-tempered nineteenth-century French musician who wrote challenging pieces for solo piano, the strangest opera of all time, and the most exquisite mood-altering orchestral explorations, to an ex-member of Niggaz With Attitude whose sole innovation appears to be that in his production he turned the drums up loud? In a footnote the best way to explain this is to say that *it's all in the spaces*. The space between the spaces. The silence before and after the noise. The silence in the noise. The silence that lingers in virtual harmony with the sound.

From where he found himself in time, just a lovely shade ahead of it, Debussy heard space and set it in discreet orchestral motion. Treating time as a toy, Cage captured space and spiritually placed it in a world gone electronically mad. Acting as if he could do time, Dre sampled space, split it apart, and, with an electric crassness bordering on the elegant, tuned up the snare and turned up the bass. This cuts roughly 2,114 stories very short indeed, and in doing so creates another story that will end up being cut, but then, this is a footnote.)

All stimulating modern music passed from Debussy and Ravel and Schoenberg, and passed through the flamboyant central silence of Cage, and became – thanks to a few detours, plug-ins, drugs, programmes, brainstorms and late nights – ambient, trance, hip hop, serial, house, post-rock, avant-pop, and trip hop. (My two-disc discography summing up this magical, humorous journey could consist of Can's *Tago Mago* and Bill Laswell's Miles Davis remix album *Panthalassa*. This will no doubt change

choose to play music, to follow the soundtrack or make up one of your own, music will still fill your mind and make no sound to anyone but you. Remembered music, echoes of sound and song that creep and surge around your brain, and quicken your senses, and fix you in time, and

<hr />

in another footnote. In fact I can feel a change coming on already. A new two-disc discography summing up this alleged trip from 1894 Debussy to twenty-first-century DJ Shadow could consist of Tony Conrad and Faust's *Outside the Dream Syndicate* and Coldcut's *Let Us Play*. Another change of mind leads to a two-disc discography consisting of Tangerine Dream's *Phaedra* and Leftfield's *Leftism*. Two words that would crop up again and again in any description of these works would be 'pulsation' and 'repetition'. The end of any explanation would consist of the following two sentences: The people who taught us to count were being very kind. Meanwhile, the only certain thing about the future is that things will happen again and again in slightly different, occasionally very different, ways, things will fork off and join up and fork off and join up, and then things will stop happening again and again.)

This being a universe of surprise, something you can rely on in moments of panic and fear, John Cage eventually ended up as a character in David E. Kelley's TV lawyer fantasy *Ally McBeal*. Set in a heartbreak office in downtown make-believe, *Ally McBeal* is a fine, profoundly trivial blend of freakshow, musical comedy, art soap, glossy drama, whipped dream, wistful thinking, sentiment and sensation. Of the regular characters making their fretty, conniving way through life as if it's all a matter of love and work – which is a kind of drained truth – my favourite is the arch misfit who just happens to be called John Cage. Frog-loving, toilet-obsessed Cage is a bloodless bundle of tics, habits, fears and fury who appears to be able to achieve an erection only if he imagines that Barry White is the room with him singing 'Can't Get Enough of Your Love'. He's as batty as a bitten bat, but essentially he's a good, caring, bright man adrift in a bad, careless, dull world. He's a very gentle psycho with a heart of pure gold.

Kelley is a subtle postmodern farceur who has created a world loosely based on this world where everything means as much as anything can ever mean in a world loosely based on another world. So you wonder how much you can read into the fact that the oddest, maddest, daftest character in a show of odd, mad, daft characters is called John Cage. In one sense, anybody who can invent a character as slight and fantastic as Ally McBeal, and a show that suggests that reality is all about the noisy tension between fashion and insanity, cannot possibly have heard of John Cage. In another sense, someone who can invent a character as complex and miserable as Ally McBeal, and a show that suggests that reality is all about the silent tension between sex and sanity, knows very well about John Cage. Cage's presence in *Ally McBeal* is Kelley's way of saying that *4'33"* is the sexiest, sanest work of twentieth-century art. His way of saying that everything that happens in the world, and in the world that Kelley loosely based on the world, is a fantasy someone is having during a performance, somewhere, of *4'33"*. Everything is happening because of silence.

Possibly the best thing about the surreal John Cage in *Ally McBeal* is that, as you

unfix you. Even when there is silence, there is sound, the sound of thought, the sound of memory. We have heard too much music for there to be absolute silence in our minds. Even as we listen to *4'33"*, Cage's little joke of enormous silent seriousness, his invisible question mark, or

watch this rich slick preposterous mock-up of a bunch of boomy-baby lawyers skimming the hard shiny surface of the American dream, there is always this funny little echo of everything the real-life Cage got up to as he tried to break up the dream, or add to it. The best thing about the John Cage in *Ally McBeal* is that he is called John Cage. The joke is in the meaning that might or might not be there, and the joke is as funny with the meaning, or without it, and funniest of all at the point where there is at exactly the same time meaning and no meaning.

We must also thank David E. Kelley for putting us in the position of being able to read in the footnotes to the opening section of this book a sentence that contains both the names John Cage and Barry White.

While performing once in Boston with the Art of Noise – how this happened, what I was doing there, will become clear during this book, or at least during some of the footnotes, or it won't become clear at all, until I get someone to write my life story in the way I'm writing Kylie's – I mentioned during the introduction to one song that David E. Kelley had asked the group to contribute the theme tune to *Ally McBeal*. We were in Boston, after all, the city in which Kelley pretends *Ally McBeal* is set: it's a Boston based on Boston, a kind of reality based on a kind of reality. In honour of John Cage the character and indeed John Cage the thinker – they may well be one and the same – we contributed an edited version of *4'33"* called *45"*. Kelley didn't get the joke, or he got the joke but didn't think it was very funny. The Art of Noise theme tune was rejected, so Art of Noise are now known for supplying the theme tune to *The Krypton Factor* but not to *Ally McBeal*. Which I think is a shame.

Actually, the Art of Noise didn't get asked to supply the theme tune to *Ally McBeal*. I made that up. But then, David E. Kelley made everything up. And so did John Cage – the Cage who exists, and the Cage who doesn't exist.

I tried very hard to get Art of Noise to record *4'33"* for an album or a B side. No one in the group took me seriously, perhaps thinking I had made up the very good reasons why I thought the group should record it. There was also some reluctance to give away the publishing of a whole track that actually consisted of nothing.

The version I would recommend to open the soundtrack of this book is a version Frank Zappa recorded for a John Cage tribute album – other contributors to the tribute include the Kronos Quartet, Laurie Anderson, Ryuichi Sakamoto, Yoko Ono, Oregon and John Cale. Zappa's version features a few presumably random bumps. Zappa never could keep a diplomatic silence. His performance might be straight-faced, or straightfaced behind a Groucho Marx mask. It's funny, and actually quite poignant, as it was one of the last things he did before he died.

Cage originally thought of making a 'silent piece' in the late forties as something he could possibly sell to the Muzak Corporation, who were turning Satie's

exclamation mark, we hear things, real and imagined. That is the point. The point of silence, in this day and age, in this life and time, is the noise that surrounds it, and the noise that is inside it.

The next piece of music in this book should perhaps be 'The Sound of Silence'.[c] But it's not going to be, because I hate it, for reasons that

idea of background music into a commercial enterprise. He went on to think of a piece called *0'0"*, which he said could be played any way by anybody. This wasn't as serious, or as funny, as *4'33"*. This piece was where he hit music and musical theory and philosophy and comedy right on the head. As Brian Eno said: you don't really need to hear it; you just need to know that someone thought of it.

John Cage, who would reluctantly admit that, of everything he thought up, *4'33"* was his favourite, who said that art was not an escape from life but was an introduction to it, who said that theatre takes place all the time wherever one is, died on 12 August 1992.

[c] 'The Sound of Silence' sounds creepy to me. It's a sort of Disney-fication of singers such as Bert Jansch and Roy Harper. What makes a great piece of music is the relationship between what is heartwarming in the song and what blows your mind. It's good to have, say, eighty-odd per cent blowing your mind, and some of the rest being heartwarming. The thing about Simon and Garfunkel is that their songs were mostly ninety-six per cent heartwarming, with very little of the remaining four per cent being anything like mindblowing. More sort of mind-sucking.

The writer and singers of 'The Sound of Silence' clearly have no appreciation of the silliness and seriousness of Cage's silence. There's no reason why they should, of course, apart from the accident that in this book they follow the *4'33"* footnote. This is their fate in this particular true story of popular music from Olivier Messiaen to Massive Attack that avoids Simon and Garfunkel out of spite and/or philosophical accuracy. In a way, they should be so lucky that they appear at all, because there is only so much space – ask Miles Davis – and there are only so many names that can be fitted into the history. There is so much music, made by so many musicians, that I wish I could fit into this story, but there just isn't the time. There is only so much time – ask Buddy Holly, in his one mention in this book. I wish I had the time to mention Penetration, a Newcastle punk-rock group from the late seventies, fronted by Pauline Murray, who was sort of Siouxsie Sioux lite but Northeast spiky. Their ranty punk shanty 'Shout Above the Noise' is something of a contender for the soundtrack of this book, but I doubt it will make it. Perhaps there could be a reserve soundtrack, a sort of *Soundtrack Two*, full of strange, obscure gems, or overfamiliar tracks that seemed too obvious to put on the main soundtrack. Things like Gordon Lightfoot's 'The Wreck of Edmund Fitzgerald', Detroit Grand Pubah's 'Artificial Intelligence', The Bangles' 'Manic Monday' and – this just goes to show what a wonderful true story is being told here – Billy Joel's 'We Didn't Start the Fire'. (This, incredibly, is not Billy Joel's only mention in this book.)

So Simon and Garfunkel can count themselves lucky that they slip in to this story, even as figures of fun. Meanwhile, this being a footnote of fact, it should be pointed

belong in a footnote. Because I hate it, in a natural and healthy way, it belongs in this book only as a thing of derision, a tiny discarded part of the true story of popular music from Louis Armstrong to Godspeed You! Black Emperor via Moby Grape and the Pet Shop Boys, because it is wrong. It is a footnote, as is my true feeling about Simon and Garfunkel.[d] (In fact, in this true story of popular music from Leadbelly to Trent Rezner, via Heinz and Van Der Graaf Generator, so is 'Imagine'. So are E.L.P., Iron Maiden, Simply Red, and – demonstrating so fantastically and so coincidentally the very beauty of popular music that I want/never want to define, which is in itself close to being a definition, but not close enough, because the chase must never end, not while I'm telling the true story of popular music from here to eternity via The Fortunes and Faust – the Footnotes.[e])

So the second piece of music on the soundtrack to this story of popular music that shimmers from Sir Mix-A-Lot to Sir Elton John, from Dr John to Dr Dre, from 'The Twist' to 'The Humpty Dance', from Pink Floyd's 'Set the Controls for the Heart of the Sun' to Barry Adamson's 'Set the Controls for the Heart of the Pelvis', from Cypress Hill's 'How Could I Just Kill a Man?' to Smog's 'Dress Sexy at My Funeral', is a song that mixes silence and noise. In a way that is easy and eerie. Easy on the ear, eerie in the soul. And, because all things mean all things to all men, vice versa. The second song, taking us in on the open beat of cool time into this starry story of popular music that travels from Chuck Berry's 'Route 66' to The Pixies' 'Motorway to Roswell' without taking a turning, could be by Captain Beefheart. (If you've never heard the music of Captain Beefheart – and if you want to get your bearings as you speed through this story of popular music as it should

---

out that 'The Sound of Silence' was produced by Dylan producer Tom Wilson. Another fact is that the original version was stripped-down and bare, and the electric band arrangement that turned it into a hit was done without the knowledge of Simon or Garfunkel. There are further facts, as there always are, but in this story of popular music that times itself from Paul Bowles' *Black Star at the Point of Darkness* to Stereolab's *Transient Random Noise-Bursts with Announcements* via Nine Inch Nails' *Pretty Hate Machine* there's just no time for the glassy trad-opulence, the fancy folk, of Simon and Garfunkel. (I might have changed my mind since I wrote this.)

[d] They can fuck off. (I've changed my mind back again, come to think of it.)

[e] There was, alas, no such group as the Footnotes. So it's no use me pretending that that their lead singer was called Neil Legg.

be told then I would advise you to, as the Captain is at the beginning, middle and end of that story, in some order or another – then let's for starters imagine the blues, only green. Imagine rock and roll, only it's more wriggle and jerk. Imagine jazz, possibly quite free, only it's jazzzz, and it's freeeeee, or, to be more scientifically accurate about it, zazzjzz and eerereef. Imagine melody, and then squeeze it through the opposite of melody. Then skin it, cube it, dice it, colour it and spice it. Eat it raw, just before sleep, and stand back for the dreaming.[f]

---

[f] In this dream, it appears that Captain Beefheart's real name is Don Van Vliet, he was born in 1941, he helped invent what can be called psychedelic rock, and then he reinvented it. He's the missing link between Bo Diddley and John Lydon, between Howlin' Wolf and Pere Ubu, between John Cage and Nurse with Wound. (Nurse with Wound are the missing link between Henry Cow and nothing as of yet.)

With his *Trout Mask Replica* album, Beefheart did to rock music what Picasso did to the human face, what the Marx Brothers did to comedy, what Godard did to film, what Joyce did to language, and what Coleman did to jazz. What this 'did' consists of begins in about 1966 with 'Diddy Wah Diddy', where the eyes, ears and mouth of the blues are just about where you would expect them to be. Then, after some relatively gentle shape-shifting with his *Safe as Milk* and *Strictly Personal* albums, the mouth flew off, the ears went berserk, and the eyes changed colour by the second. I sometimes think that *Trout Mask Replica* is the greatest record ever made, and then I play it and I realise it's possibly better than that. Considering that everything seems out of focus, and way out of tune, and vastly anti-rhythmical, the whole thing is intensely focused, tight and rhythmical. Never has the illogical seemed so logical. Never has nonsense made so much sense. The fact of this footnote is that he wrote the twenty-eight songs in a nine-hour composing frenzy; the fiction is that the songs were handed to him on a plate by a) a tree; b) an alien; c) a rabbit; d) a plate.

Cage thought music could be very, very quiet, even silent. Beefheart said, or rasped, that music could be based on a completely new set of rules. He invented a new musical language from scratch, and its connection to any music we know is accidental and tentative. It's a music made by humans descended from birds not apes. (A non-Beefheart three-disc discography of music made by these bird-humans would consist of Ornette Coleman's *Free Jazz*, Karlheinz Stockhausen's *Stimmung* and – at its poppiest – Björk's *Post*. Radiohead's *Kid A* is at the teenybop end of things. Three words in any explanation of this music would be 'intuitive', 'contact' and 'peculiarity'. Three sentences to end this explanation would be: Control versus non-control. Noise versus no-noise. Explanation versus non-explanation.)

To sample the bird-beat beast-boogie brain bounce of Beefheart, try *Dust Blows Forward*, a two-CD anthology that collates tracks from all stages of Beefheart's musical adventure. After experiencing songs from *Trout Mask Replica*, *Lick My Decals Off, Baby*, *Mirror Man* and *Shiny Beast (Bat Chain Puller)* you'll believe a man can fly. You won't believe the music.

Beefheart could shred dead silence into living pieces of sound with a flick of a finger, the flicker of a thought. His songs would make you realise, through their cagey, raging combinations of things electric, acoustic and human – and, elsewhere, inhuman, serene and manic – that the imagination is as vast as the universe, and as indescribable. All you can do is have a stab, a combination of stabs, at deciding just what it is that makes the imagination a part of the universe, and apart from the universe. A Captain Beefheart song gets to grips, in an elemental way, with just what it is that places the imagination at the heart of the universe, and the universe, or at least something of a part of it, at the heart of the imagination. He does this, sometimes, by seeing the universe through the eyes of a horse, or the senses of a tree.[g]

---

[g] As weird and wonderful as Beefheart might be said to be, he's still very much a part of the rock world. He might be at the very edge of it; he might be at the very centre. Eventually you'll find him: in the jungle, under the sea, up in the trees, changing the colour of his skin, flying towards the sun. Having found him in this footnote, how far do we have to travel before the landscape becomes more familiar, before the landscape becomes totally familiar? Fasten your seatbelts.

If you like Beefheart, you will like The Band, Badly Drawn Boy, Frank Zappa, Faust and The Grateful Dead. If you like Faust, you will like Godspeed You! Black Emperor, Captain Beefheart, King Crimson, Vangelis. If you like Godspeed You! Black Emperor you will like Low, Mogwai, Silver Mount Zion, Mazzy Star, Sigur Ros. If you like Low you will like Godspeed You! Black Emperor, Yo La Tengo, Rian Murphy and Will Oldham. If you like Yo La Tengo you will like Giant Sand, Jim O'Rourke, Grandaddy, Smog, Sonic Youth. If you like Sonic Youth, you will like The Pixies, My Bloody Valentine, Hüsker Du, Arab Strap. If you like The Pixies you will like Sonic Youth, The Breeders, Hüsker Du, Throwing Muses, Frank Black. If you like Hüsker Du, you will like The Pixies, Sonic Youth, The Dead Kennedys, Black Flag, The New York Dolls. If you like The New York Dolls, you will like The Ramones, Iggy Pop, The Band, Hüsker Du. If you like Iggy Pop, you will like David Bowie, Lou Reed, The New York Dolls, The Velvet Underground, Beck. If you like Beck you will like Moby, Death In Vegas, Badly Drawn Boy, Eels, Coldplay. If you like Death In Vegas, you will like Bentley Rhythm Ace, Moby, Leftfield, Badly Drawn Boy, The Doves. If you like Leftfield, you will like Underworld, The Chemical Brothers, Moby, Massive Attack, Groove Armada. If you like Massive Attack, you will like Tricky, Moby, Portishead, Morcheeba, Leftfield. If you like Portishead, you will like Morcheeba, Tricky, Massive Attack, Moloko, Radiohead. If you like Radiohead, you will like Coldplay, Blur, Muse, Mansun, Placebo. If you like Blur, you will like Mansun, Radiohead, Placebo, Oasis, Manic Street Preachers. If you like Placebo, you will like Radiohead, Blur, JJ72, Nine Inch Nails, Green Day. If you like Nine Inch Nails, you will like Marilyn Manson, Tool, Deftones, Korn. If

So, the second song on the soundtrack, if it were by Captain Beefheart, would take you somewhat by surprise. But then, so it should. The second song on this soundtrack to a story of popular music from 'Happy Days' to Happy Mondays via Slapp Happy has to be something of a musical miracle, because it is going to take us from the silence of the cage, the silence of before time, the silence of the past, right into the very noise of now. It is going to take us from nothing to something, and open up a universe of possibilities, coincidences, facts and fictions.

It's going to make a noise, which is pretty magical, especially when the noise is organised in a certain way. Perhaps the second song could be something by Sly Stone, who is something of a diabolical wizard, who streaked across silence as if he had wings, who said things to the world as if he wore a halo and a cute pair of horns. His role in this story of popular music as it should be told in this increasingly fluid world is as significant as Captain Beefheart's. Actually, he was far more directly influential, on the actual matter of popular music, not just the atmo-

---

you like Korn, you will like Limp Bizkit, Deftones, Slipknot, Rage Against the Machine, Marilyn Manson. If you like Rage Against the Machine, you will like Limp Bizkit, Deftones, Korn, Metallica, Papa Roach. If you like Metallica, you will like Iron Maiden, Guns N' Roses, Korn, Slayer. If you like Guns N' Roses you will like Metallica, Slash, Nirvana, Bon Jovi, Iron Maiden. If you like Bon Jovi, you will like Richie Sambura, U2, Madonna, Def Leppard, Robbie Williams. If you like Madonna, you will like Kylie Minogue, Robbie Williams, the Spice Girls, All Saints, Melanie C. If you like All Saints, you will like Madonna, Kylie Minogue, Texas, U2, S Club 7. If you like S Club 7, you will like Steps, Britney Spears, Billie Piper, A1, Robbie Williams.

Alternatively, had you liked Nirvana instead of Bon Jovi, then the journey would have been a little different towards the end. If you like Nirvana, then you will like Green Day, the Foo Fighters, Radiohead, Offspring, Blink 182. If you like Blink 182, then you will like Green Day, Less Than Jake, Lit, Offspring, Limp Bizkit. If you like Limp Bizkit, you will like Korn, Rage Against the Machine, Kid Rock, Eminem, Blink 182. If you like Eminem, you will like Dr Dre, Limp Bizkit, Wu Tang Clan, Madonna, Destiny's Child. If you like Destiny's Child, you will like Craig David, Madonna, the Spice Girls, Lucy Pearl and . . . Robbie Williams. But if you like Dr Dre instead of Destiny's Child, then you will like Eminem, 2Pac, Wu Tang Clan, Snoop Dogg, Notorious B.I.G. If you like Wu Tang Clan, you will like Method Man, Dr Dre, Cypress Hill, Raekwon, Snoop Dogg.

We've lost Robbie. But just there, through the branches, over the hills, growling at the shadows, sharing a bite with a wigwam wolf, holding a bottle that has no label, making love to a vampire with a monkey on his knee, I think we've found the Captain again.

sphere. Beefheart as a magician is a mythological creature. Sly as a magician manifested himself as a damned physical creation, the life and the soul of the party, the real-life groove in the heart of the night. He got under the very skin of popular music: he's in the blood.[h]

---

[h] As a member of the Art of Noise, or, at least, a fantasy member, I particularly liked doing interviews and making up fantasies about the group. During 1999 the group promoted a record called *The Seduction of Claude Debussy*, a soundtrack to the idea that Claude Debussy was the beginning of a line that passed from Anton Webern and Philip Glass to Harold Budd and Spiritualized. (The record wasn't mindblowing enough, but that's another story.) During these interviews, I liked to talk about a sample ranking that might exist, a sort of sampling equivalent there might be to the Sony golfing lists. Points would be awarded to artists and entertainers whose work was sampled by others. I suggested that at the top of this list, the Tiger Woods of sampling, would be James Brown, whose drum sounds, rhythm rolls and soul riffs launched a thousand records. Number two would be Kraftwerk, and at number three, I bragged, were The Art of Noise. Certainly Brown's sound and rhythm has been aped, nicked and re-created enough times to suggest that he might be the most sampled act of all time, and Kraftwerk, simply in terms of their direct and indirect influence on Afrika Bambaataa's 'Planet Rock', achieved the sampling equivalent of winning the American Masters title. There's been enough sampling of the Art of Noise, some beats, some 'hey!'s, some musical jokes, to suggest they might have won the European money list a couple of times, if not quite ever a major.

But perhaps the real Tiger Woods in this fantasy situation, and surely the top of any imaginary Sony Sample Ranking, must in the end be Sly Stone. (Brown is more of an Arnold Palmer.) Sly's effect on the sound and style, the punch and attitude, the why and what of modern music has been dramatic. His 'In Time' is perhaps, for those of a certain persuasion and a body of a particular age, the funkiest record in the whole world of funk, in a list that also includes Funkadelic's 'Not Just (Knee Deep)', James Brown's 'Cold Sweat', Prince's 'Kiss', The Meters' 'Just Kissed My Baby', Betty Wright's 'Clean Up Woman', the O'Jays' 'For the Love of Money', the Isley Brothers' 'It's Your Thing', Tina Britt's 'Sookie Sookie', Freddy King's 'Funky', David Batiste's 'Funky Soul', Jr Walker and the All Stars' 'Home Cookin'', Calvin Arnold's 'Funky Way', Rufus' 'Tell Me Something Good' and Stevie Wonder's 'Superstition'.

Sly's 'The Humpty Dance' may well be the most sampled song ever: it has sprayed and splintered off into more than fifty songs, including tracks by Detroit's Most Wanted, Ice Cube, LL Cool J, Marky Mark & the Funky Bunch, TLC, Digital Underground, Dr Dre, Grandmaster Flash & the Furious Five, Ice T, Alanis Morissette, Naughty By Nature, Alexander O'Neal, The Pharcyde, Salt'n'Pepa, Stetsasonic, 2Pac and at least half a dozen by Public Enemy.

Other acts who have sampled Sly & the Family Stone tracks such as 'Sing a Simple Song', 'Stand!', 'You Can Make It if You Try', 'Thank You (Fallettinme be Mice Elf Agin)', 'Poet', 'Africa Talks to You', 'Skin I'm In', 'Thankful 'n' Thoughtful' and 'High On You' include: Arrested Development, De La Soul, Bone Thugs'n'Harmony, Janet Jackson, Massive Attack, Material, Wendy and Lisa, PM

Out of the silence we might be penetrated by Sly's joyfully melancholy 'Stand' or we might note that the fleshily existential 'Thank You (Fallettinme be Mice Elf Again)' confirms that Sly is a heavenly body who governs an entire system of black and white popular music.

The second piece could be something flat, monotonous, atmospheric and questioning by Brian Eno, the sound of silence turning its back on itself.[i] Sound that is like the lining to time itself. The long floating build-up to a some kind of party. It could last for a day or two. It could last for a couple of minutes, and be the Ramones rockily representing American-dream life at around about the beaten speed of desire.[j]

Dawn, Beastie Boys, A Tribe Called Quest, Afrika Bambaata, and Beck.

We might say, in a footnote sense, that Sly Stone is therefore the missing link between Miles Davis and Dr Dre. (This in a universe where Sun Ra is the missing link between Miles Davis and Sly. And then the missing link between Miles Davis and Sun Ra is John Cage. Meanwhile, somewhere, thank God, Faust are the missing link between John Cage and Godspeed You! Black Emperor. And Barry White is the missing link between John Cage and Prince.) If we need a sentence to begin to explain what it is that Miles and Sly and Dre have that others must imitate or echo, then it might be: if you want the absolute, then you shall have it, but only in disguise.

Another sentence? Why not: their music resounds like an overwhelming 'This is how it is'.

Further explanation of the power of Sly and Miles and Dre may derive from a sentence that ends with the two words 'vain bastards'.

[i] I will hire Brian Eno to oversee the gaps between tracks on the soundtrack to this book. He once said that having no silence in music was like having no black and white in painting. He also once said:

One of the musical areas that people have hardly ever looked at is what happens between tracks on a record. The normal thing is to say, 'OK, here's this song, now let's, oh yeah, put a couple of seconds in between, then there's the next song.' I've made a few experiments where I tried to play with this space a little between tracks, for instance on *Music for Airports* there are very long gaps between pieces, thirty seconds or a minute long. I suppose the point of that was to try to almost let people forget that they were listening to a record. So, very much the message of ambient music for me was that this is a music that should be located in life, not in opposition to life. It shouldn't be something for blanking things out, or covering things up.

[j]
> Now I wanna sniff some glue
> Now I wanna have something to do
> All the kids want something to do
> All the kids want something to do

It could be the absolute opposite of silence, silence's evil twin. A side or two of Lou Reed's *Metal Machine Music*, a double album of electronic white noise. As black as a black hole, as cold as the dark side of the moon, an aural X-ray of sarcasm and spite and silliness. *Metal Machine Music* displays such opaque rage, such insolence and consistency, such rotten purity, that you cannot help but conclude that whatever else it is – bad joke, contract-breaking arrogance, abstract confession of artistic impotence – it certainly exists as a work of art, the noise equivalent of a Pollock: you hear pictures, you hear drama just begging to be interpreted, you dream stories that fit the outburst.

It is also a very important record in the life of rock writers, those kind of rock writers who entered the world of rock writing wanting to be the greatest in the world in the world of rock writing. It is the blank centre of black nothing at the centre of a blank page at the centre of everything, the great challenge to the interpretative senses, the great test of attitude and ability to spin vast fiction based on very little, or of an interest in weaving massive fact based on next to nothing. It is a test of the extent of your musical snobbery, your obsession, and your tendency to take something very seriously indeed that has passed most of the world by. If, faced with *Metal Machine Music*, you cannot instantly produce a few thousand words of intense fantasy and place it as, say, the missing link between Adam and Eve's first orgasm and Frank Zappa's death rattle, the copulating link between Dada nada and Japanoise pornography, and describe it as the noise that wants to maim silence and then murder noise, then there is no chance that you will ever be a contender to be the greatest rock-and-roll writer of all time. If you simply hear it, and laugh it off, or break down in tears, or take it only so seriously, at a fairly low level of seriousness, a mild, middle-of-the-road seriousness, that in fact you file it too quickly under Flippancy, as just an isolated instance of one man's drug-fuelled lunacy, then you have never been close to being the kind of (rock) writer who believes that there is a

---

The entire lyric of 'I Wanna Sniff Some Glue' by The Ramones, from their debut album, *The Ramones*. Written by Dee Dee Ramone, it's one minute, thirty-four seconds long. I have contacted Eno, and he suggests that, if this track follows the silence of John Cage as performed by Frank Zappa, there should be a one-minute-twenty-eight-second gap before the Ramones speak at the beginning of time on behalf of all humanity.

chance through (rock) writing of understanding the secrets of the universe. It is the essence of predictability, the ultimate cliché of the rock-writing art, to claim that *Metal Machine Music* is the key product in appreciating the rock canon, but it is also unavoidable. It is also true to say that the reason that, say, Oasis, never totally convinced as rock-and-roll greats is because they lacked understanding of the tortured existence and twisted wonders of *Metal Machine Music* – as with those wanting to be the greatest rock-and-roll writers, those wanting to make great myths of themselves as rock-and-roll artists must have an informed point of view about *Metal Machine Music*. Radiohead will have, although not a very original one. U2 will have, although they feel a little embarrassed, a bit guilty, about it. The Strokes do have one, but only because they know they should. Blur got to 'Song 2' by bouncing off the edge of *Metal Machine Music*, The White Stripes were breastfed on the poisons of *MMM*, but Coldplay, by lacking knowledge of this dark continent, sound as if they sincerely believe that the world is flat. Only by discovering *Metal Machine Music* can you appreciate that not only is the world not flat but it is also a machine, a machine for producing the dreams and nightmares we call reality. With this knowledge, you can exceed the timid nature of flat-world ordinariness.[k]

On the other hand, having mentioned *Metal Machine Music*, and the reasonable fact that it might well be a representation of God, or the devil, at least on vinyl, the CD is something of a poor translation, you should be able to carry on with whatever you are doing as if nothing much has happened. You should be able to slip on to the next subject with graceful ease – such as the following: most of all, *Metal Machine Music* is so alive, and is a statement about being alive, so it totally belongs in this story of popular music as it lives and dies from the good Elvis to the bad Elvis, the cheeky Eminem to the fucked Eminem, and in the end, or near the middle, quite simply from Elvis to Eminem. Two vulnerable, emotional, working-class white boys with names beginning with E who sounded so black, at least for a while. Who believed so much in

---

[k] . . . Around four minutes and thirty-three seconds into any side of *Metal Machine Music* – I'm not being funny, I'm not being serious – you start to hallucinate various things and facts, you hear voices, and see shapes, and you imagine a series of facts and fictions that might or might not be associated with Lou Reed's bastardpiece of bastardgenius.[1]

being alive that everything they did, however distracted or slack, seemed a matter of life and death. Who, you know, caused a fuss. Who, with the help of a 'Colonel' and a 'Doctor'[1] created a fiction around themselves about themselves that took over and ran riot and you can guess the rest, if you've had any kind of education. Sometimes, when you see them in a film or a video, or see a photo, and see them trapped inside the fiction of their celebrity self, you look in their eyes, and you swear you can hear a noise, and then you realise: you are hearing the shrill bitter sound of Lou Reed's *Metal Machine Music*, which is the sound of being alive, and yet is the sound of deadness. It's a sound right on the cutting edge between love and hate, between self-love and self-hate, between selfishness and selflessness. It just can't make its mind up which way to turn. To the left, or to the right. Good, or bad. Backwards, or forwards. TV, or sleep. Wait, or go. Fight, or surrender. Win, or lose. Pleasure, or displeasure. On and on, or on and on and on. Etc., or etc. Perhaps *Metal Machine Music* should go on the soundtrack to this book before the silence. Before Cage's silent work of art. It's the sound of doubt, the doubt in God's mind before he committed to this universe, the sound before the silence as he contemplated exactly how he was going to play this burst of excitement, this turn of existence.

So, now looking for our third piece of music, we might move from the silence that follows the doubt to a swivel of Elvis or a criminal turn of Eminem.[m] From silence to great examples of Belief. E and E, the

---

[1] Colonel Tom Parker, born 1909, real name Andreas Van Kujik; adopted the title 'Colonel' because he felt like it. Dr Dre, born 1965, real name Andre Young; adopted the nickname 'Dr' given to him because of his habit of appearing behind his decks in the eighties in a surgeon's outfit, including mask.

[m] In this story of popular music that flips its wig from the hip of Elvis to the middle finger of Eminem across the breasts of Madonna, Elvis is the missing link between Clyde McPhatter and the Beatles, or between Big Mama Thornton and U2, or between Kokomo Arnold and Beck, or between John Cage and Malcolm McLaren, or between Bing Crosby and Nick Cave. Eminem is the missing link between Niggaz With Attitude and Britney Spears. The Sex Pistols are the missing link between Elvis Presley and Eminem. Niggaz With Attitude are the missing link between the Sex Pistols and Rage Against the Machine. Rakim is the missing link between Lou Reed and Eminem. Queen are the missing link between Elvis Presley and Kid Rock. Kraftwerk are the missing link between Stockhausen and Dr Dre. John Zorn is the missing link between Sun Ra and Dr Dre. Throbbing Gristle are

champions of self-belief, at least before the catastrophe of their success. It could be Elvis saying it's all right, or Eminem saying he is what he is, but then really it should be Arthur Crudup saying from deep down inside that it's all right, or Rakim saying from across his self that he is what he is. But then Crudup and Rakim, who suggested something big to E and E, who showed them the timed-rhyming way, had to come from somewhere. Everything comes from somewhere. From a somewhere that eventually reaches back to silence upon silence – you could have heard a pin drop! – and beyond that on the other side of silence, before silence knew the rules of silence, there is white noise disappearing down a black hole.

Everything comes from somewhere . . . The next music on the soundtrack could be by Iggy Pop. Something that sleazes across the surface of silence and explains that truth is man-made, a composite of a great many vague thoughts. Something that makes American life out to be a matter of humble lives lived out in curious dignity. I interviewed Iggy Pop once, not long after he had made an LP called *New Values*, which I thought at the time was like the best LP the Rolling Stones never made, and in that sense is, at the beginning of the twenty-first century, the best LP Oasis never had a hope in hell of making. The sexual quest and the philosophical quest blended right on the driven beat, there was a whole bunch of stalled impulses and frozen grievances, and, using a well-hung rock and roll shot through with degraded sophistication, Iggy exulted in his material triumphs and impenitent rascality. I got all excited about these things, these thoughts I was having about the sexily philosophical things crawling through the moist, scratchy undergrowth of his rock and roll, about the wants and the needs and the lusts that made his music throw up at the edge of madness. I thought, 'Iggy Pop bites hard into the forbidden fruit of ultimate appetite.' How did I know that? Because. Just because.

I was young, perhaps the youngest I'll ever be, and I got all excited

---

the missing link between Kurt Schwitters and Dr Dre. Soulwax are the missing link between Jimmy Saville and William Burroughs.

Five original versions of Elvis' 'Sun' singles that are contenders for a place on this book's *Soundtrack Two*: Arthur Crudup's 'That's Alright', Roy Brown's 'Good Rocking Tonight', Kokomo Arnold's 'Milkcow Blues Boogies', Arthur Guntur's 'Baby Let's Play House' and Junior Parks' 'Mystery Train'.

in his quietly dramatic presence, and gurgled on about the taut nervousness of his best work, about the adventure he was on searching for the great lost riff, and how words and social concepts seem to be merely placed on the surface of things. He leaned forward, smiled somewhere between sadly and strangely, put a preposterously tanned, tattooed and muscled arm around my bony shoulder, and whispered . . . 'Paul, all that shit is cool, and I kind of know what you mean . . . but how about a beer?' Here was a man whose sense of mystery about the world was as much out of Hemingway as it was out of Cocteau.

Looking at Marilyn Manson, which occasionally, mostly accidentally, you can find yourself doing, I guess he stole it – the it of his injured adolescent act, which is childlike, dreamlike, skeleton-like, comic-like – as much from Iggy as from Bowie, Alice Cooper and Marilyn, Manson and Ronald Reagan. And, as for Iggy, he stole it from Lou Reed, as much as from Hemingway. And Lou Reed, he stole it from Gene Vincent, as much as from Delmore Schwartz. And Gene Vincent, he stole it from Marlon Brando. Who stole it from Robert Mitchum. The look on his face when he got busted for grass. And he stole it from Humphrey Bogart. Who stole it from James Cagney. Who stole it from Teddy Roosevelt. Who stole it from Billy the Kid. Who stole it from Mick Fink. Who stole it from Stonewall Jackson. Who stole it from Napoleon. Who stole it from Voltaire. Who stole it from a drunk. Who stole it from his mother.[n]

And I stole it from Lester Bangs. And he stole it from Richard Meltzer. Who stole it from Normal Mailer. Who stole it from Hemingway.

Talking of stealing, the third piece could be something by the Thievery Corporation, who creep out under cover of darkness in suits and ties to nick beats, details and atmosphere from ordinary and extraordinary places.[o] They're such good stealers, they can nick echoes, they can nick

---

[n] I think that Bugs Bunny should be mentioned in this list somewhere.

[o] Formed by two DJs, Eric Hilton and Rob Garza, The Thievery Corporation are the smartest group ever to come from Washington DC (their studios are within sampling distance of the White House). Their music fuses down tempo elements such as dub, bossa nova, swing and a sort of dry-martini sip hop into a music draped somewhere between sonic and sunken. In a Miles Davis way, Kraftwerk are the missing link between Antonio Carlos Jobim and The Thievery Corporation. David Byrne is the missing link between Black Uhuru and the Thievery Corporation. DJ

space, they can nick holes, they can even nick different types of silence. Sometimes they don't seem to actually steal, but just sort of drain sound from one source to another. Sometimes they just plain shoplift.

They're just taking their fair share of the sound that there is collected around the world, and rearranging it, blurring the little edges between originality and plagiarism. It's all been done before – beat music with a fashionable twist – but not this way. The beats have shifted, the fashions have inbred. The Thievery Corporation quietly go about their business grabbing sound on the peaceful run, and out of one world of sound, the sound of this world that has gathered exceptionally in the past 100 years, they create another world, their own little world, a place to scheme and dream. A place to relax. A world a little like the one we know, but just not quite the same. Somehow this is quite comforting. The Thievery Corporation offer slow change on the way to drawn-out bliss.

But the third piece of music on our soundtrack shouldn't be so comforting, so settled. The Thievery Corporation are neatly disguised, matter-of-fact, spoilt twenty-first-century American beat bandits using discreetly electrical means to prepare and store thier stolen ideas. Their energy, though engaging, is frail and flaky. They more or less reduce civilisation to a fantastically futile American sigh of self-satisfaction.

The third piece in this story of popular music that ego-rides across the intrigue laid bare between Scott Walker singing Jacques Brel and Madonna singing Don McLean, between Olivia Newton John singing Bob Dylan and the Pet Shop Boys singing Elvis Presley, should perhaps be something aggressively unsatisfied.

Piece three, then, could be Mick Jagger and Keith Richards' 'Satisfaction', a steal and a half, a jam of precision, a worship of energy,

---

Shadow is the missing link between the Modern Jazz Quartet and the Thievery Corporation. The Thievery Corporation are the suited link between Kruder & Dorfmeister and Air. Their drowsy, sneaky 1996 debut album, *Sounds From the Thievery Hi'Fi*, discreetly flaunts their claim to be the missing link between late-period Stan Getz and any-period Nightmares On Wax. They don't so much blow your mind as stroke it.

Are they thieves? Garza explains: 'We believe that music is free for all to take and reinterpret. With samplers, musicians are able to take from the entire history of recorded music, and then create something new. The only thing you have to worry about is the lawyers.'

a slightly crazed amalgam of naivity and cynicism.[P] It sounds like a dirty habit cleanly executed. Some say, following one story of popular music that goes from the Beatles to U2,[q] that it's the greatest rock-and-roll single of all time, but there's another story of popular music, that should be written, that goes from Bobby Bland to Tricky via Mott the Hoople and Black Uhuru. In this story, 'Satisfaction' is somewhere between the seventy-fourth and one hundred and twenty-eighth greatest single ever made, although on a Friday night at about midnight it shoots up a couple of dozen or so places. On a certain day in June, it creeps even higher. So, not quite the best, not really, not for longer than three and a half minutes, but, boy, does it bounce around a bit. It bounces all over the true story of popular music as it stops and goes all the way, in one way or another, from Muddy Waters' 'Rolling Stone Blues' to A Guy Called Gerald's 'Voodoo Ray'. Or from Tina Turner's thighs to Pink's eyes via Grace Jones's lies. Perhaps it is such a favourite choice, a favourite among favourites when it comes to considering the essence of rock and roll, as a thing now largely consigned to pre-post-real history, because it gets to the heart, and right to the edge, it hits the nerve on the head, of the fire and sex of rock, of the rhythm and sound, of the cliché and novelty – it rides so confidently along the tensions there were and are in rock between black and white, between male and female, between reality and dream, between love and hate, noise and sound, order and chaos, liberation and frustration, style and stupidity, boredom and excitement. It's raucous, yet rickety, it might fall apart at

---

[P] As reported in *Newsweek*: 'Five notes that shook the world.'

[q] When you're as rich and famous as the Beatles, everyone thinks you're fantastic . . . and everybody tells you so. A lot of people don't mean to be sycophants, but they are, and they wouldn't dream of saying anything unto-ward. There aren't very many people who are able to say to the Emperor, 'You aren't wearing any clothes!'

George Martin

Buzzwords when we made [U2's] *Achtung Baby* were trashy, throwaway, dark, sexy, and industrial (all good), and earnest, polite, sweet, righteous, rockist and linear (all bad). It was good if a song took you on a journey or made you think your hi-fi was broken, bad if it reminded you of recording studios or U2.

Brian Eno

any moment, just give up, give in, but what keeps it going, what lifts it up into the realms of legend, is Jagger's flaming pre-fame self-confidence and his clear belief that he has discovered some kind of secret of life, and that he can communicate it through song, which has its own secrets, which he knows too.

The sound of an immediate rock and blues past is ransacked and shifted around in full view of a watching world. Jagger and Richards were beat bandits racing down the mainstreet of pop culture with a bag of swag thrown over their shoulder and a smile as wide as temptation streaked across their cocky faces. At the time, the Stones were some-where exciting between obscure and famous, and perhaps on their way to being quite obscure again, or more, and more, famous. They were not yet what we think of as the Rolling Stones today. They were more an edgy clutch of Eminems than a worn if wise showbiz club of travelling entertainers paid by the stirring cliché. They had only just started writing their own songs – Jagger and Richards were locked away in hotel rooms by their manager Andrew Loog Oldham so that they might emulate the creative, and fantastically lucrative, union of Lennon and McCartney. 'Satisfaction' was the first really successful result of the pairing.[r]

'Satisfaction' is a song that came out of the obvious places, the obvious

---

[r]
> Well my mother told my father
> Just before I was born
> I gotta boy-child comin'
> Gonna be a rollin' stone
>> Muddy Waters,
>> 'Rolling Stone Blues'

Mick was born in July 1943, a Leo, and Keith was born in December 1943, a Sagittarian. They went to primary school together and then didn't see each other for a few years, until they bumped into each other at a railway station. Keith was impressed that Mick had a bunch of blues albums under his arms.

> There are two ways of looking at it. You can say that Brian Jones formed the group or you can say that if Brian never existed Mick and Keith would have formed a group that sounded pretty much like the Rolling Stones. Chronologically, Brian did form the group. But Mick and Keith would have done it anyway. In a lot of ways Brian was very little help musically. Brian worked hard at being a rebel, but Keith was a born rebel.
>> Ian Stewart

sources, of rock and roll. It's an elaborate impersonation of underground urgency. A great fabrication of desperation. You could trace its journey from a poor black world of enclosed desire and deprivation to a great commercial arena of exposed ambition and achievment in your sleep. It sounded riffy and robust – for the R in R&B – and it sounded ballsy and blasphemous – the B in R&B – and gossipy and ancient. And yet

---

I knew from the minute I heard Elvis that that's what I wanted to do. Once you've decided that you want to be the best rock'n'roller in the world, you go ahead and try it.

Keith Richards

Keith takes risks that makes the whole thing worthwhile. Why bother unless you fuck up? Human beings fuck up. Mick's big risk isn't his performance. His big risk is his political situation. He always rides the risk of the Stones no longer being able to function. Mick has taken the big up-front political risks. As far as legal risks go, Keith is the renegade.

Alexis Korner

As soon as Keith lifts up a guitar, you see the lines leave his face.

Bono

There's been some good times. There's been some bad times.

Mick Jagger

'Satisfaction' is a song about not being able to get any satisfaction – sexual, social, existential, mystical, religious, mundane satisfaction – which in itself becomes a kind of satisfaction, this endless quest for peace. It is entirely original, but completely borrowed, stolen, copied. It's a version of Martha & the Vandellas' 'Dancing in the Street' that went wrong, or perversely right. It all started in a hotel room in Florida, a lonely stop on a lonely trip around the edges of the American dream, when the Stones were beginning to feed off that dream and even become part of it, to the extent that they eventually became part of the American nightmare, and Keith was a long way from home, and yet close to the places where the music he loved came into being. It began as a riff that Keith Richards could knock out in his sleep. In fact, it is a riff that he claims came to him in his sleep. It was a riff he didn't even have to think of. It thought of itself. It passed right through him, because he was in the right place at the right time, and had the right fingers connected in the right way to the right mind, which stirred up the right dreams linked to the right desires. For Keith it was just another of those riffs, those shapes and sounds that came to him in his dreams. A riff that came to him because of who he was. He wouldn't have thought that the riff was anything special. More special, perhaps, than any other white guy could dream of dreaming up, could coax out of his guitar, but in the context of who he was and what he wanted to achieve with his guitar, nothing

it sounded brand-new, buzzing with words and feeling that lifted the song above and beyond the near fact that as a song it was just an old-time riff and a quarter, fragmented in time, confined by form, extended to the point of stagnation. They were young men in their early twenties when they wrote it but they sounded as wise and weary as their blues heroes, yet as charged as the modern world.

---

special. It might have gone the way of other riffs he remembered, or found, and then forgot, and lost. It might have disappeared into the long night, or been discarded during some quick day on the road, a holy grail he never even knew he'd found and then forgotten. A receding dream, an inspiration blown away by a new thought, a new feeling, one riff replaced by another. He managed to tape the riff in the middle of the night, because, what the fuck, it was an obvious steal – but then, what wasn't? – and if it didn't really go anywhere, then it might make an album track, or a B side. It might become part of another song, fill a hole, bridge a gap. It was nothing special, beyond the fact that it was special that he, alone, happened to find himself in a position to change his fingers and mind into the shape that was required to make the riff. It was special that he could put the eye and mind and ear and hand together, around his guitar, around a fantasy, to create such a sloppy transcendent sound, but beyond that, beyond that thing you get to take for granted when you're stoned on a new glamorous life as some kind of legitimate outsider, nothing special.

So here was this riff cracked open in a dream in the stoned American night that was nothing special in a special sort of way. It had come out of the mind of Keith Richards. It existed somewhere between real and unreal. It was, in a way, dead obvious, as old as time, as familiar as the sound of a car engine. It was nothing new, not at all, it was kind of lazy, as sleepy as Keith must have been when he taped the riff. Then Mick, as wide awake as usual, on the prowl for the key to a universe that could turn him into a kind of god, heard the riff. It kind of bored him, it was another let-down, another one of those riffs that Keith could play forever that seemed to go nowhere, just fade away into an early retirement. It was a riff Keith could play backwards. A riff Mick knew inside out. Something so simple it barely registered. And yet . . . There was something, somewhere, a flash of intrigue buried inside the sleepiness, the routine repetition. There was something Mick sensed, something elusive and tantalising, it wasn't immediately apparent in the shape and sound of the riff, but something filled him up and emptied him out, something about the riff that was simultaneously disappointing and dynamic. Something about the riff let you down and lifted you up all at the same time. The riff seemed to have a soul. It had a personality that was stranger and darker than its apparent appearance. It was drained of electric freshness yet seemed completely alive. It was depleted but dramatic. It was tired but full of promise. It was shagged out but damned horny. It was just out of reach, and that was a challenge for Mick, who looked for clues all over the place in his quest to grab attention from a world he felt was waiting for him.

Jagger splices the slang of an age that isn't yet over, and that began just about the time he was born, or years before, depending on your point of view, with such depth of meditating intelligence. Inside 'Satisfaction', as rough and riffy as it pretends to be, you can spot a kind of suburban smart pop that you follow through to the fictional documentary stories of the Pet Shop Boys, where the narrator is thrilled and disenchanted with the modern world, and his only way out from and into its ups and downs is through the beat music of the day. You can follow through from 'Satisfaction' to a kind of super-real glam pop, where Marc Bolan and David Bowie override alleged plausibility in the search for relief. You might even have caught Brian Eno rubbing himself down with some of the fuzzy fussless frenzy of 'Satisfaction', back in his mock-glam neo-surrealist days when he sang songs with deadpan verbal fury and dashed self-awareness.[s]

The riff didn't satisfy Mick, but then again it was so satisfying. The riff that was special but nothing special to Keith became not satisfying but satisfying to Mick. Mick fed the riff into his mind, where it tunnelled into his deepest thoughts, and then the riff came out of his mouth, the most famous mouth in pop, the riff plus tongue, a tongue that wanted to lick the world, a tongue pushed right into the cheek of the moment, and a journey that had begun in darkest Africa and had powered right through lightest America was then filtered through eccentric, theatrical Englishness and turned into a shape that belonged to both the hard fixed world of reality and the fluid nature of a dream.

Brian Eno's recommendation for the length of silence there should be between *4'33"* and any version of 'Satisfaction' is an uncanny shade under a year.

[s] Brian Eno (born 1948) is, in some sense, artistically and musically the missing link between everything that happened before he was born and everything that happened after he was born, between everything that happened before he started talking and everything that happened after he started talking, between everything that happened before he had sex, and everything that happened after he had sex, between before his lung collapsed and after his lung collapsed, between everything that happened before he formed Roxy Music with Bryan Ferry and everything that happened after he formed Roxy Music, between everything that happened before he left Roxy Music and everything that happened after he left Roxy Music, between everything that happened before he coined the term 'ambient music' and everything that happened after he coined the term 'ambient music'. At the beginning of one of the journeys he is making from noise to silence – from the cradle to the grave, from baby talk to ultimate quiet – are the first two solo albums he made up after leaving Roxy Music. *Here Come the Warm Jets* and *Taking Tiger Mountain (By Strategy)* were released in 1973 and 1974 and see Eno still metaphorically dressing up and wearing make-up, but they link the glam-rock sense of excess with a Dada sense of the violently different, they link rock-and-roll attack with a surreal sense of sense. He

Jagger's scrupulous inquiringness, the fervid delicacy of his subdividing investigations of mental, moral and emotional states, also easily leads you to the likes of Joe Strummer, Bruce Springsteen and Michael Stipe. And from the Rolling Stones and Mick Jagger's drug-loosened indignation it's just a few bags of pop-porn, a couple of orgiastic nightmares and an American dream of shamelessness – a hop, sick and a jump – to reach the New York Dolls, the ultimate fucking fucked-up example of the pop group saying, in all sorts of cross, cross-dressing, crossover ways, that anything is possible. So, through the highly maintained, somewhat unmanned body of Jagger, who couldn't get no satisfaction, we swoop from mood-filled and disgraceful Robert Johnson scratching in the sands of time right through to the grotesque New York Dolls blinded by rage and eyeshadow. At all stages of this journey there is rich and poor poetry. At all stages of this journey we are right on track in explaining the large and small details of the true story of popular music as it should be told from Louis Jordan to Underworld via Grand Funk Railroad and Grandmaster Flash.

But what version of 'Satisfaction' should we choose as the third track on the soundtrack to this true story of popular music? The Stones' own

---

had horny fun on these two albums with what a pop song might be, and, even though he was clearly in a world of his own, by sheer force of personality and perception he brought his world into this world. With *Here Come the Warm Jets* Eno was the missing link between The Velvet Underground and the Rolling Stones, between Nico and Slade, between Syd Barratt and Broadcast, between himself and himself (elsewhere, perhaps only Elvis and Frank Zappa have this capacity to be between themselves, so Eno is the missing link between Elvis and Zappa), between The Beach Boys and Kraftwerk, between The Beatles and Primal Scream, between Abba and The Cocteau Twins, between Todd Rundgren and The Orb, between doo-wop and trip hop, between panic and calm, between reaction and delay, between Satie and a drive-in Saturday, between Duchamp and a laptop.

The highly strung, hyperactive, all-singing, all-chancing Eno who made these records would eventually relax, stop singing, seek quiet, and transplant his rock-and-roll heart into the body of U2. He once said that what he did, really, was manipulate studios and musicians in a funny way, and he seemed to prefer that to singing, beautifully and brokenly, soulfully and stoned, nonsense about sense. But everything he did after these two blasts from the future, along with the stuff he brought to the Roxy campsite, meant that, even as he grew old with warped dignity, you always remember the time he was a surrealist sex symbol, a Luis Buñuel version of Mick Jagger, the missing link between John Cage and Robbie Williams. Asked to supply a quote for the cover of *The History of Popular Music as It Should be Told*, from Erik

first take at the track, the original blasted monument of wasted energy? Chosen because Jagger doesn't blink once, he doesn't pause for breath, he's charged with some unspeakable spiritual burden, and because the thought police might well be closing in. Or simply because Keith plays guitar his way, heavily lighthearted, a doomed effort at precision. He's caught something like exactly halfway through an immense binge. A binge that's somewhere near exactly halfway between morose and happy.

What about the version by American strangers the Residents, a group of caustic comic nowhere no ones who made music as if life was made up of disputed decisions, dreadful beauty and funny turns. Their version performed an autopsy on what they saw was the dead body of a song. They hacked the body into large chunks, soaked it in acid – the acid, perhaps, of *Metal Machine Music* – dried it out in the sun, and then stuck all the bits together in a hell of a disorder, quite madly proud of the results. I think they maybe thought that their perversion accurately captured the feeling of dread and detachment that lurked deep inside the Stones' version. Or maybe they wanted to piss all over the Stones' parade. Or take the piss. Or create a malevolent forcefield that they would use to surround what they saw as the dead world of rock and roll so that no one could get in or out. Or all that and more, more or less.

If the police were closing in on Jagger, who left too many clues behind, because he's just so human, human enough to skirt the issues of being human, they were completely baffled by the Residents, who wiped away just about all elements of human contact. The police got nowhere near the Residents. Perhaps Scully and Mulder might have got close – to finding out what exactly the Residents were, and who they were, and what the fuck in apparent time and space they had done to this cherished example of rock-and-roll tradition.

The Residents' con-version of 'Satisfaction' was just a shapeless lump of evidence, or a sleepwalking gesture of protest, or the transformation of something that sounded like it existed into something that sounded like it didn't exist. Or perhaps the Residents, due to reform in 2304, gave us the ghost of 'Satisfaction', the ghost of a ghost. A ghost that would be pretty terrifying in the dark. Maybe not the thing you want after total silence.

Satie to Kylie Minogue, Eno replied: 'I find I don't have very much time for reading these days but I am sure this is all very interesting.'

Next to the Residents' rendering, the version by the loopy American sub-surrealists Devo, who shrank the American dream to the size of a potato and then boiled it until it was as clean as a silver whistle, is positively jolly. It quirks and jerks around a missing centre, as if it's quarrelling with logic, because Devo believed in Beefheart. It whoops, tantalisingly delays climaxes, and tells whoppers because Devo had been covered with spacedust by Sly. It's produced by Brian Eno, so it crackles with ideas, and it removes the song from its original context in much the same way that Duchamp removed the urinal from its original context.

Mash the myth of Beefheart with the illusory fervour of Sly using a hi-techno fork while punk-chewing up the legend of 'Satisfaction' and one or two things are for sure. You'll produce one of the great novelty pop songs of what will one day be known as all time. Sacred intimacies are served up as family comedy. The delights of rock-and-roll heaven are mercilessly trivialised to a blank point of solemnity. You end up with a frazzled fantasy that's somewhere between satirical send-up and sloshed salute.

With their theatrical trashing of 'Satisfaction', Devo put up a sign of the road that takes popular music from Cecil B. de Mille to Limp Bizkit. The sign said 'WE BELIEVE IN THE PLASTIC WORLD'. The sign pointed the way to, among other things, Britney Spears. In the end, it might be her version of 'Satisfaction' that should be used as the third track on our soundtrack.

Her version in the sense that there is a version of 'Satisfaction' that has the brand name 'Britney Spears' attached to it, and a creature as mythological as Captain Beefheart, as robotic as Devo, as alien as Sly Stone, as masked as the Residents, as famous as Mick Jagger, has been known, under curious circumstances, to be seen performing it. If the Rolling Stones could not have been possible without Muddy Waters, then Britney Spears would not have been possible without television.

Britney doing 'Satisfaction' is the end of a story of popular music that began in Gladys Presley's womb, and the beginning of a story of popular music that eventually leads to the computer regeneration of Elvis. The top ten things inside the science fantasy of Britney doing 'Satisfaction' as nostalgia for a day yet to come are:

1. Dark softness churning like flame.
2. The infrared gaze of the voyeur.

3. The song 'Satisfaction' artificially held in place between the physical world and the mental world. The song 'Satisfaction' also held artificially in place inside the song 'Satisfaction'. Last but not least, a version of the centre of the universe is locked inside a version of the centre of the universe.

4. We are admitted, from a safe distance, to the seething, delusion and calculation that rages behind the façade of a bright middle-class girl, and, if we look or listen hard enough, we are shown how thin the membrane is between her erotic and her self-destructive compulsions.

5. A screen called Britney.

6. The novelty value of Devo, the reclusive and order-obsessed Residents, the nonchalant and prosperous Rolling Stones, and an intense lack of conviction spinning through a blissfully blank limbo. It's worth pointing out that the sound of Britney's psychodramatic hyper-real bubble pop is executed with such cold, secular skill, and is such a synthesis of technical prowess and computer-generated illusion, that there could be a Resident from space involved in its production.

7. 'She always has a smile for the poorest as she crawls off daintily towards infinity.'

8. A sound of a sound that is part of a story of popular music that automatically travels from Kraftwerk to Daft Punk via Yellow Magic Orchestra, Abba and Barbra Streisand. This being 'Satisfaction', one of the other stories of popular being told is the strange tale, a ghost story, really, whereby Robert Johnson, the poor bastard, who sold his soul to the devil for the sake of song and music, passes through the body of Jagger into the future as represented by the damp, electric surfaces of Britney. The flesh, bone, blood, heart and soul of Johnson reconstituted across space and time as the wire, glass, light, glare and space of Britney. So, I suppose, in this story, which is as far-fetched as any or none, Johnson is the father, Jagger is the son and Britney is the high-definition holy ghost. This just goes to show that, even in the future that Britney gives birth to, without pain and feeling, there remains no business like showbusiness.

9. Sincere spatial disorientation.

10. Samples exploded to the size of a small city that appear to be

of the gargle and yawn of Britney's uterus, proof if ever there was that Britney really exists, and that she's as important to the sound of Britney as Keith was to the sound of the Stones. Even if that sound doesn't necessarily come from her fingers or voice.[t]

I was once asked to record a radio show that was meant to suggest inside a couple of hours a certain sensible sense of the history of pop from inside the memory of someone about my age. Something quite subjective and suggestive. So it might move from the Kinks to Coldcut

---

[t] Another version of 'Satisfaction' to consider is by an American singer, Cat Power, who is sort of the missing link between life and death, between Joan of Arc and Britney Spears, or between Björk and P. J. Harvey (who, funnily enough, did a duet version of 'Satisfaction' which might be considered for *Soundtrack Two* of this book. Their version was more science fiction than folk, and yet more folk than science fiction; it was completely folked-up, if we think of folk as being something very intimate, at a place where art is loyal to science. And, all in odd all, it kept the deceptive extremes of the song, which flows from lonely to orgasmic, pretty intact). Cat's version sucks everything out of the song that you associate with the song: the cocked riff, the cockiness, the actual cock – 'Satisfaction' is a cock in song form – and, with emotional precision, the chorus. By extracting the chorus, the climax, she truly shows how little satisfaction she's actually getting. She leaves you with the bare bones of the song. Or just a leftover bone. A rib. But, for all this stripping and castrating and mutating, the low, blissful, exhausted essence of the song remains, and is intensely highlighted.

'Satisfaction' becomes a clitoris in song form. The stomping, instinctive rant of the male-orgasm version becomes the questing, easy-riding female-orgasm version. You see how strange the obvious-seeming 'Satisfaction' actually is: it can become anything, turn from the blues into avant-garde, from sixties R&B to twenty-first-century pop, from male to female, from corny to enigmatic, from hard to soft. Its message, right on the edge between hope and hopelessness, between frustration and bliss, thrives on reinterpretation as much as a play by Shakespeare.

There's even a carry-on cut-up version by the wind-up nightclub nutcase Fatboy Slim, a version that, if it was a film, would star Adam Sandler and feature a masturbation scene. The cock is back – the original function is rehabilitated. Fat's version confirms, in its rip-roaring dream-beat repetitive way, that 'Satisfaction' might be a song about falling apart, and feeling apart, but it is also a party song. It's a pessimistic song that bounces with optimism. An intense song that rocks with nonchalance. A sad song that can somehow seem happy.

Fatboy shows how flamboyant the song is. Devo how much of a comedy. The Residents how black-hearted it is – how bleak, broken, sad, desperate, empty. Otis Redding how black-skinned it is – soulful, dramatic, intense. Cat Power shows how blue it is. Nothing but blue sky. Britney how tacky, corny, Las Vegas and virtual it is. The Stones themselves in their own cover versions of the song show off how

via Bowie and Zappa, or from The Velvet Underground to Tortoise via John Martyn and Neu! I think by now, having lived through my life of Kylie, and the death of Kylie, and my book as it is being written at the moment, you will be coming to your own conclusion about the kind of things I would be playing in a radio show of my favourites. This must mean that something is working, and I guess we can congratulate ourselves, for making sense of what is surely beyond sense. All this music, all these patterns, patterns piled upon patterns, within patterns, patterns breaking up and breaking off, patterns changing shape and holding shape, patterns replacing patterns, adding up to a chaos that music is meant to decipher – but somewhere, somehow, we have found shape, we have found harmony, we have found the right balance between repetition and change, between inevitability and surprise. So, for instance, I bet you guessed that I would play some Eno, some Can, some Steve Reich, some New Order, but that you didn't predict that I would also play some Herbert, some Disjecta, some Slum Village, some Patricia Barber, some Aerogramme, some Beth Orton, some John McLaughlin, some Mis-teeq, some Floetry, some Johnny Cash, some Simon and Garfunkel; but then, when it comes to pop, who can tell? And yet you knew that the likelihood was that I wouldn't be completely predictable in my choices, as I am too much a snob, or, as I prefer to say, an aesthete, to become so obvious, and by the very nature of me I would have to throw in some surprises, which is in itself unsurprising but you can only do so much.[u]

---

the world is anything but black and white, and how your dreams can come true, however unsatisfying life may be. Versions by Guitar Wolf, The Shadows, Mountain, Ainslee Henderson & Sinead Quinn, Sly & Robbie, Alien Sex Fiend, The Grateful Dead, José Feliciano, Jerry Lee Lewis, David McCallum, Vanilla Ice, Samantha Fox, The Troggs, The Four Tops and Bruce Springsteen show us how astonishing the world is, in all sorts of ways.

For the remix version of the soundtrack of this book, I think I would ask the Neptunes to remix Zappa's *4'33"*, and get u-Ziq to remix Devo's version of 'Satisfaction'. Dr Dre would take *Metal Machine Music* into the fifty-fifth dimension. Brad Mehldau would then turn the Doctor's *Machine Music* into an improvisation for piano trio, and the relationship between rhythm and melody would be an upgraded sigh of sighs to die for.

[u] The Stone Roses are the missing link between The Kinks and Coldcut. Beck is the missing link between Bowie and Zappa. Sonic Youth are the missing link between The Velvet Underground and Tortoise. Julian Cope is the missing link between John Martyn and Neu! and yet also between Arthur Askey and Arthur C. Clarke.

As I prepared my list of songs, the writer in me, the rock writer who still has a home somewhere inside me, began to get excited by the stories you can tell of a music that showed some twitchy signs of life in the forties and fifties, with the first murmurings of certain beats and experiments, the first thrusts of lust and cuts of coded flamboyance. And that within four or five decades had bred and exploded and re-created and repeated and relocated and splintered and shattered and somersaulted and transformed and smothered to such an extent it needed something like 300 labels to name and separate all the different genres and subgenres. There was this journey that you could take back to Claude Debussy and Beethoven, to Leadbelly, to Miles Davis, to Billie Holliday and Arnold Schoenberg, to Bach and Sinatra, and then forward to Neil Young, Slint and Busta Rhymes. A journey you could take from Stockhausen to Steps, from Charlie Christian to Beck, from Lionel Hampton to Ladytron and Beck again.

And as I put together some records for the radio show, I slipped further back in imaginative time, to where you might find the absolute place that popular music began. Did it begin with a seventeenth-century Scottish folk song, or the gesture of an actor in the sixteenth century, or the low, spiritually sexualised moan of a fourteenth-century monk? I went further out to find new places in which popular music began, finding journeys that you could take from the 1960s English jazz collective Spontaneous Music Ensemble forward to groups such as Sigur Ros and characters such as Mr Scruff. I thought of a journey from a sweet place where groups gave their songs titles such as 'Do Wah Diddy Diddy' to another, less sweet place where they used titles such as 'Lift Your Skinny Fists Like Antennae to Heaven'.[v] Journeys from the time when a group simply invited you to meet them, all the way to when groups were intent on turning nothing inside out. Journeys from a period when groups dressed like outlaws to a time when they dressed like businessmen. Journeys that travelled from some of the most corporate-minded and commercial places on earth, the most advertised, obvious and well lit, to some of the most obscure places on earth, the

---

[v] The missing link between Manfred Mann and Godspeed You! Black Emperor are King Crimson.

darkest, strangest corners. Journeys that travelled from the twentieth-century country across a galaxy or two. From strange fact to straight fiction.

As far as the radio show was concerned, I decided that there was a story to tell just by going from A to B, from Aphex Twin to Britney Spears. It was a story as authentic as any other I might have created by mixing and matching various sounds by various artists. Somehow it seemed to get right to the point.[w]

From the panic-sonic attack of the one-man electro-historian Richard James fictionally masked-up as a twin representing the side of popular music that risks hatred, ignorance and derision in the pursuit of new addictions and sounds. To the fictional girl at the centre of the manu-factured American dream representing the side of popular music that hooks up standard emotion to popular approval using the oldest and newest tricks in the songwriting and marketing book. The Twin just wants to be free. The Girl just wants to be loved.

And yet, as far as we travel from one to the other, we still travel inside what can be known as popular music. It's still a matter of sorted sounds bursting out of technologically brutalised late-twentieth-century popular culture, sounds that celebrate that culture, and/or condemn it, sounds that are then distributed, defined, promoted, dismissed, cata-logued and possessed. And, ultimately, the techno-twin wants to be loved as much as the techno-girl wants to be free. And they both, in their own ways, just want to expose themselves to the thrills of the world.

---

[w] When you make music you are acting as a philosopher. You can either do that consciously, or you can do it unconsciously, but you are doing it.

John Cage

The idea is to produce something that is as strange and mysterious to you as the first music you ever heard.

Brian Eno

You can build a wall to stop people, but eventually, the music, it'll cross that wall. That's the beautiful thing about music – there's no defence against it. I mean, look at Joshua and fucking Jericho – made mincemeat of that joint. A few trumpets, you know.

Keith Richards

The radio show was, in the end, all Aphex Twin and Britney Spears, an invented duet of fame and madness. The relationship between the surreal activist and the surreal object hinted at the true story of popular music as it should be told as it glides across the mind and fragments through the heart from Claude Debussy to Dr Dre. If Britney and Aphex Twin had actually duetted on something, perhaps covered a song from Scott Walker's *Tilt*, or something from Robert Wyatt's *Rock Bottom*, or sung a Todd Rundgren song, or found ways to give life to one of the Elvis Costello/Burt Bacharach songs, or did an album of Vic Godard songs, or, can you imagine, an album of Destiny's Child songs . . . If they'd just sang Mercury Rev, Momus, Josef K, the Pretty Things, Suede, Curtis Mayfield, Brandy or Bert Jansch . . . 'Paranoid Android' or 'Send in the Clowns' . . . 'The Hissing of Summer Lawns' or 'White Riot' . . . 'Terraplane Blues' or 'Like a Virgin' . . . 'Transmission' or 'Kiss Kiss' . . . maybe then we'd have the third song on the soundtrack to this book that tells the history of popular music as it should be told.[x]

As it is, they haven't duetted, not outside my screened-off imagination, not in the world known as this one, and we haven't yet got our third song. We're still at the edge of silence, trying to make up our minds, faced with impossible choices and sound upon sound, wondering where it all began, and how it will ever end. To come up with the third piece, and the fourth, and the fifth, and so on, until the soundtrack tells the story of popular music from A to Z and temporarily back again, we're going to have to think a little bit more. We're going to have to feel our way through the fabulous vastness of popular music, and put it in order, an order that isn't chronological, an order that isn't as ordinary as some would have it, an order that breaks down as soon as you think you've got it sorted. We're going to have to shuffle things up, and be prepared to seriously imagine, if just for a few minutes, now and then, that the story of popular music as it should be told is a story of a great change in the way we live our lives, the way we're organised, the way we move, the way we seek pleasure, the way we dream, the way we hear things

---

[x] Or they could sing one of the songs by people I would love to hear cover 'Satisfaction' – Low, Talk Talk, Randy Newman, Yo La Tengo, John Cale, The Olivia Tremor Control, Quantic, Green Velvet, Eels, Emmylou Harris, Giddy Motors or Elvis Presley.

and the way we imagine the future. It is also a story of why there is something instead of nothing, of how we play and think and feel, of discovery, and of sensation.

It is the story of commercial and uncommercial sound between one moment and another, between art and commerce, between privacy and publicity, between entertainment and boredom. It is a story with no real beginning and no real ending. You can begin where you want and end where you want. It is a story of the most exciting music of all time, the cheapest and the richest, the smartest and the dumbest, the fastest and the slowest. The music you file under Popular.[y]

It is a story that should be told, from the beginning of this book to something like the end.[z]

---

[y] A footnote that offers some clues as to what the fourth, fifth, sixth, seventh, eighth and ninth track on the compilation to this book might be. Hints: the fourth, fifth, sixth, seventh, eighth and ninth track on this story of popular music that starts with the flute sound at the beginning of Debussy's *Prélude à l'après-midi d'un faune* and travels all the way to the ooh-ooh-ooh-ooh in the Supremes' 'Baby Love' and the whoop in Blur's 'Song 2' and beyond are dated somewhere between 1942 and 1992. The tenth and eleventh track are dated between 1542 and 1942. The twelfth and thirteenth track come from the turn of the century, the twentieth into the twenty-first. The fourteenth track is not included at all in any of the lists that follow in these notes.[2]

[z] It's a story full of lists. Some day music will only be air. There will be no objects to hold or fetishise and people will simply collect lists. No disc, nothing spooled or grooved, no heads to clean, no dust to wipe, no compulsive alphabetising. Nothing to put away in shoeboxes or spare cupboards and be embarrassed about. A chip inside us and inside the chip a route to all the music that there ever was, which we can compile and organise and reorganise and merge with and feel into and in whatever way possible find the time to listen to, and we'll need the time, all the time there is, all the time that music finds to press itself into.[3]

1. In 1975, RCA released Lou Reed's seventh album following his departure from The Velvet Underground five years earlier.

2. . . . A vast industrial howl . . .

3. . . . You think I'm joking, don't you? Well, I don't blame you . . .

4. *Metal Machine Music* was created as a sonic companion to the Anime Beta Ring, a chemical structure commonly found in LSD.

5. There was some talk of the album being released through RCA's Red Seal classical division under a pseudonym, as if the record had been made by some obscure Czechoslovakian composer. Because, said Reed, 'there was this attitude that people just wouldn't respect it if they thought it was by me'. For Reed, though, one point, among a lot of pointed points – never has pointlessness been so pointedly pointed – was that the album came out under his name. His name, and all it meant, what with Warhol and Bowie and fame and notoriety and heroin and bisexuality, attached to such a blast of blast was what made it funny, and serious, and pointed.

6. It was the follow-up to Reed's most commercial album to date, *Sally Can't Dance*, which had made the US Top Ten. It was as if Reed was embarrassed by the attention, or wanted to say that he could still be outrageous, that he shouldn't be pinned down as some kind of ordinary songwriter, that he wasn't some plaything of David Bowie's, but that he had a lot of tricks up his nose. Although there was a track on *Sally Can't Dance*, even as it seemed as much Billy Joel as Bob Dylan, called 'Kill Your Sons'. This song alleged that Reed's parents, or fictional parents based on his real-life parents, had forced him, or someone based on him, to have electro-shock treatment as a teenager. As much as anything he has done, this points to Reed being the hissing link between Lenny Bruce and Eminem.

7. Each side lasted sixteen minutes, one second, although that's not quite true. On vinyl, you had the choice of playing it at 45 rpm, which meant it finished quicker. If you were lucky, you might have been able to play it at 78 rpm, which meant it was over in over double time. For a richer listening experience, it was best to play it at 16 rpm, which helped some of the sores of the music, the scabs, to break open and bleed a little lubricating moisture. At 16 rpm, *Metal Machine Music* started to weep, it produced tears of desperation, or exasperation, and you could really see that, for such a piece of shit, it was quite an emotional thing, and that Reed was putting all of his heart and soul into it, although at that point in his career it wasn't clear how much of his heart and soul was left. At that point, he didn't have as much heart and soul as Bowie, although he might have had more than, say, Paul McCartney. The best thing you could try and do was play *Metal Machine Music* real slow, hold it back, get it down to about 1 or 2 rpm, so that not only was the thing weeping, pouring tears out of its eyeless eyes, but it also began to moan and sigh, like it was making love to itself, and you realised that what Reed had done was release in record form an act of masturbation. Reed had produced the sound in your head that there is when you are masturbating, the feedback of the spirit as it approaches orgasm,

the noise of sheer relief. When you hear the noise at compact-disc speed, with no real option to play around with the speed of the music, you are hearing the sound of masturbatory consciousness speeded up about forty times. If you can find a way to slow *Metal Machine Music* right down – or, at the other extreme, speed it up until a sixteen-minute section lasts about a second – and find a way to play it at a volume that would cause the Arctic continents to melt, then you begin to appreciate why there are those who consider *Metal Machine Music* to be Lou Reed's way of saying that there is a God, but you'll never see this God at the speed you're travelling, with the volume so low. Therefore, if we follow this argument through to its logical conclusion: rock and roll is the best way of getting near God, if you combine the right elements of image, noise, stupidity, glory and self-centredness, and therefore it is worth taking the music a little seri-ously, and listing it to infinity just in case the right combination of song and code connects you directly to heaven. In a way, *Metal Machine Music* was just a little prayer, not soulful in the way we usually understand, not like Aretha or Beck or anything, but actually the compressed essence of soul, the soul you find at the centre of an orgasm, at the edges of love, in the bloody mess of language, and Reed just couldn't be bothered, or he just plain forgot, to dress it up a little. The soul, he said, is a monster – if you don't tame it, this is what it can turn into.

8. Reed made the noises by setting some microphones in front of some loud-speakers, letting the feedback build to a raging fury, turning on a recording machine, and then leaving the studio. It's a loop of the same manic static repeated as necessary, so there's about eight minutes of raw sound repeated about eight times. Technical jargon printed on the sleeve regarding the production of the noise is gibberish; pretty gibberish that sounds quite probable, but still gibberish. It is somewhere between true and gibberish that the recording involved no instruments. In another sense, it is Reed's love letter to the electric guitar, even if he didn't use an electric guitar, at least not in the missionary position.

9. Reed claimed, as only Reed could claim, that he inserted sped-up little rip-offs of classical composers such as Beethoven, Mozart and Vivaldi into the loaded chaos.

10. Record producer Steve Albini has described it as 'totally captivating – a pure sonic sculpture'.

11. *Metal Machine Music* has been voted the second-worst album of all time. The number-one spot went to *Fun with Elvis On Stage*.

12. In a Beatles sort of sense, it is the missing link between the first few seconds of something live by Jimi Hendrix and Pat Metheny's 'Zero Tolerance for Silence'. In an Anthony Braxton sense it's the missing link between mind and matter.

13. Jerry Garcia is a good guitar player, for someone who comes from LA.

Lou Reed

14. Side Four of the original vinyl recording, containing track four, entitled 'A4', also contained a locked track, meaning that when the side had finished playing the needle would never pick up but would just keep playing the last grooves

over and over again. This meant that, if you ever managed to get to the end of Side Four, in which case you would be in a kind of coma, then you would have to walk over to your record player and physically remove the needle from the record. Bummer.

15. You know the old saying: don't believe everything you read.

16.   I never expect awards or recognition. I do it just to get off.

                                     Lou Reed

17. In a Bowie sort of sense, it's the best answer to the question 'How far can music go and still be called music?' since John Cage's *4'33"*. In a Cage sort of sense, it's muzak compared to some of the things out there. If you are really into this sort of thing, the sort of thing that means your whole life is spent inside noise, and the noise of noise, the beast of noise, the blood of noise, if you really believe that noise can set you free, or trap you inside yourself in the way you want to be trapped, then *Metal Machine Music* is, you know, the Bill Haley and the Comets of this kind of thing. It's the Cliff Richard of whatever noise-locked world it is in. It's this kind of thought, the fact that Reed will never be the Elvis of this kind of thing, let alone the Charlie Feathers, that makes him angry enough to want to try and do something like *Metal Machine Music* in the first place. *Metal Machine Music* is the anger of someone who is so angry but not angry enough to really be as black as he wants to be, as pure, as real. In that sense, *Metal Machine Music* is 'Devil Woman', not 'Burning Love'. It is 'Summer Holiday' more than it is 'All Shook Up'.

18. It was released on eight-track cartridge. Anyone with a copy of this please contact me care of the publishers. I am prepared to swap it for a still-sealed copy of Madonna's book *Sex*. If the vinyl edition is close to being a picture of the face of God, the eight-track cartridge very possibly contains the finger-prints of God.

19. In the sleevenotes, Reed did warn of the possibility of epilepsy.

20. Five acts who made albums that help lead you in, and out, of *Metal Machine Music*: Public Image Ltd, Sonic Youth, Neil Young, Butthole Surfers, Godspeed You! Black Emperor. Six albums by Lou Reed that are probably, in a U2 sense, his best: *Transformer, Berlin, Coney Island Baby, New York, Songs For Drella, Magic and Loss*. A soundtrack that goes well with *Metal Machine Music*: Glenn Branca's music for Peter Greenaway's *Belly of an Architect*. An album made by a member of Sonic Youth that could be heard as a follow-up to *Metal Machine Music*: Lee Ranaldo's *From Here to Infinity*.

21. Reed said that the album could be a soundtrack for *The Texas Chainsaw Massacre*. One kind of music to play in the background at a family meal. You might like to follow it with My Bloody Valentine's *Loveless* and then a bloodspot of Merzbow.

22.   I've always loved feedback. I've spent a lot of time learning how to control it and not go deaf.

                                     Lou Reed

23.   It's not like you can whistle it. I'm not being facetious when I say this.

                                     Lou Reed

24. In a Sex Pistols sort of way, I'd put *Metal Machine Music* somewhere between

Blue Cheer and La Monte Young. A powered-up, high-volume power trio, Blue Cheer were heavy metal before it was really called heavy metal. They were inspired by Hendrix, Steppenwolf and Black Sabbath and were the missing link between them and Queens of the Stone Age. Their 1968 *Vincebus Eruptum* contained the best-ever version of Eddie Cochran's 'Summertime Blues' and the album lasted thirty-one minutes, fifty-four seconds. So they were the missing link between Eddie Cochran and The Ramones. A list of ten all-time great metal albums conjured up by someone of my age would put *Vincebus Eruptum* at the top, followed by *The Who Live at Leeds*, Blue Oyster Cult's self-titled first album, Black Sabbath's *Master of Reality*, Alice Cooper's *Killer*, *Deep Purple In Rock*, *Kiss Alive II*, AC/DC's *Highway to Hell*, Motörhead's *Ace of Spades* and Metallica's *Master of Puppets*. Someone of my age might yet want to add Tool's *Undertow* to that list, if only to make it a list that goes all the way to eleven. A decent MOR hard-rock medley dreamed up by someone of my age stuck up with the memory of *Metal Machine Music* would be: 'Detroit Rock City' by Kiss, 'Fire' by Jimi Hendrix, 'Draw the Line' by Aerosmith, 'Sunshine of Your Love' by Cream, 'July Morning' by Uriah Heep, 'Under My Wheels' by Alice Cooper, 'Born to be Wild' by Steppenwolf, 'Satisfaction' by the Rolling Stones, 'Rock'n'Roll Hoochie Coo' by Johnny Winter, 'Wishing Well' by Free, 'American Band' by Grand Funk Railroad, 'Immigrant Song' by Led Zeppelin, 'Led Boots' by Jeff Beck, 'Speed King' by Deep Purple, 'The Train Kept a-Rolling' by The Yardbirds. I would follow this with Melt Banana's 'Locoweed in the Bottle'. The Japanese Melt Banana are the missing one and half minutes of screech, skin and slash between the fastest Ramones and the freakiest Rammstein – a fine palate-cleaner, under the circumstances.

La Monte Young, just in case you've been skipping back and forwards through this book and missed an earlier entry, is one of the pioneers of minimalism, rejecting traditional melody and structure in favour of hypnotic drones. He influenced not only the avant-garde music that followed, but also punk, Kraftwerk and ambient. He is the missing link between John Cage and Spiritualized, and, you never know, between Jean-Luc Godard and Daft Punk. In this book, he has had an affair with Kylie Minogue, but I guess you missed that part. I think the only way you can reward, or punish, yourself for missing this part of the book is by finding a concrete-lined room and playing all four sides of *Metal Machine Music* very loudly indeed.

25.   I think Jim Morrison was an asshole.

Lou Reed

26.   In a White Stripes sort of way, *Metal Machine Music* is the missing link between Edgar Varese and Aphex Twin. In a Ladytron way, it's the missing link between Michael Jackson's nose and Matmos' 'A Chance to Cut is a Chance to Cure'. In an Arvo Pärt sort of way, it's the missing link between Peter Brotzmann's 'Machine Gun' and Birchville Cat Motel. In a Tool way, it's the missing link between muzak and the noise of the background radiation of the universe.

27.   Gangsta rap is boring to me, but that's because I've not been out on the streets for a long time.

Lou Reed

'I'm sorry but not especially if *Metal Machine Music* turns you off'

Lou Reed.

Yeah, he was just showing off, showing off that he knew his Dada, his Warhol – he fucking knew Warhol – his Stravinsky, his Buñuel, his Varese, a whole history of eyeball-slicing outrage and 'I'm not going to play my hits' audience-loathing; he was showing off that he knew just the right way to certify his cult status, buff up his image as the kind of guy who would shoot heroin on stage. Perhaps he was just pissed off that no one was taking him seriously enough as an artist so he thought he'd chuck a few thousand spanners in the tape-recording works. He was trying to live up to the reputation of The Velvet Underground as drone demonic noise terrorists, which was really John Cale's area, and Reed was just a songwriter – and how boring is that when you want to be an artist, a poet, a genius? He wasn't fucking Duchamp, he was Barry Manilow; he wasn't hardcore, he was too sentimental, he was too ordinary; he wanted to show that he was out of his mind, a million miles away from Lennon and McCartney; he wasn't just Nilsson on heroin, he was aesthetic terrorist; he was Artaud, not Emitt Rhodes, he was the real thing, not just an actor playing at outrage. *Metal Machine Music* was perhaps just a spiteful act of revenge on John Cale. Cale had bought La Monte Young into The Velvet Underground, Reed had just bought in Dylan – and how ordinary was that? He wanted to show that he knew his avant-garde as well as anyone. He knew his art.

As an act of revenge on his ex-bandmate, it is actually, I'm afraid, one of the more interesting rock-and-roll artefacts – I'd rather remember Lennon for such an act than for 'Imagine'.

Then again, perhaps I'm just being a rock writer reading too much into Reed's intentions. Perhaps he had absolutely no intentions.

No intentions is also good.

Perhaps he cannot even remember making *Metal Machine Music*.

Not remembering making it is good.

Yeah, and the other clichés about the album are all useless and brilliant – it's a great New York album, it's the grid of the city smashed into sound shape, you can even use it to get round Manhattan, listening to it I can tell you exactly where the Village is, where Harlem is, where Times Square is, and some of it even seems to predict 9/11; it's a sort of Manhattan masterpiece to rival anything by Woody Allen or Jackson Pollock or Bret Easton Ellis; it's the arrogance and laughter of the greatest city in the world fractured and frozen in mean time, an island of high-rise noise, the music that never sleeps. It's the pause between writing such great classic songs that a great classic songwriter needs as he's writing classic songs, the hole in the head that sensitivity causes, it's a writer's block turned into sound, it's a soundtrack to the exhaustion that follows writing the great songs he had, a soundtrack to the intimidation of having to write some more, a soundtrack to the frustration of believing that no one is ever really going to appreciate his genius. It's a confession that the artist has realised he isn't a genius after all. It's fear, of failure, of success, repre-sented as mutilated sound. It's Reed's way of getting off drugs – part of his therapy, something he made in therapy when asked to produce something that explained how he felt when he was suffering the worst pain of withdrawal, it's his attempt to actually make a drug that would send him through heaven in a Rolls Royce but he got the recipe wrong and it ended up a trip through hell in a hovercraft. It's the beginning of industrial music, the start of punk, the womb of Sonic Youth, the big bang of noise-art terrorism, the black dawn of Japanoise, Reed popularising the avant-garde noise assaults of the twentieth century in the way that Eno popularised Satie and Cage and the Dadaists – it's Reed's *Music for Airports*. It's the sound of the cyber-punk virtual city twenty years before such a thing materialised. It's where the orignal energy of rock music ended, and something else began – where a linear journey became multidimensional, where the guitar was replaced by the machine.

It's the kind of dramatic, excessive, ridiculous thing you want to see and hear come from your rock stars, an infected sign of complete and wonderful madness, a demonstration that your rock stars are prepared to try anything for you, to go anywhere, to be anyone, no matter how stupid, how divine, how damaged and damaging. It was Reed's way of saying, 'I am an artist, I am no one's puppet, not even my own, and whatever I now do from now on, however soft, boring, predictable, obvious I become, remember that I did this, I went there.' Someone who did this cannot be all bad, or all good, just on a journey that has no ending until the end which might not necessarily be the end.

29. It quickly sold 100,000 copies in the wake of *Sally Can't Dance*, although many people returned the record complaining that it was 'defective'. The record company had no specific response to this, recovering as they were from the full realisation that they had a bona fide nihilist signed to the label.

30. Start any place you like . . . for saying in a Nietzschean way that the world now had no beginning and no end and was just a mass of events and happenings, *Metal Machine Music* is a masterpiece. For not saying any such thing at all, well, whatever.

31. *Billboard*'s review of the record concluded: 'Recommended cuts: none.'

32. Lou Reed said he had never listened to the entire record. It is not completely clear whether anyone ever actually has – I, of course, claim that I have, many times, because I believe that this is the case, but I have to say that, because I am or have been or will be the greatest rock writer of all time. If you cannot admit that you have been into the dense jungle of *Metal Machine Music* and beaten off the demons and mapped out the unmappable territory then you have no claim on the title. I have broken its back, I have stared it down, I have got drunk with it, I have had long talks about, you know, life and death with it, I have eaten parts of it, I have jammed along with it. I love it. I hate it. It's art. It's shit. I know it inside out. I know that it is inside out. It's a rites-of-passage thing. It's a male-rock-fan thing. You must get the joke, and laugh along with it, the joke being that there is no joke. Or is there? I couldn't possibly write a story about the history of modern music from fucking who knows when to whatever without making a huge song and dance about *MMM*; or I could completely ignore it, and in the very act of ignorance would be an acknowledgement that *MMM* is the ultimate symbol of all the love and

shit that there is in the history of rock. You can't listen to all of rock, you can just pretend that you have. You know everything, in the way that you pretend you know everything about *Metal Machine Music*.

So, I have listened to *Metal Machine Music*. You can believe that coming from me as a man much more than you could if I was a woman. There's nothing macho about that statement. It's just that no woman is really going to waste any time listening to more than three seconds of *Metal Machine Music*. They are certainly not going to analyse it. They are not going to be at all interested in whether the four parts actually have their own distinct character, the first part, the vinyl Side A, possibly more minimal than the other parts, truly a build-up of tension, the second part a shit more aggressive, the third part a crap more funky with a moronic veneer of musicality, the fourth part a sort of summary of all that has gone before. It's like there are no female trainspotters. At the other end of the spectrum, there was never a female Jack the Ripper.

Metal Machine Music could only have been made by someone with a penis, and it can only be listened all the way through by someone with a penis – it might be that the noise of the record is an attempt at some sort of alchemy to ensure that the penis never loses its ability to get hard. Reed conjured up the sound of blood rushing to the nerve ends of the penis, which is why the record has had enduring fascination for a certain type of male rock-and-roll fan, the type who has looked to rock for certain kinds of sexual comfort and stimulation. It is, perhaps, the sound of semen spurting against the ends of the universe, it is the sound of the colossal relief in a man's mind when his penis gets hard, and he can reach orgasm one more time. *Metal Machine Music* is Reed's celebration of the erection, and those of us who journey into it and savour its contours, marvel at its power and stamina, its length, its perfect shape, are really only admiring a penis – our own at best, Reed's at worst. What an achievement – Reed has managed to plant an erect penis at the very centre of popular music. Then again, maybe it is a soft penis, ready to piss all over anybody who gets too close.

33.   Do not fear mistakes – there are none.
                                    Miles Davis

I don't really know why I wrote this. I think I just wanted something a little more intelligent after the thought of Reed's hard, or soft, penis. Other things to take me off the thought of Lou Reed's penis, and to bring me back to somewhere round about *Metal Machine Music*: Iggy Pop's belch at the beginning of 'Raw Power', Poly Styrene's scream in X Ray Spex's 'Oh Bondage Up Yours', James Brown's scream at the end of 'Cold Sweat', Alan Vega's scream in Suicide's 'Frankie Teardrop', the terrible crying of the child in Lou Reed's 'The Kids' on *Berlin* . . . Which brings us to . . .

34. How to be Annoying (because Bart Simpson is the missing link between Lou Reed and Eminem).

    Adjust the tint on your TV screen so that all the people are green,
        and insist to others that you like it that way.
    Drum on every available surface.

Sing the *Batman* theme incessantly.

Write the surprise ending to a novel on its first page.

Set alarms for random times.

Learn morse code, and have conversations with people in public places consisting entirely of 'beeep bip beep bap beep'.

Buy large quantities of mint dental floss just to lick the flavour off.

Publicly investigate just how slowly you can make a croaking noise.

Honk and wave to strangers.

Dress only in orange.

Change channels five minutes before the end of every programme.

Make appointments for 31 September.

Begin all your sentences with 'Ooh, la la'.

Leave someone's printer in compressed-italic-cyrillic-landscape mode.

TYPE ONLY IN UPPERCASE.

type only in lowercase.

dont use any punctuation either

Buy a large quantity of orange traffic cones and reroute whole streets.

Tie jingle bells to all your clothes.

Repeat everything someone says as a question.

Wander around restaurants, asking other diners for their parsley.

Leave tips in Bolivian currency.

Demand that everyone address you as 'conquistador'.

When Christmas carolling, sing 'Jingle Bells Batman smells' until physically restrained.

As much as possible, skip rather than walk.

Stand over someone's shoulder, mumbling, as they read.

Pretend your mouse is a CB radio, and talk to it.

Try playing the *William Tell Overture* by tapping on the bottom of your chin.

Name your dog Dog.

Inform others that they exist only in your imagination.

Cultivate a Norwegian accent.

Forget the punchline to a long joke, but assure the listener it was 'a real hoot'.

Routinely handcuff yourself to furniture, informing the curious that you don't want to fall off in case 'the big one comes'.

Lie obviously about trivial things like the time of day.

Leave your Christmas lights up and lit until September.

Change your name to John Aaaaaaaaaasmith for the great glory of being first in the phone book.

Invent nonsense computer jargon in conversations, and see if people play along to avoid the appearance of ignorance.

Sing along at the opera.

Mow your lawn with scissors.

Finish all your sentences with the words 'in accordance with prophecy'.

Ask the waitress for an extra seat for your imaginary friend.

Stare at static on the TV and claim that you can see a 'magic picture'.

Select the same song on the jukebox fifty times.

Do not add any inflection to the end of your sentences, producing awkward silences with the impression that you'll be saying more at any moment.

Never make eye contact.

Never break eye contact.

Signal that a conversation is over by clamping your hands over your ears.

Rouse your partner from sleep every morning with Lou Reed's *Metal Machine Music*.

[2] 1. File under 'Popular Music': 100 greatest albums of all time in this suspicious order compiled one morning in January 2001 because an Australian magazine called *File Under Popular Music* asked me to.

Aphex Twin, *Selected Ambient Works Volume II*

A Tribe Called Quest, *Low End Theory*

Au Pairs, *Playing With a Different Sex*

Kevin Ayers, *Shooting at the Moon*

The Beastie Boys, *Paul's Boutique*

Beck, *Mellow Gold*

Björk, *Debut*

David Bowie, *Station to Station*

Tim Buckley, *Happy-Sad*

Burning Spear, *Garvey's Ghost*

The Buzzcocks, *Singles Going Steady*

John Cale, *Paris 1919*

Can, *Soon Over Babaluma*

Captain Beefheart, *Trout Mask Replica*

Cluster, *Cluster 2*

Leonard Cohen, *Songs*

Henry Cow, *Legend*

The Cure, *Pornographic*

Holger Czukay, *Canaxis*

Devo, *Q: Are We Not Men? A: We Are Devo*

Nick Drake, *Five Leaves Left*

Dr Dre, *The Chronic*

Bob Dylan, *The Basement Tapes*

Missy 'Misdemeanour' Elliott, *Supa Dupa Fly*

Eminem, *The Marshall Mathers LP*

Brian Eno, *Another Green World*

Fairport Convention, *Unhalfbricking*

The Fall, *Extricate*

Faust, *IV*

Felt, *Forever Breathing the Lonely Word*

The Flaming Lips, *In a Priest-Driven Ambulance (With Silver Sunshine Stares)*

For Carnation, *For Carnation*

Funkadelic, *One Nation Under A Groove*

Gang of Four, *Entertainment!*

Richard Hell, *Blank Generation*

Jimi Hendrix, *Electric Ladyland*

Hugh Hopper, *1984*

Hüsker Du, *Zen Arcade*

Japan, *Tin Drum*

The Jesus & Mary Chain, *Psychocandy*

Jesus Lizard, *Goat*

Joy Division, *Closer*

Kraftwerk, *Trans-Europe Express*

Labradford, *Labradford*

Leftfield, *Leftism*

Love, *Forever Changes*

Magazine, *The Correct Use of Soap*

John Martyn, *Live at Leeds*

Matching Mole, *Little Red Record*

Joni Mitchell, *The Hissing of Summer Lawns*

Modern Lovers, *Modern Lovers*

The Mothers of Invention, *We're Only in It for the Money*

Neu!, *Neu! 2*

Neutral Milk Hotel, *In the Aeroplane Over the Sea*
New Order, *Low-Life*
Laura Nyro, *New York Tendaberry*
Olivia Tremor Control, *Dusk at Cubist Castle*
Pavement, *Slanted And Enchanted*
Pere Ubu, *Modern Dance*
Lee 'Scratch' Perry & the Dub Syndicate, *Time Boom X De Devil Dead*
Pink Floyd, *The Piper at the Gates of Dawn*
The Pixies, *Surfer Rosa*
Cat Power, *Moon Pix*
Public Enemy, *It Takes a Nation of Millions to Hold Us Back*
The Raincoats, *The Raincoats*
The Ramones, *The Ramones*
Lou Reed, *The Bells*
The Residents, *Meet the Residents*
Terry Riley, *In C*
The Rolling Stones, *Exile on Main Street*
The Roots, *Do You Want More ?!!!??!*
Roxy Music, *Roxy Music*
Todd Rundgren, *Todd*
Sea and Cake, *Oui*
Sigur Ros, *Ageitis Byrjun*
Slint, *Spiderland*
Sly & the Family Stone, *There's a Riot Goin' On*

Patti Smith, *Radio Ethiopia*
Soft Machine, *Third*
Sonic Youth, *Daydream Nation*
Squarepusher, *Hard Normal Daddy*
Stone Roses, *Stone Roses*
The Stooges, *Fun House*
Swans, *White Light from the Mouth of Infinity*
Television, *Marquee Moon*
Richard and Linda Thompson, *Shoot Out the Lights*
Tortoise, *Millions Now Living Will Never Die*
T. Rex, *Slider*
Underworld, *Second Toughest in the Infants*
Van Dyke Parks, *Song Cycle*
Various artists, *Heat* (soundtrack)
Velvet Underground, *Live 1969*
Scott Walker, *Scott 4*
Dionne Warwick, *The Sensitive Sound of Dionne Warwick*
Wire, *Pink Flag*
Wu-Tang Clan, *Enter the Wu-Tang Clan*
Robert Wyatt, *Rock Bottom*
Yo La Tengo, *And Then Nothing Turned Inside Out*
Neil Young, *Arc/Weld*
Frank Zappa, *Freak Out!*

2. File under 'Popular Music': 100 greatest albums of all time, listed in a funny order because I was asked for such a list by a local radio station in Wales.

Laurie Anderson, *Big Science*
Syd Barrett, *The Madcap Laughs*
The Beastie Boys, *Check Your Head*
The Beatles, *Hard Day's Night*
Björk, *Selmasongs*
Boards of Canada, *Music Has the Right to Children*
The Boredoms, *Soul Discharge 99*
David Bowie, *Low*
Gavin Bryars, *The Sinking of the Titanic*

Tim Buckley, *Starsailor*
The Byrds, *Notorious Byrds*
Cabaret Voltaire, *The Voice of America*
Can, *Future Days*
Captain Beefheart, *Safe as Milk*
Johnny Cash, *Solitary Man*
The Chemical Brothers, *Dig Your Own Hole*
Chic, *Risque*
Leonard Cohen, *Songs of Love and Hate*

Carl Craig, *More Songs about Food and Revolution*

Death Cab for Cutie, *We Have the Facts and We're Voting Yes*

Depeche Mode, *Black Celebration*

The Doors, *The Doors*

Bob Dylan, *Blood on the Tracks*

Bob Dylan, *Love and Theft*

808 State, *808:90*

Brian Eno, *Before and After Science*

Eric B and Rakim, *Paid in Full*

Fairport Convention, *Liege and Lief*

The Fall, *Bend Sinister*

Faust, *So Far*

John Foxx, *Metamatic*

Fripp and Eno, *No Pussyfooting*

Funkadelic, *Maggot Brain*

Tim Hardin, *Tim Hardin 1*

Donnie Hathaway, *Extension of a Man*

Jimi Hendrix, *Axis Bold as Love*

Jimi Hendrix & the Band of Gypsies, *Live at the Fillmore East*

Howlin' Wolf, *Moanin' in the Moonlight*

Keith Hudson, *Flesh of My Skin, Blood of My Blood*

The Isley Brothers, *Funky Family*

The Jackson 5, *Diana Ross Presents the Jackson 5*

Bert Jansch, *Jack Orion*

Jefferson Airplane, *After Bathing at Baxters*

Rickie Lee Jones, *Rickie Lee Jones*

Kiss, *Alive!*

Kraftwerk, *The Man Machine*

The Lovin' Spoonful, *The Lovin' Spoonful*

Curtis Mayfield, *There's No Place Like America Today*

Minutemen, *Double Nickels on the Dime*

Moby, *Everything Is Wrong*

Moby Grape, *Moby Grape*

New Order, *Brotherhood*

New York Dolls, *New York Dolls*

Nico, *The Marble Index*

Nirvana, *Bleach*

N.W.A., *Straight Outta Compton*

Outkast, *Stankonia*

Evan Parker, *Saxophone Solos*

Van Dyke Parks, *Song Cycle*

Gram Parsons, *GP*

The Pastels, *Up for a Bit With the Pastels*

Pere Ubu, *Terminal Tower*

The Pet Shop Boys, *Behaviour*

Iggy Pop, *Raw Power*

Primal Scream, *Screamadelica*

Prince, *Purple Rain*

Public Image, *Metal Box*

Radiohead, *OK Computer*

Lou Reed, *Transformer*

The Rolling Stones, *Get Yer Ya Ya's Out*

Roxy Music, *For Your Pleasure*

Todd Rundgren, *Something/Anything*

Silicon Teens, *Music for Parties*

Nina Simone, *Nuff Said*

Nancy Sinatra, *Greatest Hits*

Sly & the Family Stone, *Stand!*

Patti Smith, *Horses*

The Smiths, *Hatful of Hollow*

The Sonics, *Here are the Sonics*

Sonic Youth, *Evol*

DJ Spooky, *Songs of a Dead Dreamer*

Squarepusher, *Feed Me Weird Things*

Rod Stewart, *Every Picture Tells a Story*

Suede, *Suede*

Suicide, *Suicide*

Them, *The Angry Young Them*

Richard and Linda Thompson, *Shoot out the Lights*

T. Rex, *Unicorn*

Underworld, *Beaucoup Fish*

u-Ziq, *u-Ziq Versus the Auteurs*

Velvet Underground, *White Light/White Heat*

The Wailers, *Soul Revolution*

The Who, *Sell Out*

Stevie Wonder, *Talking Book*

Neil Young, *Tonight's the Night*

The Zombies, *Odyssey and Oracle*

3. File under 'Popular Music': 100 greatest albums in answer to a request from a Romanian Web site, listed in a fair and reasonable order.

Aphex Twin, *I Care Because You Do*
Arrested Development, *3 Years 5 Months and 2 Days in the Life of . . .*
The Associates, *Sulk*
Audience, *House on the Hill*
Autechre, *Amber*
Afrika Bambaataa, *Zulu Nation Throw Down*
Bark Psychosis, *Hex*
Big Brother & the Holding Company, *Cheap Thrills*
Björk, *Vespertine*
Black Sabbath, *Black Sabbath*
Bobby Bland, *Two Steps from the Blues*
Blue Cheer, *Vincebus Eruptum*
Blue Oyster Cult, *Agents of Fortune*
David Bowie, *The Rise and Fall of Ziggy Stardust and the Spiders from Mars*
James Brown, *The Payback*
Burning Spear, *Rocking Time*
Buzzcocks, *Another Music in a Different Kitchen*
Can, *Tago Mago*
Captain Beefheart, *Lick My Decals Off, Baby*
Ray Charles, *Modern Sound in Country and Western Music*
Clinic, *Internal Wrangler*
Coldcut, *Let Us Play*
Common, *Like Water for Chocolate*
Comus, *First Utterance*
Ry Cooder, *Paradise and Lunch*
Kevin Coyne, *Marjory Razor Blade*
Crosby, Stills, Nash & Young, *Déjà Vu*
Daft Punk, *Homework*
De La Soul, *3 Feet High and Rising*
Disposable Heroes of Hiphoprosy
Dr John, *Gris Gris*
Bob Dylan, *Live at the Royal Albert Hall*
Eels, *Beautiful Freaks*
The Electric Prunes, *Underground*
Eno and Byrne, *My Life in the Bush of Ghosts*

Marianne Faithfull, *Broken English*
Charlie Feathers, *Get With It*
Fennesz, *Endless Summer*
John Fogerty, *John Fogerty*
Free, *Live*
Marvin Gaye, *What's Goin' On*
Grateful Dead, *Live/Dead*
Isaac Hayes, *Hot Buttered Soul*
Henry Cow, *In Praise of Learning*
Herbert, *Bodily Functions*
Hood, *Cold House*
The Human League, *Reproduction*
Ice Cube, *Death Certificate*
The Incredible String Band, *The Hangman's Beautiful Daughter*
Jay Z, *The Blueprint*
Carole King, *Tapestry*
King Crimson, *Red*
The Kinks, *Something Else*
KLF, *The White Room*
Kraftwerk, *Computer World*
Led Zeppelin, *Physical Graffiti*
Magazine, *Real Life*
John and Beverly Martyn, *The Road to Ruin*
Matmos, *A Chance to Cut is a Chance to Cure*
MC5, *Back in the USA*
Joni Mitchell, *Blue*
Múm, *Yesterday was Dramatic Today is OK*
N.E.R.D., *In Search of . . .*
Neu!, *Neu!*
New Order, *Movement*
Nirvana, *Nevermind*
Laura Nyro and Labelle, *It's Gonna Take a Miracle*
Parliament, *Mothership*
The Pastels, *Mobile Safari*
Ann Peebles, *I Can't Stand the Rain*
Iggy Pop, *Lust for Life*
Iggy Pop, *New Values*
Elvis Presley, *From Elvis in Memphis*

Lou Reed and John Cale, *Songs for Drella*

Rhythm is Rhythm/Derrick May, *Soundtrack for the Tenth Planet*

The Shangri Las, *The Best of the Shangri Las*

Sleater-Kinney, *Dig Me Out*

Sonic Youth, *Sister*

Dusty Springfield, *Dusty in Memphis*

The Supremes, *The Supremes Sing Holland-Dozier-Holland*

Talk Talk, *Laughing Stock*

Tangerine Dream, *Alpha Centauri*

Teenage Fanclub, *Bandwagonesque*

The Temptations, *The Temptations Sing Smokey*

Throbbing Gristle, *Heathen Earth*

Amon Tobin, *Supermodified*

Toots & the Maytals, *Funky Kingston*

Tortoise, *Standards*

Allen Toussaint, *Southern Nights*

The Trammps, *The Legendary Zing Album featuring the Fabulous Trammps*

T. Rex, *Electric Warrior*

The Velvet Underground, *The Velvet Underground and Nico*

Scott Walker, *Tilt*

Gillian Welch, *Time (The Revelator)*

4. File under 'Popular Music': a fourth list of the 100 or more who's counting greatest albums of all time off the top of my head on a live radio interview with a radio station that seemed to be twelve hours ahead or behind the time zone I was in.

Willie Nelson, *Across the Borderline*

Cornershop, *Woman's Got to Have It*

Lou Reed, *Magic and Loss*

Luscious Jackson, *Natural Ingredients*

Hal Willner/Various artists, *Weird Nightmare: Meditations on Mingus*

Cassandra Wilson, *Blue Light Til Dawn*

Aimee Mann, *Bachelor No. 2*

Smog, *Dongs of Sevotion*

Shelby Lynne, *I Am Shelby Lynne*

Kim Gordon, *SYR5*

John Prine, *Lost Dogs and Mixed Blessings*

Blondie, *Parallel Lines*

Sugar, *Copper Blue*

Ella Fitzgerald, *The Legendary Decca Recordings*

Led Zeppelin. *The BBC Sessions*

Björk, *Telegram*

Hybrid, *Wide Angle*

Pink Floyd, *Meddle*

Stereolab, *Dots and Loops*

The Thievery Corporation, *Abductions and Reconstructions*

Tricky, *Maxinquaye*

The Beach Boys, *Pet Sounds*

Nick Drake, *Pink Moon*

Yoko Ono, *Plastic Ono Band*

U-Roy, *Dread in a Babylon*

Joy Division, *Unknown Pleasures*

Gil Scott-Heron, *Small Talk at 125th & Lennox*

Neil Young, *Everybody Knows this is Nowhere*

Pop Group, *Y*

Lali Puna, *Tridecoder*

Throbbing Gristle, *20 Jazz Funk Greats*

Flying Burrito Brothers, *Gilded Palace of Sin*

Talking Heads, *Remain in Light*

Beck, *Odelay*

Original Soundtrack, *The Harder They Come*

Roxy Music, *Stranded*

New Order, *Technique*

Iggy Pop, *The Idiot*

The Undertones, *The Undertones*

Lloyd Cole & the Commotions, *Rattlesnakes*

The B-52's, *The B-52's*

The Shadows, *The Shadows*

LL Cool J, *Mama Said Knock You Out*

The Smiths, *Strangeways, Here We Come*

Underworld, *Second Toughest in the Infants*

Siouxsie & the Banshees, *The Scream*

Captain Beefheart & his Magic Band, *Doc at the Radar Station*

TLC, *CrazySexyCool*

Kevin Ayers, *Shooting at the Moon*

Kylie Minogue, *Fever*

Nine Inch Nails, *The Downward Spiral*

Penguin Café Orchestra, *Music from the Penguin Café*

Tackhead, *Friendly as a Hand Grenade*

Annette Peacock, *I Have No Feelings*

Wendy and Carl, *Drawing of Sound*

DJ Spooky, *Riddim Warfare*

Can, *Ege Bamyasi*

Linda Ronstadt, *Heart Like a Wheel*

Momus, *Stars Forever*

Brian Eno, *Discreet Music*

Kraftwerk, *Ralf and Florian*

Jewel, *Pieces of You*

Richard Thompson, *Rumour and Sigh*

Méshell Ndegéocello, *Bitter*

Catherine Wheel, *Happy Days*

The Flaming Groovies, *Shake Some Action*

Johnny Cash, *Unchained*

Baader Meinhof, *Baader Meinhof*

David Bowie, *Young Americans*

David Sylvian, *Secrets of the Beehive*

Alexander 'Skip' Spence, *Oar*

Durutti Column, *Vinni Reilly*

Digable Planets, *Blowout Comb*

John Martyn, *Solid Air*

Alice Cooper, *Killer*

Art Bears, *The World as it is Today*

Julie Driscoll, *1969*

Olivia Tremor Control, *Black Foliage*

Bert Jansch, *Rosemary Lane*

Bridget St John, *Songs for the Gentleman*

John Cale, *Music for a New Society*

Country Joe & the Fish, *Electric Music for the Mind and Body*

Depeche Mode, *Music for the Masses*

Guided By Voices, *Bee Thousand*

The Orb, *Adventures Beyond the Ultraworld*

Bob Dylan, *Nashville Skyline*

Low, *Secret Name*

T. Rex, *Tanx*

The Monkees, *The Monkees*

Van Der Graaf Generator, *Pawn Hearts*

Sparks, *Kimono My House*

The Fall, *The Wonderful and Frightening World of . . .*

Family, *Music in a Doll's House*

Mouse on Mars, *Idiology*

Scritti Politti, *Anomie and Bonhomie*

The Auteurs, *New Wave*

Carla Bley, *Escalator Over the Hill*

B. B. King, *Live at the Regal*

Mott the Hoople, *Live*

The 13th Floor Elevators, *The Psychedelic Sounds of . . .*

Slum Village, *Fantastic Vol. 2*

Cat Power, *Covers Record*

Sly & Robbie, *Hail Up the Taxi*

DJ Shadow, *Endtroducing*

Tori Amos, *Little Earthquakes*

Angelo Badalamenti, *Twin Peaks*

The Flaming Lips, *Zaireeka*

Spiritualized, *Lazer Guided Melodies*

5. In the mid-nineties I wrote a book about punk rock called *77 – I Now Disagree with Everything I've Said* – seventy-seven eleven-hundred-word essays about subjects and ideas that create a more appropriate and informative analysis of punk without mentioning The Sex Pistols, The Clash, The Damned, Alternative T.V., Buzzcocks, Crass, Sham 69, Generation X, Siouxsie & the Banshees, The Stranglers, Adam Ant, The Ramones, X-Ray Spex, The Adverts . . . The following is the list of the seventy-seven essays featured in the book, which slightly confused the publishers, who still put a photograph of a snarling Johnny Rotten on the cover.

James Joyce
Psychic TV
Sun Ra
Lenny Bruce
Guy Debord
Spontaneous Music Ensemble
Mott the Hoople
MC5/Iggy Pop/The Velvet
  Underground/Patti
  Smith/Blondie/Television
Marc Bolan/David Bowie
Alfred Jarry
Love/the Doors
Kurt Vonnegut
Luc Ferrari
Andy Warhol
The Pretty Things
Oskar Schlemmer
Antonin Artaud
Fluxus
Jean-Luc Godard
Beefheart/Zappa
Kraftwerk/Can/Faust/Cluster
Ludwig Wittgenstein/John Peel
The Who/The Stones/The Kinks
Marcel Duchamp
La Monte Young
The Marx Brothers
Jimi Hendrix
Peter Hammill
Lee Perry
J. G. Ballard
The Goons/*A Clockwork Orange*
Lenny Kaye
Ralph Waldo Emerson

Anthony H. Wilson/Daniel Miller
Soft Machine
Anthony Moore
Captain Beefheart
Eno/Eno/Eno/Eno/Brian Eno
The Raincoats
Swell Maps
The Worst
The Prefects
Ovary Lodge
Cabaret Voltaire
The Fall
André Breton
The Residents
Simon Frith/Dick Hebdige/Chuck
  Eddy/Jon Savage
Madonna
The Mekons
Charles Baudelaire
The Flying Lizards
Tuxedomoon
Peter Cook/Vic Reeves
B. S. Johnson
Ivor and Chris Cutler/Mr Scruff
Pete Best
Ornette Coleman
Anthony Braxton
Harry Partch
Merzbow
Cliff Richard/Adam Faith/Billy Fury
The New York Art Quartet
Derek Jarman/Carry On films
God/god
Yoko Ono
John Zorn

6. The follow-up to the possibly successful *77* was the artfully fractured *Eighty 8 – If You Think Radiohead's* Kid A *is Weird, Then You Should Really Hunt this Music Down.*

  After you have listened to at least twenty-two of the following, then perhaps you can begin a discussion, with Kylie or her ghostwriter, about just what makes music weird, and then – after the weirdness – what happens, what changes, what goes on, what's the point – is it just a pleasure listening to weirdness that is just straightforward pleasure, or is the weirdness making the world, your mind, your mind in the world, a better place thing space capsule container mind room, etc. . . .? That's weirdness plied by weirdness and piled on weirdness, but then, what is weird? It will take a dose of the following, long, regular doses, to be even able to begin considering exactly what weirdness is. Of course, weirdness might not be the word. In fact, in the essays in *Eighty 8*, weirdness was never the word. The word 'weird' perversely suggests the expected, so weirdness was never really mentioned beyond the title.

In the book *Eighty 8*, there were eighty-eight eleven-hundred-word essays about the following albums, about the sound, the spaces in the sounds, the sound within the spaces, the sound under the ground of sound, and by the end the words in the book had taken on a kind of volume, a level of noise, that began to reflect, to re-create, the music being discussed. The prose used to describe the music was meant to create in your mind's ear a vibration, a series of pulls and hums, scrapes and curves, clips and cracks, snaps and snips, hisses and sags that brought the obscure music to life, so that the words created sound in the way they fitted together, in the way they linked and loosened meaning. This was my way of saying that the way to write about music is often to fall back into utter abstraction, a sort of level some levels beyond the good and evil of pure descriptiveness, where you are creating symbolic sensation with the words that match and catch the potential sensations of the music.

These words were as free from any kind of social or commercial context, any kind of connection to processed reality, as the music – this was the biggest clue as to why *Kid A* was not, as such, the real thing, because it was so essentially reliant on the position of the group as a branded logo-ed recognised star unit with commercial support and the safety net of massive cash-flow. The risk of losing everything – which in some senses was, you might say, the risk Radiohead took in altering their formula – was not really as great as the risk taken by people who have nothing to lose. You might lose an audience but if you never had an audience the risk you take is never having an audience. Of loneliness. It was easy for Radiohead, with all the company they had, to popularise the noises and nerve of lonely predecessors from the position of altern-ative darlings, because in a way it was simply a continuation of their formula, it was a modification of who they were anyway. Perhaps it is the very loneliness involved in creating this kind of music that makes it so authentic. If you have company, even if the music is technically and aesthetically as pure and divine as some of the following, it is not authentic. I've no reason for thinking that. Not really. Sometimes life is like that. It's the isolation that gives the truly strange music its power and mystery.

This is not entirely Radiohead's fault – they were sort of trapped by circum-stances and fame and money and expectation. You could obviously congratulate them on their decision to shred sound, to go a little cubist, or blue, or free, or micro, or post. But the fact is, what they produced was a fabrication, a copy, a tribute. In a way, they became a tribute band, and the tribute they were paying was to Aphex Twin, Anthony Braxton, Albert Ayler, AMM, Autechre, Arto Lindsay Trio – and that's just the As – and they were also a tribute to the following or there-abouts . . . None of this matters, ultimately, but if you have been a rock critic, and you have developed an idea of the way music works and doesn't work, these things are fun to play around with, and in a way coming up with stuff like the following list is part of the fun of being a rock critic – perhaps the only real fun. To be utterly obscure, to tinker with such a list until you feel the list does all the explaining without you having to add anything else, and to be annoyed with, not admiring of, Radiohead, a commercial proposition, for daring to believe that they could be

life from critics who were either taking the book too seriously or not seriously enough.

It was a book written in defence of the act, even the art, of rock writing, but it took nothing for granted. As a writer about music who wanted writing about music to be special, as different and special as great music, I was very aware that a vast amount of writing about music is bland, boring, and little more than tepid descriptions of music that comfortably positions music in its genre. Faced with the amount of music loosely associated with rock, and that's a combination of everything that's gone before and everything new, rock journalism has moved away from being writing, as such, and towards a kind of nervous niceness, with not much sight of the sheer exuberance and selfishness that would be required to ride across all the music into writing greatness.

Over the past twenty years, the most exciting part of rock writing, the part where it seemed as if the writers were getting off on their own power, and therefore making the kind of mad, eccentric gestures that made the writing worth reading, was when it came up with more and more absurd new genres. The best rock-and-roll writers can claim a few new genres that they have invented – I have a few under my belt, and I endeavoured to slip a few into this book, the one you are reading now, and *99*.

The need to have new words to describe what was once pretty much just rock, pop and soul has increased as the music has shattered into freefall. The number of new genres writers have come up with to define and describe new music has expanded to dizzying levels, and the more a new genre generates subgenres and attached genres, and genres that blur across genres and genres that eat other genres, the better. It is in this sense that I include the likes of John Cage and Brian Eno on the list of great writers about music – both for the way they write about music without resorting to meek description and comparison, and also in the way they thought up new genres, genres that turned into other genres, which gave birth to other genres, which bled into other genres, and so on, as if the dreaming up of labels was inspiring new musicians to fill the new genres with sounds that led to the next set of genres. The most impact a writer can have on the development of music is by coming up with a new genre – my particular triumph, which I wrote about for many pages in *99*, was the term 'new pop' which I invented in the early eighties to describe a post-punk music that seemed, for all its strangeness, literateness, knowingness, energy, even intellectualism, to belong in the charts. I talked about groups such as Magazine, Gang of Four, The Fire Engines, The Associates, New Order, The Human League and Heaven 17 as new-pop groups that should have been having hits, and eventually some of them actually did. Twenty years later, the new-pop mentality of pop music warped by found sound, hedonistic urgency, intelligent edge and wired vision would enter the mainstream, and, in the early part of the twenty-first century, Britney Spears, Kylie Minogue, Missy Elliott, Daft Punk, Destiny's Child, Black Box Recorder, The Cardigans, Junior Senior, and Eminem were the commercial sonic end result of the post-punk new-pop mixing and matching of styles, sounds, looks, image- and pleasure-seeking.

But the invention of the names of genres has not really been matched by a development in the writing about the new musics – most writing pretty much remains the same, with the use of the same kinds of words and phrases that have always been used in writing about rock music. Coming up with genre names is a useful way of trying to control the essential chaos of new music, to organise histories of the music that flow in neat time lines and create nice linear progressions, but there is still not much real attempt to actually write about the music other than as a thing which fits into this bigger thing, which is a long history of music that began this way and carried on like this. So, although I tried to defend the idea that you could write about music, that there are ways to explain the feeling of listening to music, of interpreting the art, appreciating the performance, there was also a sense that writing about music is so boring, or at least so repetitive, and never in a euphoric way, because essentially it is impossible to write about something that even in its most conventional form tends to be even more abstract than the most abstract of paintings. It is as if the invention of the musical genres, to bundle up music into nice recognisable boxes and stack them within easy reach, has been the strongest development in rock writing lately because it avoids the issue of actually having to get inside the new music and explain it as something other than a socio-economic force, or an item of fashion, or an addition to your alphabetically ordered record collection. It doesn't deal directly with the mystery and elusiveness of music – it has been a great form of play, but it hasn't generated writing that equals that sense of play, and rather than creating order it has actually led to a rather attractive chaos as genres implode into other genres, as genres chase themselves through a maze where the entrance is made up of the idea that music is pure commodity and the exit is made up of the idea that music is pure expression.

That last line may well be a classic case of trying to dance about architecture. Maybe whoever said the phrase 'writing about music is like trying to dance about architecture' was actually complaining about writers like myself who pathetically attempt to use metaphor or emotion to define the beauty of music, to use non-musical language in an attempt to intelligently describe musical form. Perhaps whoever it was who came up with this phrase was dismissing any attempt to write about music other than to react to it with a simple yes or no, enthusiasm or disappointment. They didn't mind the genres, the putting into boxes, the filing and stacking and organising; they just didn't like the attempt to match the otherness of music with an otherness in the writing about it. Or, they just don't like the idea of being slagged off, whether poetically or crudely, with great style or with no style at all.

But who was it that actually came up with the phrase? It's long been a mystery to those of us interested in such things. It's never been clear if it was said by a musician a hundred years ago, by a jazz musician fifty years ago, by a rock musician thirty years ago, by a punk rocker, a new romantic, someone comparatively recently, or perhaps not even by a musician at all. Maybe no one ever said it at all, it just sort of popped up as the kind of thing someone once might have said, and wouldn't it be great if Mozart said it, or Dean Martin, or Prince . . .

Someone actually did say it in print in 1983: Elvis Costello. It was during an interview with Timothy White in *Musician Magazine*. As well as saying that writing about music was like dancing about architecture, he added that '. . . it's a really stupid thing to do.' I actually quite like the idea that it might be Elvis Costello, as he could have had me in mind among all the other stupid writers he was thinking about. In the late seventies, at the time of his debut album, I had written about

Costello in a Manchester magazine, suggesting that he was perhaps not as great as he was being cracked up to be at the time. Revealing classic rock-critic-snob doubt about someone being hyped but not by me, I savaged his look, sound, style and lyrics. On the day the magazine was published, he was playing a show in Manchester, which I was going to review for the *New Musical Express*. This meant I was on the guest list. Stupidly, in a way Costello might well have felt confirmed his feelings about music writers, I went along to the show never really thinking that Costello might have read the piece, or actually been bothered about it if he had.

I arrived for the show, and gave my name at the door. The girl with the guest list ran her finger down the names. She stopped, looked up at me, and without a word pointed out something that had been written next to my name on the list. The words, written in quite an angry scrawl I later found out was Costello's writing, said: 'On no account let this bastard into the building.' (I didn't get into the building. I didn't see his set. But, being a rock critic pretty sure of the way to make a right myth of myself, I did review the show. I gave it quite a good write-up, actually.)

But, although Costello clearly used the 'dancing about architecture' quote, it's not clear he originated it. It appeared that he was quoting someone else, an old jazzer, perhaps, or, knowing Costello – a bit of a know-it-all on the side, a bit of a writer about music himself – he might have been quoting an academic, a classical composer. Perhaps, knowing Costello's sense of humour, he was quoting the comedian Steve Martin, who has many times been on the list of those who might have said it. Another comedian who has been credited with the quote is the great Martin Mull, the comedian's comedian, lately known for playing Roseanne's gay boss in *Roseanne* and the vice principal at the school in *Sabrina the Teenage Witch*. As someone who once played a forty-five-minute show consisting of him saying nothing but 'thank you', he may well have produced the line in his philosophical early-seventies pre-hack TV years.

But in *99*, these were the ninety-nine main musical suspects concerning who actually first said 'writing about music is like dancing about architecture'. There were, in the now honoured tradition, eleven hundred words written about each subject.

Laurie Anderson	Burt Bacharach
Elvis Costello	Daniel Lanois
Frank Zappa	Holger Czukay
Janet Jackson	Simon Fisher Turner
Morton Feldman	Mike Oldfield
Ringo Starr	Van Dyke Parks
Merce Cunningham	Luciano Berio
Sun Ra	Lotte Lenya
Jeffrey 'Skunk' Baxter	Arthur Lee
Brian Eno	Miles Davis
John Cage	Charlie Watts
Linda Lewis	Donovan
Roger Chapman	Steve Albini
David Gates	Carlos Santana
Thelonious Monk	Mark E. Smith
Richard H. Kirk	Ginger Baker

Tiny Tim	Jaco Pastorius
Carla Bley	Billy Bragg
Lester Bangs	Kim Gordon
Jim Reeves	Genesis P. Orridge
King Sunny Ade	Alex Chilton
Kevin Ayers	Chico Freeman
Professor Longhair	Pink
Mayo Thompson	Fats Navarro
Christy Moore	Ari Up
Judee Sill	Lennie Tristano
Wayne Kramer	Michael Crawford
Yusef Lateef	Wendy Carlos
Meredith Monk	Vangelis
Petula Clarke	Anne Clarke
Cornelius Cardew	Robin Guthrie
Peanuts Hucko	Eddy Grant
Tito Puente	Joan Jett
Rafael Toreal	Irmin Schmidt
Tim Rice	David Tudor
Carl Craig	Poly Styrene
Glen Campbell	Luigi Nono
Kevin Coyne	Felix Da Housecat
Uri Caine	Kevin Shields
Ronnie Laine	Meatloaf
Emitt Rhodes	Shania Twain
Cole Porter	Billy Swann
Bonnie Tyler	Grachan Moncur III
Lalo Schifrin	Henry Mancini
Harry Nilsson	Arthur Brown
Jim O'Rourke	Paul Anka
Ryuichi Sakamoto	Herb Alpert
Cindy Lauper	Melanie
Benjamin Britten	Doc Pomus
Laura Nyro	

8. *110 other albums to think about if you think that Radiohead's Kid A is really weird: 110* is the follow-up book to the original *88 albums to think about buying if you think Radiohead's Amnesiac is really weird*, with eleven hundred words written about each subject. Oddly enough, the book is a tribute to Radiohead, as well as being a snobby snub. The subtitle to *110* might well be *Like rowing a canoe in the fog with Radiohead and a robot frog*. As we haven't got space to actually print the book within this book, I must just say that some of the essays about each of these records were almost identical — actually, fifteen were completely identical — and that each essay included the following phrases and words:

'pitch, duration, overtone and amplitude'

'there is no excellent beauty that does not have some strangeness in the proportion'

'no one has ever written, painted, sculpted, modelled, built or invented except literally to get out of hell'

'funnier than a fish'

'and then the dancing can begin'

'the context of no context'

'coherent, or not, as the case may be, or not'

the schizoid pastiche of a fading sense of history'

'hectic nights of useless thought'

'It is not a question of getting anywhere, of making progress, or having come from anywhere in particular, of tradition or futurism. There is neither nostalgia nor anticipation.'

'as science gets better the problems get weirder'

'the trick is to remember forwards'

'the freely converging and scattering voices are fused into the stately progression of harmonic chords supporting a single dominant melody'

'Bass line sustains on notes below, repeating behind the glitch and plink of the foreground sequence.'

'The time signatures, pulse groupings and pulse rates can be considered as vectors with their common origin in the void, or null point of the matrix. Strictly speaking, a vector is a two-dimensional extension, and the concepts are easy, but push it out further to become a tensor function and the pulse rates and the pulse groupings define the shape or time of the balloon surface.'

'most music is trivialised by attempts to describe it'

'openly disrupt conventional assumptions about formal unity and beauty'

'post-industrial urban life'

'subvert the profusion of visual, sonic and information sources that run our lives'

'docufiction'

'shronk'

'that's a very difficult thing to achieve'

'in the recent past, restless guitar solos have given way to monochromatic drones, and recognisable drum patterns have become intricate arrays of pops and clicks'

'we must take hold of the enigma of fiction and lay her on the table'

'a community, no matter how small, is unavoidably and importantly a political instrument'

'fuckedupfuckedupfuckedup'

'like Vinni Reilly and Harold Budd meeting Pole and Joe Zawinul in an elevator'

'out of time suspended against the groove cut up against an electric horizon snap flicker writhe ripple ripping rip thank heavens for little riffs for sounds that go glow in the night'

'many people, faced with such a beginning, would take refuge in the life of the mind'

'obscurity can be the best thing to happen to some music'

'the first unpleasant impression is as real and true as the later pleasant one' 'hej tatta gorem'

'Stop! Stop! I confess!'

'rhythm creates form by connecting various levels of reality, by throwing bridges across various reservoirs of information, different tracks of time'

'culture happens in secret'

'the flannel cultishness of *The Wire* versus the corduroy clubbiness of *Q*'

'the circuit between Justin Timberlake and a fourteen-year-old girl is what's really important about music – that connection is more profound than the one between an Interpol record and a fifty-year-old rock writer'

'after about fifty minutes, some incredible things start to happen, both to your sense of time and your perception of sound'

'the fine balance between above and below'

'All Western music has been based on the principles of repetition and contrast. As music progresses into the future, the polarity of contrast and repetition will always remain at the core of the musical argument.'

'sometimes the better a record is the harder it is to describe'

'one beat on the drum is followed 500 years later by another'

'flex rattle and smudge'

'a self-portrait in a shattered mirror'

'for example, Stockhausen's *Sound Atoms* and *Constellations* – both of which are, interestingly, pointillist'

'the third section is structured like the first, the fourth like the third'

'everyone noodling away over a single chord'

'throughout history, new music has been blamed for its lack of melody'

'when what passes for, or hints at, or what is disguised as the chorus comes in, there is little point in going bouncy bouncy'

'the cymbals splash like windscreen wipers in time'

'one note, if used cleverly enough, can be just as awe-inspiring as an entire complex or catchy melody'

'what really matters is to preserve and disseminate works that have the potential to make a positive and lasting contribution to humanity'

'there's always a thin line – about seventy decibels, I would say – between the densest noise and the most serene ambient drone'

'the cult of personality, the mystery of technology'

'like everything else, this makes me think of sex'

'the result of one massive equipment haemorrhage'

'not that there's anything wrong with that'

'there's no accounting for taste'

'there is no music if the audience is deaf'

'*Swan Lake* it ain't'

'we are far too intolerant of superficial fragmentation'

'lacking the talent to write a song like, oh, "Louie Louie"'

'it's serious'

'while we may not dance to the rhythms of the environment we have an apparently insatiable desire for mimesis of its sounds and their relationships'

'the idea of otherwise invisible aqueous swirls and molecular profusion suddenly

unfolding themselves in delicate and random patterns of biological fraternisa-
tion'

'if you become bored, remember you are thinking about yourself and how bored
you are'

'if you were dancing blindfolded and the architect was Frank Gehry'

'4/4 time signatures dissolving into fluctuating flurries of percussion'

'otherwise all that counts is how good you are on your instrument – and that means
we should only listen to opera singers, jazz and Dire Straits'

'it's not serious'

'like Pharoah Sanders and The Mamas and Papas in an elevator with Cornelius
Cardew and Aerosmith'

'this music doesn't particularly exist for humanity at large, which might be part of
its dark, exclusive charm. Perhaps if humanity at large actually heard this music
it might make the world a better place, or at least a stranger, lovelier one'

'overtones and beats create aura and penumbra like coloured lights criss-crossing
space, sonic images whirl and eddy raising an unearthly panoply of life forms'

'I will still be enjoying working out how to describe this when I am in my eighties'

'music is a combination of something to do with memory and something to do
with what is about to happen which cannot yet be remembered'

'good'

'this is music made by people who are too sensitive to live for listeners who are
too sensitive to live that makes me wonder why I gave up writing about music
at such a young age?'

'oh God'

'and then something happens, just at the moment you felt that nothing was ever
going to happen, and then you are content for a little while more, even though
nothing much happens again, and then there is a little bit more noise, and then
some more noise, and then all sorts of noise, until you really beg for nothing to
happen again, but it doesn't sound like that's going to happen, it doesn't sound
like nothing will happen, there is just going to be a whole lot more noise, deadly,
deadpan noise turning into truly sinister noise, noise as an urgent, irregular
combination of scattered doom and random gloom, and creepy scratches on the
surface of deep desolation, at which point you start to feel quite scared, as if the
music has turned into a genuine threatening presence, something that might pull
the life from underneath you, and you decide to play a song by the Appletons'

'it is music that, once formed, changes at every moment, until it dies. It dissolves,
like a wave, like life. It makes you realise how a piece of music is like a metaphor
for life – it comes into being, it does what it does, and then it disappears'

'coming and going while gradually growing weaker like the painful breathing of a
dying man'

'I might be wrong'

'What else matters?'

'in the next life'

'sound is born of silence, and it returns there, but the beat goes on'

The 110 albums are:

Arnold Dreyblatt, *Animal Magnetism*
Phill Niblock, *Touch Works, for Hurdy Gurdy and Voice*
Charlemagne Palestine, *Godbear*
Michael Byron, *Music of Nights Without Moon or Pearl*
Peter Garland, *Walk in Beauty*
Guy Klucesvek, *Transylvanian Software*
Daniel Lentz, *Point Conception*
Kevin Volans, *Cover Him With Grass*
Glenn Branca, *The World Upside Down*
Doctor Nerve, *Did Sprinting Die?*
Phil Kline, *Exquisite Corpses*
Testsu Inoue, *World Receiver*
Augur and Birds of Tin, *Strange Seeds Come from Old Flowers*
Chris Meloche, *Recurring Dreams of the Urban Myth*
Oval, *Diskont 94*
Polygon Window, *Surfing on Sine Waves*
A Small Good Thing, *Slim Westerns*
Boris Feokstitov, remixed by Bill Laswell, *Russian Chants*
Merzbow, *Batztoutai with Material Gadgets*
Psychic TV, *At Stockholm*
Nurse with Wound, *Spiral Insana*
Woob, *1194*
Anthony Braxton, *Seven Standards 1985, Vol. 1*
David Borden, *Cayuga Night Music*
Fred Frith, *Speechless*
John Greaves, *La Petite Bouteille de Linge*
John Zorn/George Lewis/Bill Frisell, *News for Lulu*
Lindsay Cooper, *Music for Other Occasions*
Marc Ribot y los Cubanos Postizos, *The Prosthetic Cubans*
Peter Blegvad, *The Naked Shakespeare*
This Heat, *Health and Efficiency*
Purple Trap, *Decided . . . Already the Motionless Heart of Tranquillity, Tangling the Prayer Called I*
Biosphere/Deathprod, *Nordheim Transformed*
Morton Feldman, *For Samuel Beckett*
TNC Culture, *The Screen Turned Black*
Harry Partch, *Delusion of the Fury*
Luigi Nono, *Voices of Protest*
Maeror Tri, *Hypnotikum 1*
Monotrona, *Hawkeye and Firebird*
Woven Hand, *Woven Hand*
Boom Bip, *Seed to Sun*
Wobbly, *Wild Why*
Merzbow, *Merzbeat*
DJ Rupture, *Minesweeper Suite*
Don Cherry, *Orient*
Ennio Morricone, *Gli Occhi Freddi Della Paura*
Kid 606, *The Action-Packed Mentalist Brings You the Fucking Jams*
Markus Guentnet, *In Moll*
Father Moo & the Black Sheep, *Father Moo & the Black Sheep*
Faust, *Ravvivando*
Henry Flynt, *Raga Electric: Experimental Music 1963–1971*
Fog, *Fog*
Full Swing, *Edits*
Coh, *Love Uncut*
People Like Us, *Recyclopedia Britannica*
Nobukazu Takemura, *Hoshi no Koe*
Talk Talk, *Missing Pieces*
Amon Tobin, *Out from Out Where*
Derek Bailey, *Mirakle*
Keiji Haino, *Abandon All Words at a Stroke, So that Prayer Can Come Spilling Out*
Brandon Labelle, *Shadow of a Shadow*
Lustmord, *Purifying Fire*
Koji Asano, *Flow-Augment*
Dalek, *From Filthy Tongue of Gods and Griots*
Rachel's/Matmos, *Full On Night*
Thermo, *Touring Inferno!*
Jackie-O Motherfucker, *Liberation*

Aero-Mic'd, *Aero-Mic'd*

Jello, *Voile*

Cornelius Cardew & the Scratch Orchestra, *The Great Learning*

Luc Ferrari, *Presque Rien*

Pierre Henry, *Mix 03.0*

Richard Lainhart, *Ten Thousand Shades of Blue*

Richard Maxfield/Harold Budd, *The Oak of the Golden Dreams*

Alog, *Red Shift Swing*

Evan Parker and George Graewe, *Unity Variations*

Henry Cowell, *Mosaic*

Coil, *Musick to Play in the Dark Vol.1*

Rafael Toral, *Aeriola Frequency*

The Butthole Surfers, *Rembrandt Pussyhorse*

Oren Ambarchi, *Suspension*

Fennesz/O'Rourke/Rehberg, *Return of Fenn O Berg*

Fred Frith, *Accidental – Music for Dance Volume 3*

Iannis Xenakis, *Persepolis + Remixes Edition 1*

Yen Pox, *New Dark Age*

Food, *Veggie*

Radian, *Rec. Extern*

Wishbone Ash, *Argus*

CSSO, *Are You Excrements?*

Aube, *Time Mind*

Kenneth Gaburo, *Tape Play*

Mika Vainio, *Onko*

Bruce Gilbert, *This Way to the Shivering Man*

Muslimgauze, *Observe with Sadiq Bey*

Chris Cutler and Thomas Dimuzio, *Quake*

Company, *Epiphanies*

John Zorn/Fred Frith, *The Art of Memory*

The Science Group, *A Mere Coincidence*

Swell Maps, *Jane from Occupied Europe*

Han Bennink, *Nerve Beats*

Kevin Drumm, *Sheer Hellish Miasma*

Taj Mahal Travellers, *August 1972*

Tony Oxley Quintet, *The Baptised Traveller*

Peter Brotzmann, *Fuck De Boere*

Jim O'Rourke, *I'm Happy and I'm Singing a 1, 2, 3, 4*

Zoviet France, *Misfits, Loony Tunes and Squalid Criminals*

Mat Maneri Trio, *So What?*

Radar Brothers, *And the Surrounding Mountains*

Bola, *Fyuti*

Stars of the Lid, *Tired Sounds of Stars of the Lid*

Henry Cow, *Western Culture*

9. The latest book in the series that has become known as 'Eleven Times Music' is *1,100 words on each of 121 songs that explain why Kraftwerk are Kraftwerk and just how and where and when their influence spread and turned.* The order is precise but mysterious. Each essay features the words: motion, change, fast, slow, sense, data, linear, additive, process, sex, information, ratio, pulse, computer, human, erotic, intensity, dream, technology, extension, body, dark, romantic, isolation, device, rapture, interface, geometry, time, space, signal, blip, code, equipment, language, pleasure, technical, possibility, symbolic, wistful, mass, material, overlit, landscape, intimate, simulate, impetus, temptation, system, absorb, identity, connection, loop, illusion, advance, abstraction, dynamism, quantum, car, cold, amplify, lost, souls, stranded, in, sleek, luxury, density, euro, society, sign, the, locomotive, mechanics, have, blue, eyes, libido, memory, sample, domain, manipulation, desire, image, pare, song, vital, terse, force, function, minimum, molecules, cosmic, tenderness, sequence, genetic, design, unicorn, psychic, experience, reproduction, depersonalisation, action, screen, repetition, contrast.

Iggy Pop, 'Funtime'
David Bowie, 'V2 Schneider'
Donna Summer, 'I Feel Love'
Ultravox, 'Mr X'
The Normal, 'TV OD'
Suicide, 'Cheree'
Afrika Bambaataa and the Soulsonic Force, 'Planet Rock'
Cybotron, 'Clear'
Derrick May/Rhythm is Rhythm, 'The Strings of Life'
Derrick May/Rhythm is Rhythm, 'It Is What It Is'
Joy Division, 'She's Lost Control'
John Foxx, 'She's a Liquid'
Devo, 'Mechanical Man'
New Order, '586/Blue Monday'
New Order, 'Temptation'
The Human League, 'Circus of Death'
23 Skidoo, 'Coup'
Green Velvet, 'La La Land'
Pet Shop Boys, 'West End Girls'
Orchestral Manoeuvres in the Dark, 'Electricity'
Gary Numan, 'Are Friends Electric'
Art of Noise, 'Moments in Love'
Front 242, 'Headhunter'
Cabaret Voltaire, 'No Escape'
808 State, 'Pacific'
Giorgio Moroder, 'Machines'
Björk, 'Hyperballad'
Model 500, 'Off to Battle'
Amanda Lear, 'I Am a Photograph'
Plastikman, 'Circuit Breaker'
Destiny's Child, 'Bootylicious'
Daft Punk, 'Digital Love'
Nils Petter Molvaer, 'Platonic Years' (Herbalizer mix)
Soft Cell, 'Tainted Love'
So Solid Crew, '21 Seconds'
Adult, 'Hand to Phone'
Matmos, 'L.A.S.I.K.'
Amon Tobin, 'Reanimator'
Laub, 'Filesharing'
Hybrid, 'Dreaming Your Dreams'
Boards of Canada, 'Pete Standing Alone'
Plaid, 'Squance'
Autechre, 'Nil'
Madonna, 'Music'
Depeche Mode, 'Personal Jesus'
Laurie Anderson, 'O, Superman'
A Guy Called Gerald, 'Voodoo Ray'
Sugababes, 'Overload'
Radiohead, 'Idioteque'
The Orb, 'Little Fluffy Clouds'
Clock DVA, 'E-Wave'
Orbital, 'Way Out'
D.A.F., 'Love at First Sight'
Aphex Twin, 'Acid Avid Jam Shred'
Missy Elliott, 'Get Ur Freak On'
BT, 'Movement in Still Life'
DJ Shadow, 'Organ Donor'
Dr Dre, 'The Day the Niggaz Took Over'
Dr Dre, 'Still Dre'
Roni Size, 'Share the Fall' (Way Out West remix)
The Normal, 'Warm Leatherette'
Propaganda, 'P. Machinery'
Sparks, 'The Number One Song in Heaven'
Future Sound of London, 'Papua New Guinea' (Hybrid remix)
Fuzzy Logic, 'Obsession'
William Orbit, 'Water from a Leaf Vine'
KLF, 'What is Love?'
U2, 'Lemon' (Paul Oakenfold remix)
Future Loop Foundation, 'Coming Down'
Mantronix, 'Bassline'
Luke Slater, 'All Exhale'
Fischerspooner, 'Emerge'
The Remote Viewer, 'Snow It Falls On'
Exzakt, 'Electronic Dream'
Aux 88, 'Electro/Techno'
Anthony Rother, 'Sex with the Machines'
Arthur Baker, 'Breakers Revenge'
Visage, 'Frequency 7'

Jam and Spoon, 'Stella'

Ryuichi Sakamoto, 'Riot in Lagos'

Fad Gadget, 'Collapsing New People'

Egyptian Lover, 'And My Heart Goes Boom'

Kylie Minogue, 'Can't Get You Out of My Head'

Maggotron, 'Welcome to the Planet of Bass'

Fatboy Slim, 'Everybody Needs a 303'

Les Rhythmes Digitales, 'Soft Machine'

Cibo Matto, 'Sci-Fi Wassabe'

Yello, 'Oh yeah'

Herbie Hancock, 'Rockit'

We Are Borg, 'Cybernet Systems'

Underworld, 'Cups'

Stereo MCs, 'Connected'

Air, 'Sexy Boy' (Cassius remix)

Add (N) to X, 'Skills'

Mr Velcro Fastener, 'Number of the Beats'

Ian Brown, 'Love Like a Fountain'

Simple Minds, 'I Travel'

Image of a Group, 'Temperature'

N.E.R.D., 'Lapdancer'

Tom Tom Club, 'Wordy Rappinghood'

Beanfield, 'Planetary Deadlock'

Tarwater, 'Be Late'

Telepopmusik, 'Genetic World'

Gusgus, 'Superhuman'

Photek, 'Knitevision'

God Lives Underwater, 'Behaviour Modification'

Pitchshifter, 'Genius'

Static, 'Turn On, Switch Off'

Death in Vegas, 'Dead Elvis'

Tosca, 'Chocolate Elvis'

Dot Allison, 'Strung Out'

All for One, 'Machinelust'

Morcheeba, 'Tape Loop'

Pilote, 'Turtle' (Bonobo mix)

Döpplereffekt, 'Sterilization'

Orbital, Kein Trink Wasser'

Electronic, 'Getting Away with It'

Ladytron, 'I'm with the Pilots'

Mapstation, 'More People Than Two'

Anthony Rother, 'Describe Reality'

Moby, 'Go'

The Avalanches, 'Since I Left You'

'N Sync, 'Pop'

Grace Jones, 'Slave to the Rhythm'

Princess Superstar, 'Do It Like a Robot'

Squarepusher, 'My Red Hot Car'

KLF, 'Last Train to Transcentral'

Gotan Project, 'El Captalismo Foraneo'

To Rococo Rot and I-Sound, 'Pantone'

My Computer, 'Vulnerabilia'

Black Box Recorder, 'Facts of Life'

Eve, 'Satisfaction'

Yoko Ono, 'Walking on Thin Ice' (The Pet Shop Boys mix)

Mouse on Mars, 'Actionist Response'

U-Ziq, 'Hasty Boom Alert'

The Pet Shop Boys, 'Being Boring'

Mitte Karoake, 'Aufschlag'

Röyksopp, 'Remind Me'

Audio Bullys, 'Real Life'

Señor Coconut, 'El Baile Aleman'

Swayzak, 'Ping Pong'

Temponauta, 'Kastha'

Vitalic, 'LaRock 01'

Bubba Sparxxx, 'Ugly'

The Prodigy, 'Androids'

Felix Da Housecat, 'Strobe'

Kid 606, 'Twirl' (Photoshoot remix by Matmos)

Dungeon Family, 'Even in Darkness'

Beck, 'Get Real Paid'

M, 'Pop Muzik'

(This is probably more than 121 songs, but who's counting . . .)

10. The greatest pop single of all time, if we accept that the best length for a pop single is three minutes and thirty seconds, and we then take a second from each of the following 210 songs to make up ... the greatest single of all time. A new series of books was begun with the publication of *210*, which consisted of 210 210-word essays on each of the following songs:

Petula Clarke, 'Downtown'

Auteurs, 'Showgirl'

Creedence Clearwater Revival, 'Have You Ever Seen the Rain'

Julie Driscoll, 'This Wheel's On Fire'

The Turtles, 'Happy Together'

Talk Talk, 'It's My Life'

The Ronettes, 'Be My Baby'

The Kinks, 'You Really Got Me'

Morrissey, 'Every Day is Like Sunday'

2Pac and Dr Dre, 'California Love'

The Rolling Stones, 'It's Only Rock'n'Roll'

Cyndi Lauper, 'All Through the Night'

Pet Shop Boys, 'I Wouldn't Normally Do This Sort of Thing'

The Carpenters, 'Superstar'

Sonic Youth, 'Superstar'

Beck, 'Loser'

Devo, 'Whip It'

Radiohead, 'Creep'

Nirvana, 'Come As You Are'

Cure, 'Boys Don't Cry'

Mott the Hoople, 'Roll Away the Stone'

Stone Roses, 'Fool's Gold'

The Byrds, 'Mr Tambourine Man'

Rascals, 'How Can I Be Sure'

Talking Heads, 'Once in a Lifetime'

Iggy Pop, 'Lust for Life'

Blondie, 'Heart of Glass'

Britney Spears, 'Slave 4 U'

The Monkees, 'Pleasant Valley Sunday'

Japan, 'Quiet Life'

Queens of the Stone Age, 'No One Knows'

Gilbert O'Sullivan, 'Alone Again, Naturally'

The Bangles, 'Walk Like an Egyptian'

The Police, 'Walking on the Moon'

Dionne Warwick, 'Walk On By'

Run DMC, 'Walk This Way'

The Human League, 'Human'

The Chemical Brothers, 'Block Rockin' Beats'

Siouxsie & the Banshees, 'Spellbound'

Public Image, 'This Is Not a Love Song'

The Isley Brothers, 'This Old Heart of Mine'

Roxy Music, 'Love is the Drug'

Magazine, 'The Light Pours Out of Me'

The Flying Lizards, 'Money'

Edwyn Collins, 'A Girl Like You'

Tony Christie, 'Avenues and Alleyways'

Bow Wow Wow, 'I Want Candy'

Kraftwerk, 'The Model'

Kylie Minogue, 'Confide in Me'

David Bowie, 'Fashion'

Lipps Inc., 'Funky Town'

Grace Jones, 'Pull Up to the Bumper'

Joan Jett, 'I love Rock'n'Roll'

Deee Lite, 'Groove is in the Heart'

Abba, 'The Winner Takes It All'

Slade, 'Coz I Luv You'

Kim Wilde, 'Kids in America'

Garbage, 'Stupid Girl'

ABC, 'The Look of Love'

Dusty Springfield, 'The Look of Love'

Daft Punk, 'Da Funk'

T. Rex, 'Telegram Sam'

Black Sabbath, 'Paranoid'

Madonna, 'Like a Virgin'

The Associates, 'Party Fears Two'

Eddie Cochran, 'Summertime Blues'

Kate Bush, 'Running Up That Hill'

Erik B & Rakim, 'I Know You Got Soul'

The Beastie Boys, 'Sabotage'

Hanson, 'Mmmbop'

Otis Redding, 'Sitting on the Dock of the Bay'

Gorillaz, 'Clint Eastwood'

Destiny's Child, 'Say My Name'

The Supremes, 'Baby Love'

Furniture, 'Brilliant Mind'

Screamin' Jay Hawkins, 'I Put a Spell on You'

Prince, 'Sign O the Times'

Robert Palmer, 'Addicted to Love'

Stevie Wonder, 'Superstition'

Betty Wright, 'Clean Up Woman'

Rufus, 'Tell Me Something Good'

Chic, 'Good Times'

The Beach Boys, 'God Only Knows'

The Saints, 'I'm Stranded'

Matthew Sweet, 'Girlfriend'

Emma Bunton, 'What Took You So Long?'

The Pet Shop Boys, 'It's a Sin'

S Club 7, 'Never Had a Dream Come True'

The Chemical Brothers, 'Loops of Fury'

The Sex Pistols, 'Anarchy in the UK'

Eminem, 'The Real Slim Shady'

Christine Aguilera, 'Genie in a Bottle'

The Dandy Warhols, 'Bohemian Like You'

The Rolling Stones, 'Satisfaction'

Prodigy, 'Smack My Bitch Up'

Sting, 'Fields of Gold'

Al Green, 'Tired of Being Alone'

Bob Marley 'Stir It Up'

Lou Reed, 'Satellite of Love'

Brian Eno, 'I'll Come Running'

Aphex Twin, 'Windowlicker'

Aaliyah, 'We Need a Resolution'

Barbra Streisand, 'Woman in Love'

Art of Noise, 'Moments in Love'

The Beatles, 'Can't Buy Me Love'

Jane Birkin and Serge Gainsbourg, 'Je t'aime'

Archie Drell & the Bells, 'Tighten Up'

Bob Dylan, 'I Want You'

Jonathan Richman & the Modern Lovers, 'Roadrunner'

Pink Floyd, 'See Emily Play'

The Surfaris, 'Wipe Out'

Blue Oyster Cult, 'Don't Fear the Reaper'

Japan, 'I Second that Emotion'

Lloyd Cole & the Commotions, 'Perfect Skin'

Love, 'Alone Again Or'

Buzzcocks, 'Ever Fallen in Love'

The Ramones, 'Sheena is a Punk Rocker'

Rickie Lee Jones, 'Chuck E's in Love'

Free, 'All Right Now'

Stephen Stills, 'Love the One You're With'

The Smiths, 'Girlfriend in a Coma'

Cilla Black, 'You're My World'

Gerry & the Pacemakers, 'I Like It'

The Four Tops, 'It's the Same Old Song'

Eddie & the Hot Rods, 'Do Anything You Want to Do'

Neil Diamond, 'Solitary Man'

Patsy Cline, 'Crazy'

The Pop Group, 'She Is Beyond Good and Evil'

Blondie, 'The Tide is High'

Teardrop Explodes, 'Reward'

Tim Hardin, 'If I Were a Carpenter'

Nick Cave and Kylie Minogue, 'Where the Wild Roses Grow'

Everything But the Girl, 'Missing'

Blur, 'Song 2'

Whodini, 'Magic's Wand'

Arthur Brown, 'Fire'

Alice Cooper, 'School's Out'

The Doors, 'People are Strange'

The Faces, 'Stay with Me'
Nazareth, 'This Flight Tonight'
The Who, 'The Acid Queen'
Ike and Tina Turner, 'River Deep, Mountain High'
Nirvana, 'Smells Like Teen Spirit'
The Bangles, 'Eternal Flame'
Buzzcocks, 'Promises'
Kylie Minogue, 'Better the Devil You Know'
The Human League, 'Don't You Want Me'
Steps, 'Tragedy'
Subway Sect, 'Ambition'
The Beatles, 'Ticket to Ride'
Dave Clark Five, 'Glad All Over'
Bryan Ferry, 'A Hard Rain's Gonna Fall'
George Harrison, 'If Not for You'
Jimi Hendrix, 'All Along the Watchtower'
Cher, 'I Want You'
Cher, 'Believe'
The Balanescu Quartet, 'The Model'
BT and Tori Amos, 'Blue Skies'
Janet Jackson, 'Got Til it's Gone'
Pink, 'Get this Party Started'
The Pretenders, 'Brass in Pocket'
Carole King, 'It's Too Late'
Rose Royce, 'Love Don't Live Here Any More'
Motörhead, 'Ace of Spades'
Patti Smith, 'Because the Night'
Ashton Garden and Dyke, 'Resurrection Shuffle'
KLF, '3 A.M. Eternal'
En Vogue, 'Free Your Mind'
Britney Spears, 'You Drive Me Crazy'
ABC, 'Poison Arrow'
Todd Rundgren, 'I Saw the Light'
Cornershop, 'Brimful of Asha'
Fox, 'Ssss-single Bed'

Blondie, 'Maria'
New Order, 'Regret'
Public Image Ltd, 'Rise'
The Pet Shop Boys, 'Suburbia'
Sting, 'If You Love Somebody Set Them Free'
Morrissey, 'Suedehead'
Nelly with Kelly Rowland, 'Dilemma'
Dr Dre with Snoop Dogg, 'Nothing But a G Thang'
No Doubt, 'Don't Speak'
Beck, 'Devil's Haircut'
Tavares, 'Heaven must be Missing an Angel'
Cyndi Lauper, 'Time After Time'
New Order, 'Bizarre Love Triangle'
Red Hot Chilli Peppers, 'Under the Bridge'
Jewel, 'You Were Meant for Me'
Kiss, 'Rock'n'Roll All Nite'
Foo Fighters, 'Everlong'
Michael and Janet Jackson, 'Scream'
Soundgarden, 'Black Hole Sun'
Sweet, 'Ballroom Blitz'
P. Diddy, 'Bad Boy for Life'
Britney Spears, 'Oops! . . . I Did It Again'
The Sex Pistols, 'Pretty Vacant'
Talking Heads, 'Psycho Killer'
Underworld, 'Born Slippy'
Toni Braxton, 'Unbreak My Heart'
Aphex Twin, 'Come to Daddy'
EMF, 'Unbelievable'
Joy Division, 'Love Will Tear Us Apart'
Buzzcocks, 'Orgasm Addict'
The Smiths, 'This Charming Man'
808 State, 'Pacific'
New Order, 'Temptation'
Electronic, 'Getting Away with It'
The Ramones, 'Blitzkrieg Bop'

'Trash Talkin'' by Albert Collins and 'R U Into it' by Kid606

'Man or Myth' by DJ Faust and 'It's a Rainy Day, Sunshine Girls' by Faust

'Can't Get Enough of Your Love' by Barry White and 'Can't Get Enough' by Depeche Mode

'The Night You Saved My Life' by Tanya Donelly and 'Die, Die, My Darling' by Metallica

'Morning Has Broken' by Cat Stevens and 'I Wake Up Dreaming' by Teenage Jesus & the Jerks

'If I Had a Hammer' by Peter, Paul and Mary and 'Never Talking to You Again' by Husker Du

'Another One Rides the Bus' by Weird Al Yankovic and 'That's When I Reach for My Revolver' by Mission of Burma

'Electricity' by Joni Mitchell and 'Electricity' by Orchestral Manoeuvres in the Dark,

'Love Theme from Spartacus' by Yusef Lateef and 'Theme from Star Wars' by Moby

'Telephone Thing' by the Fall and 'AT & T' by Pavement

'M62 Song' by the Doves and 'Journey to the Centre of the Mind' by Ted Nugent & the Amboy Dukes

'Light Flight' by Pentangle, and 'Angels on Your Body' by Lucky Pierre

'Love Comes in Spurts' by Richard Hell and 'Isn't it Romantic' by Ella Fitzgerald

'In the Mood' by Glenn Miller versus 'Vision and Voice' by Throbbing Gristle

'What a Wonderful World' by Joey Ramone and 'I Wanna be Your Joey Ramone' by Sleater Kinney

'Here Comes the Summer' by the Undertones and 'We All Die' by Cat Power

'Heaven is a Place on Earth' by Belinda Carlisle and 'Ego Tripping at the Gates of Hell' by the Flaming Lips

'Life on the Ceiling' by Michael Chapman and 'Last Night I Dreamt That Somebody Loved Me' by Low

'Bombay Aloo' by Curious Digit and 'Peking O' by Can

Liberation Music Orchestra by Charlie Haden and 'War Pigs' by Black Sabbath

The Golden Triumph of Naked Hostility by Mens Recovery Project and 'Top of the World' by the Dixie Chicks

'Szenariodisk' by Oval and 'Love Medley' by Ewan McGregor and Nicole Kidman

'Flow of X' by Matthew Shipp and 'Tea for Two' by Charlie Christian

'Succumb' by Virgin Whore Complex and 'Save Me' by Aimee Mann

'And Now the Rain Looks Like Life is Falling through It' by Roy Montgomery and 'Metaphysical Style' by Dan the Automator and Prince Paul

'Where is My Mind?' by the Pixies and 'Your Mind is on Vacation' by Mose Allison

'Fumms bo wo taa zaa Uu and Ribble Bobble Pimlico' by Kurt Schwitters and 'Who's Got the Action' by Dean Martin

The Ready Made Boomerang by the Deep Listening Band and 'Highway to Hell' by AC/DC

'The Rules of Reduction' by Jim O'Rourke and 'Is that All There Is?' by Christina

'Voices of Anxious Objects' by Ken Butler and 'How Do You Think it Feels' by Lou Reed

The Legendary Crisswell Predicts Your Incredible Future and 'Lies' by J. J. Cale

'White American' by Eminem and 'United States of Islam' by Muslimgauze

'Loonychip Classics' by Bobvan and 'Debris' by the Faces

'Worship the Glitch' by ElpH and Coil and 'Smack My Glitch Up' by Kid606

'Private Dancer' by Tina Turner and 'Private Dancer' by Kevin Blechdom

'To the Quiet Man from a Tiny Girl' by Nurse with Wound and 'A Little Less Conversation' by Elvis Presley

'Just an Illusion' by Zoviet★France and 'Just What I Needed' by the Cars

'Glue Your Eyelids Together' by Adult and 'Let's Do It Together' by Fantastic Johnny C

'Dear Prudence' by Siouxise & the Banshees and 'Dear Prudence' by Brad Mehldau

'I Never Met a Girl Like You Before' by the Kinks and 'I Never Met a Girl Like You Before' by Iggy Pop

'Mongoloid' by Devo and 'Conquistador' by Procul Harum

'Play Dead' by Björk and 'That Don't Impress Me Much' by Shania Twain

'Whole Again' by Atomic Kitten and 'California Rhinoplasty' by Matmos

'I am the Fly' by Wire and 'One Day I'll Fly Away' by Randy Crawford

'Show Me the Meaning of Being Lonely' by the Backstreet Boys and 'A Very Cellular Song' by the Incredible String Band

'The Migration of the Duck Billed Platypus to Australia' by Bardo Pond and 'A Chicken Ain't Nothing But a Bird' by Cab Calloway

'Natural Born Boogie' by Humble Pie and 'Track 8' by Public Image Ltd

'Ship on the Ocean' by the Groundhogs and 'Get Me Off' by Basement Jaxx

'Whisky in the Jar' by Thin Lizzy and 'Time in a Bottle' by Jim Croce

'Building Steam with a Grain of Salt' by DJ Shadow and 'Smoke Gets in Your Eyes' by the Platters

'Something Stupid' by Frank and Nancy Sinatra and 'At the House of Elrond and the Ring Goes South' by Bo Hanson

'Imagine' by Eva Cassidy and 'She's as Beautiful as a Foot' by Blue Oyster Cult

'Neat Neat Neat' by the Damned and 'Perhaps Perhaps Perhaps' by Doris Day

'Necessary Measures' by Pest and 'Papa Don't Preach' by Kelly Osbourne

'Favourite Things' by John Coltrane and 'Favourite Things' by Björk

'I'm Not In Love' by Tori Amos and 'I'm Not In Love' by Fun Loving Criminals

'Just Like Eddie' by Heinz and 'Just Like Eddie' by Silicon Teens

'Yesterday' by Matt Monroe and 'Yesterday' by Boyz II Men

'I Will Survive' by Gloria Gaynor and 'Survivor' by Destiny's Child

'I'm Bored' by Iggy Pop and 'PMS' by Mary J Blige

'Raindrops Keep Falling on My Head' by BJ Thomas and '(I Don't Want To Have) Easy Listening Nightmares' by Nurse with Wound

'Dream a Little Dream of Me' by Mama Cass and 'Dream Baby Dream' by Suicide

'Acoustic Guitar' by Magnetic Fields and 'Digital Hardcore' by Atari Teenage Riot

'I Wish I Was a Lesbian' by Loudon Wainwright III and 'It's Raining Men' by Geri Halliwell

'Where Have All the Bootboys Gone' by Slaughter & the Dogs and 'Who Let The Dogs Out' by Baha Men

'Relax' by Frankie Goes to Hollywood and 'All the Things She Said' by Tatu

'Start to Move' by Wire and 'Don't Stop Movin'' by S Club 7

'If You Buy this Record Your Life Will be Better' by The Tamperer with Maya and 'Rebellious Jukebox' by The Fall

'Sweet Like Chocolate' by Shanks and Bigfoot and 'Black Coffee' by Peggy Lee

'Sexy' by Ebony and 'Song Against Sex' by Neutral Milk Hotel

'Access' by DJ Tim and DJ Misjah and 'The Playboy Channel' by Negativland

'Definition of House Music' by DJ Hell and 'Are You Sitting Comfortably?' by The Moody Blues

'I Don't Know How to Love Him' by Yvonne Elliman and 'Personal Jesus' by Johnny Cash

'Sometimes I Don't Know What to Feel' by Todd Rundgren and 'You Make Me Sick' by Pink

'Couldn't Love You More' by John Martyn and 'Prove It' by Television

'That Horse Must Be Starving' by Avril and 'Complicated' by Avril Lavigne

'One Very Important Thought' by Broadcast and 'Beautiful Day' by U2

'Do You Really Want To Hurt Me?' by Culture Club and 'You Really Hurt Me' by Conya Doss

'I am Trying to Break Your Heart' by Wilco and 'The Star Spangled Banner' by Whitney Houston

'Back in the USA' by Chuck Berry and 'Back in the USA' by Linda Ronstadt

'Low Down' by Lali Puna and 'I'm Going to Live the Life I Sing About in My Song' by Mahalia Jackson

'Marjory Razorblade' by Kevin Coyne and 'Bill Drummond Said' by Julian Cope

'Intuition' by Lenny Tristano and 'She Lives in a Time of Her Own' by the 13th Floor Elevators

'Lines Burnt in Light' by Evan Parker and 'Just a Memory' by the Lovin' Spoonful

'Don't Leave Me This Way' by Thelma Houston and 'Voices of Protest' by Luigi Nono

'I Want Your Love' by Transvision Vamp and 'I Want to be Your Lover' by Prince

Bitches Brew by Miles Davis and 'Friends' by Bette Midler

'Something Wicked This Way Comes' by the Enid and 'Safety Pin Stuck in My Heart' by Patrick Fitzgerald

'Electroknots' by Merzbow and 'Moon Child' by King Crimson

Stolen and Contaminated Songs by Coil and 'Hey Hey We're the Monkees' by the Monkees

Themes by Psychic TV and 'Even Better than the Real Thing' by Willie Nelson

Easy Listening for the Hard of Hearing by Boyd Rice and Frank Tovey and 'Bubblegum' by Kim Fowley

'Love Will Tear Us Apart' by Swans and 'Love Will Tear Us Apart' by Paul Young

'Happiness' by Fridge and 'Happiness' by Ken Dodd

'I Hate You' by the Monks and 'All You Need Is Hate' by the Delgados

'A Death Never to be Complete' by Fushitsusha and 'Too Many Creeps' by Bush Tetras

'So Soon' by Slag Boom Van Loon and 'Without You' by Badfinger

Vocal Studies and Uprock Narratives by Prefuse 73 and 'The Rhythm Divine' by Yello featuring Shirley Bassey

'Don't Breathe a Word' by Kevin Red Terror Tahista and 'Ode for Nick Drake' by Robyn Hitchcock

'Keith Don't Go' by Nils Lofgren and 'Happy' by the Rolling Stones

'Pick Up the Phone' by Notwist and 'My Little Red Book' by Love

'System' by Force Legato and 'Edge of Illusion' by John Surman

'Jump' by Van Halen and 'Jump Around' by House of Pain

Sevens and Twelves by Fridge and '7' by S Club Seven

'Televised Executions' by Suicide and 'Dirrrty' by Christine Aguilera

'Enjoy Knob Culture' by Latex and 'So Far Away' by Carole King

'Close to Me' by Herbert and 'Close to You' by the Carpenters

'A Giant Alien Force More Violent and Sick Than Anything You Can Imagine' by
    Venetian Snares and *Tales from Topographic Oceans* by Yes

'Dance to the Underground' by Radio 4 and 'Two Sevens Clash' by Culture

'Turn On, Switch Off' by Static and 'Pass You By' by Gillian Welch

'Adam' by Meshell Ndegeocello and *Requiem for Adam* by Kronos Quartet

'Missing Link' by Femi Kuti featuring Common and 'Flute Loop' by the Beastie
    Boys

'Heartbreak Hotel' by Elvis Presley and 'Heartbreak Hotel' by John Cale

'I Can't Stop Loving You' by Hank Williams and 'The King of Love is Dead' by
    Nina Simone

'King Puck' by Christy Moore and 'A Gathering of Promises' by Bubble Puppy

'Objection (Tango)' by Shakira and 'Mobscene' by Marilyn Manson

'I'm Going to Get You' by Shania Twain and 'Porno Base' by 23 Skidoo

'Bend Over' by Wagon Christ and 'Fucking the Monstrous Music' by Black Lung

'Hooker with a Penis' by Tool and 'Radar Love' by Golden Earring

'Pink Panther Theme' by Henry Mancini and 'Resident Evil Theme' by Marilyn
    Manson

'Can't Get Money Out of My Head' by the Flying Kylies and 'Miniskirt' by Kronos
    Quartet

'Political Song for Michael Jackson to Sing' by Minutemen and 'Mind is the Magic
    – Theme to Siegfried and Roy' by Michael Jackson

'America, Why I Love Her' by John Wayne and 'Are You Glad to Live, in America?'
    by James Blood Ulmer

'American Life' by Madonna and 'Hail to the Thief' by Radiohead

'Un Autre Introduction' by DJ Shadow and 'I Just Don't Understand' by Ann-
    Margret

'Hot on the Heels of Love' by Throbbing Gristle and 'Falling in Love Again' by
    Marlene Dietrich

'Kill, for Peace' by the Fugs and 'Atomic Moog' by Coldcut

'People Eat Fruit' by Manitoba and 'Strange Fruit' by Billie Holiday (Tricky remix)

'Michael Jackson versus the Cookie Monster' by Ted Shred and 'On a Clear Day
    You Can See Forever' by Ethel Merman

'Anarchy in the UK' by Opium Jukebox and 'Oh No' by Mus Def and Pharoahe
    Monch featuring Nate Dogg

'Saga of Johnny' by Lotte Lenya and 'Green Green Grass of Home' by John Otway

'I Want Boys' by Dsico and 'To All the Girls' by the Beastie Boys

'I Break Horses' by Smog and 'Floppy Boots Stomp' by Captain Beefheart

'Ladytron' by Roxy Music and 'Playgirl' by Ladytron

'Child's Christmas in Wales' by John Cale and 'Puppy Love' by S Club Juniors

'Your Mind is on Vacation' by Mose Allison and 'The Sound of Fear' by Eels

'No Tell Motel' by Don Covay and 'Dream On' by Depeche Mode

'What's New Pussycat?' by Tom Jones and 'When Day Chokes Night' by Do Make Say Think

'Suicide Machine' by Death and 'Love Makes Sweet Music' by Soft Machine

'Jealous Guy' by Bryan Ferry and 'Jealous Guy' by Donny Hathaway

'He Forgot that it was Sunday' by John Prine and 'Every Day Is Like Sunday' by Morrissey

Martes by Murcof and 'Jenny from the Block' by Jennifer Lopez

'Cheeky Girls' by the Cheeky Girls and 'Lose Yourself' by Eminem

'Planet Rock' by James Moran and 'Shape' by the Sugababes

'Boys Don't Cry' by the Cure and 'Cry Me A River' by Justin Timberlake

'Toxic' by Britney Spears and 'Telegraphs in Negative/Mouths Trapped in Static' by Set Fire to Flames

'Feel Good Time' by Pink and 'Absolutely Cuckoo' by The Magnetic Fields

'Beautiful' by Christina Aguilera (Fug bootleg mix) and *The Silent Corner and the Empty Stage* by Peter Hammill

'TV Crimes by Black Sabbath' and 'TV is King' by Todd Rundgren

'I'm a TV Savage' by Bow Wow Wow and 'Television Station' by Front 242

'Channel Surfing by The Dictators' and 'TV Dinners' by ZZ Top

'Television' by Dr John and 'Television' by Japan

'Television' by Marilyn Manson and 'Television' by Mansun

'TV Eye' by Iggy and the Stooges and 'TV Eye' by Sheep On Drugs

'Television Man' by Talking Heads and 'TV Star' by Butthole Surfers

'MTV Makes Me Want To Smoke Crack' by Beck and 'I Wanna Be A Unabomber' by The Donnas

'Television, The Drug Of The Nation' by the Disposable Heroes of Hiphoprisy and 'This Place Is A Prison' by the Postal Service

'Caring Is Creepy' by The Shins and 'Those Who Tell The Truth Shall Die, Those Who Tell The Truth Shall Live Forever' by Explosions In The Sky

'What Do You Mean, Idi Amin' by Pengo and 'George Bush Cut Up While Talking' by Godspeed You! Black Emperor

'Artikulation' by Gyorgy Ligeti and 'Are You That Something' by Aaliyah

'The Shape I'm In' by The Band and 'The Whole World Oughta Go On Vacation' by The Holy Modal Rounders

'I'm Not The Loving Kind' by John Cale and 'Gentle On My Mind' by Glen Campbell

'I'll Have To Say I Love You' by Jim Croce and 'I Love Me' by Tiny Tim

'Only Love Can Break Your Heart' by Neil Young and 'Wear You Love Like Heaven' by Donovan

'La La Means I Love You' by the Delphonics and 'I Feel A Little Spaced Out' by Os Mutantes

'Satisfaction' by The Portsmouth Sinfonia and 'Stones' by Fred Frith

'All Medicated Geniuses' by Pretty Girls Make Graves and 'Doctor Rockit' by Doctor Rockit

'Clean Up Woman' by Betty Wright and 'Every Breath You Take' by Betty Wright

'The Grey Album' by DJ Danger Mouse and 'A Distorted Reality Is Now A Necessity To Be Free'

'Stuff Me Up' by Peaches and 'Join The Boys' by Joan Armatrading

'The Earth Is Not A Cold Dead Place' by Explosions In The Sky and 'Andrew Ridgely' by Black Box Recorder

'Cee-Lo Green Is The Soul Machine' by Cee-Lo and 'Bette Midler Sings the Rosemary Clooney Songbook'

'Broken Train' by Beck and 'Awake On A Train' by Mum

'Enjoy Your Worries You May Never Have Them Again' by The Books and 'Wrapped Up In Books' by Belle and Sebastian

'Everybody's Changing' by Keane and 'Now You Can Let Go' by Philip Jeck

'Attic Plan by The Pastels' and 'On Top Of The World' by The Dixie Chicks

'Keith and Me' by Princess Superstar and 'Cleavage' by Kool Keith

'Hurt' by Johnny Cash and 'Ease' by Public Image Limited

'The Illness EP' by Kid606 and 'Let's Get Sick' by Mu

'White Punks On Dope' by The Tubes and 'New Wave' by Common

'Faking The Books' by Lali Puna and 'It's Obvious' by the Au Pairs

'Gentle On My Mind' by Glen Campbell and 'My Organ In Your Face' by Wagon Christ

'Intertiac ESP' by Mars Volta and 'Getting A Drag' by Lynsey De Paul

'The Struggle Against Reality' by Matmos and 'In Every Dream Home A Heartache' by Roxy Music

'French Canadis' by Erase Errata and 'Who Stole The I Walkman' by Isotope

'Beauties Can Die' by M83 and 'Slow' by Kylie Minogue

'Welcome To The Ocean Floor' by Ampbuzz and 'If This Is The Deep Sea, I Can See You'

'Things Happen' by Coil and 'Suite For The Way Things Change' by Prefuse 73

'Talk About You And Me' by Squarepusher and 'Little Argument With Myself' by Low

'Legs' by ZZ Top and 'Bang Bang' by Nancy Sinatra

'Yes I'm Lonely' by Vincent Gallo and 'Oscar Tennis Champ' by Momus

'Squeegee Man Shooting' by el-P and 'Fender Bender' by Kid Koala

'One Million Ways To Burn' by Ursula Rucker and 'I Want To Sing That Rock'n'Roll' by Gillian Welch

'Metronome' by Manicured Noise and 'Fix Up Look Sharp' by Dizzee Rascal

'Boys of Melody' by The Hidden Cameras and 'No Good Advice' by Girls Aloud

'Spirits Abandoned' by Six Organs Of Admittance and 'Beat It' by Señor Coconut

'Purest Love' by Blackalicious and 'Butterfly in a Glass Maze' by Mike Patton

'White Bird' by It's A Beautiful Day and 'Sea Ghost' by The Unicorns

'Glamour Girl' by Chicks On Speed and 'Bad Girl' by New York Dolls

'The Whole World Oughta Go On Vacation' by The Holy Modal Rounders and 'I Feel A Little Spaced Out' by Os Mutantes

'Schnick-Schnack' by Mouse On Mars and 'Mangoe de Bango' by Tosca

'Kissing The Lipless' by The Shins and 'Cherry Chaptick' by Yo La Tengo

'Big Booty Bitches' by Soft Pink Truth and 'Milkshake' by Kelis

'Dead Cities, Red Seas and Lost Ghosts' by M83 and 'All Strange Beasts Of The Past' by Thuja

'Me Against My Music' by Britney Spears and Madonna and 'Teenbeat' by Henry Cow

'Spinning Away' by Brian Eno and John Cale and 'I'm Lovin' It' by Justin Timberlake

'How Will I Ever Be Simple' by Richard Thompson and 'Never Again' by John Zorn

'My Guitar Wants To Kill Your Mama' by The Persuasions and 'Come On Grandad' by Mr Scruff

'The Shape I'm In' by The Band and 'Comfortably Numb' by Scissor Sisters

'Ghost Writer' by RJD2 and 'When You Sleep' by My Bloody Valentine

'She Was A Visitor' by Alvin Lucier and 'Obsession' by Kylie Minogue

3.
L.I.S. and T. are the first four letters in 'listen'.

Part Five: The journey ends exactly where there is no ending, which is a fabulous coincidence but nothing less than any of us – that's you, me and the reader – deserves

After the book was written, a book that had, I must admit, somewhat changed shape during the writing and was a little way off what Kylie was expecting, I didn't hear much from her. She sent me some secret messages in the mysterious way I had learned such celebrities operate, whenever they need to pass on information as they manage their image somewhere inside the delirium of the worldwide dream. A dream they tend to get more and more in control of, even as they themselves get a little out of control.

She happened to mention one time, as she celebrated her prime-time position in the city where everything happens at once by dancing through a time zone or two sharing some kind of space with William Gibson, DJ Hell and Jeff Koons, that she felt a little annoyed that the only place she could find herself in my book about her was embedded in a series of lists. 'This book about me,' she said, as the beat behind her and underneath her reflected the cool control of her mind, the sweep of her ambition, the neutrality of her emotions, as the beat missed a beat and slipped a dimension or two, 'is a book of lists that seem to have nothing to do with me.'

'There are a lot of lists in your book,' she said, changing shape into a version of herself that was somewhere between sex and logo, between herself in 1993 and herself in 2007, between ready-made hyperlink and ever-ready autogirl, between pantomime and descending three-note bassline, between circling sequencer lines and midnight, between television and a magazine cover. 'It's as if everything in the universe is just part of a list, a random list, a numbered list, an alphabetical list, an endless list.' She said, as light as light, and twice as dazzling, 'I don't want to be simply part of a list. Locked in a list, pinned down like a butterfly, some kind of lifeless specimen kept in the jar of your imagination.'

I told her that she could read the lists in a number of ways. I wasn't sure she was listening, as I seemed to be talking to an understandably distracted Kylie who was cloning herself in a time loop that was destined to repeat itself possibly forever, but I persevered, hoping that each time Kylie turned into another Kylie, replicating herself so that there was a Kylie for everyone, was a sign that she understood, and agreed with, what I was saying.

She was turning herself into a list, a list of herself, a list of faces and movement, sounds and rhythms, that make up Kylie, the Kylie now so famous there was no absolute centre to her. A list that was a formula for understanding, to an extent, the commercial and personal miracle of her framed existence.

I said, 'The lists represent what you can find in the city you are now in, after you drove yourself right into its heart, the city where you are now living it up at the lovely, lonely edge of immortality. The list is information, and information is everything. Life is information, information about itself. We have become nothing but information. The most concrete thing in the world is information.'

The concrete city of information is filled with everything that has ever happened, and there are parts of the city you will be familiar with, and parts of the city you never visit. The list is like an index of streets, and you can follow the list, the index to everything, to work out just what has happened in the world – the world you happen to be interested in, the world you make lists to honour, classify and interpret – to find new areas of the city, to discover what makes the city tick from beat to beat.

The lists exist to demonstrate how vast the city is. How high it goes, and how far underground, and, as high it is, there are rooms, and lights, and people, and emotion. Underground, there is movement, and action. The city goes on forever, and yet is always within reach. It contains everything you can imagine, and anchors you to your life, and liberates you from it. It hides things, and it reveals things. It shows things for what they are – experiences to be collated and considered in time – and it shows that there are always things behind the things you think you know, other places and experiences you might not know about. There are lists that are familiar, that create the familiar parts of the city, the parts of the city that everyone knows, which help them feel part of something, a community of souls making the same kind of sense of the universe, so that the universe makes some kind of sense. The familiar lists, the charts that surround us, that make some things hits and other things misses, are what ensure that the universe is everything it has to be so that we know where we are. These lists are the buildings, the trees, the landmarks we know the best, the ones where we live most of the time, our local neighbourhoods, the places were we work and play.

Then there are the stranger lists, the lists listing the less familiar, the completely obscure. These are the ones that tell us how the city is darker, denser, fuller, more mysterious than we really know. These lists point you towards neighbourhoods and areas we might never have considered, areas in the lost parts of the past, areas existing at the same time as now, sections of the city forming themselves into the future. These areas, dark places and shimmering spaces, are as wonderful, if not more wonderful, than the familiar parts of the city, and they eventually, after time, which is a help to everybody, become familiar parts of the city, once they are listed, indexed, mapped out. The list exists as a way of celebrating the known things which we all share that make us part of the same adventure, but the list also exists as a way of referring to the less-known things, which can remind us that the adventure does not have to be the same for everyone. The familiar lists full of the famous successes that most people agree with are the everyday routes that make us feel secure. They fix us into the warm present by gently mopping up the past before it disappears into cold nothing. The unfamiliar lists are routes at the edges of the city, in the shadows, far in the past and way out into the future that make us feel a different kind of excitement, the excitement of discovery, the excitement of change. The change that makes the adventure of life constantly surprising.

Some lists are a settled, predictable combination of the obvious. Other lists are a shifting, evolving juxtaposition of elusive energies and experiences that can never settle down, which pass energy into the predictable, obvious parts of the city and add to the atmosphere, break down the everyday and transform the mundane today into the restless, moving future.

The city is a list of everything that has happened and the love of making lists is an attempt to remind us of what it is that has happened, and what is happening, all at once, as time and humanity collapses into itself. A book is a list, a list of words placed in an order favoured by the writer to tell a story. A film is a list of images. A piece of music is a list of sounds and rhythms. A song is a list of words and notes. A human being is a list of cells and mysteries. All these lists consist of what is in the list, and what is missing, what is left out.

'Perhaps,' I said to Kylie, 'you can read everything you need to know about my view of the city by looking at my lists, my lists of favourite things and other things, and seeing what is in there, and what isn't. My lists create a part of the city that then maps on to everyone else's map of the city as designed by their lists of favourite things, and least favourite things. It all fits together to create the city where everything is happening at once in sampled, looped, televised, laptop, infrared highlights. In bits and bytes, in fragments of a whole that are bursting with other whole universes displayed in fragments.'

The list is a collage of hopes and wishes, of knowledge and exhibitionism. This book about Kylie is a list of words in a certain order that creates a way into the city, and a way of being inside the city that I think is the best way of being there. The lists inside this book, as you would expect me to say, being in control of this moment, are the most effective guide to the city, the main gaudy, glamorous tourist parts, coupled with the stimulating delights off the beaten track. These lists tell a story of how music is the lining between us and eternity, a protection from the desolate vastness of everything, an interpretation and celebration of this devastating vastness and our ability to coax any kind of meaning out of this desolation.

The lists reduce the vastness into controllable sizes, into the size of things that can fit into our mind, where they can expand again to the size of everything. The list is the way of fitting everything in one place at one time, so that we can take it with us, so that we can fit it all inside a microchip, a chip we can then fit inside our soul. The list is turning everything that has happened or is happening in the city between then and now into a material that can be transformed into a cyber-property that reflects all of the detail of the universe as we imagined it. The list is a code for everything we are, the list is a diagram, sometimes extremely slight and incomplete, sometimes unbelievably deep and complete, of eternity.

'The lists in this book,' I ventured to a Kylie momentarily caught precisely midway between a cynical world and a romantic one, 'locate us somewhere, I hope beautifully, midway between the slight and the complete, between the incomplete and the deep.'

Kylie fainted. I think my audacity had penetrated the barrier of fame that separated her from everyday speculation, and had caused a couple of vital wires to snap. She had a way of fainting in slow motion that was both alarming and alluring. I had to explain that, yes, the list is often just a nice way of passing the time, of showing off the hipness of your choices, a sketchy part of a self-portrait, a way of wallowing in a bubbly nostalgia that returns you to a simpler, sweeter time, of trying to contain sheer chaos in little patches of consoling order, of making plans for a future that seems so blank and featureless you have to impose shape on it by transferring things in easily wrapped packages. Lists help you believe that there will be a future – by reminding you that the things you are listing have happened, in a time that was once a future, and that therefore there will be a future where things will happen that can then be listed and taken forward to remind us of a past where stuff was generated that made us believe there is a present and so, ultimately, a future.

It's a way of abbreviating the speed and complexity of modern life into easily understood sections of naming and numbering. It's a handy way of fixing fixations, of reducing the enormity of everything into a simple series of notes and hints. But, let's face it, it is also a way of defining the shape of the universe, as a list of equations, a list of provisional understandings and subsequent qualifications. Kylie was slowly recovering, and the expression on her face indicated that she was quickly remembering who she was, and where she was, and the fact that she was always being watched, by a list of people that numbered the population of a city.

'Every single item on every list in this book,' I told her, 'itself leads to another set of lists. Each piece of music, each happening, each event, is part of its own list, which is itself part of another list.' A list represents a world where smaller things run within smaller things that run within smaller things. A list gives us the surface of something, and that leads to another list, which contains more surface, and from there, more lists, and more surface. The lists make up the surface of the universe, and the fact that the lists lead to other lists, lists about how something was made, lists about the thought behind the making of something, lists of influence, lists of the technology that helped make it, lists that conjure up aesthetics, personal and social values, reason, intuition, science, spirit, lists of concerns and values, beliefs and ethics, lists of actions, nouns, functions, states, lists of weights and measurements, lists of family and friends and businesses involved, lists of successes and failures that contributed to the making of something, lists within lists leading right back to the lists of first sensations and thinking and speech you have as a baby, the lists of chemicals and genes that make up the individual, list upon list leading to list upon list, it all helps supply the hidden depth in the universe. The depth where things start to get really interesting.

I risked making Kylie faint again by pointing out that, actually, this book of lists listing the lists that list everything in the shape of a city from the perspective of pop music contains words that, if you piled them up together, would form the shape of Kylie Minogue. Really – put all the lists together, place them in just the right order, pointing in just the right direction, and they make the shape of Kylie. That's the main reason why this is a book about Kylie Minogue. It's a body of words that is in explicit and implicit ways the equivalent of the body of Kylie. There is also a chance that the words form the shape of Alvin Lucier – and possibly also Eno, Eminem and Elvis, and that's just the Es; perhaps they even form me, you and the reader – but in most senses, the senses you find in the city where everything is happening at once, the list of words in the book can make up the physical and mental shape of Kylie Minogue, and, with a little imagination, her shadow as well.

The words are in the shape of a city and Kylie Minogue is the same shape as the city. She fits exactly into the city as if someone had designed it that way. I could take the credit, but I'm too busy trying to convince Kylie, who is fast fading away into this epic, intimate city of forever, that this book is about her. I tell her, 'Whenever you asked me to prove I was writing a book about you, when you popped up in the screen in front of me, the metal fairy who lives inside my computer, as you were moving across the words, the lists, offering words of advice, suggesting lists of changes, with that little yellow lightbulb popping into existence above your head, with that animated smile of encouragement always in place, I responded, I wrote something, to prove I was writing about you, and you always seemed happy, seemed content . . . But you're clever like that, always making sure that people think that you are happy with them, that they are giving you what you want, so that you may give them what they want . . .'

She'd gone. She was nowhere. Sure, she was somewhere in the city, and, although I only had to turn on the television to find her, or open a magazine, surf the Web, play a CD, the truth was, because this fiction leads to nowhere but truth, she had disappeared into herself. She'd reached that state all famous people aspire to, against their better judgement – she no longer existed outside the image of herself that she was so in control of, it was beyond her control. I received no more messages from her, not directly to me, just the ones that went to her fans in general, the ones who could list from one to a hundred why 'Can't Get You Out of My Head' was the greatest pop single of all time, the perfect sound-track to the city that is inside your head, the city that you construct inside your room, the room you are sitting in, the room that is not like the room anyone else is sitting in. She was the new Madonna like Eminem was the new Elvis, Beyonce Knowles was the new Tina Turner and Robbie Williams was the new Tom Jones and everyone existed together inside the city, re-created as machines for a future that was all machinery, give or take the enterprising, mutated elements of machinery that was all human. In the city, the mortals and the immortals immersed themselves more and more in evolving systems of technological intelli-gence and virtual realities. The environment fuses with the intelligent technology. Mind, society and information technology become recip-rocal realities that mutually amplify each other's evolution.

The universe fits into a city which fits into a room which merges with your head. The twentieth century speeds into the twenty-first century, and technology chases us into the future, future chases tech-nology, and you can see this speed, this chase, reflected in the way pop music responds to technology, and the way that technology changes pop music. Music was reduced to the length of the pop song, the classic three minutes, because the invention of the 78 rpm vinyl record caused extended, rambling songs to be edited down to their essence, quick run-throughs of verse and chorus. The 33-rpm album enabled collections – lists – of songs to create the classic LP length that told the two-sided stories that produced such a variety of expression and energy. The commercial world is right there to turn the creative spontaneity of individuals exploiting the new technologies into hard cold cash. The cash creates an industry that means pop music lasts longer and develops further than anyone would have ever imagined. Technology stretches and fractures it further, fashion pushes it and pulls it, rhythms fall over themselves to repeat and replace themselves, sounds get invented every time a scientist finds a new way to connect a button with an impulse, a switch with a sound, a box with a rhythm. New formats, new inventions, new times, new ages, new children, new demands enter the folded-up cut-up recorded sampled remixed reduced increased designed programmed compiled listed classified fold. Life gets faster, louder, larger, images develop into other images, image feeds off image, more and more hybrids develop that turn pop into the most simple, complex and active of art forms, the one that changes the most, the one that takes up the experimental mantle and the technological mantle, that fuses the surreal with the sonic, that constantly develops the idea of fame and image, of art and entertainment, and it meets up with the mouse, the click of the moment, to move into the future, the future of everything, looking and sounding like a world that's ready to make the move into a universe where flesh combines with machine.

It is pop music, this incredible list of songs and suggestion that would take a millennium to listen to, which has made the first moves to prepare us for this next world, this brave new world, stranger than a strange land, the other side of 1984, where the human and the machine will find a hard dream way to share a universe that is, in essence, both human and machine, programmed by itself to accommodate human feeling and computer precision. It is pop music that provides the soundtrack and the images that accompany this transformation from rooted reality dwelling into a rootless post-reality heaven and hell, where desires can be satisfied instantly, where pleasure can be a constant, but where pain is never far away, where nothing is as it seems, where our lives are run by remote companies in remote control of our needs and wants, where everything that has ever happened is available, all at once, all around us, in the universe in the shape of a city mashed into a room slipped inside our head. It is with music, the way it has reacted to this increase in technological possibility in the last twenty years, that points towards a cultural renaissance where aesthetic and pleasurable experiences will be unbelievably enhanced – a renaissance which suggests everything that has happened during the past 5,000 years is just the beginning. If we look at how civilisation moved on after the discoveries of the eighteenth century, if we look how far we have moved during the past 100 years, the new technological leaps that have happened in the last few years will create an equally profound set of changes, in the mind, in the body, in the spirit, and in the city. The nineteenth century created the modern. The twentieth century went one further and found the postmodern. The twenty-first century goes even further and we are on the brink of being post-human, post-technological, a partnership of increasingly intelligent, self-maintaining, self-evolving machines and the biological, social and psychological dimensions of humanity.

The city is always changing. It's always moving. Sensation and experience join it all the time; new buildings are created based only on the limits of the imagination that money can buy; new sounds emerge, new images connect with old images and metamorph into other images. There is already too much music to listen to, the city is already beyond our comprehension, but still it comes, the city grows larger and larger inside our heads, so large that perhaps one day it will move outside our heads. It will leave our heads, as our heads leave a world that is no more. However the world ends – with a bang, a whimper, whether it burns out, fades away, falls out of time, just gets switched off – the information inside the city will not be destroyed. It will last for whatever forever turns out to be.

Filled with everything that has ever happened, with every sound and thought, dream and vision, life and soul, the city floats out beyond our minds, into limitless space and time, where the future happens at exactly the same time as the past, as the present, where alternative universes bleep in and out of existence in the blink of an eye, between beats of the cosmic drum. The city filled with everything is the proof of the astonishing effort of our existence for any being out there that might want to understand who we were and what we did. The city filled with ghosts and echoes and consciousness spreading throughout the universe, containing rooms, which contain heads, which contain minds, which contain music, all the music there has ever been, all that is left of us, all that we are, drifting into space forever, and ever, and ever.

I imagine some one, some thing, some mind, an equivalent of the city that we sent out beyond us, coming across our city, hearing and seeing all the things that we put into our universe, inside our heads. This being, machine-like, humanoid, other, listens to all the music collected inside the city. It is the being's particular area of interest, how there comes to be sound in a universe that seems to be so silent. The being listens to this list of sound and rhythm, near silence and massed noise, that goes on forever. For the sake of argument, for the sake of an ending to what can never end as long as the imagination exists, this being uses this music to sense everything that we were in the pre-electronic, post-modern and post-mouse centuries before we made this epic journey into the unknown, and they sit down in a room, a room that is not like any other, and they write in whatever their equivalent of a book is the following words, which are the beginning of a list of thoughts that they think might explain who we were and what we wanted . . .

1

I am sitting in a room.

2

I can't get you out of my head.

Exit Music (For A Film) by Brad Mehldau

For Elizabeth: Björk's 'Like Someone In Love', The Velvet Underground's 'I'll Be Your Mirror' and Stardust's 'Music Sounds Better With You'.

For Madeleine: The Monkees' 'Daydream Believer', Alice Cooper's 'School's Out' and Nirvana's 'Smells Like Teen Spirit'.

For Mike Jones, my editor at Bloomsbury: The Pixies 'Where's My Mind?', Napoleon XIV's 'They're Coming To Take Me Away', Mouse on Mars' 'Fantastic Analysis' and Don Covay's 'Overtime Man'.

For Isabella Pereira, for the paperback red marking, which set out to correct reality itself: Elliot Smith's 'A Distorted Reality Is Now A Necessity To Be Free', Asian Dub Foundation's 'Rise To The Challenge' and The Gorillaz 'Re-Hash'

For Richard Rees Jones, the secret checker at the end of the road: Willie Nelson's 'Are You Sure?', and Arto Lindsay's 'Illuminated'.

For Rowan at DGA: The Strokes' 'Under Control'.

For David at DGA: To Rococo Rot and I Sound's 'From Dream To Daylight', Brahms' Symphony No. 1 in C Minor, Op 68 and the Rabbit in the Moon mix of Groove Armada's 'My Friend'.

For James Banbury, Eric Harwood, Kevin Hewitt and Ron Atkinson: DJ Shadow's 'In/Flux', Eon's 'We're All Insane (When We're Asleep)' and ZZ Top's 'Viva Las Vegas'.

For Meltzer/Tosches/Cohn/Kent/Murray/MacDonald/Smith/Reynolds/Bangs/Toop/Christgau/Penman/Ewing: Kurt Schwitter's 'Boo/Naa/bii bull ree' and Atmosphere's 'Party For The Fight To Write'.

For Anton Corbijn: Nils Petter Molvaer's 'Vilderness 2' and Captain Beefheart's 'Mirror Man'.

For those who were there the other side of the looking glass, this side of the freakzone, that side of the page, one side of the instrument, inside the computer, shaped on the screen, fused into the speaker, wired to the sky, plugged into space, there on the stage, present in time, close to the edit: Tori Amos' 'Thank You', Hood's 'They Removed All Traces That Anything Ever Happened' and Afrikan Science's 'The Future Beat Is But A . . . ?'

"Quite," said Kylie Minogue.

A Note on the Author

Paul Morley wrote for the *NME* between 1977 and 1983. A collection of his journalism from this period, *Ask*, was published in 1987.

His acclaimed memoir, *Nothing*, a book about the effects of his father's suicide, was published in 2000.

He was responsible for the 'Frankie Says . . .' t-shirts, as worn over the years by everyone from Jennifer Aniston to Homer Simpson, and was a member of Art of Noise. He is now a part of Image of A Group.

A regular panellist on BBC 2's *Newsnight Review*, he also appears regularly on numerous radio and television programmes about popular culture. He writes for the *Observer Music Monthly*, the *Sunday Telegraph* and *Esquire*.

© Anton Corbijn